STEPHEN CHARLES NEILL, an Anglican, was born in Edinburgh and studied at Trinity College, Cambridge. From 1939 to 1945 he was Bishop of Tinnevelly, India. Since 1962 he has been Professor of Missions and Ecumenical Theology at the University of Hamburg (this is believed to be the first time a British theologian has become a professor in a German theological faculty).

HANS–RUEDI WEBER, a pastor in the Swiss Reformed Church, was born in Ruchwil in the canton of Berne and studied at Biel and at the University of Berne. He is Associate Director of the Ecumenical Institute, Château de Bossey, Céligny, Switzerland. He was formerly Executive Secretary of the Department on the Laity, World Council of Churches.

THE LAYMAN IN CHRISTIAN HISTORY

THE LAYMAN IN CHRISTIAN HISTORY

A Project of the
Department on the Laity of the
World Council of Churches

EDITED BY
STEPHEN CHARLES NEILL
AND
HANS-RUEDI WEBER

The Westminster Press
PHILADELPHIA

PRINTED IN GREAT BRITAIN
Published by The Westminster Press_R, Philadelphia 7, Pennsylvania

CONTENTS

ABBREVIATIONS

CIL	*Corpus Inscriptionum Latinarum*
CSEL	*Corpus Scriptorum Ecclesiasticorum Latinorum*
DACL	*Dictionnaire d'archéologie chrétienne et de liturgie*
DCB	*Dictionary of Christian Biography*
H.E.	*Historia Ecclesiastica*
PL	Migne, *Patrologia Latina*
PG	Migne, *Patrologia Graeca*

PREFACE

THIS book is an enterprise of the Department on the Laity of the World Council of Churches.

Only very rarely does it happen that a writer, or a team of writers, can maintain that a genuinely original book has been produced, or that unmistakably new ground has been broken. The present team ventures to hope that, with all becoming modesty, it may make exactly this claim. As the reader will become aware, the writers have between them surveyed with astonishing erudition the whole history of the Church of Christ from New Testament times till the present day, and have gathered together a vast amount of information such as has never before been brought within the covers of a single book. The editors have both been concerned for a considerable number of years in the lay movements in the Churches; they have been astonished at the wealth of material here for the first time made available through the researches of their colleagues. And it is interesting to observe that not one of these colleagues has made reference anywhere to any book comparable to that in the production of which we have collaborated. There have been detailed surveys of some areas and some periods. But we think it possible to affirm with some confidence that this is the first general survey ever made of the life and witness of the lay membership of the Church of Christ.

It is clear that, in the past, church history has been written almost exclusively in terms of prelates, councils, movements and heresies. Every now and then some outstanding layman—Sir Thomas More, Hugo Grotius, William Wilberforce—demands for himself a place in the pages even of church history. But perhaps Goethe was all too right when he wrote:

> Mit Kirchengeschichte, was hab ich zu schaffen?
> Ich sehe weiter nichts als Pfaffen.
> Wie's um die Christen steht, die Gemeinden,
> Davon will mir gar nichts erscheinen.

It is easy to see why this is perhaps inevitable. Yet everyone who has ever been engaged in pastoral work knows that the true life of the Church, the essential apostolic succession, is to be found in those simple and inconspicuous Christian laymen (and let it be said here once for all that in this book the word 'laymen' is to be taken not in an exclusively masculine sense, but as convenient shorthand for 'laymen and laywomen'), who without theological precision have humbly accepted the fact of Christ, and have set themselves to fashion their lives after the pattern of his life. Most of these, naturally, belong to the unrecorded past:

> There be of them that have left a name behind them,
>   to declare their praises.
> And some there be, which have no memorial;
>   who are perished as though they had not been,
> And are become as though they had not been born;
>   and their children after them. (Ecclus 44.8–9)

It is time that some kind of memorial was raised to these forgotten saints, in the firm conviction that:

> Their seed shall remain for ever
>   and their glory shall not be blotted out. (Ecclus 44.13)

The production of a composite book of this kind is always attended by certain difficulties; indeed, the editors of such books are inclined to think that the difficulties vary directly and in geometrical progression with the number of authors concerned. This book has not escaped its share of problems and misfortunes. The worst of these affected the chapter on Britain in the seventeenth and eighteenth centuries. This had been undertaken by that outstanding scholar Dr Norman Sykes, Dean of Winchester. Pressure of other responsibilities led Dr Sykes to withdraw his offer of co-operation; not much later his lamented death deprived his colleagues of the services of an invaluable guide and counsellor. Fortunately, Dr Sykes had drawn up a fairly full outline of what he thought should go into the chapter, and it is on the basis of that outline that the chapter printed in the book has been prepared. A very distinguished Roman Catholic scholar who had been approached in connection with Chapter 13 did not receive from higher authority the permission which would have made it possible for him to contribute. Not all the writers found it possible to keep to the schedule of dates originally drawn up. Unfortunately, the last chapters to come in were precisely those of Professor Meinhold, Professor Schmidt, and Dr Grootaers, which had to be translated from German and French, and thus further delays were inevitable. Not only so; the last-mentioned two chapters were far too long in their original form for the maximum space that could be allotted to them in the book, and Bishop Neill, who undertook the translation, had at the same time to perform the delicate task of shortening the chapters down to an acceptable length—happily, to the satisfaction of the writers concerned.

Each writer is responsible for his own chapter. But all the writers have seen most of the chapters, and many have been helped by pertinent comments that have come in from their colleagues. There are, inevitably, certain differences of style and presentation, and at certain points editorial co-ordination may be held to have been defective. But this really is a book, and not simply a collection of detached essays. A single aim was set before the writers and a single spirit animates the book. Many of the writers are personally known to one another or to the editors; all have found it possible to co-operate with an almost angelic spirit of patience and mutual forbearance. *The Layman in Christian History* is a monument to a notable piece of ecumenical team-work. Somehow, rather too many Anglicans seem to have slipped into the team; but our Roman Catholic, Orthodox, Lutheran, Reformed and Free Church colleagues seem to have given a very good account of themselves, and we do not think that the presentation can be justly accused of being at any point tendentious or sectarian.

To whom will this book be useful?

We think that it will be found of real value by both teachers and students of church history. Both are aware that, while they must inevitably concentrate for the most part on prominent people, notable movements and crucial events, the reality and continuity of their subject is to be found only in that unchanging faithfulness of the ordinary lay Christian of which we have written above. This book may help them to view their work in a somewhat unusual perspective, and to estimate the significance of the unusual and the striking in its relation to the continuities of ordinary and everyday life.

We hope that many laymen in the Churches will find time and patience to read the book. Some of it may be rather heavy going for them. But we have tried to keep technicalities to a minimum, in so far as this is compatible with the demands of exact scholarship; and we do not think that there is anything too difficult for the ordinary layman to grasp, if he is willing to take the time needed for rather patient and exact reading of the book. We have all been encouraged by the resurgence of the self-consciousness of the laity in the Churches, and by the range and variety of lay activity today. Much of this we imagine to be wholly new. The layman who reads the book may be both surprised and encouraged to find that almost everything that we are doing today has its precedents in the past, and that in every age the ingenuity and devotion of laymen have been exercised in countless ways in the service of the Church.

We hope that this pioneer work may be the jumping-off place for many pieces of further and more detailed research. We are grateful to our authors for all that they have given us; but we are convinced that there are almost inexhaustible treasures still to be discovered. Of many notable Christian laymen no satisfactory biography exists. At point after point we have had to say simply, 'We do not know.' We have hazarded certain conjectures on the basis of available information, knowing that the evidence which may turn them from conjectures into established facts has still to be dug up. Here is an extensive field into which the student can advance in the confidence that exciting and relevant discovery awaits him.

Inevitably there is a certain academic flavour about this book. Almost all the writers have been or are or will one day be professors. It is, however, notable that no less than five of them are laymen (in this one instance only laymen means lay *men*); this is perhaps a favourable omen, a valuable example of ecumenical co-operation in one of the many fields of co-operation into which the Spirit of God is leading the Churches at the present time.

S.C.N.
H.-R.W.

Stephen Neill

INTRODUCTION

STRICTLY speaking neither a history of the laity nor a theology of the laity can be written. The whole Church is the *laos*, the people of God. If its history is correctly written, the life of the Church will be displayed in all its manifold variety and in all the complexity of its relationships with the world outside itself. The whole body of the Church is priestly. A true theology of the Church will set it forth in its priestly relationship to its members, to society, and to the whole universe on the godward side of which it stands; each separate office or ministry will be seen, and its significance considered, only in relation to the priestly character of the whole.

Yet, when this has been said and taken seriously, there is a case for the separate study, both historical and theological, of the laity in the Church. The distinction between ordained and lay, between those whose sphere of service is primarily the Church and those whose sphere of service is primarily the world, is a real one. Nothing is gained by minimizing or overlooking it. A great deal of attention has been paid to the ordained ministry of the Church, its nature, its authority and its functions. The laity tend, by way of contrast, to be taken very much for granted, as though in their case no special problems arise. But such an attitude can hardly be justified. It is mainly through its laity that the Church enters into contact with the world which, though redeemed by Christ, stands to him in a relation different from that of the Church. It is at this meeting-point of the Christian and the non-Christian, the sacred and the profane, the religious and the secular, that the layman stands, and here that he encounters his problems. To say that to the Christian nothing is profane is simply to beg the question. It is true that all things are to be brought under the dominion of Christ, and that everything is susceptible of sanctification as it is brought into contact with his redeeming power. But how this is to be done is not by any means always obvious; the ministry of the layman has its difficulties, and is no less deserving of study than that of the ordained minister of the Church. It is with the layman on the frontier of the Church that we are in this book primarily concerned.

Much confusion has been introduced into the study of this subject by a failure to define exactly the area under consideration and to distinguish the various senses in which the terms 'lay', 'layman' and 'laity' can be used.

It is generally taken as axiomatic that the essential distinction is between 'ordained' and 'lay'.

This distinction will serve very well as a starting-point. Almost every Church and Christian body in the world has found it necessary to develop a class of men who have been solemnly set apart for the service of the Church, equipped with all the authority necessary to carry out the ministry of the word and sacraments, and in most cases required to devote the whole of their time to the service of the Church. In most Churches canonically, and in some countries legally, ministers of the gospel are debarred from taking up any form of lucrative employment, and from gaining their livelihood outside their service of the Church. In exceptional circumstances Churches may find it necessary to do without such a whole-time ministry, as the Church in the very earliest times seems to have done. But it may be thought likely that this will always remain the exception, and that the development, training and support of a whole-time ordained ministry will be the normal practice of the great majority of the Christian bodies.

But there is another distinction which is of fundamental importance in the history of the Church—that between those who live of the gospel and those who live of the world.

This distinction can, it appears, be traced back to the words of Jesus Christ himself; the affirmation that the labourer is worthy of his hire is the basis for the view, generally held in the Church through the ages, that one who is engaged in the service of the gospel may reasonably claim to be set free from the cares of making a living in an ordinary or 'secular' avocation. Paul states the same principle, basing it expressly on a command of the Lord: 'the Lord commanded that those who proclaim the gospel should get their living by the gospel' (I Cor. 9.14). He does not make use of this privilege himself; but his case is a particular one, linked to a special vocation; he fully recognizes the duty of the

Christian congregation to support those who labour for its advantage, and the right of such servants to expect that what is necessary for their livelihood will be forthcoming.

From the earliest times the number of those who have 'lived by the gospel' has far exceeded the numbers of the fully ordained ministry. To put it in another way, the Church has always found it necessary to develop a far richer variety of ministries than is suggested by the use of the singular 'ministry'. At an early period no less than seven 'minor orders' grew up. These still survive in a somewhat fossilized form, as part of the ladder which must be climbed in the Roman Catholic Church by the candidate for the priesthood. Armies of monks and nuns, of friars and lay sisters have served the Church through the centuries; some of these have been ordained priests, but the great majority have been 'laymen' in the sense in which that term is generally used. At the present time the majority of the missionaries of the older Churches who are working overseas are women; they are wholly supported by the contributions of the faithful through the Churches and are wholly occupied in their missionary endeavours. In almost all the younger Churches, the structure provides for a comparatively small number of ordained ministers, of Western or local origin, and for an enormously greater number of catechists, evangelists, teachers and others, who while not ordained to any specific ministry are dependent on the Church for their livelihood, and are supposed to be giving their undivided strength to the service of the Church. Thus in the area best known to me in South India, a diocese with a staff of rather less than a hundred ordained ministers maintained in the villages about two thousand teachers in mission schools; a large number of these combined with their school work the office of catechist, and were responsible for the church services except those for which according to Anglican practice the presence of an ordained minister is necessary. The list could be almost endlessly prolonged. It would include organists and choirmasters, and those, such as sextons and janitors, whose work, while less directly spiritual, has still been found necessary for the maintenance of organized Christian congregations.

Now all these people, while not ordained ministers, are living in and from the Church. They are part of its organization; it is their sphere. Their outlook is bound to be ecclesiastical in a variety of ways. They cannot think in exactly the same way as the lay Christian whose sphere is the world.

There is a second group of laymen who, though not dependent on the Church for a livelihood, have so identified themselves with it as to make it the centre of their existence. Much of the spare time of such men and women is given up to various church activities, financial, social and the rest. They are rarely, if ever, missing from their places when services are being held. They form the backbone of church committees. They are well-informed about all that is going on in the Church, and their conversation is larded, sometimes to the discomfiture of those who do not share their interests, with little scraps of church gossip and vaguely ecclesiastical turns of phrase. The service rendered by such people is literally invaluable; it is hard to see how the Church could get on without them. Yet as interpreters of the Church or as advertisements for it they are not always entirely successful. They sometimes give the impression of living in the Church, and making only occasional forays out from it in order to earn that secular livelihood which makes possible the ecclesiastical sector of their lives.

This description is to some extent an exaggeration, and to some extent a caricature. There are shifting degrees of ecclesiasticism among laymen. Yet it is just the fact that, when the ordinary layman hears someone described as 'a good churchman', he is at once seized with a vague disquiet; the impression given is of someone who is not quite at home in the everyday world, who is a little censorious of its standards and is likely to be a disapproving rather than a welcoming visitor.

The third type of layman is the man or woman who really lives in the world, is at home in it, and is familiar with its ways. Such a Christian cannot but be aware the whole time of the tension between the standards of the gospel and those standards which govern the life of man when unredeemed or only very partially redeemed—this tension is the recurring theme of the whole of this book. But he is neither afraid of the world as it is, nor resentful of it. However much it needs to be changed, it is still God's world, and it is also man's world. Its concerns are of genuine interest to him, and not something that he endures because they cannot be entirely avoided. He recognizes that this world has its validity—a contingent validity, indeed, since it too is at every point dependent on that will of God which keeps it in being; to treat as absolute that which can never be more than relative would be to deify the created thing and so to fall into the sin of idolatry. Nevertheless, it is precisely in this world that such a Christian feels that he is called to exercise his vocation as a Christian. This is the place in which God is to be served. The Church is the home in which he receives inspiration and instruction for this service. But it is not the battlefield, the place where the victory of God is to be won. The battlefield is the world, the place of encounter with other men. A Christian vocation is the exercise of any of the ordinary avocations of daily life in such a way that the glory of God is manifested through it.

This sense of lay vocation has always been present in the Church. But for a variety of reasons its significance is being felt anew in many sections of the Church today.

The so-called ages of faith were a good deal less attractive than the idealized picture of them painted by sentimental lovers of the days that are past. They were days of ignorance and violence as well as of beauty and devotion. But in those epochs, over the whole of Christendom, the distinction between Church and world had to a large extent been transcended. By far the greater part of the population lived in small villages. The one prominent building in the village was the church. Its rules governed men's lives. Its festivals were their holidays. When the Church said that they must not work, willy-nilly they must rest. Everyone knew everyone else. Of course men sinned; but, if they did so, all their neighbours were likely to know about it. There were generally accepted standards of right and wrong, not only in what we would today call the strictly moral sphere. It was recognized that men would not always behave as they should; but if they sinned there were means of reconciliation at hand. Excommunication from the fellowship of the Church could mean also exclusion from human fellowship, and could be a very terrible penalty; for the village-dweller lives a life of community of an intimacy that can hardly be imagined by those who have lived all their lives pent up in cities, and to be deprived of the support and assurance provided by that community is as painful for him as it is for a crab to be robbed of its shell.

Something of this ancient tradition still survives in the Christian village, whether it be in one of the lands of ancient Christian civilization, or in one of the newer areas of the Church. In such places there is little talk of lay movements, and little understanding of what this talk is all about. Village life is much more complex than is generally supposed by the city-dweller; yet it is complexity in miniature, and it is not felt as complex by those who live it, because it is so much a part of the texture of their lives that, except when it is threatened, they are hardly aware of it. Man knows his position in society; he fulfils, well or ill, his duties; he is not conscious of 'the world' as an alien and possibly hostile sphere with which he is in some way concerned.

But in two great areas of Christian life such a synthesis has either never existed, or has long since disappeared.

With the rapid spread of the gospel in recent generations, an ever-increasing number of Christians live in surroundings which have never in any way come under the influence of the gospel. They have to form their own intimate life of fellowship under unfavourable circumstances, and to maintain an existence which is always in a measure threatened by forces that they cannot control. In such a situation the danger is that the Christians will form a ghetto for mutual protection, will have no more to do with 'the world' than is absolutely necessary, and will feel little if any responsibility for it. Such a world-denying attitude is not Christian. The first duty of the Christian in such a situation is witness; the second is the exercise of that capillary action through which the transformation of even a non-Christian world can be at least begun. It is the business of the Christian, as we have said, neither to be afraid of this world nor to resent it.

More obvious is the changed situation that has come about through the growth of urban life. At the beginning of this century there were in the world only eight cities with a population of a million or more. Now there are at least seventy, with another thirty rapidly climbing up to the million mark. It may be taken as certain that this trend towards aggregation will not be halted. And inevitably life in such cities is producing a new type of man, with whose nature we are as yet hardly familiar. It is almost impossible for those who have grown up otherwise to imagine the mentality of a child who has never seen a cow, other than those contented cows which serve as advertisements for Carnation milk. And, though we use the word 'cities' of these sprawling accumulations of streets and houses, the word is really a misnomer. A city was a place with a centre, with great and beautiful buildings marking the reality of its civic existence, and inspiring men with the dignity of being citizens of no mean city. The modern city is no more than a collection of conurbations, endless streets where there are no dignified or splendid buildings, and where even the churches no longer have those highly non-utilitarian steeples that make the skyline of some ancient cities still a joy to behold.

The disaster of modern industrial life lies not simply in the size of all its operations, in the anonymity and impersonal quality of existence, grievous though these are. The real trouble lies deeper still.

The traditional unity of man's being has been broken up. In the past everything held together; there were different spheres of activity, but they were all related to one another. All ancient religions, including the simple beliefs of primitive man, have found their expression in a culture which recognized the religious elements in its formation. Every culture, until the twentieth century, owed its origin to a set of religious convictions, even though it might rebel against the traditional expressions of them. Now the various activities of man's mind and hands seem to have fallen apart. Religion has become interested in religion, and has in consequence become anaemic. Culture has declared its emancipation from its religious past, and has therefore become demonic.

This sad state of affairs may be illustrated by what seems to be happening to education in the modern world. It appears to be concerned in the main with technological instruction calculated to make the pupil an efficient cog on one or other level of the industrial machine, and with those processes of adaptation which will make him a socially acceptable creature in a predetermined order of society. Not much time is left for the contemplation of the ultimate verities, for the training of the mind to be at home in the great dimensions of beauty and of truth. Education no longer recognizes its religious origin, and its fundamentally religious concern. Religion is either excluded, or catered for in a special department of religion—as though religion could ever be departmental, or live other than an unhealthy existence when separated from all the other branches of human knowledge.

A similar claim to autonomy is made by government and by industrial process. We now know that there are no such things as laws of nature; there are only certain observed and statistically measurable uniformities. But it is still no uncommon thing to hear talk of the economic laws which are autonomous, self-acting and invariable. It is supposed that 'biography is about chaps', but economics is about things —an illusion than which nothing could possibly be more disastrous. Economics too is about chaps; and government and administration are about chaps; and medicine is about chaps, and everything else too. It is through the disregard of the personal that Western civilization has come to grief, and landed itself in contradictions from which no one at present can see the way out. And behind the personal stands God, since it is only in fellowship with God that man is fully personal, and therefore God stands as the judge over every human tradition and activity and organization—and illusion too.

To some extent the Churches are to blame for the secularization of modern society. They have been too closely wedded to existing patterns of social organization to exercise a genuinely critical function in relation to them. They have too easily allowed themselves to be thrust back into the purely religious sphere. They have too easily allowed themselves to be intimidated by such slogans as that 'the Church must keep out of politics' and by one or two cataclysmic errors made when the Churches have strayed without due caution into the political field. They have often failed to think theologically about the situations with which they have been confronted. But it must not be forgotten that circumstances have been against them. The Churches with their still medieval form of organization were ill-adapted to meet the challenge of the population explosion, which began in Europe about the beginning of the nineteenth century, and for the shift of population which denuded the countryside and crowded the population into ill-built mushroom cities. The parochial system, admirably adapted to the stable village population, has proved inadequate to meet the needs of the modern day. The 'sects', less tied than the established Churches to bricks and mortar and to traditional ways of doing things, have been more successful than any other Christian groups in finding their way into the largely alienated world of the great city; but certain limitations in their outlook tend to confine their usefulness within rather narrow limits. The industrial world of the great city is for the most part a place in which the voice of the Church is not heard.

This is the point at which the layman is beginning to come into his own. If the Church is ever again to penetrate this alienated world and to claim it in the name of Christ, its only resources are in its convinced and converted laymen. There are vast areas, geographical and spiritual, which the ordained minister can hardly penetrate; the laymen are already there, and are there every day. What happens to society in the future will largely depend on the use that they make of their opportunities, of their effectiveness as Christian witnesses in a new and as yet imperfectly charted ocean of being.

The Christian layman living in the world is challenged in four different ways to be a Christian.

There is, first, the demand for simple personal integrity in all his doings. On a certain level this problem presents itself as fairly simple. The craftsman must be a good craftsman, doing his work as well as it can possibly be done, for the sake of the job and not for the sake of reward. To suppose that the profit motive can be eliminated from human affairs is purely Utopian; men do and always will expect a just reward for their work. The profit motive becomes satanic only when the reward is regarded as being more important than the work, when men begin to be more interested in making money than in making beautiful and durable things. But at the level just above that of the craftsman, difficulties begin to throng and increase. In the industrial world we are dealing not so much with individuals as with structures, entities that seem to have a quasi-personal and demonic life of their own. The Christian is not always faced by clear-cut decisions as between right and wrong; he is often condemned to dwell in a strange twilight, in which the effects of decisions, and their impact on the life of other men, are largely unpredictable. To act at all times as a Christian may prove to be much more difficult than appears to one who merely observes from outside.

Secondly, the Christian is called always to regard himself as the servant of society, and to estimate the quality of his work as service. Here, again, on certain levels the relationship between work and the needs of society may be fairly obvious. The engine-driver and the pilot of a jet aircraft can literally see what they are doing; appreciation of their work is not often expressed but is probably often felt by those whom they convey with such skill in safety to their destination. It may be questioned whether it is a good thing that so many people should seem to desire so intensely to be somewhere else. But journeying is part of human life as God has ordered it; and, if so, to journey safely and swiftly is no bad thing; those who serve the traveller are truly servants. But once such direct contact is lost, apprehension of the servant relationship between the Christian and society becomes much more difficult. It is hard for the man whose day is spent in making a few not very interesting movements on a conveyor belt to find his work enriching or inspiring. Indeed the Christian in such a situation may conclude that a society which demands such well-paid slave labour of some of its members has gone so disastrously astray that only the most radical reconstruction will bring it back to the point at which it can again be regarded as being in some sense a Christian society. But even such radical criticism may be a form of service, provided that the concern of the servant is with service.

On a third and deeper level the Christian layman is challenged to think out the Christian significance of his work. This is perhaps best illustrated from the concerns of such professional men as the doctor and the lawyer. What difference does it make to the professional work of a doctor whether he is a Christian or not? Some would answer that the question is really meaningless and therefore irrelevant. But the Christian, just because he is pledged to wholeness of life, cannot allow himself to be put off by such a denial. The relationship between doctor and patient is always human and personal; it cannot but be profoundly affected by the doctor's understanding of what human nature is, and of the place of man in the universe. The doctor who recognizes this and tries to understand it is being far more realistic than the prosaic 'realist' who scorns such fancies.

The situation of the lawyer is similar. What is law? Is it merely the codification of the prejudices and ignorances of man, the rationalization of the claims of a possessing class to possession? Or are there profound and eternal principles to the maintenance of which the lawyer is pledged? Law is concerned with the relationships of men in society. The Christian is convinced that there is a divine ideal for the life of man as a social being, an ideal after which man has dimly striven all through the centuries, which was clearly revealed in the life of Christ and in the pattern of the Church, but the realization of which in any particular situation is hindered by the purblindness and recalcitrance of man. He cannot see his work otherwise than *sub specie aeternitatis*.

In such difficult fields the individual is likely to feel himself lost. This is the kind of area in which the meeting of mature and thoughtful Christian minds is extraordinarily fruitful; and this is also the point at which 'the Church' in the sense of the professional Church, can come to the help of the layman in the world. The trained theologian cannot as such pronounce on any of the complex problems by which the godly layman is perplexed. But he should have some knowledge of the theological principles to which all these problems are related. Between the rarefied air of abstract principle and the down-to-earth world of practical decision there is the strange and beautiful world of the 'middle axioms', by means of which pure Christian truth can be related to fields which are ill-adapted to the reception of it in its pure form.

When he has reached this point, the Christian layman is likely to find himself impelled to ask the fundamental question as to the relationship between what we have called for convenience 'the Church' and what we have called for convenience 'the world'. To what extent is the separation between them that we have recognized artificial or transitory? Or is it really so radical that we must regard the world as being basically hostile to God, and to all those things for which the Church stands?

The Christian layman does not regard his world as intrinsically evil. The great discoveries of physical science are in his eyes a genuine form of communion with the living God who made all things, even if the scientist who made the discoveries fails to give, as he should, the glory to God. Technocracy, on which so much Christian vituperation has been poured, has for the first time made possible the abolition of degrading poverty—possible, though as yet far from actual. The great Roman lawyers who laid down the great series of maxims by which lawyers are still guided were not idolaters; they were moved by respect for man and by a real perception of his needs to those imperishable formulations. The hard-won emancipation of so many areas of thought and action from the tyranny of a theology that had failed to recognize its own limitations is one of the great and permanent achievements of the human mind. Are all these accomplishments to be regarded simply as products of the erring human mind and intelligence? Or is there also a divine element in them? Are they, perhaps, to be accepted as evidence that what we have called the world is also in some sense under the direction of God, and that his operations extend far beyond the limits of the visible Church? Have we drawn too sharp a distinction between Church and world? The two spheres are not the same; each has its independence, and methods of operation appropriate to that purpose for which it exists. Yet is it possible to make any rigid separation between them? Is it not inevitable that, where the Church exists at all, its relationship with the world should be that of mutual interpenetration rather than of mutual exclusion, let alone hostility?

Here we touch one of the most complex fields of theological thinking, and one that bristles with as yet unsolved problems. We raise the whole mystery of the providential ordering of the world by God. We raise the question of what has been called traditionally 'the two realms'. We confront the question of the kingdom of God, and of the extent to which the realization of it in the kingdoms of men is possible.

These theological issues are not the subject of this book, which is to be historical in its approach and treatment of its theme. But the theological questions will always be present in the background; they are mentioned here as a reminder that life is always lived and experienced as a whole, and that the division of it into compartments or aspects or whatever we like to call them is necessarily artificial. In every form of Christian living the whole problem of the Christian faith is involved; even when the layman himself is least aware of it, his existence is a theological existence in the presence of God.

Our book is concerned essentially with the layman in the third of the three senses which we have distinguished above. Our subject is the layman in the world; the layman who makes his living in the world, is dependent on it, is in some degree threatened by it, is called to confront it, at times to oppose it, and to establish the claim of Christ to be Lord of his world as of all other worlds. It is clear that the vocation of the Christian layman in the twentieth century is a difficult and exacting one; if he is to fulfil his vocation worthily, the layman no less than the ordained minister will need a sense of the divine calling and of the divine presence.

It is, in the first place, essential that he should be a member of a worshipping community. In a world as difficult as this the lone individual is likely to be lost in his own isolation. Not only so; worship opens up the divine and eternal dimensions, without which human life cannot be genuinely human. Perhaps the real distinction between 'Church' and 'world' is that the Church lives or should live always in immediate awareness of the divine, whereas to the world the divine is present only as a remoter background. Yet, as Coleridge has sublimely said, even terrestrial charts can be drawn only with the help of celestial observations; and as he struggles to find his way through the jungles of this world the Christian feels particularly his need of the guidance that comes only from the eternal world. Intelligent lay participation in every act of worship is one of the signs of a living Church.

Secondly, it is necessary that the Christian layman should be theologically literate. It is hardly possible for him to be theologically expert. But in his field of operation mere goodwill is not enough. He must have a real understanding of the Christian faith—its content as divine revelation, and its practice as the attempt to bring all things human under the sovereignty of Christ. Increasingly it should be the task of the ordained ministry to train and educate the lay folk, to turn every parish into 'the layman's university', in such a way that the layman does not go out to his difficult task unprepared and unequipped.

Thirdly, the layman must be alert, aware of his surroundings, and able to communicate with them as a Christian. It is still possible for the Christian living in the world to exercise what Milton called a fugitive and cloistered virtue, to use his Christian faith as a protecting guard between himself and the world rather than as his chief instrument for the penetration of that world. The Christian layman should be fired by imaginative sympathy with his world, wholly identified with it in its needs, though wholly independent of it in its mistaken desires. He must listen before he speaks, and make no hasty or over-confident judgments.

Above all, the Christian layman must have the courage to bear witness to the faith that is in him. The trouble is that there are just too few converted and committed Christians in the world. We have spoken of structures and their almost demonic power. But after all the structures have been built up by men and are operated by men. The trouble is that the men who built them up seem so often to have been selfish, ambitious and uninspired. It is idle to suppose that there can be extensive change in the structures unless there is widespread change in the attitude and convictions of the men and women who have to live and work within these structures. The restoration of society depends on the restoration of human nature; the Christian knows of only one way in which human nature can be restored, and that is through the deliberate and conscious submission of man who stands in need of redemption to the redeemer. Ways and methods of bearing witness are manifold, and in this field as in all others there is great variation between the gifts of different individuals. But the Christian layman is not fulfilling his vocation, unless he is actuated at all times by a deep concern that all with whom he is brought in contact should find their way to that faith in Jesus Christ which is the mainspring of his actions and the source of all his happiness.

The Christian layman who takes his vocation seriously is unlikely to feel that he is faced by any easy task; he is much more likely to cry out with the apostle, 'Who is sufficient for these things?' It may encourage him to learn that he stands in a great apostolic succession, stretching from the days of the New Testament to our own time, of lay folk who have proved themselves courageous and effective witnesses for Christ. Problems and situations change; methods which were appropriate to one time would not have a chance of success in another time or clime. But the situation in all its basic elements remains the same—a world which ceaselessly runs to escape from its Creator, a Creator who is never weary of reconciling the world to himself, and is pleased at all times to use men as the ministers of that reconciliation which has been once and for all accomplished in Jesus Christ. 'Who is sufficient for these things?' The apostle's answer is that our sufficiency is from God who has been pleased to make us effective ministers of his new covenant with men (II Cor. 2.16; 3.4–6).

1

George Huntston Williams

THE ANCIENT CHURCH*

AD 30–313

Introduction: Christian People, a Royal Priesthood and a
Priestly Kingdom

FROM the point of view of official Judaism, Christianity arose largely
as a lay movement. Its recruits were seldom from the priestly class.
Unlike John the Baptist, Jesus was not born of a priestly family. When
the time came to trace his ancestry, the evangelists stressed a royal
rather than a priestly lineage. Yet, seeing in Christ the eternal High
Priest (Heb. 4.14), the early Christians came to think of themselves by
virtue of their baptismal incorporation into him—priest, prophet, and
king[1]—as constituting collectively a priestly kingdom (Rev. 1.6) and a
royal priesthood (I Peter 2.9), and as such carrying into the world the
promises and the prerogatives of the ancient People (*laos*) of God
(I Peter 2.10). It would therefore be a misconception of the eschatologically royal-priestly character of the New Covenantal People to
imagine that the universal priesthood of all believers (the customary
Protestant phrase) betokened anciently an amorphous, egalitarian fellowship. These terms suggest, rather, a strenuously self-disciplined
company of believers who *as a royal priesthood* programmatically appropriated selected parts of the ethical code of the superseded priestly
caste, sharpening its strictures by interiorization and democratization,
and who, at the same time, *as the priestly kingdom*, annulled with

---

* The chapter represents a revision of an article which first appeared as 'The Role of the
Laymen in the Ancient Church', *The Ecumenical Review* X (1958), pp. 225–48, which was
reprinted with the original notes in *Greek and Byzantine Studies* [later: *Greek, Roman, and
Byzantine Studies*] I (1958), pp. 9–42; and which was translated into Spanish as 'El papel
de los laicos en la Iglesia antigua', *Cuadernos Teologicos*, No. 27–28 (Second Semester,
1958), pp. 45–66.

Messianic authority other parts of the Law, confident that they would soon be co-ruling with Christ and judging all things, judged by none.

We best understand their bold mixture of legalism and antinomianism if we, instructed by the parallels among the Pharisees and among the Essenes of the Qumran community,[2] see in it the consequence of their claim to being, in Christ, the righteous remnant of the People of God. On the one hand, no jot or tittle of the Law was to be unheeded (Matt. 5.18); for if their righteousness did not exceed that even of the strict Pharisees, they would not enter the (high-priestly) kingdom of heaven (Matt. 5.20). On the other hand, they knew that Christ had fulfilled the Law and that a new law, an inner law annulling some of the outer Law, had been vouchsafed to them. Theirs was thus a strenuous ethic, at once priestly and eschatological. In the beginning this strenuous ethic of the priests of the Old Covenant[3] and of the saints of the latter days was presumably incumbent upon all who, by dying to the world in baptismal regeneration, were ordained members of the royal priesthood.

Then, as this Church of the Saints, sharing all goods in common under James and Peter, evolved into a tenaciously organized *imperium in imperio*, which three centuries later found favour in the sight of a calculatingly devout emperor, a process of gradual differentiation took place between the clergy and the laity of the *laos* of God. While the clerical leaders of God's People managed (as still later the monks) to perpetuate and institutionalize the virtues of the fervent believers of the first and second generations (at the same time giving ever greater sacerdotal specificity to their own liturgical role in the corporate eucharistic participation in the sacrificial action of the only High Priest), the other members of this People, the laity in the modern sense of the term, for the most part accommodated themselves to a less rigorous implementation of the priestly-eschatological ethic of the formative generations. Content to live by the minimal evangelical precepts, many lay men and women nevertheless, here and there, now and again, as confessors and martyrs, continued to heed also the more stringent maximal counsels. In any event, throughout the pre-Constantinian period, the Christophorous laity never entirely lost consciousness of their royal-priestly responsibilities and prerogatives, to which they were called by baptismal ordination and which they continued to exercise in the realms of liturgy, discipline, teaching, philanthropy, and testimony in the world at large, even though they became for the most part satisfied to supply and protect their clergy as the pre-eminent and exemplary embodiments of their strenuous rigoristic ethical ideal.

To be true to the fulness of our theme, we shall be attentive both to the whole royal-priestly People of God (clergy and laity) as leaven in the lump or scattered or seeded in the workaday world generally and specifically to the laity alongside their clergy gathered for worship, instruction and discipline.[4]

I · Laymen as Participants in the Royal Priesthood by Virtue of their Baptism

Clement of Rome was the first Christian writer to use *lay man*. In a letter to the church in Corinth written about AD 95, Clement, the presiding presbyter or proto-bishop of the Greek-speaking church in Rome, makes brief reference to the participants in the liturgy with the assertion: '. . . the lay man (*ho laïkos anthrōpos*) is bound by the lay (*laïkos*) ordinances'.[5] In assigning the layman a liturgical role along with but subordinate to that of the presbyters and that of the deacons ('Levites'), Clement was at once reflecting general Greek usage of the word 'lay' and turning it in a specifically Christian direction. Up until this time the Greek term was used as an adjective to distinguish the mass of people from their leaders. In translations of the Old Testament Hebrew into Greek it was commonly used to distinguish ordinary or profane from cultic usage, and was usually applied to things rather than to persons. Clement used the term both of persons and things (the ordinances) and in so doing also insisted on the liturgical competence of the layman, however limited it might be. It is of interest that when Clement's letter was translated into Latin perhaps half a century later, becoming thus the earliest extant *Latin* Christian document, the translator preserved something of the older pagan *Greek* feeling about the impropriety of applying *laikos* to persons; for, though he wrote in Latin *lay ordinances* (*laicis praeceptis*), he preferred for 'the *lay* man' the socially tinctured phrase *plebeius homo*.[6] However plebeian or humble the role of the layman, he was nevertheless from the beginning a participant in liturgical praise of the Creator and the Redeemer and not merely a spectator of the cultic mysteries.

We appropriately begin our account of the role of the layman in the ancient Church with his 'ordination' to the royal priesthood by virtue of his baptism. It is significant that the generic term for the non-clerical members of the Church is intimately related, by way of I Peter 2.9 f., with the eucharist. For in this *locus classicus* of the doctrine of the priesthood of all believers[7] the royal priesthood (*basileion hierateuma*),

God's own people, was thought of as engaged in the corporate but spiritual sacrifice of the eucharist:

But you are a chosen race, a royal priesthood, that you may declare the wonderful deeds of him who called you out of darkness into his marvellous light. Once you were no people but now you are God's people (*laos theou*) . . .

Not only were Christians the new Israel, says the preacher of the baptismal sermon, but also the only authorized or effectual priesthood. Collectively, Christians constituted the succession to the priesthood in old Israel, having been vouchsafed the right of *corporate* but otherwise direct access to God through the unbloody or spiritual or rational sacrifice of thanksgiving made possible through Christ.

The apologist Justin Martyr (d. *c.* 165) restated the principle of the priesthood of all believers when he wrote: '. . . being inflamed by the word of his [Christ's] calling, we are the true high-priestly race of God'.[8] The contemporary Athenian apologist Aristides asserted that all Christians could trace their genealogy from the High Priest Jesus Christ.[9] Irenaeus in Gaul (d. *c.* 200) could say: 'All who are justified through Christ have the sacerdotal order.'[10]

'Ordination' to the laity was effected by the sacrament of baptism and the accompanying unction (later, in part, differentiated as the sacrament of confirmation).[11] In the baptismal unction catechumens were enrolled in the royal (and prophetic) priesthood, for it was likewise by anointment that Israel's kings and priests had been consecrated. Tertullian (d. *c.* 220) stressed the priestly character of baptismal unction when he wrote:

Thereupon as we come forth from the laver, we are anointed with the holy unction, just as in the Old Dispensation priests were anointed with oil from the horn of the altar. Whence the term *Christus*, from the chrism which is the anointing, a name that is now appropriated to the Lord.[12]

Tertullian held that baptismal 'ordination' qualified the recipient of grace to baptize in his turn, for 'what is equally received can be equally given'.[13] At the same time, for the sake of order, he, before joining the Montanists, argued that what was lawful might not be expedient and that lay *men* only should perform the sacrament and only in the absence of a cleric; that lay women should never presume to baptize in any circumstance.

Although the indelibility of baptism was long in dispute in the ante-Nicene Church in connection with the admission of heretics and schismatics, the theological ideal of an indelible character came firmly to undergird the three sacraments of baptism, confirmation, and ordination.

Besides his ordination as royal priest, the laic in some quarters, notably in the Alexandrian tradition, could aspire to the status of the ideal gnostic, whose gradual, post-baptismal illumination and growth in inner discipline and grace enabled him to go through the *spiritual* grades of deacon, presbyter, and bishop, some day 'to sit down on the four-and-twenty thrones, judging people', even, perhaps, the less spiritual clergy.[14]

To sum up, the laic in the ancient Church had an indelible 'ordination' as priest, prophet and king, no longer in bondage to the world, but freed through Christ to know the truth in the illumination of the Spirit, to exercise sovereignty over the inner temple of self, to join in the corporate thanksgiving of the redeemed, and to forgive the brethren in Christ's name. The laity was a true order (*taxis*) with its own often distinctive liturgical, constitutional, eleemosynary and witnessing role in the gradual differentiation of the People of the Mission into laity and clergy.

The later Fathers will speak freely of the specialized priesthood of the ordained clergy as derivative from or participant in that of the heavenly High Priest; but with equal propriety one may add that both genetically and theologically the functional priesthood of bishops and presbyters was mediately derived from the corporate royal priestly *laos*, since the cleric but concentrated in his person an action that continued to belong to the whole baptismal community of the reborn in Christ. During the period of the persecutions, when some of the secrets of the faith were guarded by the faithful even from prospective converts (the *disciplina arcana*), the laity was clearly an order not to be confused with the catechumenate and still less with the 'world'.

It will now be our task to ascertain what exactly were the laic's specific rights, duties, and achievements in the realms of liturgy, constitution, discipline, philanthropy, and propagation of the faith in the period before Constantine.

II · *The Layman at Worship*

Paul described in a lively manner (I Cor. 14.26) how all the faithful were active in worship: 'When you come together, each one has a hymn, something to teach, a revelation, a tongue or an interpretation thereof.' The problem was not to create more active participation, but to order it in the right way. Paul recommended prophetic interpretation more highly than unintelligible tongues, because it served all present, including the stranger, who might be converted. The responsive and confirmatory 'Amen' made it possible for all to identify themselves with the prayers of the leaders (I Cor. 14.16). The heavenly hymns of the angels and saints in Revelation transcribe the primitive liturgy of the royal priestly people.

Laics in their eucharistic role of bringing in the bread, wine, and other offerings were commonly called *prospherontes*. Clement of Rome made specific what he meant by the 'lay ordination' when he wrote:

> Let each of us, brethren, in his own order make eucharist (*eucharisteitō*) to God, keeping a good conscience and not transgressing the appointed rule of his liturgy.[15]

We have two subsequent glimpses of laics at worship in Rome, enabling us to fill out the picture into the third century.

Justin Martyr, in his Apology for pagan eyes, remains intentionally general in his account of the eucharist but describes both a baptismal and an ordinary Sunday eucharist, remarking that after the prayers of the liturgical president (the bishop), 'all the laity present shout assent, saying "Amen" '; and he proceeds to explain the affirmative meaning of the Hebrew.[16] In arguing with Trypho the Jew he can be somewhat more specific about the eucharist and about the role of the laic therein:

> . . . *we* are now the true high priestly race of God, as God himself bears witness [Mal. 1.11], saying that in every place among the Gentiles there are those bringing (*prospherontes*) pure sacrifices acceptable to him.
>
> God therefore has long since borne witness that all sacrifices offered by his name, which Jesus the Christ enjoined, namely, at the *eucharistia* of the bread and the cup which are presented in every place on earth by the Christians, are well pleasing to him.[17]

It is clear from this passage that Justin has in mind the liturgy of the whole priestly people and not merely that of the more specialized celebrants.

Hippolytus (d. *c.* 236), the rigoristic rival of Bishop Callistus of Rome, provides us in his *Apostolic Tradition*, about half a century after Justin, with another glimpse into the liturgical action of laics. Here we see them as *prospherontes*, offering at the eucharist not only the bread and

B

the wine, but also occasionally oil, cheese, and olives for eventual distribution. The instructions to the bishop on receiving the oil can be
quoted to evoke the whole liturgical scene in Rome *circa* 200:

> If any one offers oil, he [the bishop] shall make eucharist as at the obla-
> tion of bread and wine. But he shall not say word for word (the same
> prayer) but with similar effect, saying:
> 'O God who sanctifiest this oil, as thou dost grant unto all who are
> anointed and receive of it the hallowing wherewith thou didst anoint kings
> and priests and prophets, so grant that it may give strength to all that
> taste of it and health to all that use it.'[18]

Another manual, *The Testament of Our Lord*, of much later recension,
preserves or elaborates important formularies chanted by the laity in
the canon of the Mass. For example, after the bishop, it bids the laity
say likewise:

> Remembering therefore thy death and resurrection, we offer to thee
> bread and the cup, giving thanks to thee who alone art God for ever and
> our Saviour, since thou hast promised to us to stand before thee and to
> serve thee in priesthood. Therefore we render thanks to thee, we thy
> servants, O Lord.

At communion each lay recipient chants:

> Holy, Holy, Holy Trinity ineffable, grant me to receive unto life this
> Body, and not unto condemnation. And grant me to bring forth the fruits
> that are pleasing to thee. . . .[19]

The degree of participation of the laity, in the Syriac tradition represented by the *Testament*, is extraordinary. But at an even later date, in
the absence of their bishop[20] the Christian *populus* of Rome, fearing
God rather than the emperor and a certain bishop, 'author of wickedness
and a murderer', felt free to congregate in the cemeteries of the martyrs
and celebrated '*stationes sine clericis*' (stations at which no clerics were
present). Whether these 'stations' were penitential or eucharistic
gatherings is uncertain. In the Greco-Roman world it was ordinarily
only among heretics that laics could, in the absence of the clergy, pro-
ceed to the enactment of the eucharist on their own. Tertullian, after
he had become a Montanist, asked the question:

> Are not even we laics priests? It is written in Revelation 1.6: 'A king-
> dom also and priests to his God and Father, hath he made us.' It is the
> authority of the Church and the honour through the sessions (*concessus*)
> of the *ordo* sanctified to God which has established the difference between

the *ordo* and the *plebs*. Accordingly, where there is no session of the ecclesiastical *ordo*, thou offerest the eucharist, and baptizest (*tingues*) and art a *sacerdos* (priest) for thyself; for where three are, there is the Church, albeit they be laics.[21]

Besides the eucharistic liturgy there was the love-feast, sometimes accompanying it, sometimes observed separately in the homes of the more affluent members and to which the bishop would be invited in order to break the bread. Tertullian describes such an *agape* and, by good fortune, mentions the role of the laics:

> After washing of hands and the lighting of lamps individual members are invited to stand out and sing to the best of their ability either from sacred scriptures or something of their own composing. . . .[22]

He goes on to say that 'the feast ends, as it began, with prayer'.

We have already quoted Tertullian, even while still orthodox, on the lawfulness of the lay performance of baptism in the absence of a cleric. Long before him the oldest church manual of discipline, the *Didache* ('Teaching of the Twelve Apostles') assumed that any Christian, including a laic, might baptize provided he fasted, like the one to be christened, 'for one or two days beforehand'.[23] A later writer,[24] looking back on the early days, says 'everyone baptized'. The Iberian Council of Elvira (*c.* 306) in canon 38 makes rather specific the meaning of such necessity:

> During a sea voyage, or in general if no church is near, a laic who has not soiled his baptismal robe and is not a digamist [twice married as a result either of widowerhood or religiously prompted divorce from an unbelieving spouse] may baptize a catechumen who is at the point of death.

It should be added for completeness that, in the baptism and unction of female catechumens, widows and deaconesses who were essentially lay persons had, from the beginning, taken an active part in helping the bishop or presbyter in all but the anointment of the head.

We turn now from cultic practices to the constitutional role of the laity.

III · The Lay Role in the Constitution and Discipline of the Churches[25]

The choosing in Acts 1.15 of a successor of Judas in the presence of precisely *one hundred and twenty* of the 'multitude' (this same number was requisite in a Jewish community in order to elect members to the

Sanhedrin) and in Acts 6.5 the choosing of the deacons, also by the whole multitude, served as a pattern and apostolic sanction for the lay election of clerics throughout the ante-Nicene period.

The *Didache*, after dealing with inspired prophets and teachers visiting as itinerants, goes on quite simply:

> Elect therefore for yourselves bishops and deacons of the Lord, men meek, and not lovers of money, and truthful, and approved; for they too minister to you the ministry of the prophets and teachers.[26]

But elsewhere, and especially later, the procedure was not nearly so direct and simple. Distinctions came to be made between the divine vocation, the lay recognition of the call or election, the liturgical sacring, and the installation. Nevertheless, to the end of our period and well into the Constantinian era, the laity played an important part in the elevation of their bishop. Hippolytus in the *Apostolic Tradition* records the aforementioned refinements; but the bishop is still 'elected by all the laity'.[27]

Origen of Alexandria and then Caesarea (d. *c.* 254) observes that the chief cleric must be ordained 'in the presence of the whole laity in order that all may know for certain that the man elected to the priesthood is of the whole people the most eminent . . . and . . . to avoid any subsequent change of mind or lingering doubt'.[28]

Cyprian, bishop of Carthage (d. 258), makes a similar point: 'The bishop should be chosen in the presence of the laity who have most fully known the life of each one of several possible choices, and have looked into the doings of each one as regards his habitual conduct.'[29] Cyprian also insists that, just as the laity has the power of recognition, they have also the power of withdrawing from the jurisdiction of an unworthy cleric:

> . . . the laity, obedient to the dominical precepts and fearing God, ought to separate themselves from a sinful prelate (*praepositus*) and not associate themselves with the sacrifices of a sacrilegious priest (*sacerdos*), especially since they themselves have the power either of choosing (*eligere*) worthy priests or of rejecting (*recusare*) unworthy ones.[30]

So well known was the power of Christian laics to approve or disapprove their leaders that even the Emperor Alexander Severus (222–235), who was sufficiently well informed to know about their golden rule and who desired to erect a temple to Christ as one of the gods, adopted from the Christians the practice of posting the names of his nominees to public office for the sake of securing public testimony as to their character, saying that when Christians and Jews observed this custom in announcing the names of those to be ordained, it would be 'monstrous that such a precaution should be omitted in the case of provincial governors to whom were committed the lives and fortunes of men'.[31]

The laity also participated with the presbyters and bishops in the corporate discipline of the Church. James in his epistle (5.16) laid the basis for 'sacramental' lay confession when he wrote:

> Therefore confess your sins to one another that you may be healed. The prayer of a righteous man has great power in its effects.

Of the pre-Constantinian writers it was pre-eminently Origen (d. *c.* 254) who interpreted this passage in the sense of sacramental absolution.[32] Although the hearing of another's confession long survived as a lay prerogative, the principal exercise of lay Christian counsel and rebuke was connected with the discipline of excommunication.

Excommunication of the faithless and the wayward members, an originally unforeseen disciplinary action, developed its forms more slowly and therewith also still other constitutional procedures for the readmittance of the penitents. Paul had commanded by letter (I Corinthians 5) that the Corinthian church, assembled with his spirit present, should excommunicate a particularly diseased member, consigning him to Satan. In Matthew 16 the prince of the apostles was expressly given the power of the keys, the power to bind and loose. Over against both this dominical authorization and the notable apostolic action, which would subsequently serve as a model for every bishop, was the 'competing' authorization of communal action in Matt. 18.15–20, which undoubtedly transcribed the usage of the community at an early date and then served as another authoritative pattern for assembling the whole church for a final act of corporate excommunication of an unworthy member thrice warned. But eventually the apostolic-episcopal pattern came to prevail over that of communal action.

In the first three centuries, the struggle over the authority respectively of the apostolic bishop, the college of presbyters, the confessors, and the laity, especially in the problem of dealing with members who had lapsed during persecution, was vigorously fought out. Ante-Nicene church history is the story of innumerable small and large, regional, 'national' and class schisms over the issue of rigorism and laxism. It is significant that in the numerous manuals of church law, which were commonly ascribed to the apostles but which, of course, reflected the usage and experience of the growing Church, the communal disciplinary session portrayed and authorized in Matthew 18 was gradually converted into the pattern for the lay acclamation of a bishop-elect who before the whole church was thrice declared to be faultless and hence worthy of the headship of the church.[33]

Although the clerical control of disciplinary action came to prevail in the ancient Catholic Church, as distinguished from the rigoristic schisms and some of the heretical sects, we must sample the evidence of the strong persistence of the communal voice in the disciplinary action of the ante-Nicene Church.

Clement of Rome, who deplored the constitutional revolution in Corinth, did not so much contest the right of the laity to eject their liturgical leaders as chastise them for having presumed to do so when their leaders had in fact 'offered the sacrifices *with innocence and holiness*'. Although this is more a constitutional than a disciplinary matter, we have in another apostolic father, Polycarp (d. *c.* 155), head of the church in Smyrna, a clear indication that the whole church and more specifically the laity with their presbyters had the right to depose and excommunicate one of their presbyters, Valens by name, and his wife, who had fallen into error, apparently in connection with defalcation in the matter of the communal funds. Polycarp urges the whole church to restore the couple if theirs proves to be a 'true repentance'.[34]

For North Africa we have evidence that primitive usage persisted vigorously and even developed new constitutional forms of lay authority in the realms of discipline and temporal administration. North African writers from Tertullian on mention besides the *presbyteri* (*seniores ecclesiastici*) an apparently collegiate group of *seniores laici*.[35] They may have been elected by the whole body of the faithful[36] or were more likely the most respected of the laity and, one might add, with sufficient leisure and sufficient means to serve with the bishop. There seems also to have been a distinction felt among the lay *seniores* between the weightier elders *ex plebe* or *locorum seu urbium* (who are listed after the clerical presbyters and before the deacons) and the elders of the church (*seniores ecclesiae*, who are listed after the deacons). The latter may have been limited to the caretaking tasks of fabric and furniture, but the *seniores* 'from the laity', possibly nominated by them and surely responsible to them, clearly had important administrative and judicial functions. In his *Apology*, Tertullian says that '*probati seniores* who have received the honour not by payment but by public testimony preside' at the sessions of the church which he likens to a *curia*.[37]

But the lawyer-theologian may, at this point, be adapting his speech to the pagan audience and has preferred the general term *seniores* to the more esoteric (clerical) *presbyteri*.[38]

Tertullian vividly describes the humiliating public confession of grievous sin, and points up for us the individual and collective action of the bishop, the presbyters (here there is no mention of lay elders as a distinct group) and the faithful laity:

> *Exomologesis* is a discipline consisting in prostration and humiliation, imposing on the offender such a demeanour as to attract mercy . . . to exchange his sins for harsh treatment of himself; . . . in general, to nourish prayers with fasting, to groan, to weep and moan day and night to the Lord his God, to prostrate himself before the presbyters (*presbyteri*), and to kneel before God's dear ones [*cari*, possibly the confessors]; to invoke all the brethren (*fratres*) as sponsors of his prayer for mercy.[39]

Cyprian made even more specific the rigoristic and perhaps even vindictive motivation of the laity in testing the penitent and also his own episcopal role in the readmission of schismatics, writing to the bishop of Rome:

> Oh, if you could, dearest brother, be with us here when those evil and perverse men return from schism, you would see what effort is mine to persuade patience to our brethren that they should calm their grief of mind and consent to receive and heal the wicked. At the return of the submissive they are filled with joy, but great is the outcry at the reception of the incorrigible. . . . Scarcely do I persuade the laity; nay, I extort it from them that they should suffer such to be admitted. And the just indignation of the brotherhood is vindicated perhaps in the fact that one or another who, not withstanding the opposition and gainsaying of the laity, having been admitted through my indulgence (*facultas*), have proved worse than they were before. . . .[40]

Many times the penitent schismatics and the weaker brethren who had lapsed during persecution and who were held back from readmission by the laity who were more severe than their bishop, sought out the prayers and specifically the certificates sometimes granted by confessors. These steadfast confessors (surviving martyrs), having themselves been more than meritorious during persecutions, exercised a moral authority in the community and, in some cases, arrogated to themselves the privilege of forgiving on their own their less steadfast fellow-Christians. In Cyprian's time they constituted a threat to the more orderly procedures of the Church in session. Confessors were, of course, a class that transcended the distinction between clerics and laics; but laics, being in any event more numerous than clerics, naturally predominated among the confessors. Tertullian, with characteristic irony, excoriates the grievous sinners: 'most eager to gain access to the prison [to seek out a confessor] who have lost the right of entrance to the Church'.[41]

Cyprian's contemporary in Rome, Cornelius, gives us a picture similar to that of North Africa as to the role of the laity in the corporate disciplinary action of the Church. Certain named confessors who had defected with Novatian returned:

> . . . they made known in the presence both of a number of bishops [not just the bishop of Rome, perhaps not including him], and also of very many presbyters and lay men, bewailing and repenting of the fact that for a brief space they had left the Church under the persuasion of this treacherous and malicious wild beast.[42]

One of the three simple and rural bishops whom Novatian had brought in to ordain him repented. With him Cornelius thereupon had communion, however, 'as a laic, all the laity present interceding for him'. At an earlier date under Bishop Zephyrinus, Natalius, another confessor, was lured into being ordained a heretical bishop, attracted by a salary of 150 *denarii* a month. Visited by Christ in visions, he finally desired to return to the orthodox community:

> . . . he arose at dawn, put on sackcloth, covered himself with ashes, and with all haste prostrated himself in tears before Zephyrinus the bishop; and, rolling at the feet not only of those in the clergy but also of the *laics*, he moved with his tears the compassionate church of the merciful Christ.[43]

The popular ascription of the power to forgive sins long remained associated with (lay) confessors and was to survive in the popular veneration of monks as latter-day confessors.[44] In contrast, the power of the ordinary layman, individually or corporately, to exercise the Christian duty of receiving the confession of sin from a brother in Christ and forgiving him in his name was everywhere attenuated.[45]

IV · The Layman as Teacher

As we turn from the exercise of discipline to the communication of the tradition by missionary evangelism, instruction, catechizing, and the definition of doctrine in synod, we find that here, too, after a period of rather full participation with the ordained clergy, the role of the laity declined, until it is virtually extinguished by the opening of the era of the great councils, when it will be pre-eminently the royal-priestly emperor who will 'represent' laity in the definition of the faith.[46]

Originally 'everyone taught' the redeeming faith that was his, says a later writer,[47] looking back into the ante-Nicene period before the bishops as successors of the apostles had come alone to exercise the magisterial function in the Church. He could have cited I Peter 3.15:

> Always be prepared to make a defence to any one who calls you to account for the hope that is in you, yet do it with gentleness and reverence.

Or one could have appealed to the author of the epistle to the Hebrews, who in his turn (8.11) had quoted Jer. 31.34 and had declared the ancient prophecy fulfilled in the people of the New Covenant:

> And they shall not teach every one his fellow or every one his brother, saying 'Know the Lord', for all shall know me, from the least even to the greatest.

The earliest Christian laymen knew whereon they believed, and needed no more to be taught, but they were nevertheless severally commissioned to make clear their faith to non-Christians. The pre-Constantinian period was for Christians an age of explicit (rather than merely implicit) faith for the laity no less than for the ordained leaders.

We may distinguish, in fact, the transitional emergence of a teaching order as the *choros* intermediate between the clergy and the laity. Justin Martyr and Origen were notable members of the 'choir of teachers'.[48]

That not all the evangelization and catechetical instruction took place under the leadership of such learned lay teachers or under the bishops becomes clear from Justin's description, when he admits that these teachers were often simple-minded (*idiōtai*) and uneducated. Even blind and crippled persons taught, for God, he argued, could work even with humble instruments. Of these teachers, who were also itinerants (most of them laics), Origen has the following description:

> ... as far as they are able, Christians leave no stone unturned to spread the faith in all parts of the world. Some, in fact, have done the work of going round not only cities but even villages and country cottages to make others also pious towards God. One could not say that they did this for the sake of wealth, since sometimes they do not even accept money for the necessities of life, and if ever they are compelled to do so by want in this respect, they are content with what is necessary and no more, even if several people are willing to share with them and to give them more than they need.[49]

Origen, himself the greatest theologian of his time, was for a long time an unordained member of the choir of teachers. He was rebuked by his bishop in Alexandria for preaching and teaching, on invitation, in the presence of bishops: and for this reason he left Alexandria for Caesarea. His new bishop, Demetrius, also rebuked the responsible bishops (of Jerusalem and Caesarea) for permitting another laic to sit in the episcopal *cathedra* and preach. Their self-defence is preserved by Eusebius in a document suggesting that such usage, despite their own magnanimity, was indeed on the way out. They report that Demetrius added to his letter to them:

> . . . that such a thing had never been heard of, nor taken place hitherto, that laics should preach (*homilein*) in the presence of bishops; though I [Alexander or Theocritus] do not know how he comes to say what is evidently not true. For instance, where there are found persons suited to help the brethren, they also are invited to preach to the people by the holy bishops, as, for example, in Laranda: Euelpis by Neon; and in Iconium: Paulinus by Celsus; and in Synnada: Theodore by Atticus, our blessed brother bishops. And it is likely that this thing happens in other places also without our knowing it.[50]

More significant for our present purpose than the occasional preaching by laics in the presence of certain indulgent bishops and the feats of such learned laics as Origen and the lay succession of brilliant heads of the catechetical school in Alexandria of which he was one, was the role of the unnamed and less tutored laity who seemed to have participated rather actively, not only in the disciplinary sessions of the Church, but also in the synods convened for the clarification of the faith and practice received by the Church. Our most interesting and conclusive material happens to centre in actions connected with Origen and more generally with Egypt.

In the newly discovered, stenographically recorded papyrus on the debate of Origen with Heraclides, we have first-hand evidence of the modest but essential part played by the simple laity in doctrinal formulation; for we can directly overhear the great (essentially lay) theologian himself solemnly asseverate in an Arabian synod (called to deal with problems of the Trinity and the final resurrection): 'Accordingly, with the permission of God and secondly of the bishops [there were several in the debate with him], and thirdly of the presbyters and of the *laity*, I say again what I think on the subject.' Then after summarizing his position he again takes cognizance of the laity: 'If you agree to these statements, they also with the solemn testimony of the *laity* shall be made legally binding and established.'[51] It appears that at the end of the synod the doctrinal formulations were formally set forth, the whole assembly including the laity ratifying them. Moreover, the laity probably had a good deal to do with initiating the original petitions which occasioned the synod.[52]

The doctrinal competence of the laity, in the sense of their feeling responsible for an explicit faith and of having the right to demand clarification on disputed points of tradition and scripture, comes out vividly again in a letter of Bishop Dionysius of Alexandria preserved by Eusebius. A certain Nepos, on the basis of the book of Revelation, had been teaching a rather fleshly millennium. The Church's view of the Kingdom and of the place of Revelation in the still incompletely clarified canon of New Testament scriptures was thus at stake— scarcely *adiaphora*, matters of no moment! The bishop tells how he went out to the centre of the affected region, Arsinoe, to discuss the whole problem reasonably and with charity:

> Now when I came [*c.* 254] to the [nome] of Arsinoe, where, as thou knowest, this doctrine [of Nepos] had long been prevalent, so that schisms and defections of whole churches had taken place, I called together the presbyters and [lay] teachers of the brethren in the villages—there were present also such of the brethren as wished; and I urged them to hold the examination of the question publicly.

There follows a description of a friendly give-and-take. Dionysius expresses

> ... greatest admiration for ... their firmness, love of truth, facility in following an argument, and intelligence, as we propounded in order and with forbearance the questions, the difficulties raised and the points of agreement, on the one hand [their] refusing to cling obstinately and at all costs (even though they were manifestly wrong) to opinions once held; and on the other hand [their] not shirking the counter-arguments, but as far as possible attempting to grapple with the questions in hand and master them.[53]

Dionysius goes on to admit he cannot always understand the Apocalypse himself and acknowledges further that 'if convinced by reason' on the part of these nimble-witted and earnest presbyters, lay teachers, and simple laics, he is not 'ashamed to change our [episcopal] opinions and give our assent. . . .'

When Origen countered the attack of the pagan critic Celsus that the Christians, because of the practice of itinerant evangelists, attracted only the uneducated and the poor, he pointed out that the advanced instruction for the catechumens was, after all, not given in public.[54]

The women, too, took part in this instruction. Clement of Alexandria, claiming that the wives of the apostles followed them only as 'sisters' and helpmates, proved this by saying:

> For they assisted them in ministering to women restricted to the house and through them the doctrine of the Lord could come without any seeming indecency into the women's part of the house (*gynaeceum*).[55]

Clement was portraying here, of course, the missionary practice of his own days.

The Syrian *Didascalia*, which reflects the beginnings of a more clerical form of the catechumenate, exhorts the widows to an ascetic and charitable office in the Church, and urges them not to usurp the task of teaching, which formerly they had evidently done:

> When she is asked a question by anyone, let her not straightway give an answer, except only concerning righteousness and faith in God; but let her send them that desire to be instructed to the rulers.[56]

The *Apostolic Constitutions*, also of a later date, reflect the coming to a close of the tradition of the charismatic (inspired lay) teacher when it grudgingly orders that '. . . even if a teacher be a laic, still if he be skilled in the word and reverent in habit, let him teach. . . .'[57]

V · *The Layman and Christian Service*

Luke describes in Acts (2.44; 4.32 ff.) the communism of the saints in Jerusalem as though to tell the Gentile world that its dream of the return of the golden age had in a sense been realized in the Church, as likewise the prophecies of the Old Testament had been fulfilled in this partial restoration of the goodness of paradise.

The communism of the Dead Sea Essenes has recently provided us with fresh antecedents and analogues. Here, too, the initiates had to bring their possessions into the common chest:

> All who declare their willingness to serve God's truth must bring all of their mind, all of their strength, and all of their wealth into the community of God.[58]

As in the case of Ananias and Sapphira, those who lied about their wealth were punished.[59]

The Jewish-Christian Ebionites longest retained the ideal of the community of goods.[60] Although the pre-Constantinian Church for the most part abandoned the absolute community of goods, they continued to recognize the community of things made holy in the fellowship of the liturgy.[61] The liturgical offerings of olives, cheese, and oil, mentioned above, in the *Apostolic Tradition* of Hippolytus, had as their destination beyond the altar the poor and the needy of the parish.

Pseudo-Clement, who incorporates a good many Pythagorean and Stoic ideas about the golden age and communism,[62] declares in his letter written allegedly to James as bishop of Jerusalem that 'as it is wicked for you to undertake secular cares . . ., so it is sin for every laic if they [*sic*] do not stand by one another even in their daily needs (*biōtikais chreiais*)'.[63]

Tertullian describes the common chest of a later date and in another tradition and the voluntary character of the offering:

Though we have a kind of money-chest, it is not for the collection of official fees, as if ours were a religion of fixed prices. Each of us puts in a small donation on the appointed day in each month, or when he chooses, and only if he chooses, and only if he can; for no one is compelled and the offering is voluntary. This is as it were the deposit fund of kindness. For we do not pay out money from this fund to spend on feasts or drinking parties or inelegant sprees, but to pay for the nourishment and burial of the poor, to support boys and girls who are orphan or destitute; and old people who are confined to the house; and those who have been shipwrecked; and any who are in the mines, or banished to islands, or in prison, or are pensioners because of their confession, provided they are suffering because they belong to the followers of God.[64]

The idea of bequests, a quota for the poor and for the benefit of the soul of a departed member, is first clearly demonstrable in the Constantinian age of accommodation;[65] but the *Testament of our Lord* surely preserves older usage in its instructions on bequests to the Church:

If any one depart from the world, either a faithful man or a faithful woman, having children, let them give their possessions to the Church, so that the Church may provide for their children, and that from the things which they have the poor may be given rest, that God may give mercy to their children and rest to those who have left them behind. But if a man have no children, let him have not much possessions, but let him give much of his possessions to the poor and to the prisoners, and only keep what is right and sufficient for himself.[66]

Irenaeus, without the trace of calculating charity in Tertullian and the Syriac *Testament*, movingly describes the love-inspired outreach of Christian worship and the Christian's giving of his talents to the whole world:

> Wherefore, also, those who are in truth his disciples, receiving grace from him, do in his name perform [miracles], so as to promote the welfare of other men, according to the gift which each one has received from him. For some do certainly and truly drive out devils, so that those who have thus been cleansed from evil spirits frequently both believe [in Christ], and join themselves to the Church. Others have foreknowledge of things to come. They see visions and utter prophetic expressions. Others still, heal the sick by laying their hands upon them, and they are made whole. . . . And what shall I more say? It is not possible to name the number of the gifts which the Church, [scattered] throughout the whole world, has received from God . . . and which she exerts day by day for the benefit of the Gentiles, neither practising deception upon them, nor taking any reward from them. For as she has received freely from God, freely also does she minister [to others].[67]

Justin Martyr among many others refers to the converting example of Christian lives.[68] On the occasion of a great pestilence in Alexandria the Christians there made it especially manifest that their care and concern for the brothers was not limited by death. This made a deep impression on the pagan populace. Dionysius of Alexandria writes in a letter:

> Most of our brethren were unsparing in their exceeding love and brotherly kindness. They held fast to each other and visited the sick fearlessly, and ministered to them continually, serving them in Christ. . . .
>
> The best of our brethren, some presbyters, deacons, and many of the *laity* that were exceedingly commended, transferred death to themselves. So that this very form of death, with the piety and ardent faith which attended it, appeared to be but little inferior to martyrdom itself. They took up the bodies of the saints with their open hands and on their bosoms, cleaned their eyes and closed their mouths, carried them on their shoulders, and composed their limbs, embraced, clung to them, and prepared them decently, washing and wrapping them up, and ere long they themselves shared in the same offices, those that survived always following those before them.
>
> Among the heathen it was the direct reverse. They repelled those who began to sicken, and avoided their dearest friend. They would cast them out into the roads half dead, or throw them out when dead without burial, striving to shun any communication and participation in death, which it was impossible to avoid by any precaution and care.[69]

From this tribute to lay workers in time of plague we may turn to the quite specialized religio-medical practice of exorcism in the ancient Church and the role of the laity therein. Exorcism and the renunciation of the devil and all his works was an integral part of the baptismal rite and the bishop pronounced the formulas. But besides this solemn sacramental exorcism, there was the kindred therapeutic exorcism carried on by charismatic and commonly lay practitioners. Justin says that many a layman had the gift of healing:

> And now you may learn from what goes on under your own eyes. For many devil-possessed all over the world, and in your own city, many of our men, the Christians have exorcized in the name of Jesus Christ, who was crucified under Pontius Pilate. When all other exorcists and sayers of charms and sellers of drugs failed, they have healed them, and still do heal, sapping the power of the demons who hold men, and driving them out.[70]

The healing ministry of prayer to Christ to drive out the devils of insanity and sickness on the apostolic pattern is also briefly referred to by Origen, who says, '. . . it is mostly people quite untrained who do this work'. He continues:

> Not a few Christians exorcize sufferers, and that without manipulations and magic or the use of drugs, but just by prayer and an invocation of the simpler kind and by such means as the simpler kind of man might be able to use.[71]

Moreover, since the Christians were more successful than the heathen exorcists, this made their (medical) missionary activities among their pagan neighbours highly effective.[72]

Besides the more spectacular exorcists and healers the so-called 'widows' served as humble nocturnal vigilants and nurses. Since the time of Paul these widows held a distinct place in the Church, partly given over to ascetic practices, partly to the exercise of Christian charity especially on behalf of the female members of the community. The *Canones Apostolorum Ecclesiastici* prescribes:

> Out of three widows who are appointed, two should remain in intercessory prayer for those whose situation demands it or pray for revelations if necessary. The third should assist women who are sick. She should be a good steward, sober, and notify the presbyters of what she sees and hears. After improper profits she should not crave or drink too much wine, which would impede her nocturnal service and her other charitable activities.[73]

The number of widows dependent on the charity of the Church was high. Cornelius of Rome counted besides his 46 presbyters, 7 deacons, 7 sub-deacons, 42 acolytes, 52 exorcists, readers, and janitors, not less than 1,500 widows![74] They were mainly in charge of the mission to the shut-in women, who were regularly not allowed to leave the house.

The social action of the pre-Constantinian Church and, of course, the communism of the first generation of Christians was a sharing among the holy in holy things. It was primarily a philanthropy of Christians, among Christians, sustained by things sacramental in their sight. Eventually the communistic motif would be institutionally transformed as monastic coenobism in the fourth century, and would be theologically transmuted as the ecclesiological doctrine of the *communio sanctorum*, the communion of saints, inserted into the Apostles' Creed in the fifth century. But the philanthropic impulse would remain characteristic of the great Church. Indeed the social concern for those outside the Christian community of the sacraments would, if anything, become even more prominent in the Church after its recognition by Constantine.

We now turn to the long tradition of the witness and achievement of God's *laos* in the world, of the leaven in the lump, of the Christians away from their *ekklesia* in the *diaspora*.

VI · The Laymen in Diaspora

The first three centuries were a period in which the Church existed as a rejected minority. The accusations against it included almost every imaginable crime, from sexual promiscuity to cannibalism. These suspicions were nurtured by the fact that the Christians refused to conform in certain matters with the general usage. Their doors were unadorned on the Caesar's Day, they could not be found in the circus or theatre, and they did not engage in the sports and games then popular. They were reluctant to use the public baths and cautious in the purchase of meat, which might have been previously dedicated to pagan idols. Claiming to be a third race neither Jew nor Gentile, claiming to have no emperor but Christ, it is little wonder that they aroused suspicion and hatred, not least of all among the pagans of conspicuous civic virtue.

The *Didache*, in setting forth the traditional Jewish doctrine of the two ways, does not yet, to be sure, breathe the odour of complete sanctity. The way of life includes surprisingly down-to-earth prohibitions: 'You shall not corrupt boys, you shall not commit fornication, you shall not steal, you shall not practise magic, you shall not use enchantment, you shall not murder a child by abortion or kill when born.'[75] Nevertheless, despite the tell-tale crudeness of such injunctions, the level of Christian morality and the scope of Christian philanthropy beyond their own community seems to have been sufficient to attract the sometimes grudgingly favourable comment of outsiders.[76]

The Christians of the pre-Constantinian period, for their part, had no doubt about their ethical superiority. Although there was spiritual pride and bigoted self-righteousness, we should like to think that in a moving letter from a Christian to his friend, one Diognetus, we find the best portrayal of the pre-Constantinian layman's situation among the non-Christians:

> Though they live in Greek and barbarian cities, as each man's lot is cast, and follow the local customs in dress and food and the rest of their living, their own way of life which they display is wonderful and admittedly strange. They live in their native lands, but like foreigners. They take part in everything like citizens, and endure everything like aliens. Every foreign country is their native land, and every native land a foreign country. Like everyone else they marry, they have children, but they do not expose their infants. They set a common table, but not a common bed. They find themselves in flesh, but they do not live after the flesh. They pass their days on earth, but they are citizens of heaven. They obey the prescribed laws, and at the same time surpass the laws by their lives.[77]

Equally moving is the passage in the *Apology* of the Athenian Marcianus Aristides addressed to the Emperor Antonius Pius some time after the year 138. After pointing out that the Christians were a kind of fourth nation exceeding in virtue the Greeks, the Barbarians, and the Jews, Aristides declared:

> . . . they have come nearer to truth and genuine knowledge than the rest of the nations. For they know and trust in God, the Creator of heaven and of earth, in whom and from whom are all things, to whom there is no other god as companion, from whom they received commandments which they engraved upon their minds and observe in hope and expectation of the world which is to come. Wherefore they do not commit adultery nor fornication, nor bear false witness, nor embezzle what is held in pledge, nor covet what is not theirs. They honour father and mother, and show kindness to those near to them; and whenever they are judges, they judge uprightly . . . and whatsoever they would not that others should do unto them, they do not to others . . . their oppressors they comfort and make

them friends; *they do good to their enemies; and their wives . . . are pure as virgins and their daughters modest; and their men abstain from all unlawful wedlock and from all impurity. . . . As for their servants or hand-maids, or their children if any of them have any, they persuade them to become Christians for the love that they have towards them; and when they have become so, they call them without distinction brethren. . . . And they walk in all humility and kindness; and falsehood is not found among them; and they love one another; and from the widows they do not turn away their countenance; and they rescue the orphan . . .; and he who has gives to him who has not without grudging; and when they see the stranger they bring him to their dwellings and rejoice over him as over a true brother; for they do not call brothers those that are after the flesh but those who are in the spirit and in God; . . . and if they hear that any of their number is imprisoned or oppressed for the name of their Messiah all of them provide for his needs, and if it is possible that he may be delivered they deliver him. And if there is among them a man that is poor or needy and they have not an abundance of necessaries, they fast two or three days that they may supply the needy with their necessary food.

And they observe scrupulously the commandments of their Messiah; they live honestly and soberly, as the Lord their God commanded them. Every morning and at all hours on account of the goodnesses of God towards them they praise and laud him; and over their food and over their drink they render him thanks. . . .

. . . such is the ordinance of the law of the Christians . . ., such their conduct. As men who know God they ask from him petitions which are proper for him to give and for them to receive; and thus they accomplish the course of their lives. And because they acknowledge the goodnesses of God towards them, lo! on account of them there flows forth the beauty that is in the world. §And truly they are of the number that have found the truth.**

And to me there is no doubt but that the earth abides through the supplication of the Christians. But the rest of the nations err and cause error in wallowing before the elements of the world, since beyond these their mental vision will not pass. And they search about as if in darkness because they will not recognize the truth; and like drunken men they reel and jostle one another and fall.[78]

Such was the image that Christians had of themselves as an elect race living in the Roman Empire but not entirely of it.

It was in relation to penal servitude in the mines and other public works and service in the militia and constabulary (in the Roman Empire virtually identical), and especially during the sporadic or the systematic persecutions, that Christians were most commonly called upon to witness—to use the terminology of our survey—in the *diaspora*.

One Papylas, presumably a lay member of the church in Pergamon, during the persecution under Marcus Aurelius proudly addressed the interrogating proconsul who had asked as to whether he had any children: 'In every district and city I have children in God; yes, and many of them, thanks be to God!'[79] The Phrygian physician Alexander in Gaul, renowned for his love towards God and his boldness of speech, 'for he was not without a share of the *apostolic* gift', encouraged the confessors and then was himself seized and taken with them into the amphitheatre.[80] The martyred centurion Marcellus (d. 298), by his Christian 'soldierly' example in responding to the enraged examiner, converted the pagan court stenographer, Cassian, who thereupon threw down his notebook in disgust and followed the Christian way.[81]

Sons of soldiers had, according to the later law of the Empire, the duty to serve as soldiers. One Maximilianus, a Christian, avowed his faith when the responsible officer tried to enforce his enlistment. After the officer had stated why it was his duty to serve and that he was a qualified recruit, the proconsul asked: 'What is your name?' Maximilianus replied: 'Now, why do you want to know my name? I have a conscientious objection to military service: I am a Christian.' The proconsul ordered that Maximilianus be equipped. While this was being done, Maximilianus answered: 'I can't serve; I can't sin against my conscience; I am a Christian.' The proconsul ignored this and ordered that his measure be taken—he was reported by the sergeant-at-arms as being five feet ten inches in height. The proconsul ordered the sergeant to have him sealed. Maximilianus resisted and answered: 'I won't do it; I can't serve.' The proconsul: 'Serve, or you will lose your life.' Maximilianus: 'I won't serve. You may behead me, but I won't serve the powers of this world; I will serve my God.'[82]

Martyrdom was not all valour and triumph. The goal was direct entry into paradise, the forecourt of the Kingdom, rather than slumber in the grave till the resurrection. The *Passio SS. Perpetuae et Felicitatis*, perhaps written or completed by Tertullian, shows how Perpetua's stand as a martyr destroyed a family. Her pagan father did not understand her. Full of despair he humiliated himself to save her from death. He could not comprehend why for her the impending execution was a joyous event and begged and wept in vain. He even called her 'mistress' instead of daughter to win her back. But Perpetua, though full of compassion for her father, remained firm.

It cannot be doubted that the exuberant confidence in a heavenly reward affected many wistful bystanders of the martyrdoms. Justin Martyr confessed:

> I myself . . . when I was delighting in the teachings of Plato, and heard the Christians slandered, and saw them fearless of death and of all things which are counted fearful, I understood. . . .[83]

Outstanding among the resources of the persecuted Christians of all ages and walks of life was their sense of solidarity as race elect, and their refusal to inform against each other under judicial torture. *Traditores*, as the few were called who lapsed and gave information about their brethren, were punished with excommunication. Judas, as one of the intimate circle of the original twelve, stood out as *the* example of the traitorous (from *traditor*) informer. The Council of Elvira, convened while Christians still stood in peril of the persecution under the Emperor Diocletian, enacted in Canon 73 the excommunication, without the possibility of reconciliation even on the deathbed, of any informer who had caused the proscription or death of the person informed against.[84]

We may close our account of the role of the laity in the period of the persecutions with the disdainful caricature of the little people (men, women, and children) ever ready for a martyr's death, who carried the gospel into the recesses of society and who, though nameless and despised by cultured and informed observers, probably did more even than bishops, apologists, and theologians to prepare for the sudden conquest of the Greco-Roman world at the opening of the fourth century. The words are those of the pagan critic Celsus:

> In private houses also we see wool-workers, cobblers, laundry-workers and the most illiterate and bucolic yokels, who would not dare to say anything at all in front of their elders and more intelligent masters. But when they get hold of children in private and some little old women with them, they let out some astounding statements as, for example, that they must not pay any attention to their fathers and school-teachers, but must obey *them*; they say that these talk nonsense and have no understanding, and that in reality they neither know nor are able to do anything good, but are taken up with mere empty chatter. But *they* alone, they say, know the right way to live and if the children would believe *them*, they would become happy and make their home happy as well.[85]

Disparagingly, a philosophical publicist here describes better than he knew how in fact it was the little people, the lay men and women of the ante-Nicene Church, who built the foundations of that spiritual mansion (we need not insist on the 'happy home') in which even an emperor, a very practical layman, was one day to choose to live.

NOTES

1. The full phrasing is first found in Eusebius, *Ecclesiastical History* I.3, 8.

2. Among recent studies of this theme, see William David Davies, *Torah in the Messianic Age and/or the Age to Come* (Philadelphia, 1952); Herbert Braun, *Spätjüdisch-häretischer und frühchristlicher Radikalismus: Jesus von Nazareth und die essenische Qumransekte* (Tübingen, 1957); and Matthew Black, *The Qumran Scrolls and Christian Origins* (New York and London, 1961).

3. See the forthcoming doctoral dissertation of Clarence Lee, 'The Sacerdotal Ethic of Early Christianity', Harvard University, Cambridge, Massachusetts.

4. The distinction is a basic approach in the work of the chapters of this book. The present chapter on the laity roughly parallels another study, made by the present author, of the evolution of the clergy in the ante-Nicene period: *The Ministry in Historical Perspectives*, ed. H. Richard Niebuhr and Daniel Williams (New York, 1956), ch. 2.

5. *I Clement* 40.5.

6. Ignace de la Potterie, S.J., 'L'origine et le sens primitif du mot "laïc" ', *Nouvelle Revue Théologique* LXXX (1958), p. 849.

7. Traditional Catholic and critical Protestant scholarship have until recently joined, from diverse impulses, to spiritualize, interiorize, and individualize the meaning of the sacrifice in I Peter 2.5 and 9. E. G. Selwyn, though conservative on the matter of the authorship of the epistle, sees clearly the eucharistic significance of the priesthood of the *laos. The First Epistle of St Peter* (London, 1948), pp. 295 ff.

On the priesthood of all believers, besides the recent literature cited in nn. 4 and 14 of the original version of the present chapter, *loc. cit.*, pp. 11 and 17, one may consult the comprehensive Catholic survey of the literature by R. Tucci, 'Recenti pubblicazioni sui "laici" nella Chiesa', *Civiltà Cattolica* CIX, ii (1958), pp. 178–90.

8. *Dial. cum Tryph.* 116.

9. *Apol.* 2 (in the Syriac version which is closest to the original Greek text) and 15 (in the adapted Greek text).

10. *Omnes enim justi sacerdotalem habent ordinem* (*Contr. Haer.* IV.8, 3). The original Greek text has not survived.

11. For a modern interpretation, see Max Thurian, *La confirmation, consécration des laïcs* (Neuchâtel, 1957).

12. *De baptismo* 7.

13. *Ibid.* 17.

14. Clement, *Stromata* VI.13.

15. *Op. cit.* 41.

16. *I Apol.* 65. Cf. Theodoret of Cyrrhus, *Comm. in II Cor.* *1.20*. See P. Rouget, *Amen, Acclamation du peuple sacerdotal* (Paris, 1947).

17. *Dial. cum Tryph.* 116 f. In language which suggests familiarity with this passage, Origen a century later asks:

'Or do you not recognize that the priesthood has been given to you also, that is to the whole Church of God and the nation of believers? . . . You have therefore a priesthood, being a priestly nation, I Peter 2.9. Therefore you ought to offer to God a sacrifice of praise, of prayers, of pity, of purity, of righteousness, of holiness. To offer this aright you have need of clean garments, of vestments kept apart from the common clothing of the rest of mankind; and you must have the divine fire, God's own fire which he gives to men, of which the Son of God says, Luke 12.49: "I have come to send fire on earth" '—*In Levit. hom.* 10.1.

18. *Op. cit.*, ed. G. Dix, 5.1 and 2.

19. *Op. cit.* 1.23; transl. James Cooper and Arthur Maclean (Edinburgh, 1902), p. 73; see another long formulary, pp. 83 f.

20. Damasus (366–384). See Christine Mohrmann, '*Statio*', *Vigiliae Christianae* VII (1953), p. 224. At the same period in the East, Basil of Caesarea countenanced laymen, during persecution, keeping the communion at home and partaking of it with their own hands at appropriate intervals. He cites the current usage of the laity in Egypt and the practice of hermits in the wilderness where there is no priest: *Ep.* 93.

21. *De exhort. cast.* 7.

22. *Apol.* 39.

23. *Op. cit.* 7.

24. Ambrosiaster, *Comm. in Eph.* 4.11.

25. The most recent specialized study is that of P. Trempelas, '*Hē summetochē tou laou en tēi eklogēi tōn episkopōn*', *Epistēmonikē Epetēris* of the Theological School of the University of Athens (1954–5), pp. 1–27. See also C. Jenkins, 'The Position of Clergy and Laity in the Early Church in Relation to the Episcopate', *Episcopacy, Ancient and Modern*, ed. C. Jenkins (London, 1930), and the Ph.D. thesis of Dr Charles J. Speel, II, 'The Communal Authority in the Ancient Church', Cambridge, 1956.

26. *Op. cit.* 15.

27. *Op. cit.* 2.1.

28. *In Levit. hom.* 3. The text survives only in Latin, and the key terms are *sacerdos* and *populus*.

29. *Ep.* 67.5. In *Ep.* 10.8 he speaks of Cornelius of Rome as made bishop by the judgment of God and Christ, by the testimony of the clerics, and by the vote (*suffragio*) of both the priests and the *plebs*.

30. *Ep.* 67.3.

31. *Vita Alex.* 45.7.

32. The problem has been most recently surveyed from the Catholic point of view by Jorge Sily, S.J., 'El texto de Santiago: "Confesaos los unos a los otros pecados" en los once primeros siglos de la Iglesia', *Ciencia y Fe* VI (1950), pp. 7–22.

33. Cf., for example, the wording of the electoral procedure in the *Constitutions of the Holy Apostles* VIII.4. There is a clear echo of the participation of laics (*tēs synodou kai tou plēthous*) in disciplinary action in Chrysostom, *Hom. in Act.* 27. On the episcopal monopolization of the prerogative of all spiritual men to judge all things (I Cor. 2.15), see Albert Koeniger (ed.), 'Prima sedes a nemine judicatur', *Festgabe Albert Ehrhard* (Bonn, 1922), pp. 273–300.

34. *Op. cit.* 11.

35. See most recently Pier G. Caron, 'Les *seniores laici* de l'Église africaine', *Revue Internationale des Droits de l'Antiquité* VI (1951), pp. 7–22; also his basic study, *I Poteri giuridici del laicato nella Chiesa primitiva* (Milan, 1948).

36. So, Caron, *op. cit.*, on the basis of an epitaph, but one would need more evidence.

37. *Op. cit.* 39.

38. Caron holds that they are *seniores ex plebe*.

39. *De poenit.* 7.

40. *Ep.* 59 (54).15.

41. *Ad martyres* 1.

42. Cornelius *apud* Eusebius, *H.E.* VI.43, 6.

43. The anonymous author of the *Little Labyrinth*, Eusebius, *H.E.* V.28, 8–12.

44. Karl Holl, *Enthusiasmus und Bussgewalt beim griechischen Mönchtum* (Leipzig, 1898).

45. Amédée Teetaert, Ord. Cap., *La confession aux laïques dans l'Église latine* (Bruges and Paris, 1926).

46. On the authority of the emperors see Francis Dvornik, 'Emperors, Popes, and General Councils', *Dumbarton Oaks Papers* 6 (Cambridge, 1951), pp. 1–23. Two ancient historians mention laics skilled in dialectic participating in the Council of Nicaea in 325: Socrates, *H.E.* I.8; Sozomen, *H.E.* I.17.

47. Ambrosiaster, *Comm. in Eph.* 4.11.

48. I have brought together some of this material in *The Ministry in Historical Perspectives*, pp. 46–8. See Hans Freiherr von Campenhausen, *Kirchliches Amt und geistliche Vollmacht* (Tübingen, 1953), ch. 8. [Note that Origen was in middle life ordained to the presbyterate—Ed.]

49. *Contra Celsum*, III.9.

50. Eusebius, *H.E.* VI.19, 18. Adolf Harnack notes how far-fetched the examples are and calls these men the last preaching teachers known by name besides Origen. For other pertinent material see his *The Mission and Expansion of Christianity in the First Three Centuries* (ET), 2 vols (New York, 1908).

51. *Entretien d'Origène avec Héraclide et les évêques sur le Père, le Fils, et l'âme*, ed. Jean Scherer, Publications de la Société Fouad et de Papyrologie, Textes et Documents, IX (Cairo, 1949); translated in the *Library of Christian Classics* II (Philadelphia and London, 1954), 128 and 134.

52. In two other synods at which Origen dealt with doctrinal matters the laity are known to have been present, surely in more than the role of auditors or spectators for otherwise their presence would not have been noticed in such brief accounts. Eusebius, *H.E.* VI.37; Origen, *Opera omnia* (ed. C. Lommatzsch) XVII.9. 'A great majority of the laity' were also present in the important synod of eighty-three bishops held in Carthage on 1st September 256; *apud* Cyprian.

53. *Apud* Eusebius, *H.E.* VII.24, 6.

54. *Contra Celsum* III.51.

55. *Stromata* III.6, 53, quoted by Josephine Mayer, *Monumenta de viduis, diaconissis virginibusque tractantia*, Florilegium Patristicum, XLII, Bonn, 1938.

56. *Op. cit.* 3.5.

57. *Op. cit.* VIII.31.

58. 1 QS i, 12.

59. 1 QS vi, 25.

60. On communism in the early Church, see most recently Werner Elert, *Abendmahl und Kirchengemeinschaft in der alten Kirche* (Berlin, 1954), and the article, with the literature, by A. Piolanti in *Lexikon für Theologie und Kirche*[2] IV (Freiburg, 1960), pp. 651–3. See further the chapter on the Ebionites in *The Scrolls and the New Testament*, ed. K. Stendahl (New York and London, 1957/8), ch. 13.

61. Barely suggested by F. J. Badcock, *The History of the Creeds* (London, 1930), ch. 17.

62. See Hans von Schubert, *Der Kommunismus der Wiedertäufer und seine Quellen*. Heidelberger Akademie der Wissenschaften, S.B. philo-hist. Kl., X.11 (1919).

63. *Hom., ep. Cl.*, ed. Paul de Lagarde, *Clementina* (Leipzig, 1865).

64. *Apol.* 39.

65. See Eberhard Bruck, *Kirchenväter und soziales Erbrecht* (Berlin/Göttingen/Heidelberg, 1956).

66. *Op. cit.* 2.5.

67. *Adv. haer.* II.32, 4; very similar in Aristides, *Apol.* 15, ed. Harvey 2, 49, 3 (vol. I, p. 375) (Greek-Syriac version), below at n. 78.

68. *I Apol.* 16.

69. Letter to the brethren, *c.* 252, *apud* Eusebius, *H.E.* VII.22, 7 ff.

70. *II Apol.* 6.

71. *Contra Celsum* VII.4.

72. John Foster, *After the Apostles: Missionary Preaching of the First Three Centuries* (London, 1951), p. 64.

73. *Op. cit.* 21.

74. *Apud* Eusebius, *H.E.* VI.43.

75. *Did.* 2.2.

76. Karl Holl, 'Die Missionsmethode der alten und mittelalterlichen Kirche', *Gesammelte Aufsätze zur Kirchengeschichte* III (Tübingen, 1921–8), pp. 121 ff.

77. *Ep. to Diognetus* 5.4–10.

78. *Op. cit.* 15 and 16. The *Apology* survives in Syriac, Armenian, and Greek. The full text of the Greek appears to have been compacted and rendered more elegant for use in a later Christian romance. But Greek fragments very close to the ample Syriac text have been found. The foregoing translation is largely from the original Greek fragment. It is indicated in the text by asterisks: * to **. This is taken over with a modification of the punctuation from H. J. Milne, 'A New Fragment of the *Apology* of Aristides', *Journal of Theological Studies* XXV (1924), pp. 73–7. To supplement the fragment at the beginning and at the end, the corresponding parts of the English translation from the Syriac text as published in ANF IX, pp. 277 ff., have been used. The mark § indicates a very attractive sentence which may well be an inference from the later copyist of a faulty part of an earlier copy of the *Apology*. It appears, however, in both the Greek fragment and the Syriac. On its elimination as not in the present form from Aristides, see J. de Zwaan, 'A Gap in the Recently Discovered Greek Apology of Aristides 16, 1', *Harvard Theological Review* XVIII (1925), pp. 109–11.

79. E. C. E. Owen, *Some Authentic Acts of the Early Martyrs* (Oxford, 1927), pp. 42 f.

80. Eusebius, *H.E.* V.1, 49.

81. Owen, *op. cit.*, p. 121.

82. D. R. Knopf and Gustav Krüger, *Ausgewählte Märtyrerakten* (1929), pp. 86–7; as translated by Arnold Toynbee, *An Historian's Approach to Religion* (New York and London, 1956), p. 105.

83. *II Apol.* 12.

84. G. H. Williams, 'The Reluctance to Inform', *Theology Today* XIV (1957), pp. 239 ff.

85. Quoted by Origen, *Contra Celsum* III.55.

2

William H. C. Frend

THE CHURCH OF THE ROMAN EMPIRE
313–600

I · *The Situation in 313*

THE triumph of Christianity during the last quarter of the third century had brought its own problems in its wake. In the field of doctrine, Eusebius (*H.E.* VIII.1, 7) describes the mounting tensions between rival groups of Christians that characterized the period immediately before the Great Persecution. In the field of church order, equally grave problems were arising, and these were to have their effect on the relationship between the clergy and the laity in the succeeding age. The Church in the first two centuries had been a small and closely-knit body scattered through the cities of the Roman Empire. So long as it remained such, the laity retained an important role in its organization and liturgy. When, in 197, Tertullian described the Church in Roman Africa, he calls it 'a society with a common religious feeling, a unity of discipline and a bond of hope' (*Apology*, ed. Glover, 39.1). 'Where three are together,' he says elsewhere, 'there is the Church, even if they are laymen.'[1] The Holy Spirit imposed an equality on priests and laymen alike: the services which Tertullian describes were evidently not yet standardized. The congregation met 'to read the books of God' (*Apology* 39.3), and then 'each from what he knows of the Holy Scripture or from his own heart is called upon before the rest to sing to God' (*ibid.* 39.8).

As we have seen in the previous chapter, the laity took a leading part in this liturgy, and behind these practices lay a theory of the Church, which regarded Christianity less as an organization than as a way of life under the continuous guidance of the Holy Spirit. The return of the Lord was expected as an event which Christians would witness, and therefore the 'spiritual man', and above all the martyr, was looked upon as the perfected Christian.[2] Confessors and martyrs were taken from laity and clergy alike, and theirs was the right of 'binding and loosing',[3] and of receiving commands from the Lord. The clergy administered discipline among the congregation, but Paradise was for the martyr and the martyr alone.[4]

The third century was to see some radical changes in this point of view, changes which affected adversely the position of the laity within the Church. The dual influence of the failure of the Second Coming to take place in a temporal form, and the influx of a large number of nominal Christians in the years of peace between 212–249, altered men's views about the nature of the Church. Patently, it had become a mixed body, containing sinners as well as the elect, and the bond of unity was to be found in the sacraments administered by the clergy. In both East and West the transformation can be studied in the bitter comments of Hippolytus[5] at Rome, and the nostalgia of Origen for the 'golden age' of the Severan persecution (202–203).[6]

By the middle of the century, the monarchical episcopate had become the universally recognized system of church government. Ordination was a permanent step, setting the cleric rigidly apart from the world he had renounced.[7] In 251, confessors in Carthage who aspired to forgive the sin of apostasy after the Decian persecution (249–251) were firmly rebuked by Cyprian,[8] and some, at Cyprian's discretion, were promoted to the ranks of the clergy.[9] At the same time, significant changes were going on among the clergy themselves which increased the distance between them and the mass of the faithful. 'Minor orders', of sub-deacons, acolytes, doorkeepers, exorcists and readers were being built up into a regular hierarchy of ecclesiastical grades.[10] The deacon was tending to become more pronouncedly an administrator, and thus encroaching on functions which laymen were performing in the service of the Church. In Carthage, the deacons are mentioned as supervisors of funds belonging to the Church in 251.[11] Fifty years later, the senior deacon there, the 'archidiaconus', had become the heir presumptive to his bishop's see.[12] The Holy Spirit was being firmly guided into ecclesiastical channels. Thus, at the time of the Great Persecution in 303, doubts were being cast in Carthage on the value of unregulated martyrdom as a means of obtaining divine mercy. Vigils outside prisons in which lay confessors were housed were sharply discouraged by Caecilian, the archdeacon of Carthage.[13] Martyrs and their relics were held to have no merit until duly approved by ecclesiastical authority.[14]

The Great Persecution brought the implicit conflict of authority between cleric and inspired layman into the open. In Africa this conflict formed the background to the Donatist controversy. In Egypt, a similar development set in motion the Melitian schism. Just at the very moment when more and more of the provincials were turning to an intense and eschatological form of Christianity, the government of the Church was becoming solidified on a formal, hierarchical basis. Moreover, after the Edict of Milan in February 313, the avenue of martyrdom became closed. Lay Christianity had to find new outlets. It is no accident that in the fourth and fifth centuries monasticism and various forms of ascetic life were, in the main, movements among the laity. In the East, these were regarded as deliberate substitutions for martyrdom.[15] But they were supplemented by a general and intense interest in theological problems among the Christian provincials as a whole. The fact that laymen could still influence the outlook and practice of the Church rendered their subordinate position in its organization and liturgy tolerable.

II · The Layman in the Worship and Organization of the Church[16]

'The layman should honour the good shepherd [the bishop], respect him like a father, lord and master, as the high priest of God as guide in piety.' 'He who hears the bishop hears Christ.' Thus, the *Apostolic Constitutions*, probably in the earlier part of the fourth century,[17] defined the role of the layman. In the plan of the churches which were being built all over the Mediterranean provinces of the Roman Empire, a substantial screen of stone or marble divided the nave, or *quadratum populi*, from the altar and apse whither only the clergy might approach.[18] No layman might participate in the administration of the sacraments.[19] No psalms written by individual Christians were to be sung in church.[20] Laymen were to sit 'quietly and seemly' in their places.[21]

Such were the rules, but even so, there were occasions when necessity knew no law, as when perhaps in a time of local persecution by the pro-Arian emperor, Valens (d. 378), Basil of Caesarea authorized laity to keep the communion at home and partake of it themselves (*Letter* 93).[22] There is also some evidence to show that the practice of lay preaching, exemplified by Origen during the third century, did not die out at once. Asterius the Sophist, unordained because of lapse during the Great Persecution, was apparently permitted to preach his semi-Arian doctrines in Syrian churches between 331–335, and to attend synods of bishops.[23] In the West, Pope Leo had to remind correspondents in the mid-fifth century that laymen were not to preach.[24] In Africa a layman might still teach in the presence of clergy if invited to do so,[25] and he retained the right exercised by all laymen of all ages to grumble at the services. The retired tribune, Hilarius, complained bitterly to the clergy of Hippo against a new-fangled practice introduced there from Carthage of singing parts of the Psalms before the offertory at the Eucharist. Augustine apparently gave him short shrift.[26] In both East and West, however, congregational singing was becoming established. We hear how *c*. 375 the two Antiochene ascetics Flavian, later to be Bishop of Antioch, and Diodore, later Bishop of Tarsus, had the congregation at Antioch divided into two choirs to sing the responses antiphonally.[27] Their plan was not accepted at once without opposition, but gradually it became the rule in the East. In the West, we find Ambrose of Milan instituting a similar practice. The people sang psalms and hymns in alternate choirs and their responses echoed 'like the roar of waves on the seashore'.[28] To him this was the most effective service the laity could perform in the liturgy.[29] Nearly a century later we find the same practice in Gaul.[30] 'We had assembled', writes Apollinaris Sidonius, *c*. 465, 'at the tomb of St Justus. The annual procession before daylight was over, attended by a vast crowd of both sexes which even that great church could not hold with all its cincture of galleries. After Vigils were ended, chanted alternately by the monks and the clerics, the congregation separated; we could not go far off, as we had to be at hand for the next service at Tierce, when the priests were to celebrate the Mass.'[31] It is a scene which says much. The laity have their function, to support the intercessions of the clergy, to escort them during the great processions on feast days, and on these occasions to assemble in their thousands and do them honour.

Organizationally, the West provides examples of a tendency to extend the principle of hierarchy to the laity themselves. Thus, Victricius of Rouen (*c*. 390) indicates the order in which the laity may approach holy relics in the course of a procession.[32] After the priests, deacons and clergy in minor orders, come the monks, the children, the widows, the *continentes* (laics who, while remaining in the world, had voluntarily accepted certain ascetic practices), the old men, the mothers, and finally the mass of the people. A serious effort seems to have been made to give the widows, at least, a fixed status among the laity. This was due partly to a traditional dislike of second marriages as something akin to adultery,[33] partly to the honour in which widows were held in the

Early Church.[34] The Fathers insist on the merits of the widows and attempt to define their duties. We learn from the Council of Orange in 441 that there was a formal profession of widowhood before the bishop and that those professed wore special vestments.[35] At the Council of Elvira,[36] and at Carthage in 348, regulations were laid down for the conduct of widows.[37] In Africa, we learn that at the end of the fourth century one of the tasks allotted to them was the preparation of catechumens for baptism, especially in country districts (*Statuta eccl. antiqua* 12).

Even so, the clergy seem to have been constantly on the look-out for possible encroachments on their privileges. The widows, even if learned, were not to baptize nor to teach men, we are told.[38] At the end of the fifth century Pope Gelasius forbade their veiling and benediction.[39] In the last resort, the Church was not prepared to leave them very much more than constant prayer and continuous charity on her behalf in return for a small stipend.[40] The layman of mature years who sought ordination faced an almost interminable *cursus honorum* of ecclesiastical offices before he attained the presbyterate.[41]

Even the rather mundane work of administering church finances and property was tending to become, outside of Africa, the preserve of clerics. In the mid-fourth century, the Council of Antioch (Canon 25) had advised bishops not to use their clergy for such purposes, but to employ their lay friends and relatives. In 451, however, the Council of Chalcedon decided that the office of examiner of church accounts should be held by a cleric,[42] and three years later, Pope Leo saw reason for requesting the Emperor Marcian not to allow civil judges 'in a manner without precedent' to audit the accounts of 'the oeconomos of the church of Constantinople'. He claimed that these should be examined by the bishop alone.[43] In the sixth century, it seems to have been the usual practice for the landed property of the great sees to be administered by the deacons as well as by lay officials.[44] A Roman council held in July 595 laid down that the Bishop of Rome should have no lay servants to wait on him and Pope Gregory replaced his lay attendants by clergy and monks.[45]

Some shreds of active lay participation in the internal life of the Church, however, persisted. The laity, in dire need, might still baptize.[46] They never lost the right of electing their bishop, and of approving, at least in theory, his clergy. The election of Caecilian at Carthage in 312, for instance, was said to have been by 'the voting of the entire populace', and the new bishop appealed to the 'whole body of the citizens' for their support against the charges brought against him by the Donatists.[47] Socrates's account of the synodical letter of Nicaea included the proviso that the people (subject to ratification by the Bishop of Alexandria) should elect successors to any Catholic or Melitian cleric who should die.[48] In November 374, on a celebrated occasion, Ambrose was acclaimed bishop by the thronging crowd in the cathedral of Milan, and though he was a layman at the time, this example of *vox populi, vox Dei* was adjudged binding. Both he and the cathedral clergy accepted it. On a lower plane, Jerome records that when he was ordained priest at Antioch by Bishop Vitalis, the congregation called out three times, 'He is worthy'.[49] By the same token, the Canons of the African Church laid down the need for the assent of the laity before a bishop proceeded to ordain a priest.[50] They could also object to the transfer of their bishop to another see,[51] and bring pressure on individuals such as Augustine[52] himself, or his rich friend Pinianus, to accept ordination in a particular church.[53] We hear, too, of laymen being present at church councils. At the beginning of the fourth century, the Council of Elvira was held in the presence of laymen as well as clergy,[54] and at that of Tarraco in 516[55] it was laid down that letters of summons to Councils should be sent to some laymen as well as clergy. At Riez in Gaul in 469, the Council met 'in the presence of judges and councillors and private citizens',[56] while even at Rome, Gelasius's council of 495 specifically records that members of the lay nobility were there also.[57] But, even so, the Church has moved a long way since the time when Cyprian could assert as a matter of principle that important issues, such as whether the lapsed during persecution should be readmitted to the Church, must be decided only 'with the consent of the whole people'.[58]

There was, however, one important exception to the progressive decline in the status of the laity in the Church, namely the *seniores* in North Africa. Deservedly, they have attracted the attention of scholars.[59] First, these lay representatives of the Christian congregation formed an integral part of the organization of both the Donatist and Catholic churches in North Africa in the fourth and early fifth centuries. Secondly, they are clearly a survival of lay control derived from a much earlier period. There is plenty of evidence for their existence from both texts and inscriptions. They are the *fideles seniores* (faithful elders) of Optatus, *De Schismate* 1.17, the *seniores plebis* (elders of the common people) of the *Gesta apud Zenophilum* (AD 320), the *seniores christiani populi* (elders of the Christian people) of the *Acta Purgationis Felicis*

(AD 314–315), and the *seniores laicorum* (elders of the lay folk) of the *Codex canonum Africae ecclesiae* (Canon 91). From the last mentioned, we learn that in Catholic churches, they took precedence over the *clerici*, coming immediately after the deacons. Augustine mentions their existence at Hippo (*Letter* 78), and an inscription (*CIL* VIII.17414) records a Christian 'senator' who seems to have functioned twice as a representative of the people. In the Donatist Church, the crisis involving the Primate, Primian of Carthage, in 392–393 was directly due to the complaints made against him by the *seniores* of the Donatist congregation.

Their functions were both administrative and disciplinary. Among the former duties, they co-operated with the bishop in administering and safeguarding church property. For instance, when in 311 Mensurius, Primate of Carthage, departed from his see to justify the conduct of a member of his clergy to Maxentius in Rome, the movable wealth of the Church was left under the guardianship of the *seniores* (who promptly abused Mensurius's trust!).[60] In the same period, the *seniores* of Cirta in Numidia and Apthunga in Byzacena seem to have formed an administrative council for their churches. In 320, Purpurius of Limata addresses a letter to the '*clericis et senioribus*' of Cirta.[61] Apart from these duties were others of a judicial and disciplinary character, which allowed the *seniores* a check even on the conduct of their bishop. In the inquiry concerning the alleged *traditio* (surrender of sacred books and vessels) of Felix of Apthunga the *seniores* of 'the Christian people' engage an advocate to open their case against Felix.[62] In 392 Primian, the Donatist Primate, restored a group of local schismatics and some notorious evil-doers to communion. The *seniores* at once protested, and failing to persuade Primian they went on to hold a council and decided to support the claims of a rival candidate for the see. They then drew up a document which they circulated to the Donatist episcopate as a whole, outlining their bishop's misdeeds, and demanding the summoning of a formal council to investigate their charges.[63] We also hear of the *seniores* of Musti associated with a presbyter accusing their bishop before the Proconsul in 395.[64] A few years later, a similar affair, though on a lesser scale, involved the Catholic church at Nova Germanica in Numidia. Here, too, the *seniores* brought a complaint against their bishop, which was examined by a council presided over by the Bishop of Carthage. In this case, the Council decided that episcopal arbitrators should be appointed to hear both sides and that the (Catholic) Primate of Numidia should be informed of the results.[65]

These were interesting cases, because they show that the element of lay control in the Church in Africa was still remarkably strong. It was a vigorous survival long after it had ceased in other parts of the West. Ambrose, for instance, refers to a time in the distant past when *seniores* had existed in the Church in Italy,[66] and there is no evidence for *seniores* in other provinces at this period. At the same time, the office in Africa is evidently a traditional one connected with church discipline, as Tertullian refers to *seniores*, who do not seem to be presbyters, empowered to excommunicate unworthy members of the Christian community (*Apology* 39.4).

No entirely satisfactory explanation has been given either for the origins or the survival of this office. The analogy of the local headmen, the *seniores* who ruled African native villages, has been mentioned,[67] but direct influence of this institution on that of the Church would be surprising, in view of the purely urban origins of the latter. Caron, the most recent critic, has seen the *seniores* as the lineal descendants of the plenary assemblies of members of the Church, such as met in Apostolic times (cf. Acts 1.15). When such assemblies became unwieldy, the *seniores* would naturally emerge as representatives of the people as a whole. There is something to be said for this view, in particular as Cyprian stated on several occasions that there were matters in the Church which must be discussed by the whole people, *apud plebem universam* (*Letter* 16.4). The phrase used to describe the *seniores* as '*seniores ex plebe*' (elders chosen from among the common people) is a further reason for accepting the representative character of the office. Caron also takes its origin back to the very beginnings of Christianity. This, too, is useful, for it seems evident that many of the peculiar features of the organization of the African Church may be explicable by reference to primitive Christian, or perhaps Judaeo-Christian, influences.

Various facts point in this direction. For instance, the 'sacerdotalism' of the African bishop has long been attributed to an Old Testament attitude towards priesthood, which would account for the bishop (or priest) being regarded as subject to the same taboos of purity as the Levite.[68] It has also been recognized that the ethical code imposed by the rigorist element in the African Church, bore a striking resemblance to the Jewish *halaka* of the day. Detailed comparisons can be made between Tertullian's prescriptions for avoiding contact with pagan society, contained in the *De Idololatria*, and those to be found in the Jewish *Aboda Zara* of the same date.[69] Christians and Jews were apparently buried side by side in the cemetery of Q'mart at Carthage,[70] and now it has been pointed out that the Western text of the Bible, in use in North Africa, may have been influenced by the Judaeo-Christian *Gospel of Thomas*.[71] Thus, it is reasonable to look for parallels to the *seniores* further afield than Africa, perhaps in the organization of the most primitive Church in Palestine. It may be worth recalling that at Qumran the highest direction of the Sect of the Dead Sea Scrolls lay in the hands of a council of three priests and twelve laymen. These decided administrative and disciplinary matters.[72] If we are confronted by a similar oligarchy of lay and priestly officers in the churches in North Africa, it may be that the explanation must be sought in a Jewish or Judaeo-Christian environment out of which the North African Church developed.

Another lay office which appears to have been purely Western is that of defender of the Church (*defensor ecclesiae*). In the African Church these *defensores* are mentioned twice in the *Codex canonum*. The Emperors are requested by African Catholics *c*. 400 to order their establishment. They were to be lawyers (*scholastici*) and their duties were to be first, to act with the bishops to prevent oppression of the poor by the rich,[73] and secondly, to act as advocates for the Church in lawsuits in which the interests of the Church were involved.[74] We do not know how effective they were, and they do not seem to have survived the Vandal conquest.

In the Roman Church, however, the *defensor* was to have a long career as lay supervisor of the enormous patrimony of St Peter. By the end of the fifth century this included not only land in Italy, but great estates in Sicily, North Africa, Dalmatia, Corsica and Sardinia.[75] Thus in the pontificate of Gelasius (492–496) we find the *defensor* Faustinus associated with the archdeacon Justinus in the management of church property.[76] Their duties included the supervision of the settlers on the land (*coloni*), acting as assessors in the bishops' courts, and above all, administering the poor relief provided by the papal bounty.[77] Lay *defensores* continued to be employed in the sixth century until Gregory the Great replaced them by ecclesiastics as part of his general policy of clericalization.[78]

It seems, therefore, evident that a real change, to the detriment of the laity, came over the organization of the Church after the conversion of Constantine. Not very much remained of the 'royal priesthood' shared by all members of the People of God of the first three centuries. Only among the Donatists of North Africa do we find explicit solidarity

C

between the clergy and people. There, the people 'shared in battle against the Devil', participating in the suffering of the righteous which was the mark of the true Church from eternity to eternity.[79] But this was a theology of a bygone age. Elsewhere, unity of Church and world emphasized the Sacraments and their impersonal dispensers as the guarantors of salvation.[80] The elevation of the priesthood to the status it was to hold throughout the Middle Ages was the natural consequence.

III · *The Layman in the Life and Thought of the Church*

To consider the layman, however, in terms of church worship and organization alone would give a false impression of his influence in the life of the Church during the Patristic period. The fourth and fifth centuries saw the completion of the Christianization of the Mediterranean, and its spread beyond the bounds of the Roman Empire. From now on, except for the interlude under Julian 361–363, the Emperor was a Christian, and Christianity was the religion of the Roman Empire. The Church received valuable tax remissions and other privileges,[81] Christians were often favoured in the Imperial service, and the inhabitants of townships could sometimes invoke their devotion to Christianity as a means of winning Imperial favour.[82] The Emperors believed, like their pagan predecessors, that material prosperity depended on the observance of right religion, and that right religion was practised by the orthodox representatives of the Church.

In this new situation, the laity, though deprived of their former powers in the inner life of the Church, found scope as its advocates and benefactors. The closeness of the relationship between Church and State required the skilled diplomacy of Christian administrators, and the influence of these powerful lay officials on church affairs could be very great. The Church Council was modelled on the Senate, and its president was the Emperor (as at Antioch in 341 or Milan in 355), or his delegate who would be a senior official. At the same time, the persistence of the classical tradition in education had the effect of training Christian laymen to think in the philosophical terms in which the doctrine of the Church was being expressed. So long as that tradition survived the laity produced theologians every whit as instructed as the clergy themselves. And always present were the traditions associated with eschatology and martyrdom which formed the background to the monastic and other movements of lay asceticism.

Let us first take some examples of the influence exercised by the educated laity in important ecclesiastical issues. Senior officials had become notorious for their intervention in church affairs by the reign of Constantius II,[83] and they played a large part in the perennial struggle for power between the three great sees of the East, Constantinople, Antioch and Alexandria, from 381–451.[84] Thus, the eunuch Eutropius was among those responsible for the choice of John Chrysostom as Patriarch of Constantinople in 398. In the next generation, Counts Candidian, John and Irenaeus were active behind the scenes at the Council of Ephesus in 431. For his part, Cyril of Alexandria spent enormous sums in bribing important officials, such as the Chamberlain Chrysoretus,[85] whose support against Nestorius he considered essential. Another Chamberlain, Chrysaphius, was patron of Eutyches in 449. In the West, we find Count Marcellinus, a friend of St Augustine, presiding over the conference at Carthage in May 411, to decide whether the Donatists or Catholics constituted the 'Catholic Church' in Africa. These men acted as representatives of the Emperor, a reminder that the guiding hand in church affairs was his.

More beneficial, but less widely known, was the missionary influence exercised by Christian merchants trading beyond the frontiers of the Empire, or by Christian captives in barbarian hands. The story of the conversion of the kingdom of Axum in northern Ethiopia is an astounding one. We are told, admittedly a century after the event,[86] how Frumentius and his brother Edesius were captured by the 'Indians' on the Red Sea coast, and that having risen high in the service of their king, began their work of evangelization about the year 320 (or even earlier). They were then helped by Christian merchants trading in Ethiopia; they set up churches, and finally returned to Alexandria with the story of their doings. At this point Frumentius was ordained by Athanasius and appointed bishop, but all the spadework had been done by him and his helpers as laymen. Much the same chain of events was taking place at this time in the Black Sea kingdom of Iberia. Here, too, the chosen instrument was originally a Christian captive called Nina, who herself preached the gospel, and caused churches to be built before the arrival of a bishop and consecrated clergy.[87] A century later, the same combination of a Christian captive from a Roman province and Roman merchants was to bring about the conversion of Ireland by St Patrick. In Justinian's reign Longinus and his companions travelled far up the Nile to plant Christianity in the hitherto pagan kingdom of Merowe. They even got as far as the neighbourhood of Khartoum.

Within the Empire itself, lay influence and example had an enormous effect in promoting a real Christianization of values among the population as a whole. Imperial policy sought to secure religious uniformity as needful for the survival of the Empire, without, however, showing overmuch concern for the application of Christian standards of conduct. If Constantine facilitated the emancipation of slaves,[88] prohibited gladiatorial shows[89] and the infliction of branding in the face,[90] other equally cruel punishments were retained by him and his successors.[91] Even regarding so vital a subject as marriage, the Church was unable to enforce its views on the Emperor and his advisers. Marriage was and remained a civil contract, dissoluble by either party on certain accepted grounds, throughout the period covered by this chapter.[92] In these circumstances, Christianity in its deeper meaning was largely a matter of home influence. This is confirmed by an interesting remark made by the pagan philosopher, Libanius, *c.* 390, probably concerning Antioch. He is speaking of efforts being made by a friend to win back support for the traditional rites of paganism. 'When men are out of doors, they listen to your plea for the only right course, and they come to the altars. But when a man gets home, his wife and her tears and the night plead otherwise, and draw him away from the altars.'[93] This statement rings true, and is borne out by what we know of the part played by the Christian womenfolk in the early lives of Ambrose, Augustine, John Chrysostom and Basil of Caesarea. Each of these owed much to a sincerely Christian mother or sister.

It was in the example of ordinary daily life that the Christian layman showed himself to such advantage over his pagan contemporary. The Emperor Julian (d. 363), one of the best observers of social conditions of his time, contrasted the apathy of the pagan priesthood in Asia Minor and their lack of interest in the religious education of their families, with the devotion of the Christians to works of charity. 'The Hellenic religion', he wrote to the high-priest of Galatia in 362, 'does not prosper as I desire. . . . Why do we not observe that it is their benevolence towards strangers, their care of the graves of the dead, and the pretended holiness of their lives, that have done most to increase atheism (Christianity)?'[94] There were no pagan Fabiolas,[95] founders of hospitals for the sick in Rome. It is not surprising, perhaps, that when in 365 a great earthquake struck Cyrene, the capital of the province of the same name, the pagan shrines were not rebuilt. The churches were.[96] By the end of the century 'even the Egyptian Serapis' had become a Christian.[97]

Christian example extended to Christian giving. Here, the Church benefited from the example of Constantine. In the very year of the Edict of Milan, the Emperor had handed over the Lateran Palace, which belonged to his wife Fausta, to the Bishop of Rome, together with a wealth of gold and silver.[98] From then on, his gifts to that see were on a magnificent scale. They included two great new basilicas, those of St Peter and St Paul, with extensive endowments which brought in respectively 3,710 and 4,070 *solidi* a year.[99] In the East he rebuilt the cathedral of Nicomedia, destroyed during the Great Persecution in 303; he built the Golden Church at Antioch, and a vast new basilica on the supposed site of the Holy Sepulchre at Jerusalem.[100] His example was widely followed. The prefect Rufinus, whose reputation Claudian has blackened for posterity, had an enormous church built in his villa at Drus (The Oak) near Chalcedon, *c.* 395.[101] The pilgrim Etheria records having seen a church near Jerusalem which had been built by a tribune.[102] In North Africa, the chapel in honour of St Salsa at Tipasa (west of Algiers) was embellished during the fifth century by a layman named Potentius,[103] and in Donatist Numidia three tribes are recorded as having combined to build a church in the village of Henchir Zerdan.[104] Very rich and very poor united in these services to the Church.

All this time legacies and gifts were flowing in. Since 321 it had been legal to bequeath property to the Church,[105] and advantage was freely taken of this. In addition, the Church transformed the pagan custom of leaving money for sacrifices for the dead into a demand on the laity to bequeath a certain part of their incomes to the Church.[106] This sum was regarded both as an insurance against the flames of hell,[107] and more constructively as a contribution towards the relief of the poor. It is interesting that St Basil, who was the first churchman to link the monastic vocation to a system of ordered social reform, should have been the first to define the scope of this Christian duty among the laity. He urged that a fixed sum, amounting even to as much as half the value of an estate, should be set aside for the benefit of the soul, before the remainder of the estate was divided among its heirs.[108] His friend, Gregory of Nazianze,[109] was equally emphatic. 'We must share our wealth with Christ, so that it may be sanctified, and shared with the poor.' One finds the same advice to rich laity in Ambrose,[110] Augustine,[111] and Salvian of Marseille[112] (*c.* 440). Though the Roman bishops of the late fourth century were stigmatized for their active legacy-hunting,[113] it was sometimes a question of clergy dissuading pious laity from impoverishing their children by over-generous gifts to the Church. Augustine records a case in which a rich lady in a fit of pique had given a whole fortune away to two monks.[114] Almost invariably Catholic families left money or property to the Church.[115] Even the Donatist Church in Africa, which drew its support for the most part from the poor, shared in legacies,[116] while the Catholics were enriched by the proceeds of the enormous estates of Melania and Pinianus. Other rich Christians, like Paulinus of Nola, did likewise for their own churches. The foundations of the immense wealth of the medieval Church were laid in the century after the conversion of Constantine.

These are not isolated instances of Christian piety. In this Indian summer of the Ancient World,[117] when standards of education still remained high and the framework of the city-state held together, theology was the ruling passion of the Christian provincial. It was not only in Constantinople, the capital of the Empire, that abstruse points of doctrine were argued in bazaars and market-places. There, to be sure, the laity seem to have thought of little else. 'If in this city', states Gregory of Nazianze in 379, 'you ask anyone for change, he will discuss with you whether the Son is begotten or unbegotten. If you ask about the quality of the bread, you will receive the answer that the "Father is greater, the Son less". If you suggest that a bath is desirable, you will be told that "there was nothing before the Son was created".'[118] What Arianism was to the inhabitants of Constantinople, Modalism was to the people of Ephesus. In 431 this helped Cyril of Alexandria on the way to his victory over Nestorius. A true politician, Cyril knew the value of public relations, and on the morrow of the Council he wrote a long letter to his friends in Alexandria describing how 'from morning until nightfall' crowds demonstrated in the streets of Ephesus in favour of his doctrine. The town was illumined and Cyril's supporters were fêted.[119] Here, too, the abstruse formula worked out by the professionals merely put into the language of Platonist theology the aspirations of the mass of the laity of Egypt and Asia Minor.

In the West, at Rome, we find Roman ladies petitioning Constantius for the restoration of Pope Liberius in 357,[120] and Roman mobs engaged in bitter struggle over his succession.[121] A generation later, in Africa and later in Italy, the early career of Augustine gives ample evidence for the passionate interest in theology which existed among his intellectual contemporaries. We can see him at the age of 18 or 19 discussing with his friends at the university of Carthage the merits of Manichaeism as a more rational and authentic form of Christianity.[122]

We see him fourteen years later, in 387, still a layman, urging the case for Catholic Christianity with his friends and pupils in the villa at Cassiciacum.[123] Four or five years later, crowds gather in the baths of Sossius at Hippo to hear him debate in public against the local Manichaean champion Fortunatus.[124] In his later years Augustine used the appeal of direct propaganda to the Donatist laity in his efforts to overthrow their Church. We hear, even, that the questions of free-will and grace mooted in Pelagianism were debated 'in synagogues and marketplaces' in Italy and Africa.[125] It is the same story of popular religious activity and enthusiasm in the Greek and Latin worlds of this period.

In North Africa the bitterness of the religious conflict throws some unexpected light on the part the laity was playing in the daily life of their churches. We have mentioned St Augustine, but we find that Donatist lay discussion groups existed in rivalry to him at Hippo[126] and in other North African towns. These laymen knew the story of their Church and could answer their great antagonist when it came to debate.[127] One of these laymen, Cresconius the grammarian from somewhere in Proconsular Africa, has left a record of his views, which Augustine was obliged to answer in four longish books written in 405–406.[128] Cresconius was an ordinary well-read layman who aspired no higher in his profession than primary schoolteacher. He was not a rhetorician, and he was not a philosopher. Nor had he any formal training in theology. Yet when Augustine's first book against Petilian of Constantine came into his hands about the year 405 he had no qualms about setting to and answering it. He performed commendably enough. He knows that his Church is the heir to that of Cyprian in its views on baptism and the relationship between Church and society (*Contra Cresconium* II.31, 39). He can defend the legitimacy of schism; he can appeal to the right of religious toleration for minorities on the legitimate ground that truth develops from minority opinion,[129] and he can drive his argument home with an apt text from Scripture. He makes a classic definition of schism as opposed to heresy.[130] At the same time, his work is a curious mixture of biblical fundamentalism and conventional rhetorical quibble. On the one hand, he takes his opponents to task for calling the Donatists 'Donatistae' instead of 'Donatianae';[131] on the other, he defends Petilian's failure (temporary, as it proved) to reply directly to Augustine's work by citing the example of Ezekiel who declared that Israelites should speak only to Israelites,[132] and he upbraids Augustine for using pagan metaphors in Christian religious writing.[133]

This latter point illustrates the ever-present tension between the traditional pagan-inspired education and the new Christian knowledge and values. Cresconius evidently had immersed himself in the latter without ridding himself of the influence of the former. Indeed, in the African Church neither Cyprian nor his Donatist successors ever quoted pagan works, even if they wrote in faultless Latin. This African layman was also well informed about other events in the Christian world. It is he who quotes the Council of Serdica against Augustine to show that the Donatists were in fact in communion with Churches outside Africa (*Contra Cresconium* III.34, 38), and he indicates that Augustine's Manichaean background, embroidered with some additional details, was common knowledge among the Donatist laity.[134] Altogether, Cresconius testifies to the existence of a remarkably high standard of instruction and alertness among the Donatists at the turn of the fifth century.

Cresconius is represented as an ordinary, instructed layman.[135] If one accepts this description, it is not difficult to understand how it was possible for laymen to gain a degree of theological knowledge which enabled some to make significant and far-reaching contributions to Christian thought. In this connection the all-important factor was the Christian attitude towards classical education. The division between the predominant, orthodox Greco-Latin Christians who, with some heart-searchings and reservations, favoured its retention, and the native, provincial Christians in Egypt and Syria, and the heirs to the Judaeo-Christian tradition in North Africa, who opposed it, was of vital significance. The former accepted the relevance of the present world and sought to Christianize the classical tradition; the latter, their eyes fixed firmly on the Day of Judgment and the expectations of Christ's Church at that time, rejected both the world and its learning. Thus the third-century *Didascalia Apostolorum* which for a long time enjoyed considerable influence in the Syriac-speaking Church states bluntly, 'Have nothing to do with pagan books.'[136] The Bible provided both for supernatural and cultural needs. The rest came from the devil. The result of this outlook was schools, like that of Nisibis, on the Persian side of the Romano-Persian frontier, whose curriculum was founded entirely on the Christian sacred writings, and whose aim was the propagation of the Christian ascetic ideal unalloyed by classical influences.

The ascetic tradition was destined to triumph within the Roman frontiers as well. But, up to the fall of Rome in 410, loyalty to the classical cultural tradition was just strong enough to provide a medium through which men educated in it could contribute to Christian thought without a sense of incongruity. After that, consciousness of a real decline from the standards of the past induced a fatalistic acceptance of the view that the end of the world was approaching, and that the world therefore should be renounced. In this atmosphere both classical culture and a spirit of inquiry into the secrets of the universe were regarded as irrelevant.

But until the catastrophes of the early fifth century a different spirit, more hospitable to educated lay participation in theological questions, prevailed. Attempts made to adapt the old wine of the classics directly to the new bottles of the Christian Scriptures were indeed short-lived failures. The two Apollinarii, father and son (*flor.* 350–370), for instance, do not appear to have progressed very far in their effort to turn the Pentateuch into heroic verse, when in 362 Julian forbade Christians to teach the pagan classics.[137] The pious Paula, Jerome's friend, found few followers to chant the psalms in Hebrew;[138] but, in contrast, Prudentius (348–410) realized that Christian ideas could easily be expressed in classical metres, and the former governor of the province of Tarragona, a layman, became the first great poet of the Christian Church. He demonstrated the feasibility of using the classical heritage as a vehicle for conveying the ennobling truths of Christianity.

Thus, the last part of the fourth century became the great age of the lay theologian in the early Church. Synesius, before he was induced to become Bishop of Ptolemais in 409, and Marius Victorinus are examples of laymen whose background of Neo-Platonism was of vital importance. Both men underwent a long period of hesitancy and sympathetic inquiry before accepting Christianity. Synesius had prayed in the churches of Constantinople and married a Christian,[139] while still nominally a pagan. Victorinus had had a long friendship with the Christian priest Simplicianus.[140] Both seem to have regarded Christianity as a fulfilment of Platonism, assuring to the believer, however, a salvation from sin which Plato could not give. Victorinus was the founder of the tradition of Christian Platonism in the West, and his influence on Augustine was of prime importance. The application of Neo-Platonist categories to the interpretation of Scripture in the West enabled the Church to win back the allegiance of intellectuals, such as Augustine, who otherwise would have preferred Manichaeism.[141]

Another layman who made an important, but quite different, contribution to scriptural exegesis in the West was Tyconius (*flor.* 380). Tyconius was not a Platonist; indeed, he was a Donatist from Proconsular Africa, and Greek influence was entirely absent from his work.[142] He seems to have set to work with the characteristic African concern for the doctrine of the Church and little else in mind. Granted the truth of the prophecy of Isa. 53.10–12, that Christ and his Church formed one whole, how could the 'immense forest of prophecy' which occupied most of the Old Testament be interpreted to demonstrate this? Tyconius's answer was his *Liber Septem Regularum*, the Seven Rules of Interpretation, by which all prophecies could be referred in some way to Christ or his Church. He used immense ingenuity to arrive at his results, including a fantastic numerology, by which almost any number mentioned in Scripture could mean any other, but his work (thanks to Augustine's recommendation) remained a textbook of exegesis in the Western Church throughout the early Middle Ages.[143]

Important, too, was his contribution to the philosophy of history accepted in the Western Church. This was the direct result of his study of Scripture and of his preoccupation with the doctrine of the Church. Tyconius had taught in three of his Rules that humanity was organized under two great institutions, the institution of Christ which was the Church, and the institution of the world which was ruled by the devil. Like the Jewish writers of three centuries before,[144] and like his younger contemporary Petilian of Constantine,[145] Tyconius demonstrated how the Bible told the story of two societies, that of Cain and that of Abel, the lust for power contrasted with righteous suffering. These societies were eternal and for ever in conflict. They were worldwide and not local, membership of each being determined by the will of the individual. 'One aimed at serving Christ, the other at serving the world. The one desires to dominate in this world, the other flees from this world. Each labours in common, the one towards its own damnation, the other towards salvation.'[146] The two societies were two Churches. In Tyconius's mind, the righteous would include the African Donatists, but more besides. Though his more strait-laced colleagues were shocked at the idea of the existence of righteousness among those who were not in communion with them, and he was censured,[147] he did not leave the Donatist communion; in spite of this Augustine valued his work greatly.[148] He became one of the major formative influences in Augustine's doctrine of grace; and his concept of the Two Cities, and hence his thought, that of a layman inspired by the African Bible, contributed to the development both of Western theology and Western medieval political ideas.

Two other lay theologians, both Westerners, should be noted here, namely Ambrosiaster and Pelagius.

Of the former very little is known, though much has been speculated. That he was a layman seems certain, and the most convincing evidence points to his identification with the Roman official of consular rank Hilarius Hilarianus (*flor.* 370–410).[149] In any event, he was a widely read and widely travelled individual, one who has a hearty contempt for 'the boastfulness of the Roman deacons', as he put it,[150] and whose attitude towards the internal organization of the Church was that of a candid critic and observer. However, his surviving works, the *Commentaries* on the Pauline Epistles and the *One Hundred and Twenty-seven Questions on the Old and New Testaments*, tell a story of profound meditation on Scripture. Like Tyconius, he was a biblicist, but unlike him was not the slave to one aspect of Christian doctrine alone. His service was to set the foundations for a study of St Paul which did not run counter to human justice and reason. Utterly opposed both to Manichaeism and to Judaism, he emphasized personal responsibility and freedom from legalistic interpretations of Christianity. One recognizes a kindred spirit in another layman, Helvidius (*flor.* 380–390), who laughed at the idea of the superiority of the celibate over the married man, and had modern views about the reality of Jesus' home circle.[151] It is not surprising that one of those whom Ambrosiaster influenced was a younger contemporary named Pelagius.[152]

It would be out of place to discuss Pelagius's theology in any detail.[153] From the point of view of the laity in the Church his importance is twofold. First, his career demonstrates the vital part which the lay teacher was still playing in spreading the Christian message in the West at this time. Secondly, the advice which he gave to his hearers appealed to that sense of individual responsibility and self-reliance on which civilized society must ultimately be built. Pelagius regarded Christianity as his profession in the world and not as an escape from the world. 'I want you to be a Christian, not to be called monk, and that you possess yourself of virtue for its own worth, rather than a foreign name', he writes to one correspondent.[154] His closest friends, such as Celestius, his disciples, like James and Timasius,[155] were laymen, and his correspondents, like Celantia, Demetrias, Marcella and Claudia, lay aristocrats of the type who sat at the feet of his rival and opponent, Jerome.[156] At times, he places special emphasis on a text because he sees it has particular application to the laity. His appeal was directed above all to the younger members of the noble Roman houses who might be expected to become the Empire's leaders in the early years of the fifth century.[157]

His message was well adjusted to his hearers. Like Ambrosiaster, he saw that reason and equity lay at the core of the Divine Providence, that God was no respecter of persons, and that he did not ask the impossible of any man.[158] The same Providence, he pointed out, enforced constraints on man and nature alike, and these were constraints intelligible to the human mind. His view of human knowledge was the opposite therefore of that of the Christian ascetic who denounced the search after the secrets of nature as irrelevant to salvation. On the contrary, faith, taught Pelagius, was not enough to save a man.[159] It must be reinforced by active good works and good conduct. A man's will-power, aided by grace, which, however, could be won by good inclinations and supported by an active charity, would secure him a pure life, free not from temptation, but ultimately from sin.

It was an optimistic theology, blending a theory of Christian morality with active social reform directed against the excessive riches of the Roman senatorial class.[160] It would have been well-fitted to a vigorous society willing and capable of setting its house in order. But this was not the society of the last century of the Western Empire.

Ambrosiaster and Pelagius each had his devoted following among the Roman laity. From Pelagius's opponents, Augustine and Jerome, we catch sight of other aristocratic laymen more world-renouncing perhaps, but equally at home with theological issues. It was in answer to questions put to him by Flavius Marcellinus, the high official who presided over the conference between the Donatists and Catholics at Carthage in May 411, that Augustine started to write the *De Civitate Dei* ('The City of God'),[161] and his first two books on the subject of Sin and Free-will[162] in 412. From Jerome's circle we have a letter from a Roman noble named Oceanus, who had interested himself both in the problem of Origenism[163] and later in the Pelagian controversy.[164] Pammachius, a mutual friend of Augustine and Jerome, forwarded to the latter Jovinian's criticism of the grosser aspects of the ascetic's life,[165] which called forth the most scurrilous of all Jerome's tracts, the *Adversus Jovinianum*. At the same time, he so impressed the old man that he was described as 'thoroughly learned in the law of the Lord' and capable of instructing others[166]—no mean compliment from one so jealous of his scholarship as Jerome.

Thus, the turn of the fifth century sees some extraordinarily fruitful work in the Church carried out by educated Christian laymen. The Church was enriched intellectually and materially by their efforts, and the clergy were forced to define their terms in response to the pressure of their interest and arguments. Why did this movement fail to last? Why had Europe to wait for a thousand years before the lay theologian reappeared? No single answer can be given. A number of factors combined to prevent the continuation of intelligent lay interest in theology. It depended, as we have seen, on the existence of a comparatively large and ultimately optimistic educated class of provincials. This in turn depended on the continuance of security and stability in the Roman Empire in which classical education might flourish. In the West this did not happen. The massive invasion of Gaul in 406–407 by Franks, Vandals, Alamans and Goths, followed by the sack of Rome by Alaric in 410, destroyed for ever the confidence of the Romanized middle classes in the Western Empire. As Marrou points out,[167] the invasions resulted in a complete breakdown of Roman life, and the disappearance of the old schools where the classical traditions had been preserved. It seems fairly certain that in Gaul, for instance, the generation that came after Ausonius, the Christian Gallic poet who had been tutor to the Emperor Gratian (375–383), was the last to be familiar with the normal system of classical education. For about seventy years after this, until about 470, the torch is kept alive by individual tutors attached to noble Gallo-Roman families, like that of Sidonius Apollinaris (*flor.* 460), and an active interest in theology is maintained among the laity.[168] After that, the old culture fades out. In the sixth century the only education was the ascetic religious education given by the Church. 'Alas, for our age,' writes Gregory of Tours, in 576, 'the study of literature has perished among us, and the man is no longer to be found who can commit to writing the events of the time.'[169]

In Africa and Italy, the process was more drawn out. The Italian kingdom of Theodoric the Ostrogoth produced lay Christian philosophers, such as Boethius (executed 523) and Cassiodorus (d. 584), but there, too, the days of the secular school, and with it of the lay theologian, were numbered. In Africa the classics scarcely survived the 'Vandal peace'.

Material calamities brought their psychological repercussions. The humane, balanced approach to theology was the product of a classical background, but it had little attraction to men and women who believed that the Last Days were at hand. With each successive crisis the certainty of this dread event took deeper hold. From Salvian (*flor.* 430–440) onwards, the West has its fill of prophets of doom. At such a time, 'the same mouth', said Pope Gregory, 'could not sing the praises of Jupiter and praises of Jesus Christ.'[170] It was a grave scandal for bishops to engage in human sciences, he tells Desiderius of Vienne, who was lecturing in literature.[171] To the Christian layman little now remained but the alternatives of ordination or the ascetic life of the monastery.

This was already taking place during the latter half of the fourth century. The laymen who have left their mark on the correspondence of Jerome and Augustine were nearly all ascetics at heart. Increasing distaste for the formal, bourgeois Christianity represented by Jerome's parents or the poet Ausonius was combined with deepening pessimism over the future of the world in which they were living. Christian as well as pagan society in Rome was empty and uninspiring. Jerome could write to Eustochium, *c.* 382, 'I would not have you consort with matrons. I would not have you approach the houses of nobles. I would not have you see what in contempt you have renounced in order to remain a virgin.'[172] Ammianus Marcellinus, a pagan critic, was equally strong in his denunciation of the lives of the Senatorial nobility: 'the few houses', he says, 'that were formerly famed for devotion to serious disputes now teem with the sports of sluggish indolence, re-echoing to the sound of singing and tinkling of flutes and lyres.'[173]

In these circumstances the reactions of the serious-minded laity tended towards other-worldly asceticism. As early as 355, we hear of Ambrose's sister, Marcellina, solemnly taking the veil at the hands of Pope Liberius.[174] From Augustine[175] we learn of the enthusiasm which the story of Antony and his companions aroused among the more idealist of the Roman nobility. Among these was Marcella, at whose house on the Aventine Jerome and his pupils used to meet to study Hebrew and join in prayer. Her influence, backed by a remarkable knowledge of theological literature, contributed largely to the condemnation of Origenism by Pope Anastasius in 401.[176] It was from her circle that Jerome recruited his companions Paula and Eustochium to share in his self-imposed exile at Bethlehem in 385.

Aristocratic lay ascetism was not confined to Rome and Italy. In Spain, about 375, a rich nobleman, Priscillian, was converted by an Egyptian holy man to an extreme form of the ascetic life.[177] His following included the Christian poet Latronianus, clergy and wealthy women. Whatever strange practices, inherited from a surviving Gnostic legacy, they may have indulged in, this too was partly at least a revolt against the worldliness of an established ecclesiastical order. In 385 Priscillian and his companions paid for their views with their lives; but in the next century Priscillianism was a clandestine religious movement which dominated Galicia in north-west Spain.[178] In Africa, too, the success of Manichaeism, with its demands for a world-renouncing life, on young intellectuals of Augustine's generation, and Augustine's own preference for monasticism until he was persuaded to accept ordination,[179] are further examples of the tendency of laymen in the West to neglect their responsibilities to society, and ultimately the culture to which they owed their intellectual being, for the benefit of their own souls. 'Après moi le déluge' could have been said by Paulinus of Nola or Priscillian as well as by Louis XV.

In the West, asceticism was a symptom of a declining culture. In the East it was part of a mass movement. In both, it was a protest against Greco-Roman society and some aspects of the Greco-Roman Church. In Egypt and Syria also it was the concern of laymen, closely allied to the rising regional and native cultures that had been emerging into new life towards the end of the third century. Antony, Hierakas, Pâkhom and Amoun were Copts. They thought in Coptic, and if they wrote, they wrote in Coptic.[180] Their flight to the deserts bordering the Nile valley may be interpreted as a revolt both against the still-predominant pagan Hellenistic culture and against social and economic injustice. Their religious outlook, however, contrasted with the progressive standardization of church services and orders which we have noted in the early part of this chapter. The monks of Egypt and Syria were reviving a much earlier tradition of Christianity, that of the prophet, wonder-worker and martyr. Their enemies were demonic powers both here and hereafter, and these they fought through the Holy Spirit. The Bible and the Holy Spirit replaced dogmatic Creed and Logos. The layman's church of the martyrs which had been the main victim of the alliance between Church and State in the East, returns in the form of the monk's cell. 'The monks', as Leclercq so justly writes, 'were the successors of the martyrs.'[181]

Contemporary accounts leave no doubt as to the enormous influence of biblical study on the lives and views of the monks. Antony, for instance, is reported to have told his monks that the Bible was enough for instruction, and that through its power they could overthrow the demon.[182] Hierakas, his contemporary, was said to know the whole Bible by heart in Coptic.[183] In 431 Schenute of Atripe could equate 'proclaiming the gospel' with 'becoming a monk'.[184] As a result, metaphysical speculation concerning the Divine Logos or the Person of Christ was entirely alien to their outlook. Christ was Saviour, or, more potently, Judge. Heretics were names of curse-laden individuals, whose doctrines, like those of Nestorius, were denounced but not understood.[185] Like the confessors of the previous era, the monk believed himself to be in direct contact with the Lord and received visions and revelations from him. The martyrs were his supreme object of veneration.

The monk was not anti-ecclesiastical, especially after Antony's friend Athanasius became patriarch. He was simply non-ecclesiastical, regarding orders as on a different footing from his own vocation. Monks such as Ammonius would mutilate themselves rather than accept ordination.[186] Others adopted passive resistance. The priesthood was either something too holy to be aspired to, or was not strictly relevant to monastic life. As Duchesne points out,[187] Antony could hardly have received communion from clergy during the twenty years he was in seclusion. Basil of Caesarea, indeed, confirms (*Letter* 93) the fact that the hermits in the Egyptian desert partook of the communion sacrament at their own hands. One feels that the local bishop and his eight priests who ministered to the 5,000 or so monks at Nitria every Saturday and Sunday must have been somewhat exotic.[188] Progress towards sanctity was a matter of individual progress under the direction of master ascetics who also were laymen.

This tradition of individual lay asceticism may be traced back to the prophetic, Spirit-guided movements which opposed the Great Church in the second and third centuries. In Asia Minor it is possible to establish a personal link in Eutychian, a Novatianist layman of Bithynia who was also a monk.[189] Here, one can see the process at work, whereby a lay monastic movement grew out of the individualistic religion of the puritan sect. Among the equally puritanical Egyptian Melitians monasticism was also characteristic.[190] In Africa, one may point to the Donatist Circumcellions who, though not monks in any orthodox sense, combined lives of the wandering ascetic with a fierce lust for martyrdom and hatred of social injustice.[191] In this, too, they shared the outlook of Schenute's followers in the White Monastery. In the same non-ecclesiastical, individualistic context we may place the numerous ascetic sects, such as Messalians, Adamites, Pastores, Gyrovagi, Stylitesi, etc., which infested Asia Minor and Syria in the fourth and fifth centuries.[192] These are the forerunners of the ascetic lay heresies of Europe in the Middle Ages.

The austerities of the Egyptian and Syrian monks resulted in one final contribution to lay religious practice from the West, that of the pilgrimage to the Holy Land and to the great monastic settlements in

Palestine and Egypt.[193] By 350 there was a regular pilgrims' route from Gaul to Palestine. Towards the end of the century one lady named Etheria travelled from Galicia in north-western Spain to Mount Sinai, Jerusalem, Antioch, and, 'having satisfied my curiosity', Constantinople. She has left us a careful account of her travels, and of the services and ceremonies in which she had taken part. One such, the description of the service at daybreak on Good Friday, may be quoted. 'And when they arrive before the Cross the daylight is already growing bright. There the passage from the Gospel is read where the Lord is brought before Pilate, with everything that is written concerning that which Pilate spake to the Lord or to the Jews.' Then after an address by the bishop, still before sunrise, 'they all go at once with fervour to Sion to pray at the column at which the Lord was scourged'. Later, 'a chair is placed for the bishop in Golgotha behind the Cross which is now standing: the bishop duly takes his seat, and a table covered with a linen cloth is placed before him. The deacons stand round the table and a silver casket is brought in which is the holy wood of the Cross.' The Cross is touched with the eyes and foreheads of the people passing by in procession (ed. McClure and Feltoe, pp. 73–4). We are here coming very near to the Middle Ages, and the popular piety of later times.

We conclude, therefore, on the note of subordination. The Roman Empire is Christian. The clergy are the chosen servants of God, the laity his people. Even so, not all laymen could be fitted into this logical pattern. What of the Emperor himself? In the East, Eusebius of Caesarea regarded Constantine as the representative of the Divine Logos on earth,[194] whose authority extended therefore to religion as well as to secular affairs. Throughout the period covered by this chapter, the patriarchs of the great sees in the East were in practice though not in theory dismissible by the Emperor and appointed by him. No Council would decree contrary to the Emperor's known will, though the Emperor did not himself presume to determine the formularies of the faith.[195] In the West, however, non-Platonic and more deeply influenced by Judaeo-Christian ideas, Church and State were always separate. 'The Emperor is within the Church, not above it' of Ambrose[196] repeated only a little more violently Donatus of Carthage's question, 'What has the Emperor to do with the Church?'[197] Behind these differences of outlook lay basic doctrinal differences between East and West which eventually would rend Christendom in twain.

The Emperor's position, however, safeguarded that of the laity as a whole. The Emperor was a layman himself, yet no one denied his sacred character, nor his right to legislate on ecclesiastical matters. In his person the 'royal priesthood' of the whole people of God had its representative, and thus the layman could never be completely ignored. In this period, as the Ancient World melts into the Middle Ages, the laity played an astonishingly active part in the intellectual and moral life of the Church. The succeeding age was to be less fruitful, but once the pessimism that had descended on the Western world in the fifth century had lifted, the way was open again to full lay discipleship. The Later Roman Empire provides an example of this for our own day.

NOTES

1. Tertullian, *De Exhortatione Castitatis* 7 (ed. Oehler, p. 744), and see also *De Baptismo* 6 (ed. Reifferscheid, *CSEL* XX, p. 206).

2. See Tertullian, *De Pudicitia* 22; *Apol.* 50.16.

3. Eusebius, *H.E.* (ed. Kirsopp Lake) V.2, 5, regarding the martyrs of Lyons.

4. Tertullian, *De Anima* 55 (*CSEL* XX, p. 389).

5. Hippolytus, *Elenchos* 9.12 (ed. Wendland). See G. L. Prestige, *Fathers and Heretics* (London, 1954), pp. 33 ff.

6. Origen, *Homil. in Jeremiah* 4.3 (ed. Klostermann, p. 25).

7. Cyprian, *Letter* 1.1 (ed. Hartel, *CSEL* III.2, p. 466).

8. Cyprian, *Letter* 27 (ed. Hartel). See also, *The Apostolic Constitutions* (ed. Robertson and Donaldson, 1870) VIII.23.

9. Cyprian, *Letters* 39.1 and 40.

10. For the situation in Rome *c.* 250, see Cornelius's letter to Fabius of Antioch, cited by Eusebius, *H.E.* VI.43, 11.

11. Cyprian, *Letter* 52.1.

12. Optatus of Milevis, *De Schismate Donatistarum* 1.16 (ed. Ziwsa, *CSEL* XXVI, p. 18).

13. *Acta Saturnini* 17 (*PL* 8, 701 A).

14. Optatus, *De Schismate* 1.16. Lucilla's martyr was not yet formally accepted as such by the Church.

15. Note, for instance, the interesting statement preserved in the seventh-century romance, *Barlaam and Joasaph* (ed. Woodward and Mattingly) 12.103: Monasticism arose 'from men's desire to become martyrs in will, that they might not miss the glory of them that were made perfect by blood'.

16. See J. Gaudemet, *L'Église dans l'Empire romain* (Paris, 1958), pp. 185–91. H. Leclercq, art. 'Laïques', in *Dict. d'archéologie chrétienne et de liturgie* VIII, 1063–4, and J. R. Palanque, G. Bardy and P. de Labriolle, *De la Paix Constantinienne à la Mort de Théodose* (vol. III, in *Histoire de l'Église depuis les origines jusqu'à nos jours*, ed. A. Fliche and V. Martin, 1947), pp. 398 ff. For Roman Africa, P. Monceaux, *Histoire littéraire de l'Afrique chrétienne* III (Paris, 1905), ch. 4.

17. *Apostolic Constitutions* II.16 and 21.

18. For examples, see H. Leclercq, art. 'Basilique' in *Dict. arch. chrét. et de liturgie* II. 1, 540. Also, *Council of Laodicea* (ed. Bruns, *Canones Apostolorum et Conciliorum*, Berlin, 1893, I, p. 75), Canon 19.

19. *Apost. Canons*, Canon 40.

20. *Council of Laodicea*, Canon 59 (Bruns, *Canones* I, p. 79).

21. *Apost. Canons*, Canon 57.

22. This is an important letter, because Basil adds that 'long custom had sanctioned the practice from very force of circumstances' (ed. De Ferrari, p. 146).

23. Athanasius, *De Synodis* 18 (*PG* 26, 713 B–C); Socrates, *H.E.* 1.36.

24. Leo, *Letters* 119.6 and 120.6 (*PL* 54, 1045 and 1054).

25. *Statuta ecclesiastica antiqua* (= *Statuta*; ed. Bruns, *Canones* I, p. 140) 98.

26. Augustine, *Retractationes* (ed. Bardy) II.11.

27. Socrates, *H.E.* 6.8. Cf. Basil, *Letter* 207.2–4.

28. Ambrose, *Hexaemeron* III.5.23 (*PL* 14, 165 D).

29. Ambrose, *Sermo contra Auxentium* 34 (*PL* 16, 1017).

30. Apollinaris Sidonius, *Letters* V.17.3 (ed. O. M. Dalton, *Letters of Sidonius* II, pp. 71–2).

31. Note, in this connection, the pilgrim Etheria's description of the laity at Jerusalem, c. 390. (*Pilgrimage of Etheria*, ed. McClure and Feltoe, pp. 45, 52 and 96.)

32. *De Laude sanctorum* 3 (*PL* 20, 445).

33. Athenagoras, *Supplicatio* 33, *Canones Apostolorum* (ed. Bruns, *Canones* I, pp. 1 ff.) 16 and 17; Gregory Nazianze, *Oratio* 37; Canon 19 of Council of Ancyra (Bruns, I, p. 70); Canon 7 of Council of Neo-Caesarea (Bruns, I, p. 71).

34. Polycarp, *Philippians* 4, Tertullian, *De Jejunio* 8, Augustine, *De Bono Viduitatis* 12, 15, Ambrose, *In Ep. Tim.* 1.5 (*PL* 17, 476 B and C).

35. Canon 27 (Bruns, *Canones* II, p. 126).

36. Canon 72 (Bruns, II, p. 11).   37. Canon 4 (Bruns, I, p. 113).

38. *Statuta*, c. 99 and 100 (Bruns, I, p. 150).

39. Gelasius, *Letter* 9.21 (*PL* 59, 54 C). Also, 9.13. In the sixth century Rome is consistently hierarchically-minded. Thus, Pope Sylvester is reputed to have forbidden laymen to bring a suit against a priest!—*Liber Pontificalis* (Loomis, p. 45).

40. *Statuta*, c. 103. See J. Gaudemet, *L'Église dans l'Empire romain* III, p. 189.

41. Canon 13 of Council of Serdica (Bruns, I, p. 99). Gelasius, *Letter* 9.2 and 3 (*PL* 59, 49).

42. Canon 26. See W. Bright, *Notes on the Canons of the First Four General Councils* (1882), p. 191.   43. *Letter* 137.2 (*PL* 54, 1101).

44. For instance, Peter the Sub-deacon, who administered the Papal estates in Sicily, in the pontificate of Gregory the Great, and to whom many of Gregory's letters are addressed.

45. Gregory, *Decreta* 5.2 (*PL* 77, 1335 B). Cf. F. Homes Dudden, *Gregory the Great* (London, 1905), p. 262.

46. Council of Elvira, Canon 38. Augustine, *Contra Epistolam Parmeniani* II.13, 29 (*PL* 43, 71).

47. Optatus, *De Schismate Donatistarum* 1.18 (Ziwsa, p. 20).

48. Socrates, *H.E.* 1.9.

49. Cited from J. Steinmann, *Saint Jérome* (Paris, 1958), p. 83.

50. *Statuta* 22.   51. *Ibid.* 26.

52. Possidius, *Vita Augustini* 5 (*PL* 32, 37–8).

53. Augustine, *Letter* 126.3.

54. *Council of Elvira*, Preface (Bruns, *Canones* II, p. 2).

55. Canon 13.   56. Canon 10 (Bruns, *Canones* II, p. 121).

57. Gelasius, Concilium Romanum II (*PL* 59, 183 B).

58. Cyprian, *Letters* 14.4 and 16.4 (Hartel, pp. 512 and 519).

59. See P. Monceaux, *Histoire littéraire de l'Afrique chrétienne* III, pp. 83–4; P. Caron, 'Les *Seniores laici* de l'Église africaine', *Revue internationale des Droits de l'Antiquité* VI (1951), pp. 7–22; W. H. C. Frend, *Journal Theol. Stud.* N.S. XII (1961), pp. 280–4.

60. Optatus, *De Schismate* 1.17 and 18 (Ziwsa, pp. 19 and 20).

61. *Gesta apud Zenophilum* (Ziwsa, p. 189).

62. *Acta Purgationis Felicis* (Ziwsa, p. 198). Also, *ibid.*, p. 201.

63. Augustine, *Enarratio in Ps.* 36.20 (*PL* 34–5, 377–9).

64. Augustine, *Contra Cresconium* III.56, 62 (*PL* 43, 529).

65. *Codex canonum Eccl. Afr.* 100 (Bruns, *Canones* I, pp. 185–6).

66. Ambrose, *Comment. in I Ep. ad Timoth.* 5.1 (*PL* 17, 475 D): 'I do not know what neglect caused this custom to fall into disuse.'

67. P. Monceaux, *op. cit.*, p. 83, n. 10. P. G. Caron, *art. cit.*, pp. 20–1.

68. Tertullian, *De Baptismo* 17 (*CSEL* XX, p. 214). Cf. J. B. Lightfoot, 'Essay on the Christian Ministry' (pp. 179–267 in his commentary on *Philippians*, 1869), pp. 243 ff.

69. W. A. L. Elmslie, 'The Mishna on Idolatry, Aboda Zara', *Cambridge Texts and Studies* VIII.2 (1911), p. xxiv.

70. P. Monceaux, *Rev. des Études Juives* (1902), p. 12, and *Histoire littéraire* I, pp. 8–12. Here, too, strict adherence to Talmudic funerary prescriptions is evident.

71. G. Quispel, 'The Gospel of Thomas and the New Testament', *Vigiliae Christianae* XI (1957), p. 199.

72. *The Manual of Discipline* VIII.1. Discussed by B. Reicke, 'The Constitution of the Church', in *The Scrolls and the New Testament*, ed. K. Stendahl (New York and London, 1957/8), p. 151.

73. *Codex canonum eccl. Afric.* 75.   74. *Ibid.* 97.

75. F. Homes Dudden, *Gregory the Great* (London, 1905), Bk II, ch. 3, and E. Spearing, *The Patrimony of the Roman Church in the time of Gregory the Great* (Cambridge, 1918), pp. 6 ff.

76. Gelasius, *Letter* addressed to Justin and Faustinus (*PL* 59, 149 C).

77. E. Spearing, *op. cit.*, pp. 33 ff.

78. John the Deacon, *Vita Gregorii* 2.15. Cf. F. Homes Dudden, *Gregory the Great*, p. 300.

79. Cited from an anonymous fourth-century Donatist sermon, published by A. Pincherle, *Bilychnis* XXII (1923), pp. 134–48.   80. Cf. Optatus, *De Schismate* 2.1.

81. See, for instance, Sozomen, *H.E.* V.5; Ammianus Marcellinus XXI.16; and *Cod. Theod.* XVI:2:8, 9 and 15.

82. For instance, in about 325, the people of Orcistus in Phrygia petition Constantine for the rank of *civitas* on the grounds *inter alia* that they are all Christians. Published by W. M. Calder, *Monumenta Asiae Minoris antiqua* VII, No. 305.

83. See, for instance, Hosius to Constantius in 355, 'Do not use force, write no letters, send no Counts . . .': Athanasius, *Historia Arianorum* 44.

84. See N. H. Baynes, 'Alexandria and Constantinople: A Study in Ecclesiastical Diplomacy', *Byzantine Studies and Other Essays* (London, 1955), pp. 97 ff.

85. Figures in J. B. Bury, *History of the later Roman Empire* (reprinted 1958) I, p. 354.

86. Socrates, *H.E.* (written *c.* 440) I.19. Sozomen, *H.E.* II.24.

87. Socrates, *H.E.* I.20. See P. Peeters, 'Les Débuts du Christianisme en Géorgie', *Analecta Bollandiana* 50 (1932), pp. 5–58.
88. *Codex Theodosianus* (ed. Mommsen and Meyer) IV:7:1.
89. Socrates, *H.E.* I.8. See also, *Cod. Theod.* IX:40:8 of Valentinian I.
90. *Cod. Theod.* IX:40:2.
91. Such as swallowing molten lead or being eaten by bears (Ammianus Marcellinus, *Rerum gest.* XXIX.3, 9, on Valentinian I). On the tendencies in Constantine's legislation, see A. Alföldi, *The Conversion of Constantine and Pagan Rome* (ET by H. Mattingly, Oxford, 1948), p. 128.
92. Note the complaint by Ambrosiaster, *c.* 380, *Quaestiones in Vet. et Nov. Testamentum* 114: 'Here, in the city of Rome, which is called the most holy city, women are permitted to dismiss their husbands.'
93. Libanius, *Letter* 1057 (cited from B. J. Kidd, *Documents Illustrative of the History of the Church* II, p. 131).
94. Julian, *Letter* 22 (ed. W. C. Wright).   95. Jerome, *Letter* 77.4 (ed. F. A. Wright).
96. See R. G. Goodchild, *Cyrene* (1958), p. 23.   97. Jerome, *Letter* 107.2.
98. *Liber Pontificalis* (ed. Mommsen), pp. 52 ff. Cf. A. Alföldi, *The Conversion of Constantine and Pagan Rome*, pp. 51–2.
99. Cited from A. H. M. Jones, *Constantine and the Conversion of Europe* (London, 1948), p. 215. For the vast extent of the patrimonies of the Western churches, especially Rome in the sixth century, see F. Homes Dudden, *Gregory the Great*, Bk II, ch. 3; L. R. Loomis, *The Book of the Popes* (1916), p. 43.
100. Eusebius, *De Vita Constantini* 4.58–60; Socrates, *H.E.* I.16.
101. See L. Duchesne, *The Early History of the Church* II (ET, London, 1931), p. 495.
102. *The Pilgrimage of Etheria* (ed. McClure and Feltoe), p. 30.
103. *CIL* VIII.20914 (after AD 442).
104. S. Gsell, *Monuments antiques de l'Algérie* (Algiers, 1901) II, p. 341.
105. *Cod. Theod.* XVI:2:4.
106. E. F. Bruck, *Kirchenväter und soziales Erbrecht* (Göttingen, 1956), p. 36.
107. See Gregory of Nazianze, *De Pauperum Amore* 22 (*PG* 35, 885).
108. Basil, *In Divites* 7.39 (*PG* 31, 299).
109. Gregory of Nazianze, *De Pauperum Amore* 18 (*PG* 35, 880).
110. Ambrose, *In evang. S. Lucae* 8.79 (*CSEL* XXXII.4, p. 432).
111. Possidius, *Vita Augustini* 24 (*PL* 32, 53).
112. Salvian, *Ad Ecclesiam* (ed. Pauly), II.12, 13.
113. *Cod Theod.* XVI:2:20 (July 370), and Jerome, *Letter* 52.6 (*PL* 22, 532).
114. Augustine, *Letter* 262.5 (ed. Baxter, p. 507).
115. Augustine, *Comment. in Ps.* 103.16 (*PL* 36, 1371).
116. Augustine, *Comment. in Joh. Ev.* 6.25 (*PL* 34–5, 1436).
117. The spirit of the fourth century is nowhere better described than by T. R. Glover, *Life and Letters in the Fourth Century* (Cambridge, 1901).
118. Gregory of Nazianze, *Sermon concerning the Deity of the Son*: *PG* 46, 557.
119. *Letter* 24 (*PG* 77, 137). Cf. L. Duchesne, *The Early History of the Church* (ET by Claude Jenkins, London, 1948) III, pp. 244–6.
120. Theodoret, *H.E.* II.17 (ed. Parmentier, p. 137).
121. Ammianus Marcellinus (ed. Rolfe), XXVII.3, 11–13.
122. *Confessions* III.10 and 11. Cf. J. O'Meara, *The Young Augustine* (London, 1954), pp. 64 and 81 ff.

123. In *De Beata Vita*, *De Vera Religione* and *De Ordine*. See Ch. Boyer, *Christianisme et Néo-Platonique dans la Formation de Saint Augustine* (Paris, 1918), ch. 4.

124. Possidius, *Vita Augustini* 6 (*PL* 32, 38). For popular participation in this debate, Augustine, *Contra Fortunatum* X.19 (*PL* 42, 121).

125. Julian of Eclanum, cited by Augustine in *Contra Julianum opus Imperfectum* IV.37 (*PL* 44–5, 1356–7).

126. That of Centurius, Augustine, *Retractationes* II.19, 46.

127. Augustine, *Letters* 43 and 44.

128. See P. Monceaux's full account of Cresconius in *Histoire littéraire de l'Afrique chrétienne* VI, pp. 87 ff. On other Donatist lay writers and chroniclers, *ibid.*, pp. 233–58.

129. Augustine, *Contra Cresconium* III.66, 75 (ed. Petschenig, *CSEL* LII, p. 480).

130. *Ibid.* II.3, 4: 'Heresy is division between those who follow diverse principles; schism is separation between those who follow the same principle' (Petschenig, p. 363).

131. *Ibid.* II.1, 2.   132. *Ibid.* I.10, 13.   133. *Ibid.* IV.65, 81.

134. *Contra Cresconium* IV.64, 79.

135. P. Monceaux, *Histoire littéraire* VI, pp. 86 ff.

136. *Didascalia Apostolorum* 3 (ed. Connolly, 1929, p. 13). For this attitude in North Africa, see *Passio Marculi*, *PL* 8, 760 (*c.* AD 350).   137. Socrates, *H.E.* III.16.

138. Jerome, *Letter* 108.27.   139. T. R. Glover, *op. cit.*, pp. 337 and 347.

140. Augustine, *Confessions* VIII.2, 14. See P. Henry, *Plotin et l'Occident* (Louvain, 1934).

141. See P. Courcelle, *Recherches sur les Confessions de Saint-Augustin* (Paris, 1950), p. 137.

142. See P. Monceaux's essay on Tyconius in vol. VI of the *Histoire littéraire de l'Afrique chrétienne*, pp. 165–219; E. Buonaiuti, *Il Cristianesimo nell' Africa romana* (Bari, 1928), pp. 335 ff.; and F. C. Burkitt, 'The Rules of Tyconius', *Cambridge Texts and Studies* III.1, Cambridge, 1894.

143. Burkitt, *op. cit.*, p. xxiv.   144. Cf. *4 Maccabees* 17.21.

145. Petilian of Constantine, a lawyer before being elected Donatist bishop of Constantine *c.* 395, cited in *Contra Litteras Petiliani* II.92, 202 (*CSEL* LII, pp. 123 ff.).

146. Tyconius, *Comment. in Apocalypsim* (*apud* Beatus of Libana, Madrid, 1772, p. 507). See T. Hahn, *Tyconius-Studien* (Leipzig, 1900), p. 29.

147. Augustine, *Contra Epist. Parmeniani* I.1.

148. Augustine, *De Doctrina christiana* III.41, 46.

149. See A. Souter, 'A Study of Ambrosiaster', *Cambridge Texts and Studies* VII.4, pp. 183–5, and Dom G. Morin, *Revue Benedictine* XX (1903), pp. 113–24.

150. *Quaestiones in Vet. et Nov. Testamentum* 101 (*PL* 35, 2301).

151. Jerome, *Adversus Helvidium* (*PL* 23, 183 ff.).

152. For Ambrosiaster's influence on Pelagius, G. de Plinval, *Pélage, ses écrits, sa vie et sa réforme* (Lausanne, 1943), pp. 86 ff.

153. See Plinval, *op. cit.*; J. Ferguson, *Pelagius* (Cambridge, 1956); and particularly, J. Tixeront, *Histoire des Dogmes* II, ch. 11.

154. Pelagius, *De Divina Lege* 9 (*PL* 30, 115 D); Plinval, *op. cit.*, p. 103.

155. Augustine, *De Gestis Pelagii* 23.47 (*PL* 44, 347).

156. On Jerome's lasting hostility towards Pelagius, Plinval, *op. cit.*, p. 53.

157. Plinval, *op. cit.*, pp. 211–16.   158. Pelagius, *De Vera Circumcisione* 2.

159. Pelagius, *Vita* 13: 'man is not justified by faith alone'.

160. Cf. Augustine, *Letter* 156 (Hilarius of Syracuse to Augustine): *PL* 33, 674; Pelagius, *De Divitiis* 9 and 10; Plinval, *op. cit.*, p. 221.

161. Augustine, *De Civitate Dei* I.1.

162. The *De Spiritu et Littera*, and the *De Peccatorum Meritis et Remissione*. See *Retract.* II.33 and 37. Marcellinus was also a friend of Jerome. He and his wife wrote to the latter asking for information about the origins of the soul (Jerome, *Letter* 126, ed. Wright).

163. Jerome, *Letter* 8.3 (*PL* 22, 743).   164. Jerome, *Letter* 126 (*PL* 22, 1085).

165. Jerome, *Letter* 48 (*PL* 22, 493).

166. Jerome, *Letter* 126 to Marcellinus and his wife Anapsychia. For an account of Jerome's circle of lay acquaintances, F. A. Wright, Appendix I to *St Jerome Select Letters* (Loeb ed., 1954).

167. H. I. Marrou, *A History of Education in Antiquity* (ET, 1956), p. 343.

168. Sidonius Apollinaris, *Letters* II.9.5 (ed. Dalton, I, p. 49).

169. Gregory of Tours (ed. Dalton): Preface to *Historia Francorum*.

170. Gregory, *Letter* 11.34. Verses of the poets were 'unfit to be recited even by a religious layman'. In general, G. Bardy, 'L'enseignement au Ve. siècle', *Mélanges F. Cavallera*, pp. 191 f.

171. Gregory, *ibid.* Cf. Homes Dudden, *op. cit.*, p. 286.

172. Jerome, *Letter* 22.16 (ed. Wright).

173. Ammianus Marcellinus, XIV.6, 18 (ed. Rolfe).

174. Ambrose, *De Virginibus* III.1 (*PL* 16, 219–20).

175. *Confessions* VIII.15.   176. Jerome, *Letter* 127.6 (ed. Wright).

177. Sulpicius Severus, *Chronicon* (ed. Hahn, *CSEL* I) II.45–8. Cf. A. d'Alès, *Priscillien et l'Espagne chrétienne* (Paris, 1936), and art. 'Priscillianus' in *DCB* IV, pp. 470 ff.

178. See Council of Braga I, of 448; seventeen canons directed against Priscillianism, and Council of Braga II, of 563, Canon 10 (ed. Bruns, *Canones* II, pp. 30 and 42).

179. Possidius, *Vita Augustini* 5 (*PL* 32, 37).

180. Cf. Epiphanius, *Panarion* 67.2 and 6 (ed. Holl, p. 133); Athanasius, *Life of Antony* 1 (*PG* 26, 840 B) and 77 (Antony spoke Greek through an interpreter); K. Heussi, *Der Ursprung des Mönchtums* (Tübingen, 1936), pp. 58 ff.

181. H. Leclercq, art. 'Monachisme', *DACL* XI.2, 1848.

182. Athanasius, *Life of Antony* 16.

183. Epiphanius, *Panarion* 67. See Heussi, *op. cit.*, p. 59.

184. Cited from Leipoldt, *Schenute von Atripe* (Texte und Untersuchungen, XXV, 1904), p. 42.   185. *Ibid.*, p. 88.

186. Palladius, *Lausiac History* (ed. Lowther Clarke), p. 64. Socrates, *H.E.* 4.23.

187. L. Duchesne, *Early History of the Church* II, p. 390.

188. Palladius, *Lausiac History* VII (Lowther Clarke, p. 58).

189. Socrates, *H.E.* 1.13. From Phrygia comes another Montanist inscription, set up by Aurelius Kyriakos, dated to the late third or early fourth century, commemorating an 'ascetic', now in the Museum of Afyon.

190. H. I. Bell, *Jews and Christians in Egypt* (Oxford, 1924), pp. 48–9. Cf. Epiphanius, *Panarion* 68.1, for monastic support of Meletius against Peter when both were in prison in Alexandria in 305.

191. See W. H. C. Frend, *The Donatist Church* (Oxford, 1952), pp. 171–5.

192. Listed by H. Leclercq, art. 'Monachisme', *DACL* XI.2, 1829–31.

193. See ch. on 'Women Pilgrims', in T. R. Glover's *Life and Letters in the Fourth Century*, ch. 6.

194. *De Laudibus Constantini* 1.6 (ed. Heikel, p. 198).

195. L. Duchesne, *op. cit.* II, p. 522.

196. Ambrose, *Contra Auxentium* 36 (*PL* 16, 1018). Cf. *Letter* 20.23.

197. Optatus, *De Schismate* 3.3.

3

R. W. Southern

THE CHURCH OF THE DARK AGES
600–1000

I · The Social and Legal Aspects of Religion

THE first thing to emphasize about the religion of the laity during this period is the extent of our ignorance. Almost nothing written by a layman has come down to us; and even when we can be sure that our documents contain expressions of lay intentions, some allowance must be made for the fact that a monastic hand has almost always prescribed their form and given definition to their thought. In one way this is a less serious obstacle than it might be, because lay thoughts about the Church and about religious observance were largely a reflection of monastic thoughts. But this applies chiefly to the upper ranges of society. We shall never know much about the religion of the 'ordinary' man. What it was that the barbarians of Europe were converted to must remain a very dark mystery. It would be naïve to suppose that the ideas of the converted always conformed to those of the missionaries, whether Catholic or Arian.

We can see that the new religion was essentially a religion of supernatural power placed at the disposal of adherents of Christ. Victory in battle did more than any other single thing to induce or confirm the faith of barbarian rulers, and their followers accepted their changes of faith almost without demur. Only in northern Germany do the Saxon wars of Charlemagne appear to have provoked a reaction self-consciously and aggressively pagan. Elsewhere the Christian Trinity replaced or supplemented the pagan gods, and performed the same function in daily life as the old rituals, whatever they may have been. This function may be briefly described as the taming of demonic forces in this world and the promise of blessedness hereafter. The demonic forces were immensely real, and ever present in plague, pestilence and famine, in flood and fire, in disease, disaster and unnatural death. We cannot understand the day-to-day religion of this period, particularly of those with no resources of book-learning or elaborate liturgical observances, unless we remember that there was no science of secondary causes of events. It was therefore only a step from the natural phenomena of daily experience to the unseen agents of the spirit-world.

For the Christian, these agents were primarily the two warring hosts of saints and devils. Above them was the commanding figure of God; beneath them, Man. The importance of the saints for man's safety was overwhelming. And, since the saints chiefly communicated with the physical world through contact with their earthly remains, this necessarily led to an extravagant veneration for their relics. Relics stirred the religious life of the period to its most animated forms of expression: they set in motion a passionate and variegated sequence of events in which prayers and devotions jostled with holy and unholy frauds, in which visionary experiences vied with commercial speculation, and works of art with acts of petty pilfering. The journeys of relics, obtained by every kind of dubious expedient, were events of the first importance in the history of cities and kingdoms. They represented a universal urge, the one level of religious activity in which the laity could engage on an equal footing with the clergy. Every king was of necessity a col-lector of relics to ensure the safety of his kingdom and his person; and even the poorest might hope to drink water in which some dust or some rag from the tomb of a saint had been dropped. It is well known, for example, that King Alfred devised a primitive clock by burning candles continuously of equal length to measure the hours, and equally it is well known that he invented a horn lantern to shield the flame of the candles from the draught; but it is less known—because it fits less easily into our picture of a ruler's cares—that these candles had the further purpose of providing a perpetual light before the relics which everywhere accompanied him.[1] These relics were his *halidom* or, in another common phrase which admirably expresses the purpose of defence and surety, the *patrocinia sanctorum* who guarded the king and his kingdom. Besides their potency in miracles and works of healing, they were an essential instrument of social and political life: the oaths, which were a chief means of settling disputes and an uncertain but indispensable guarantee of peace and order in society, were taken on these relics in the confidence that perjury would be avenged; the ordeals which were the main instruments of judicial proof took place in their presence; they were an essential feature of the frequent processions and litanies in times of sickness, danger and famine. It is therefore not surprising that the traffic in relics, which by the end of the Middle Ages had worked its way down into the lower reaches of society and led to innumerable abuses, was a matter of great interest to every important layman as much as to every important church.[2]

Important as they were as material objects on which attention could be focused, it would be wrong to isolate relics from other indications of the close bonds between religious observances and the social life of the time. The following extract will show how far law, liturgy and sacrament were bound together in an indissoluble union. It comes from a ritual for the judgment by water which is found in many English and Continental manuscripts from the tenth century onwards:[3]

> When the men whom you wish to send to the ordeal by cold water have fasted for three days with a priest, bring them into church, and there let the priest sing Mass before them and take their offering. And when they come to communion, before they communicate, let the priest say to them: I adjure you by the Father and the Son and the Holy Spirit, and by the Christianity which you have received, and by the only-begotten Son of God, and by the Holy Trinity and by the holy Gospel, and by these holy relics which are in this church, and by that baptism by which a priest has regenerated you, that you do not presume to communicate nor to come to the altar, if you have done this deed, or consented to it, or know by whom it was done. . . . When they communicate, the priest shall say: 'This Body and Blood of our Lord Jesus Christ be for you a means of proof this day.'

After Mass on these occasions there followed a long adjuration to the water which was the instrument of God's judgment. The priest addressed to the water the following solemn words:

> I adjure you by the holy name of the undivided Trinity, by whose will the element of water was divided so that the people of Israel passed through with dry feet . . . that you on no account receive these men if they are guilty of that deed with which they are charged . . . but make them float on your surface, so that no charge can be brought against you and no deceit of the Enemy can hide the fact.

The accused men then kissed the gospels and the Cross, and were sprinkled with holy water, and were lowered into the water.

Scores of similar formulas for many different occasions exist, and they illustrate better than any commentary can do the sense of a supernatural power constantly operating in the world, and accessible to man in his common occasions through liturgical and sacramental channels. This power was not just vaguely apprehended or urged by preachers on unwilling ears: it was part of the everyday furniture of life.

A great deal in the attitude of men of this time towards miracles and relics, and the tone of secular religious life as a whole, must be explained by the conditions of extreme physical misery which persisted throughout the whole period and reached an almost unendurable height in the tenth century. Never before or since has life in Europe been so grim for so large a proportion of the community. The situation which existed would perhaps best be paralleled in our own time by an intermittent, haphazard and uncontrollable series of undirected nuclear explosions at the rate of one or two a year. If anything, this underestimates the perennial dislocation of society, but it may give some idea of the mental adjustment which is necessary in appreciating the stress of disorder under which men lived.

It was an essential part of men's thoughts that they were living in the last age of the world. Too much has sometimes been made of this. Responsible theologians never accepted the view that the world would end in the year 1000 or 1033, or any other precise date. Yet the shadow of the approaching end of the world was ever present, and this expectation became more intense as the year 1000 approached. There was good reason for this. Not only was the period of a thousand years mentioned, with whatever spiritual significance, in the Bible as the length of time which must elapse before the final unleashing of Satan on the world, but many of the signs of the last days were present in apparently everincreasing ferocity. They gave additional weight to the gloomy forebodings, the severity of outlook and the lack of hope in this world, which are the most strongly marked characteristics of the whole period.

These characteristics are strikingly apparent in the ecclesiastical legislation which has come down to us. Penances of several years, requiring a degree of fasting which would have incapacitated a man for serious work, were common for sins of widely different kinds. This is readily intelligible in the light of the legal ideas of the time. The chief principle which ran through the earliest legal codes of barbarian Europe was that of compensation to be paid to the injured party, and the chief function of an expert in the law was to carry the elaborate code of compensation in his mind. If this principle is carried over into ecclesiastical legislation, as it was, the results were bound to be both chaotic and terrifying. The search for genuine compensations for spiritual offences could only lead to madness, or more rationally in many laymen to the postponement of baptism, which was itself a satisfaction for all previous sins, until the last possible moments of life. The penitential literature in which the terms on which a sinner could obtain reconciliation are laid down has rightly been regarded with abhorrence by later generations. Yet it should be read with commiseration as a monument to an impossible task which weighed for several centuries on the consciences of Christian men. In the Europe of this period there must have been many men performing heroic acts of penance over several months, and even years, for offences which in secular law could be atoned for by relatively mild compensations. And for grave crimes like patricide penitents were to be found making a hopeless tour of the shrines of Christendom over the years with the instrument of their crime eating into their flesh. We only know about those who experienced a miraculous release from their bonds at some favoured shrine, but these fortunate few are the visible witness to a large and unseen army.[4]

What happened to those who died before the completion of their penance was a subject about which it was better not to think. The doctrine of Purgatory to meet such cases had not yet been clearly developed, and there was no promise of any future remission for those who died with their penance incomplete. In practice, for the wealthy there were a number of subterfuges which nullified the effects of this severity. As early as the seventh century we hear of men who will undertake penances on behalf of others for pay. This was forbidden, but we hear of no similar prohibition of such acts of substitution without pay, and the system evidently remained in force as long as these crushing penances persisted. At the very end of our period an English compilation lays down a very practical plan by which a powerful man could accomplish a seven years' penance in three days with the help of 840 assistants who fasted with him.[5] Only the very great could call on such assistance; the case of the ordinary man was quite hopeless. The same remark must be made about the other method of commuting penances open to the rich: the method of abundant alms-giving. We find an example of this in the experience of an Anglo-Saxon nobleman Wulfin who had the misfortune ('by mischance' the account euphemistically states) to slay six priests. He went to Rome and received as a penance the injunction to provide the means of supporting six priests to pray for him in perpetuity. He came home and gave an estate to the monastery of Gloucester on the understanding that seven monks should intercede for him for ever.[6] Alms-giving on this scale was for the few and there is every reason to think that it was not undertaken in a spirit of benign munificence but of well-grounded terror. Unless alms-giving could be substituted for penances many laymen must have been obliged to abandon all hope of Heaven.

The Council of Cloveshoe in 747 speaks of the practice of commuting penances by alms-giving as a new and dangerous one. The dangers of providing rich men with an easy way to Heaven at the expense of their families and descendants were certainly very obvious, and did not diminish with time. But mere pity, if not greed and social influence, must have suggested the need for some form of relief from intolerable burdens, and in course of time the possibility of commutation of penances by alms-giving was written into the disciplinary system of the Church. There was thought to be biblical warrant for this substitution in such phrases as 'The ransom of a man's life are his riches' (Prov. 13.8) and 'Make unto yourselves friends of the mammon of unrighteousness, that when ye fail, they may receive you into everlasting habitations' (Luke 16.9); and by the eleventh century even so stern a moralist as Peter Damian took the system of commutation for granted:

> You know that when we receive lands from penitents, we relax something of their penance according to the measure of their gift, as it is written: 'The ransom of a man's life are his riches.' Consider therefore and reflect that, as a man who offers lands to the Church has his weight of penance lightened, so he who robs the Church of lands is weighed down by a just load of penance.[7]

When we inquire what hope there was for sinful man surrounded by terrors and incapable of helping himself by disbursing his riches, there can be little doubt about the answer. Their hope lay in the saints and in their miraculous powers. It is scarcely too much to say that the popular religion of those centuries was centred not on the sacraments, nor on God or the life of Christ, but on the saints and their relics.

II · The Lay Ruler and the Church

The penetration of the natural order by the supernatural, which has been noted above, was most clearly seen at the point where it affected the position of the secular ruler. At the beginning of our period the secular, barbarian rulers of the West—as contrasted with the Emperors of Constantinople—were accorded no very elevated place in the scheme of Christian thought. They attained their position by a purely secular ceremony (if ceremony there was) and the emblems of their dignity were a strange mixture of reminiscences of Roman imperial insignia and ancestral barbarian ornaments, such as we see in the Sutton Hoo burial or in the practice of King Edwin of Northumbria (d. 633), of whom Bede reports that he had a standard of Roman pattern borne before him wherever he went. One of the most obvious effects of the conversion must have been to deprive the ruler of his supernatural dignity, since it made his most treasured possession—a genealogical tree showing his descent from the pagan gods—of no more than antiquarian interest. But men abandon old ideas with reluctance. Royal blood with its tale of descent from gods, even non-existent gods, meant more than could rationally be explained; and these genealogies continued to be preserved long after their essential claim had become a matter of mythology. It was only when a family with no claim to royalty arose to supplant the greatest royal house in Europe that the need for a new sanction became imperative. It was this situation which was responsible for an innovation of immense importance for the history of the relation between the lay ruler and the Church—the introduction of a religious ceremony as an initiation into the powers of kingship. The anointing of King Pippin by Archbishop Boniface in 751 was the first act of its kind in the West of which we have any reliable record. From this moment religion and secular power became inextricably interwoven in Western Europe.

This combination had already been effected in the Empire at Constantinople. As early as 457 a ceremony of coronation by the Patriarch had become a necessary part of the act of elevation to the Imperial throne. To some extent, therefore, the West was simply copying the East in introducing a religious element into the royal position. But as so often happened, the West was not satisfied with simple imitation: in the act of imitation it struck out a new line for itself. It is quite certain that the anointing formed no part of the original Byzantine coronation ceremony. The adoption of this feature in the West came directly from the Old Testament, and was intended without doubt to refer to Samuel's anointing of David whereby 'the Spirit of the Lord came upon David'. From this time forward, and in virtue of this ceremony, the rulers of the Franks and soon those of the English could take the title, so pregnant with mysterious meaning, and assume the position of *Christus Domini*, the Lord's anointed. During the following centuries, contrary to what is often thought, the religious adulation of the lay ruler went further in the West than in Byzantium itself, and though curbed in the eleventh century it was always ready to break out into new life.

It is not to be expected that any single idea of the position and functions of the Christian ruler should persist with unanimous approval throughout these centuries. Yet there is a dominant view which can be found without much alteration from the middle of the eighth until the end of the eleventh century. This view, which summed up the practical reality of royal power as well as its supernatural grace, is very clearly expressed in a letter of Alcuin to Charlemagne in 799, shortly before his coronation as Emperor:

> There have so far been three positions in the world of the highest rank: that of the Pope who is accustomed to rule the see of St Peter, the Prince of the Apostles, as his vicar . . .; secondly the Imperial dignity and secular power of the second Rome [i.e. Byzantium] . . .; and thirdly the royal dignity, in which the dispensation of our Lord Jesus Christ has placed you as the ruler of the Christian people, in power more excellent than the other two, in wisdom more distinguished, in the dignity of your rule more sublime. On you alone depends the whole safety of the Churches of Christ.[8]

It will be seen that on this view there was an ascending order of excellence: Pope—Emperor—King, with the Christian king at the summit. The Imperial coronation on Christmas Day 800, which combined the royal and imperial dignities for the first time in a barbarian ruler, did something to upset this order, but the important point is that Alcuin placed the lay ruler—whether Emperor or King—above the sacerdotal ruler. It was the function of the lay ruler to order the affairs of the Christian community over which he was set by God, not only in their temporal but also in their religious aspect. As Alcuin wrote on another occasion to Charlemagne:

> You endeavour to purge and protect the Churches of Christ from the doctrines of false brethren within, as much as from destruction by pagans without. The divine power has armed your majesty with these two swords in the right hand and in the left hand.[9]

On the shoulders of the secular ruler was laid the care of the churches. It was for him to see that suitable pastors were appointed, that the means were available for their support, that councils were held for the settling of problems and the dissipation of heresy. In virtue of this dual responsibility, he was frequently referred to as both *rex* and *sacerdos*, and the example of Melchisedech was quoted to support the amalgamation of kingly and priestly functions.

This amalgamation can easily lead to misunderstandings. No one supposed that the lay ruler was *sacerdos* in the full sense of one who

could administer the sacraments of salvation. But the phrase expressed
the conviction that the ruler was, so to speak, enveloped in a sacerdotal
aura. This could be expressed more clearly in visible symbols than in
writing, and it is to the pictures and ceremonies of the time that we
must turn to see the light in which the lay ruler appeared to his contemporaries. We have many pictures of the Latin Emperors of the
ninth, tenth and eleventh centuries, in which we see them portrayed
in the full dignity of their semi-sacerdotal power. The Emperor is portrayed wearing a massive crown in which symbolic stones and relics
have been set, holding an orb inscribed with a Cross, wearing a dal-
matic, the vestment of a deacon, having under him archbishops and
warriors, his spiritual and secular aids respectively. A hand from Heaven
places the crown upon his head, and in some pictures the symbolism
is completed by the apocalyptic symbols of the four evangelists. The
pictures vary greatly with the taste of the artist, but the essential features which recur again and again are the direct dependence of the
Emperor on God, the subordination of the ecclesiastical persons to the
Emperor, and the semi-sacerdotal character of the Emperor's dress
and the objects with which he is surrounded. It is a striking fact that,
although they learnt much from Byzantium, the Western artists took
the symbolism a good deal further than any of their Byzantine models.
Nothing indeed could be more holy than the idea of the Byzantine
Emperor. Professor Baynes has called him an earthly Providence, and
there are many texts which bear out this description. But I do not think
that he was ever portrayed with the richness of liturgical and symbolical
ornament which the Western artists lavished upon the rulers whom they
sought to honour.[10]

There is a good illustration of this fact in the most important act in
the ceremony of coronation—the act of anointing the new ruler. It was
this which above all gave the ruler his religious character, and it has a
special importance because it was not distinctively an imperial, but a
royal, prerogative. It caught on quickly after 751, and became *par
excellence* the symbol and guarantee of royal authority.[11] The English
royal house of Mercia appropriated the rite in 787; and a century later,
it was in virtue of their anointing that each of the upstart royal houses
who divided the Carolingian Empire could claim an equal sanction as
the Lord's anointed. Hence by the beginning of the tenth century there
were four or five kings in Europe who each independently could claim
a sacerdotal character. These kings would not themselves in their official
documents call themselves *rex et sacerdos*: this belonged to the realm of

biblical analogy. But they would often, and with a full sense of its significance, use the title 'Vicar of God' or 'Vicar of Christ', and this at a time when the Pope used no higher title than 'Vicar of St Peter'. The distinction was not lost upon contemporaries. The following passage expresses the view of a writer of the early eleventh century, and it will be seen that it conforms very closely to what Alcuin had said to Charlemagne at the end of the eighth century before he became Emperor:

> Our Kings and Emperors, vicars of the Supreme Ruler in this our pilgrimage, alone arrange the appointment of bishops, and it is right that they should have authority before other men over their pastors; for it would be incongruous if those pastors whom Christ made princes after his own likeness should be under the dominion of any except those who are set above other men by the glory of benediction and coronation.[12]

We must not inquire too closely what exactly the 'glory of benediction and coronation' had conferred on the lay ruler which other men lacked. If we do, we shall be disappointed, for it is the nature of ceremonies and symbols to leave many questions obscure. Ceremonies in these centuries express more clearly than any words which have come down to us the general ambience of ideas, but it is absurd to expect them to answer all the questions which could be answered in an elaborate treatise. It must here suffice to note that the orders of coronation which were developed in this period have many distinct parallels with the order for the consecration of bishops. Both kings and bishops were anointed with the same oil, both received a ring and a staff, and in the conferring of these symbols similar words were spoken. All this suggested that the king was more than a layman. But he was also in some ways more than a priest:

> Always remember, my king, that you are the deputy of God, *your* king. You are set to guard and rule all his members, and you must render an account on the Day of Judgment. The bishop is in a secondary place, being simply the Vicar of Christ.[13]

These words were written by an otherwise unknown correspondent to Charlemagne in about 775, and they arrest the attention because what he is saying is something which never ceased to have some currency. The theological concept they express is that the king represents God on earth in his character as Ruler, whereas the priest represents Christ in his character of mediator between God and Man: the king is the representative of God in his divine nature; the priest is the representa-

D

tive of Christ in his human nature; hence the former is superior to the latter. An Anglo-Norman writer of the end of the eleventh century put the matter thus:

> Both priest and king in their office bear the image of Christ and God; the priest of the inferior office and nature, namely the human; the king of the superior, the divine.[14]

It has been necessary to dwell on these somewhat obscure points because they provided a theoretical basis for a very important practical power. Take away the divine element in the king's position, and the assumption of power over the Church would be—as it later appeared to be—an act of tyranny. But as the Vicar of God the ruler had not only a right but a duty to regulate the affairs of the Church. Throughout this period it was the king who appointed bishops; and in virtue of the same general duty of supervision, the Emperor on more than one occasion appointed a Pope with no more than a formal regard for the processes of election. The royal right in the appointment of bishops was emphasized in the most explicit way. On the death of a bishop, the members of the cathedral chapter brought the dead man's pastoral staff to the royal court, and the king gave it to his nominee as a token of his authority over the people of God. What the king conferred was not sacramental power—this came from God at consecration—but authority; and no one challenged the king's right to confer on an appropriate person a portion of the territorial and spiritual authority which he had received at his coronation. To have challenged this right would have been not only to nullify the effect of the coronation service, but from a practical point of view to throw the Church into the hands of the local aristocracy, who only too often succeeded in exercising a power to which they had no theoretical claim. We do not yet, though we soon shall, hear from ecclesiastical writers complaints about inordinate *royal* power.

From the king's point of view the control of the Church was an essential part of his royal dignity, and circumstances continued to make it increasingly important with the passage of time. The most harassing of the many insoluble problems of a medieval ruler was the problem of conserving his family fortune. This was in fact almost impossible. In order to make and keep friends he had to make gifts of land, for without friends he was lost. But men who have been given land soon forget to be grateful; and, if they themselves remember, their sons hasten to forget. So, in the uneasy task of inducing loyalty, there was a constant process of depletion of the royal estates, which confiscations, successful wars and marriages only imperfectly arrested. It was noted of the son of Charlemagne especially that he gave away in perpetuity many estates which had belonged to his forefathers. And what he began, his descendants were obliged to continue. It is easy to blame their improvidence, but it is quite impossible to think what else they could have done.

These facts, fundamental as they are to the problem of exercising royal authority, have an important bearing on the relations between the Church and the lay ruler. In the shifting sands of royal power, there was one source of strength which rulers were not slow to recognize. In the bishops and abbots of their kingdoms they had men whom they had appointed. These were often men who had been their servants before their appointment, and they had no lawful issue to succeed to their lands. Hence it is very easy to see why, for the two and a half centuries after the death of Charlemagne until the middle of the eleventh century, lay rulers came increasingly to rely on their ecclesiastical subordinates for loyalty, advice, the preservation of their influence in their kingdom, and even for the means of sustenance. It is one of the most pathetic and convincing indications that a ruler had his back to the wall when we find him increasingly accepting the hospitality of bishops and abbots and unable to support himself on his own estates. This was the position of the last Carolingians in France before the accession of Hugh Capet in 987, and to see the shifts to which they were reduced in the struggle for survival increases our respect for their tenacity. It also prepares us for the attack on lay authority over the Church which was not long in coming.

III · The Development of Tithes and Parishes

There were, therefore, many ties of duty and interest which bound together the lay ruler and the local churches of his dominions. It is not surprising that the ruler was willing to use his authority for the maintenance of ecclesiastical discipline: he was the legislator in ecclesiastical matters as much as he was in secular affairs. We have only to look at the legislation of the tenth-century English kings to see that they turned from secular to ecclesiastical matters with no sense of trespass on a domain which was not theirs by right. Here is an example of about the year 960:

> This is the ordinance which King Edgar has enacted, with the advice of his councillors, for the glory of God and his own royal dignity and the good of all his people:

1. All tithes shall be paid to the old churches to which obedience is due, and payment shall be made both from the thegn's demesne land and the land held by his tenants, from all that is under the plough.
2. If a thegn has a church of his own on land which he holds by charter, and the church has a graveyard, he shall pay a third of his tithes to this church.
3. If anyone refuses to render tithes as we have decreed, the king's reeve and the bishop's reeve and the priest of the church shall go to him and forcibly take the tenth part for the church to which it is due; they shall leave a tenth part for the man himself and divide the remainder between the man's lord and the bishop.[15]

It is impossible in a short commentary to exhaust the interest of this royal decree, but besides its proof of royal responsibility for the Church, there are two points which specially deserve notice. The first relates to the payment of tithes; the second to the growth of parishes.

In the first place this is the earliest law in English history which makes the payment of tithes compulsory under pain of secular penalties. The penalties are very severe, absurdly severe we may think, but displaying the grim poetic justice dear to early law: he who does not give one-tenth willingly shall unwillingly retain only one-tenth. This compulsory payment from all men engaged in production becomes the stable item in the ordinary revenue of the Church for the next nine hundred years.

The idea that all Christians ought to pay a tenth of their annual income to the Church was not new. Its origin is to be found in the Old Testament, for example in Leviticus 27.30: 'and all the tithe of the land, whether of the seed of the land or of the fruit of the tree, is the Lord's: it is holy unto the Lord.' In England, references to church dues of an unspecified kind, payable on pain of a heavy fine, go back to about the year 700; and tithes are mentioned by name, but without secular penalties, in royal laws from about 930 onwards. So in about 960 King Edgar was only systematizing something which had long been recognized as a moral obligation. It need scarcely be said that it was not easy to enforce payment. Only a few years after the ordinance which has been quoted the King put out another law attributing the recent plague to the failure of husbandmen to pay, and of reeves to enforce payment of, tithes; and the continued repetition of the laws on the subject shows the difficulty of making them effective. Indeed it is probably true to say that so long as it was left to the unaided efforts of royal and episcopal officers to enforce payment a very large measure of default was inevitable. But before turning to the factors which speeded up the process by which the universal payment of tithes became effective it is necessary to turn to the parallel developments on the Continent.

On the Continent, Charlemagne is once more the outstanding figure. There are traces of compulsory payment of tithes even before his reign, but it was he who extended the obligation to large areas of his newly conquered Empire in perpetuity.[16] Alcuin was moved to object to the imposition on so newly and insecurely converted an area as Saxony; but without effect. Ecclesiastical discipline was to be the hallmark of the Carolingian Empire, and the universal obligation to provide for the Church was one of the pillars of the new polity. When nearly every other institution of the Carolingian state went down, this remained. It was one of the chief legacies of the Carolingian age to the future.

But how was this huge payment from the great mass of Christian laymen to be enforced year after year? Certainly not by royal officials and bishops alone. They were too remote and powerless to be effective. It was here that a new development came into play which changed the whole aspect of the Christian world for the ordinary layman. If we look back at the law of King Edgar we see that tithes were to be paid to the 'old churches', but that if the lord or thegn had a church on his own land with a graveyard attached, a proportion of the tithe could be paid to it. We stand here at the beginning of the process which finally resulted in the system of parishes and parish churches as we know them. In earlier days the local organization of the Church had been diocesan. The cathedral, with its bishop and his staff of clergy, was the unit of church life from which everything flowed. This was reasonably satisfactory in the city polity of the Roman Empire, but it was clearly quite inadequate to the needs of a widely scattered rural society with no great centres of population. Hence there developed a system half-way between the ancient diocese and the modern parish: the diocese became to some extent decentralized with the erection of collegiate churches maintaining a small body of priests at strategic points in the diocese. These were the 'old churches', the mother churches or minsters, to which Edgar's law refers. Traces of their influence and early importance survived for many centuries. But these too were inadequate to the needs of the time, and they soon began to be supplemented by the churches which landowners built on their own lands. These are the churches to which Edgar's law allowed a certain proportion of the tithe to be paid. It was, however, too much to expect that landlords would willingly see two-thirds of their tithes go to a distant church, perhaps on another man's land, when their own church, not to say they themselves, stood in need. It is impossible to mark the dividing-line between greed, local interest and spiritual needs. The process whereby local landlords built churches and then appropriated the tithes of their tenants for the maintenance of their churches and the priests whom they appointed was complex and is largely undocumented. But by the end of our period it had, for better or worse, transformed the local organization of the church.

There were sinister features in this development, but it is not necessary to suppose (as is sometimes done) that all features were sinister. The payment of tithe was recognized as in principle good, but it is very unlikely that it could have been enforced by anyone except the local landlord; and it is very unlikely that he would have enforced it for any except his local church. This led to abuses. A landowner who was unwilling to see tithes leave his estate, might prefer to see them in his own pocket. And in these centuries there was no effective means of preventing this. Even without the evidence of later critics we might therefore conclude that the man who alone could enforce payment must often have enjoyed the proceeds. And this would be the more readily excused in times of great difficulty, when moreover the task of building and furnishing the church and maintaining the priest fell on the owner of the land. This cannot excuse the doubtless frequent misappropriation of a payment which canonically should have been divided into four parts appropriated to the bishop, the priest, the fabric and the poor, respectively. But it is important to remember that parish churches *did* get built in large numbers throughout the later part of our period, and that the whole structure of the parochial system came into existence at this time. The landlords who were responsible for this were moved by many incongruous motives, but it would be absurd to imagine that the least important of these was a genuine interest in the religious well-being of themselves and their tenants.

IV · Lay Devotion

All men, whether clerks, monks or laity, necessarily shared the same hazards and the same outlook on the world and its problems, and much the same views on religion. But in the narrower fields of theology and religious devotion there was a vast difference between laymen and monks. This distinction was much more marked in the West than in the East. There were many reasons for this. In the East, the traditions of classical education had never been completely abandoned, and the existence of a wealthy, leisured and literate laity must always be reckoned with. Moreover, in the East the language of scholarship and worship was the language of everyday speech. But in the West this had ceased to be so by the eighth century: by this time no one learnt Latin as his vernacular language, and no learned works and no liturgical or devotional literature existed in any other language than Latin. The attempt of King Alfred to build up a library of learned works in the vernacular has no parallel in these centuries: it was in any case only a measure of desperation in the face of a widespread ignorance of Latin even among the clergy, and it only touched the fringe of the problem of conveying clerical learning to those who knew no language but their mother tongue. This sharp division between the literate world of monks and clerks and the illiterate world of the laity is one of the major facts of the period. It has often been misinterpreted, as if it formed part of a clerical conspiracy against lay influence, or as if it conclusively demonstrated the sordid brutality of lay minds. Neither of these conclusions has any truth in it. Yet it is a significant fact that the laity in general (we shall speak later of the exceptions) became isolated by the barrier of language and intellectual discipline, as much as by taste and other preoccupations, from the main developments of religious life and thought. This isolation was not by any means complete, but it had momentous consequences. Whereas in Constantinople theological discussion remained one of the chief intellectual exercises of the cultured layman, in the West we hear of no theological discussions in which a layman took a leading, or even articulate, part after the time of Gregory of Tours (d. 594). Gregory gives lively accounts of the heretical opinions on the Trinity of the Merovingian King Chilperic and the Visigothic nobleman Leuvigild, and he makes it plain that such matters were best left to the bishops. Nevertheless its arguments were at least reasoned and showed a disposition towards independent inquiry on the part of the barbarian rulers. This habit of mind, however, quickly died out. The rulers of the Carolingian period, although they often acted as conveners and presided at theological debates, are seldom reported as taking any part in the discussion.[17] Charlemagne is the outstanding exception to this rule. This immensely vital and active ruler was determined to dominate every side of the life of his time, and the most important theological treatise of his long reign is ascribed to his personal authorship in the original manuscript. This ascription is misleading, and no one could suppose that Charlemagne himself composed the learned and powerful attack on the Greek attitudes to images, which went under his name. A careful examination of the manuscript, however, has brought to light a large number of shorthand notes in the margin, and in all probability these are the remarks made by Charlemagne when the substance of the treatise was read and discussed in his presence. But these notes, though they show that Charlemagne was very willing to intervene, also disclose the limitations of his capacity to discuss such topics. His remarks are limited to comments of the most commonplace kind, as he nods his head in agreement; *bene, perfecte, docte, catholice, syllogistice, optime, eleganter,* are among the reported remarks which appear with tedious reiteration.[18]

King Alfred a century later had a more refined intellectual curiosity than Charlemagne, and his personal additions to the works he translated have often been praised for their artless beauty and insight. But, though they are refreshing to meet, and though they reflect the aspirations of a virtuous man, they are quite commonplace in content.

Much more important than any attempts at independent speculation are the evidences of the religious observances of the laity. As an expression of the basic religious duties of a layman the following may be quoted from the diocesan regulations of one of the best of Charlemagne's bishops, Theodulf, Bishop of Orleans:

> All the faithful are to be admonished, from the highest to the lowest, to learn the Lord's Prayer and the Creed, and they are to be told that these two contain the foundation of the whole Christian faith; and unless a man can recite them, and believes what is said in them, and recites them often, he cannot be a Christian. It was formerly laid down that nobody who does not know the Creed and his Lord's Prayer shall be confirmed or baptized . . . unless he is of an age at which he cannot learn them.
>
> Christian laymen are also to be taught to pray at least twice in the day, morning and evening; and if anyone cannot say the Lord's Prayer and Creed, let him say, 'Lord, who hast formed and created me, have mercy on me; God have mercy on me a sinner', and let him thank God for his daily food, and for making him in his own image and for separating him from the beasts. And, after he has done this, and has adored his only Creator, let him invoke the saints of God, first St Mary and then all the saints of God, and pray that they should intercede for him before God. Let those who can go to church, pray there; and for those who cannot, let them pray morning and evening wherever they are, for the Psalmist says 'The Lord ruleth in every place', and 'Thou art in every place, and though I ascend up to Heaven there art thou', and again 'I can find no place in which thou rulest not.'[19]

Nothing could be clearer or more expressive of the rational legislation of the Carolingian renaissance than these paragraphs, or than the one relating to the observance of Sunday, which follows them in Theodulf's collection. This forbade secular work on Sundays except for the preparation of food or necessary journeys on condition that attendances at Mass and prayers were not neglected. The further regulation that all should attend Vespers on Saturday and Matins on Sunday morning before Mass must be taken as the expression of an ideal rather than the description of a general practice. How far legislation of this kind could be enforced must remain obscure; in all probability it remained a remote aspiration. But, if so, the aspiration was not confined to the clergy nor to the great centres of civilization. The attempts to enforce Sunday observance runs persistently throughout the period. In the earliest codes of English law there were savage penalties for working on Sundays, and though these became less severe in course of time they continued to form part of Old English royal legislation until the Norman Conquest.[20] These temporal penalties were reinforced by a letter reputed to have come from Heaven in which those who broke the Sunday were threatened with every kind of temporal and eternal punishment. This letter seems to have been in circulation in Spain in the sixth century, and Pope Zacharias condemned it in 745. But it continued to excite interest throughout our period, and it has a history in every language in Christendom down to the present day.[21] It belongs to that strange set of religious phenomena which know no limits of time or space. Its only importance here is its testimony that threats and fantasies were of more avail than the exhortations of milder spirits; but the total result of the campaign for Sunday observance remains unclear.

About the higher levels of society, however, we are better informed. Once more, our best source of information comes from the court of Charlemagne. He asked Alcuin to give him some advice on his private devotions. Alcuin replied:

> You have asked us to send to you . . . a brief account of how a layman in an active life ought to direct his prayers to God at the appropriate hours . . . and we shall briefly say what we think.[22]

Alcuin then gave a large selection of Psalms, Collects, Hymns and Sentences for each day of the week and for use on special occasions. Whether or not Charlemagne made any use of this elaborate prayer-book it is impossible to say. According to his biographer his daily religious observances conformed closely to the routine laid down by Theodulf, which has been quoted above:

He went diligently to church, so far as his health permitted, both morning and evening, as well as to Matins and Mass. . . . He took great pains over the reform of the lectionary and Psalter, in both of which he was reasonably learned, although he himself did not read the lessons nor take part in the psalmody except in a low voice.[23]

Everything we know about Charlemagne confirms the general truth of these statements about his religious habits. If he was no theologian, he was certainly deeply interested in the ordering of the church services in his own chapel and throughout his empire. And what is true of Charlemagne is true in large measure of his descendants and even of the families who replaced them when the Carolingian Empire broke up. These families were themselves members of the Carolingian aristocracy and shared the religious and educational ideals which were developed at Charlemagne's court. Taken altogether, they form of course only a tiny proportion of society, and it would be absurd to attribute even to this tiny fraction a uniformly high standard of religious zeal. But equally it is a mistake to speak, as is often done, as if the only interest of the lay ruler in the Church during these centuries was in its exploitation. This was a view which was widely propagated at the time of the Hildebrandine reform movement and modern historians have been greatly influenced by the propaganda of that time: it appeals to our sense of the division between sacred and secular things to look at the world in this way. But the Carolingian ruler had not learned to draw these distinctions. Government was less a matter of administration than of ceremonial, and the central ceremonies were those of the Church.

Charlemagne's family and many of the noble families of the age were carefully educated to take this responsibility seriously. Charlemagne's son, Louis, was, like his father, diligent in his observance of religious duties:

He was [according to his biographer] well instructed in the Greek and Latin tongues, though he could understand Greek better than he could speak it: but Latin he spoke like his mother tongue. He went each morning to church to pray, falling down on his knees and touching the pavement with his forehead, praying long and humbly, and often with tears.[24]

The biographer goes on to say that his preoccupation with psalmody and reading caused him to place too much reliance on his counsellors; and it is a noticeable feature of this period that the second or third generation of rulers in a family often tended to neglect their practical duties for religious exercises, just as nowadays the sons and grandsons of captains of industry neglect business for the pleasures of culture and benevolence. Many rulers, however, managed a very effective combination of secular and spiritual interests.

In England, almost every ruler from the time of Alfred to the Norman Conquest effectively combined a strong personal piety with an attention to the needs of government which was sometimes brilliantly successful and always (despite the reputation of Ethelred the Unready) intelligent. King Alfred must once more, from the nature of the evidence, be our chief example: his biographer says that he carried about with him a book of Psalms and Prayers, which provided him with a daily routine of worship.[25] Alfred's book must have been similar to, if not the very work which Alcuin put together for Charlemagne, for to judge from the number of manuscripts now in existence Alcuin's compilation enjoyed a wide and deserved fame as the best collection of religious exercises for those who could not maintain a full monastic routine of offices. It was replaced in the course of the eleventh and twelfth centuries by other compilations formed on a quite different principle, but until the year 1000 at least it had no rival.

It is when we descend below the level of kings that it becomes difficult to say anything about the religious practices of the laity. But among those who had the wealth to maintain a private chapel, and the leisure and inclination to frequent it, their round of devotions probably did not differ greatly from that of their superiors. Naturally, noble ladies had often more time than their husbands for prolonged religious observances, and their interests and tastes were responsible for many of the developments of later medieval piety. But in this early period they are distinguished only by a more active pursuit of traditional exercises. There is (or was until its destruction in the last war) a manuscript of the tenth or eleventh century at Chartres which illustrates the kind of routine which a lady of ample leisure might follow. The instructions it contains were drawn up for an unknown queen of the ninth century, and the daily discipline laid down is as follows:

> After saying the Night Office repeat the Confession which Alcuin composed for the Emperor Charles in his daily offices; then say the seven Penitential Psalms and the Litany, together with the *cursus sanctorum* and the Office of the Dead and the Office which you say at the regular canonical Hours; then go to church and hear Mass and pray for your mother and father and husband.[26]

This routine has some novel features which cannot detain us here, but it is clear that it was suitable only for a person who could spend as many as three or four hours a day in regular devotions. That there were such people among the laity we know from the life of Queen Margaret of Scotland who died in 1093. The routine of her religious exercises is known in great detail and it was a good deal more elaborate even than the one which has just been detailed. In particular the extra-liturgical Offices which are represented above in the Office of the Dead have been greatly extended to include Offices of the Holy Trinity, the Holy Cross and the Blessed Virgin Mary. But there is the same evident intention of following the monastic routine as closely as the circumstances of secular life permitted. Although Queen Margaret is somewhat outside our period there is a further detail in her Life which is perhaps worth noticing for the light which it turns on the habits of the illiterate layman of this time. The Queen had a Gospel Book which still exists. Her husband, Malcolm III, being illiterate, could not read it, but he had it bound with ornaments of precious stones and gold, and often (so the biographer says) turned it over in his hands.[27]

These devotional manuscripts of great laymen and their wives are some of the most remarkable artistic products of the age. The possession of these treasures does not of course necessarily indicate any strong devotional impulses, but they are important nevertheless as showing the position of the chapel and its furnishings in the general picture of aristocratic life. The will of one of the greatest of the Carolingian counts of the middle years of the ninth century, Everard Marquess of Friouli, is important in this respect, since it gives an account of the division of his books as well as his lands among his children. These 'books of his chapel' are too numerous to recite at length, but four of his children inherited Psalters of which one is described as the 'Psalter which he had for his own use', and another is a Psalter with a commentary which his wife used. There are also three missals, of which one is the daily missal that was always in his chapel, and there are various books of prayers, psalms, lectionaries and Lives of the Fathers. It is not so much the existence of these books in a comital family which is significant, for they might have been acquired in all kinds of ways; but the evidence for their use and careful distribution among the family is highly significant.[28] It shows the Carolingian aristocracy at its best.

It is probable that the standards of the ninth century did not survive throughout the tenth century without a serious decline at least in some parts of Europe. The circumstances of nascent feudalism were not favourable to lay literacy or devotion. But this decline did not extend to the rulers of Germany and England, and even among the feudal aristocracy, which had lost all connection with Carolingian political tradition, be found. By the middle of the eleventh century there are many signs that a new age in lay religion, as in so many other aspects of life, had begun.

NOTES

1. *Asser's Life of King Alfred*, ed. W. H. Stevenson, 1904, pp. 90–1.

2. For fuller treatment and bibliography of this subject, see Max Förster, 'Zur Geschichte des Reliquienkultus in Altengland', *Sitzungsberichte der Bayer. Akad. zu München*, 1943.

3. F. Liebermann, *Die Gesetze der Angelsachsem*, 1903, I, p. 401. For Continental formulas, see K. Zeumer, *Formulae Merov. et Karol. Aevi* (Mon. Germ. Hist., *Leges*, V, pp. 601–722).

4. For the penitential literature of this period, see H. J. Schmitz, *Die Bussbücher u. die Bussdisciplin der Kirche*, 1883, and *Die Bussbücher u. das kanonische Bussverfahren*, 1898. For the Carolingian reaction against this literature, see P. Fournier and G. le Bras, *Histoire des collections canoniques en occident*, 1931, I, pp. 84–94.

5. D. Wilkins, *Concilia Magnae Britanniae et Hiberniae*, 1737, I, p. 338.

6. W. Dugdale, *Monasticon Anglicanum*, 1817 ed., I, p. 545.

7. Migne, *Pat. Lat.* 144, 323 (cf. 351 for the practice of affixing a monetary equivalent to penances for those *qui longa jejunia perhorrescunt*. This practice, says Peter Damian, was an indulgence to the laity lest they should die with their penances incomplete and their absolution for ever unattainable. But it was also applicable to ecclesiastics, e.g. the archbishop of Milan, condemned by Peter Damian himself to a penance of a hundred years for simony, but commutable on a fixed annual tariff. Quoted by N. Paulus, *Geschichte des Ablasses im Mittelalter*, 1922, I, p. 14 n.).

8. *Ep.* 174 (Mon. Germ. Hist., *Epistolae Karolini Aevi*, II, p. 288).

9. *Ep.* 171 (*ibid.*, p. 282).

10. As a guide to the very large literature on this subject, see especially E. H. Kantorowicz, *The King's Two Bodies*, 1957, pp. 42–86, and P. E. Schramm, *Die deutschen Kaiser u. Könige in Bildern ihrer Zeit*, 2 vols., 1928, and *Herrschaftszeichen und Staatssymbolik*, 3 vols., 1954–6.

11. See W. Levison, *England and the Continent in the eighth Century*, 1946, pp. 115–20.

12. Thietmar, Bishop of Merseburg, *Chronicon*, I, 26, ed. F. Kurze (scriptores rerum Germ. in usum scholarum), p. 16.

13. *Epistolae Karolini Aevi* (Mon. Germ. Hist.), II, p. 503.

14. *Tractatus eboracenses*, ed. H. Boehmer (Mon. Germ. Hist., *Libelli de Lite*, III, p. 667).

15. II Edgar, 1–3, ed. A. J. Robertson, *The Laws of the Kings of England from Edmund to Henry I*, 1925, p. 20.

16. U. Stutz, 'Das Karolingische Zehntgebot', *Savigny Zeitschrift, Germ. Abt.* 29 (1908), pp. 180–224.

17. At best the laity might ask questions: it was for the clergy to solve them. Cf. Alcuin, *Ep.* 136 (Mon. Germ. Hist., *Epp.* V, p. 205): Vere et valde gratum habeo laicos quandoque ad evangelicas effloruisse inquisitiones, dum quemdam audivi virum prudentem aliquendo dicere, 'clericorum esse Evangelium discere non laicorum'.

18. D. de Bruyne, 'La composition des *Libri Carolini*', *Rev. Bénédictine* 44 (1932), pp. 227–234; W. v. den Steinen, 'Karl der Grosse u. die *Libri Carolini*', *Neues Archiv* 59 (1932), pp. 207–80.

19. From the *Capitula* of Theodulf, *PL* 105, 191–206. The wide influence of this work may be judged from the existence of two distinct Anglo-Saxon translations of it. (See N. R. Ker, *Catalogue of MSS. containing Anglo-Saxon*, 1957, nos. 50 and 318.)

20. The earliest English law prescribing secular penalties for working on Sundays comes from Wihtred of Kent, 695; cf. also the *Penitential* ascribed to Archbishop Theodore of Canterbury (668–90), which gives some indication of the source of this legislation, I, xi, 1: Qui operantur die dominico eos Greci prima vice arguunt, secunda tollunt aliquid et eis, tertia vice partem tertiam de rebus eorum, aut vapulent, vel vii diebus peniteant (Haddan and Stubbs, *Councils and Ecclesiastical Documents* III, p. 186).

21. See H. Delahaye, 'Note sur la legende de la lettre du Christ tombée du ciel', *Bull. de la classe des lettres de l'Academie de Belgique* (1899), pp. 171–213.

22. See Alcuin's *Officia per ferias*, with its address to Charlemagne (*PL* 101, 569–612).

23. Einhard, *Vita Caroli* 26, ed. L. Halphon, 1938, p. 76.

24. Thegan, *Vita Ludovici imperatoris* (Mon. Germ. Hist., *Scriptores*, II, pp. 594–5).

25. *Asser's Life of King Alfred*, ed. W. H. Stevenson, p. 73.

26. Chartres MS. 127, printed in H. Bradshaw, *The early Collections of Canons known as the Hibernensis*, 1893.

27. Turgot, *Vita S. Margaretae Scotorum reginae*, printed in *Symeonis Dunelmensis Opera* (Surtees Society, 51), 1867, pp. 234–54 (esp. pp. 241, 247–8, 250).

28. The list of books and beneficiaries is printed in G. Becker, *Catalogi bibliothecarum antiqui*, 1885, pp. 29–30.

4

Christopher N. L. Brooke

THE CHURCH OF THE MIDDLE AGES

1000–1500

Introduction

FROM many points of view the eleventh and twelfth centuries marked a major turning-point in European history: the papal (or Gregorian) reform, the contest of Empire and Papacy, the intellectual revival, the Crusades, the formation of the Norman states and many other movements made this a period of dramatic change. There is change, too, in the nature of the sources available to the historian. Standards of education rose among the higher clergy; Latin literature flourished; the small circle of humanists expressed their thoughts with a freedom and sophistication unparalleled since the fall of Rome; the wider circle of ascetics, theologians and lawyers left a record of themselves which makes the clerical world of the twelfth century familiar to us as no previous generation since the age of the Fathers. But if we turn to their lay contemporaries, peasants, knights, barons, merchants, even kings, we are still met with something like silence. Laymen were still illiterate, by and large, and we depend for our knowledge of them on what their clerical contemporaries chose to tell us. This is one of the notorious difficulties of studying the Middle Ages. There was no more fundamental division in medieval life than the division between clergy and laity, especially between the upper clergy, the highly educated, privileged clerks possessioner, and the lay aristocracy, illiterate, brought up to the arts of war and (in a rudimentary way) of justice and government. The difficulty is at its height between the eleventh and thirteenth centuries. Before the eleventh century the upper clergy were few in numbers and not so distinct as a class. After the thirteenth century, especially in the south of Europe, the divergence was beginning rapidly to break down. There had always been lay education in Italy, and many of the great names in Italian thought and literature, from Dante on, were laymen. Even in the north the divergence could not last for ever. A literate civil servant in the English court in 1150 or in 1250 was inevitably a 'clerk', a cleric, even if only in minor orders. Most of his successors would still in 1350 be clerics. But already laymen were appearing in the service; and by 1450 his successors were as likely to be laymen as clergy.

To this there were some exceptions. The English kings, for instance, from the twelfth century on (King Stephen perhaps excepted) were all at least formally literate; some leading barons were able not only to be patrons of literature, but to engage in intelligent discussion with their protégés. But in the twelfth or thirteenth centuries the essentials of lay education were picked up in the tilt-yard or on the battlefield, in the court-house or out in the country hunting and hawking. Not for nothing have the Middle Ages been called 'the ages of faith': there was a great deal of simple piety—as well as a great deal of simple superstition—partly hidden from us behind this veil by the obscurity of the evidence. Professor Southern has analysed the roots from which this piety and this superstition sprang, and described the long round of devotion engaged in by the more conscientious of the lay upper classes. In general terms, his picture continues to be valid for the late Middle Ages. More was done for the well-to-do to provide them with books of devotion in the vernacular; the layfolk's mass books, primers and books of hours became increasingly common and increasingly sumptuous; and many books of hours survive with splendid illustrations intended to provide an eminent or at least a wealthy layman with suitable occupation during Mass or Office. The world of thought of these laymen, however, is desperately hard for us to penetrate; and although it becomes easier at the very end of the Middle Ages, it is only very few, and usually very exceptional, laymen who reveal their thoughts to us before the sixteenth century.

The evidence is thus very uneven, and this has dictated the form of the present chapter; this, and the need to cover many topics in a brief compass, which has compelled me to deal with some problems—for instance, the layman and the parish, the status of the monarch in the Church—rather cursorily; I do so the more readily, as a foundation for their understanding has been firmly laid in the previous chapter. I have been particularly concerned to give a very broad survey some actuality by taking concrete examples of men and women working out some of the various roles that layfolk had to play. I open with an attempt to analyse the official attitude of the Church to the laity and their place in its life, and to set this in a framework of broad generalization about the trends of the period. Particular study is made of the extremes of orthodox submission and heretical revolt between which the medieval layman had to find his niche. Next I shall attempt to penetrate nearer to the heart of the problem by inspecting the ideas of two men of the early thirteenth century who reflected deeply on the role of laymen, both in *ecclesia* and in *diaspora*. In Wolfram von Eschenbach's poetry we find a profound effort to work out the role of the layman in his own world, as knight and husband. In St Francis of Assisi we find an inspired plan to reunite cleric and layman in one community. A different role, that of the merchant, emerges from one of the most remarkable private correspondences of the later Middle Ages, that of Francesco di Marco Datini, of Prato near Florence, and his friends. The letters were written in the later fourteenth and early fifteenth centuries, and in them the problems of marriage and of the layman's attitude to the clergy and to the Church are seen, as at no earlier period, in their actuality. When the merchant of Prato died the Reformation was still over a century away; but many of the forces which made it possible were already actively at work; and with some of these our survey will conclude.

I · As the Clergy Saw It

The official view of the medieval Church on the relations of cleric and layman started from the presupposition that the two were utterly different in status and function, and must be kept apart. 'Thou shalt not plough with an ox and an ass together', says the book of Deuteronomy (22.10). The second Council of Seville in 619 quoted this text in support of a canon forbidding laymen to hold offices as *oeconomi* in the Church or to act as ecclesiastical judges. It was to this canon, as quoted in Gratian's *Decretum* (*c.* 1140), that an educated cleric would first turn in the later Middle Ages if he wanted to know about the layman's place in church affairs. 'Because you are layfolk,' said Archbishop Stephen Langton in 1213, 'it is your business to believe that your prelates are men who do all things discreetly and with counsel.' 'The view of the Church as the community of the faithful was not lost sight of by the theologians,' comments Professor Cheney. 'But in the government of the Church and in everyday speech, the Church was equivalent to the clerical order. The clergy were the shepherds, the laity sheep.'[1]

Such a view was in marked contrast to the leading part played in the affairs of the Church by the monarchs of the earlier Middle Ages. Men like the Emperors Charlemagne, Otto the Great, Henry II or Henry III had been very far from submissive; nor in many respects were their successors in the later Middle Ages. What had altered was the Church's attitude to lay influence and the layman's role; between clergy and laity a great gulf had been fixed. In essence, this was the achievement of the papal reform of the eleventh century. For various reasons which the reformers felt to be not only compelling but urgent, they strove to reduce lay influence in church affairs to a minimum, and to deepen the gulf between the orders. This led on the one hand to the conflicts between *sacerdotium* and *regnum*, and on the other to an enhanced sense of the separateness, and the sacredness, of the clergy. This was a natural consequence of a theological development in which the notion of sacrament had received a new definition, and with it the office of the men who administered the greatest of the sacraments. In the twelfth and thirteenth centuries the logical consequences of these views were drawn out in all manner of ways. It was impossible to deny laymen the right to administer baptism and hear confession; and to deny that laymen themselves ministered the sacrament of marriage would have been to abolish the sacrament, since it has always been held that it is the contracting parties who are the agents. But lay baptism became increasingly rare; and confession to a layman was made wholly exceptional in the twelfth century, a marked departure from ancient tradition. As for marriage, law and theology were only slowly emerging from a deep and ancient confusion, due to the diverse customs from which medieval marriage was descended. Strenuous efforts were made to encourage folk entering marriage to plight their troth *in facie ecclesiae*, but it was only slowly (so far as we can tell) that marriage in church, or 'at chirche-dore', became common and then normal. Medieval decrees against clandestine marriage had to be renewed and elaborated by the Council of Trent.

It was the sacramental movement above all which widened the theoretical gulf between cleric and layman; just as it was the intellectual revival which widened the gulf in practice, by giving to the clergy standards of learning hitherto undreamed of. Clergy and laity performed different functions in a world deeply convinced of the importance of function. At first sight, it might seem a simple matter for them to agree on their different roles; to live and work apart. But it is notorious that there was nothing in the world more difficult than for ambitious churchmen and ambitious monarchs to agree on the limits of their spheres of activity. Two main reasons may be advanced for this. First, spiritual and temporal never have been clearly distinguished; there must be some mingling of the elements; a Church which becomes too other-worldly, or contrariwise too worldly, withers away. Secondly, the educated cleric and the illiterate warrior lived in quite different intellectual worlds. The disputes between empire and papacy, between *regnum* and *sacerdotium*, were at heart disputes between two fundamentally different ways of looking at the world.

Even in the Church's view the laity had a role to play. The king or prince had the duty of protecting the bishop and his Church. One of the most remarkable ways in which the Church accommodated itself to the feudal society in which it lived was by finding a Christian function for a community naturally warlike and aggressive. There was discussion among the early medieval reformers of the role of the 'Ordo Laicorum';[2] but the most significant development was the idea of the Crusade. Christianity has always been a religion of peace, and has found a certain difficulty in harnessing the warlike proclivities of some of its adherents. In early days the feudal warrior's role was confined to protection of the Church from damage, and protection of all those who could not protect themselves; in extreme circumstances he was viewed as the instrument of divine vengeance. In the eleventh century some churchmen began to see justification in a more aggressive kind of war. A papal banner accompanied the Normans into England, which was being recovered from the 'perjured usurper' Harold; and papal banners accompanied other armies here and there in Europe. In these adventures the idea of a Crusade was born; but it rapidly became apparent that some limit must be set to the freedom with which popes like Gregory VII (1073–85) unleashed the horrors of war for slight, if apparently righteous, causes. When the Byzantine Emperor Alexius Comnenus asked for assistance against the Seljuk Turks, Pope Urban II seized a golden opportunity to restore the prestige of the papacy and of its banners by employing them outside the frontiers of Europe, on an enterprise which might not command the unanimous support of responsible churchmen but was at least generally recognized as Christian. The First Crusade was preached in 1095 for the defence of Constantinople and (in most men's eyes) for the recovery of Jerusalem from the infidel—both of which could be regarded as defensive measures. The feudal warriors of Europe, in the eyes of the papacy, were there to protect their spiritual pastors and to defend Christendom against the infidel.

II · The Layman from Within

Many laymen, not unnaturally, viewed their role somewhat differently. Side by side with the papal view of the function and status of laymen were the series of conflicting views held by many of the lay princes of Europe; and side by side with the official view of the Crusade was a popular view, much cruder and only too effective. The views of the lay princes represented the survival of the traditions and customs of the early Middle Ages. The kings of the tenth and early eleventh centuries had sometimes been addressed as 'deputies of God' or 'vicars of Christ', a symbol of their lofty authority and of the aura which surrounded it.[3] The reformed papacy made every effort to put this authority in its place, in the end (in the course of the twelfth century) taking for itself the proud title 'vicar of Christ'. But deep traditional attitudes among the princes and their supporters were not so easily killed; and incoherent as the notion of royal and princely authority often was, it survived through the later Middle Ages to be converted into the Erastianism of the Reformation.

The papacy regarded the Crusade as a defensive war. But the popes did everything they could to stir popular enthusiasm; they backed it with an indulgence of unprecedented potency, and they and their assistants preached war with a fervour and an assurance of divine aid natural to men excessively well acquainted with the Books of Joshua and Kings in the Old Testament. The result was that they touched a spring of popular enthusiasm deeper than they had dreamed of. The popular doctrine of the Crusade was remarkably coherent. It bore a close likeness to the Muslim doctrine of Holy War, and the speed with which Pope Urban was answered in 1095 shows that it was already in circulation. War justified itself: the infidel was bound for Hell, and there was nothing wrong in speeding him on his way; infidels could be slaughtered like cattle. This was not the only motive for popular interest in the Crusade. Motives were mixed from the start, and it was the adventure of the hour; it was especially congenial to those with a taste for war but nagged by doubt whether the internecine wars of Christendom prepared a man for heaven. Religious motives, too, were mixed. But the popular doctrine in all its ugliness was one of the great forces unleashed by the preaching of the Crusade, and one of the main reasons why the first outcome of Urban's preaching was a widespread massacre of the only infidels within reach, the Jews—the first of its kind recorded in Western Europe.

The founders of the papal reform had been aware of popular movements, and prepared to enter into alliance with them. In return the earlier reformers, like Pope Leo IX (1049–54), made a deep impression on the popular mind. The reformers supported the violent popular rising of the 'Pataria' in Milan. The vanguard of the First Crusade consisted of the rabble of peasants, artisans, beggars and knights who followed Peter the Hermit. But in the long run these popular movements revealed dangerous tendencies; and the various elements which might emerge—social revolution, the expectation of a millennium, heretical beliefs and practices—became mingled and confused in the mind of clerical contemporaries as they have tended to become confused in the minds of modern historians. The rabble was unpredictable; it contradicted conventional notions of hierarchy; it could easily inspire panic.

It was the tragedy of the medieval Church that it never found a way to develop, encourage and educate the enthusiasm it could inspire. When we meet movements of this character in the later Middle Ages, they were usually being treated as heretical. Medieval heresies were diverse in their nature and are usually obscure; most of our information about them comes from their orthodox opponents, who sometimes misrepresented them. It is reasonably clear that the various heretical and semi-heretical movements which flourished in the twelfth century, especially in southern France and northern Italy, owed their success to dissatisfaction with the official Church. This was not because the official Church was corrupt and worldly—sometimes it was, but by no means always—so much as because it failed to instruct the laity, and took away from the layman all initiative and almost every opportunity to use his head in the Church's service.

Various types of heresy first appeared in Europe in the eleventh century, then grew and flourished until in the late twelfth they could challenge the popularity of the official Church in the south of France and in parts of northern Italy. The Church took fright and adopted every method of persuasion and repression it could devise. The heretical groups were severely weakened by persecution and Inquisition, but there is no definite breach of continuity between the movements of the twelfth century and the re-emergence of heresy as a major problem in England and Bohemia in the fourteenth and fifteenth centuries. The leaders of all these movements were drawn from the more educated of the lower, unprivileged clergy, and from the more active of humble laymen, small merchants, artisans, knights; alliance with an eminent academic churchman, like Wyclif himself, was a comparatively rare event. It was in communities where active and intelligent laymen naturally met, and in communities in touch with ideas from other parts of Europe and further afield, that heretical movements flourished. There are exceptions to this rule; but the heresies of the eleventh, twelfth and thirteenth centuries in particular lived with the merchant and the artisan.

Through the confusion of nomenclature and the distorting mirror of orthodox panic we can discern three main strands of opinion among the heretics: first, a dualist theology akin to the theology of the Manichees and Paulicians, deriving from the Bogomil Churches of the Balkans and Byzantium; second, a latter-day revivalism in 'pursuit of the millennium';[4] and third, a demand for a return to the simplicity of the primitive Church which anticipated many of the doctrines of the Protestant Reformers. The relative strength of the three movements is impossible to assess; the problem is made all the more difficult by the constant exchange of ideas and influences between them, and by the impossibility of distinguishing clearly between the third group and some officially orthodox communities which showed similar puritan tendencies. The dualists, Cathars or Albigensians, as they were most commonly called, regarded the world and the flesh as evil, and aimed at an extreme puritanism of life; the second group had no expectation that the world would continue, and varied in practice from extreme puritanism to extreme promiscuity. Of the third we first have serious evidence in the Petrobrusian movement in southern France in the early twelfth century; and it comes into the light of day with the followers of Waldo, the founder of the Waldensians of southern France, northern Spain and northern Italy (where they still survive) in the late twelfth century. They started as a movement preaching voluntary poverty and the reading of the Bible (preferably in the vernacular); they soon incurred persecution; and they rapidly developed the other 'Petrobrusian' doctrines, confession to laymen, denial of transubstantiation, denial of the necessity of a priesthood and even of churches, denial of Purgatory and of the cult of the saints. At the heart of the Waldensian heresy lay a clear appreciation of the role of the layman in the world as well as in the 'Church': they lived as paupers in a world of paupers.

The Church reacted sharply. The various steps which led to the establishment of the Inquisition were usually taken by men who felt that an exceptional crisis demanded exceptional measures; that the orthodox must be instantly protected against the spread of this or that epidemic. But behind the various attempts to stamp out heresy by force or by kindness a great deal of serious thought was given to the problem of eradicating the causes of the disease. Men of the calibre of Pope Innocent III (1198–1216) realized that something was amiss with the Church itself if it could not win and hold the allegiance of the rank and file of Christian folk.

Innocent believed in killing by kindness. When heretical or ex-heretical communities submitted to him, he preferred to allow them to remain as religious communities in the hope that their example would spread. The ex-heretical groups could speak the language of the heretics, and answer them in terms they understood. This view hardly appealed to the Church's leaders on the spot. The bishops tended to regard the ex-heretical groups as hardly less dangerous than the heretical; both existed as a criticism of the official Church; both were inclined to be dangerously radical in social as well as in ecclesiastical views. Ex-heretics insufficiently controlled by orthodox, academic churchmen were liable to relapse into error without noticing it. The bishops tried to insist on the enforcement of the rigid laws against heretics passed by Innocent's predecessors. But it was clear that the official Church as it was could not cope with the problem. The laity wished for opportunities to express their religious zeal; the Church failed to instruct them; the parish clergy were often discouraged from preaching, largely because the hierarchy did not regard them as sufficiently instructed to be able to preach and instruct. It was a Spaniard, Dominic de Caleruega, who propounded the view that a special Order of Preachers was needed to supplement the resources of the parish clergy—men who could set out with impeccable academic qualifications, and provide the laity with precisely the preaching and instruction they required. To this end the Dominican Order was founded in the opening decades of the thirteenth century.

III · A Great Lay Adventure

It was no coincidence that heretical movements should have sprung up and become popular in the twelfth century. Partly, no doubt, this was due to the reopening of trade routes with the East, from which the Cathar doctrines found their way to the West. But it was essentially a by-product of the intellectual reawakening of the age. The humanists were reading Cicero and Augustine with new eyes, as if they had never been read before, and finding new and exciting ideas in them; the monastic reformers were reading the Rule of St Benedict as if it had never been read before, and attempting to live by it to the letter; many different types of men were reading the Bible as if it had never been read before, and reconstructing their theological interests accordingly. Anselm, Bernard of Clairvaux and countless others found a new interest in the life of the human Jesus and everything associated with him, including his earthly home and his human Mother. The Waldensians discovered some of the many problems which direct contact with the gospel always raises, including the problem of wealth and poverty.

It was the words of the gospel heard in a church early in 1209 which decided Francis of Assisi that he was called to found an Order based on Jesus' charge to his disciples to go out two by two, and to take nothing with them—a charge which perfectly fitted his own reflection on the needs of the poor, the humble and the wretched. Francis has won the affection of countless admirers in his own day and in ours by his infectious gaiety and joy; and it has often been said that all his actions were natural, spontaneous and unselfconscious. This can be exaggerated. It is clear that his Rule and his way of life were a direct answer to a direct challenge from the gospel, but at the same time they reflected the felt needs of his society. In a hierarchical society the son of a wealthy merchant could not be naturally at ease with a beggar or a leper; he could only really make contact with them by becoming poorer and humbler than they were. And so Francis excluded everything which would tend to separate himself and his followers from the humblest members of society: wealth, money, privileges, fine clothes, books, learning, comfort and standing of every kind. He excluded all these things, and yet remained strictly orthodox: he laid great emphasis on obedience as well as on poverty and chastity, and he wished his friars to be subject to the whole clerical hierarchy.

Although his Order included clerks, and he himself became a deacon, Francis never regarded it as a clerical Order. The lay brothers were in no way inferior to the rest. In early days they were in a majority; only one of the first eleven friars was a priest. The first two Ministers-General after St Francis's death were laymen. This use of the word involves an ambiguity. *Laicus* might mean a man who was not in orders; in this sense numerous early friars were *laici*. It might also distinguish a layman from anyone who had a clerical tonsure or was literate; in this sense they were all *clerici*. But Francis himself and the early Franciscans referred to their brothers not in orders as *laici*, and it is clear that he was deeply concerned with the function of layfolk, not only in his Order, but in the world. Beside the Friars Minor, he founded an Order of nuns, the Poor Clares, and also a Third Order, the tertiaries, as they are now usually known, whose function was to continue in their temporal occupation, but to live according to a simplified version of the Rule. The tertiaries were not sworn to poverty or chastity; but they were sworn to do works of penitence and charity. The Third Order was lay in the full sense; and it is significant that Francis should have been a pioneer in providing layfolk with a function in the Church's life outside as well as within his own community.

'St Francis had emphasized that the prayers of simple laymen might save more souls than the sermons of the learned', but his successors 'thought the Order had little need of them'.[5] The Franciscan Orders have never entirely lost the simplicity and poverty of the founder; but the essentially lay character of the early friars was quickly abandoned, and with it one of the few really serious attempts to find an evangelistic function for laymen in the medieval Church.

As so often happened with new religious orders, the friars attracted recruits of very varied type and talent, not excluding men of position and of learning. The men of learning among the Minors began to consider the role of their Order with new eyes; and intelligent men devoted to the Church's cause tended in the thirteenth century to see the Church's needs not in Franciscan terms, but in Dominican. The ideals of the two Orders had much in common; but the Dominicans were essentially a learned Order of priests, a *militia Dei* organized for the practical purpose of preaching throughout Christendom, and with a special interest in preaching in those countries where heresy was rife. In course of time the learned friars transformed the Franciscan Order; it was at their instigation that the last lay General, Brother Elias, was deposed in 1239. There were many charges levied against Elias. One of them was that he promoted laymen to positions of authority in the Order; and the ringleader in his deposition, the English Haymo of Faversham, shortly afterwards (*c.* 1242) passed the crucial constitution virtually forbidding the recruitment of laymen to the Order. Forty years later, the celebrated Franciscan gossip Brother Salimbene, who had been received by Elias shortly before his fall, looked back to the influential lay friars he had known in his youth. He recalled the extinct race without regret. They were useless folk; they neither celebrated mass nor heard confessions; they 'did nothing but eat and sleep'. Salimbene's strictures need not be taken too seriously. Haymo's attack was based on grounds more positive than these. He accepted the common view that a man must have a university degree if he was to be trusted to combat heresy, error and ignorance.

In the end there could be no escape from the dilemma: a learned cleric, full to the brim with the immensely elaborate educational apparatus of the thirteenth-century universities, could hardly make contact with the humble and the outcast; but a man who identified himself wholeheartedly with the poor had to share their mental as well as their physical poverty. Francis had many followers who could do a part of what he did; but a large Order could not be composed of such men. Yet it is a mistake to fall too readily into the temptation of becoming a partisan in this argument. The world has been enormously enriched by the life of men like Francis; and the life of some of his lay brothers was remembered as evidence that laymen could give an example even to clerics. But, if the Order was to become large and influential, it is hard to believe that Haymo was wrong. It is easy to be wise after the event, to point out to Haymo and Dominic that, even allowing their premises, academics may become heretics, universities breeding grounds of heresy; in a measure they knew it, though they can be forgiven for not foreseeing the careers of Wyclif, Luther and Cranmer. What they did see is that ignorance breeds ignorance; simple faith is admirable, but it is not enough.

Two problems emerge very clearly from this analysis of the Franciscan movement and the place of the laity in it. In spite of all the founder's protests, the Order appeared to contemporaries to be a criticism of the existing parish system. Francis denied this, partly out of humility, partly because his analysis, or intuition, went deeper than the level of common criticism. To him the trouble was that the humblest levels of society were not adequately served. It is doubtful if this was true in quite the way in which it was true, say, in English industrial cities in the nineteenth century; but it is clear that in any hierarchical society a parish system could do little to break down social barriers, or to draw folk together in a community in which there is neither Jew nor Greek, neither bond nor free. Francis glimpsed what the Church is so painfully learning today after 150 years of rapidly growing economic specialization, that there is a sense in which only the poor can talk to the poor, only a layman can talk to laymen. The second problem is raised very urgently by the difference of view between Francis and those who wished later to change the nature of his Order. In the end neither side had the best of it; but that does not necessarily mean that the problem is insoluble. Both Francis's solution and Haymo's solution were for the moment—attempts to deal with the immediate situation. In the long run poverty and ignorance themselves might prove soluble, and with their solution the problem takes on a different complexion.

IV · *The Christian Warrior*

In the same decades in which Francis was struggling with the problem of the poor layman in Italy, a member of the knightly class, of comparatively humble standing, though intensely proud of being a knight, was pondering on the status and function of his own kind in the south of Germany. Wolfram von Eschenbach's most famous poem, *Parzival*, was written in the opening years of the thirteenth century; his other great poem, *Willehalm*, in the 1210's, and the author is thought to have died in the 1220's.[6] He was a poor knight with a small landed estate in south Germany (his house was so poor, he tells us, that even the mice had hard work to find a living). He wandered in the princely courts of central Germany in search of patronage; he knew from his own experience many aspects of the life of knighthood and chivalry, and he showed a deep interest in the problems of the Crusading movement, though there is no indication that he had visited the East.

In *Parzival* Wolfram explores every passage in the rambling mansion of chivalry. The story is that of the *Perceval* by Chrétien of Troyes, of the quest for the Holy Grail; but Wolfram has considerably adapted it to suit his tastes and needs. Wolfram's *Parzival* is the finest exposition of one of the greatest of medieval tales; but it is more than that. It is a searching criticism of the tastes and values of contemporary chivalry. In the context of a medieval romance, which has also the fantasy and prodigality in story-telling of its medium, Wolfram expounds his view of what is involved in being a knight; not merely the skills of warfare or the gallantry of chivalry, but a set of religious attitudes which he regards as essential to the higher chivalry, the true chivalry of the Grail. The quest for the Grail enables his hero to discover a transformed chivalry; so vital is this that he even has to swear to abandon his wife until he has successfully attained the Grail. There are thus three essential and closely linked elements in the world of Parzival—his wife, his arms and his religion; and there are many aspects of his story on which we could profitably linger. Of these, three seem particularly significant.

The poem is set in a theological context. Wolfram was not book-learned: by his own confession, he was illiterate; he knew virtually no

Latin; his knowledge of books must have been confined to the many vernacular songs which he had heard recited, and to conversation with clerical friends. None the less, in his own way, he was a theologian of strong and independent views. Parzival appears to be in the grip of divine predestination: in spite of his upbringing he must become a knight and accept a knightly vocation; by reason of what appear comparatively trivial faults, he fails in his first visit to the castle of the Grail, and has to struggle five years more. Yet it is made clear that Parzival is no mere passive instrument in God's hands. In the middle of the poem, in its most critical scene, Parzival comes to the cell of the hermit Trevrizent, his uncle, where he learns a great deal essential to his purpose, makes confession to the hermit (though the hermit is a layman)[7] and is absolved from his sins. We are given to understand that God had directed his steps to the hermitage, in part at least, because Parzival had earned his reward. He had earned it, not by faith, but by loyalty, by *triuwe*, the supreme virtue of the code of chivalry—a loyalty which includes loyalty to oneself as well as to one's order in society. This inspires Parzival to dogged perseverance: he refuses to give up, to change his ground, until he understands. The poet emphasizes that Parzival's virtue did not lie in faith, when, in the opening words of the poem he announces that its theme is *zwîvel*, doubt and despair; doubt which leads Parzival, when he learns of his early failure, to lose faith in God. This is something quite remarkable in the thirteenth century: a poem which makes religious doubt its subject; and it is clear that Wolfram knew what doubt meant, deeply religious man though he was.

Wolfram's purpose is not to search out the intellectual grounds of doubt, but to make the even more startling point that God finds merit in a man, even if he lose his faith, if he leads his life in strict accord with the code of his order. This is no formal legalism; Wolfram's account of knightly *triuwe* is a profound searching out of all that was best in chivalry as he knew it. One example must suffice. Parzival was married before he went on his unfortunate visit to the Grail castle; and his loyalty to his wife, his *triuwe* as a husband, is the first and most striking of his qualities. It is a love deeper and more abiding than the fever of courtly love or *minne*, the love of the romances, of the romantic chivalry which Wolfram condemns, and with which it is several times contrasted. Although it has to survive five years of separation, it is never strained even for a moment; and reunion with wife and children is the supreme reward of his final success. The poet seems to be saying something like this. A feudal warrior has a special function in the world, a function most clearly revealed in the life of his family and the life of warfare; his Christian duty lies first and foremost in this, to be faithful to his wife and family, faithful to his lord, faithful to himself and to the code of chivalry, and to show *triuwe* in every human situation which arises. This matters more than theological orthodoxy; if he does this, God will be with him. Human love and human loyalty were to Wolfram symbols of God, whose *triuwe* ever gives help to the world, who is himself the '*ware minnaere*', the true Lover. He sums up the good life as meaning to live without alienation from God, yet to live well and obtain recognition in this world too; a firm and clear statement of the function of the layman in a Christian world.

The third of the elements in *Parzival* which most concern us is the presence in it of two pagans, who are held up as examples of natural goodness. One or two generations earlier, the clerical author of the *Rolandslied*, in the tradition of popular theology, had happily permitted the heathen to be slaughtered like cattle. In *Parzival* the problem of the good heathen is only hinted at; in *Willehalm*, Wolfram's second great work, it is brought right into the open. The hero's wife, Gyburc, is a converted Saracen; she has been baptized, but she has not lost her sympathy with her own family and people. Willehalm the Christian is at war with her pagan relations, and her problem is central to the poem. The heathen are God's handiwork.

> hoert eines tumben wîbes rat,
> schonet der gotes handgetat.

'Hear the counsel of a simple woman, and spare God's handiwork.' The problem of Rennewart, Gyburc's brother, who fights on the Christian side, but appears unwilling to become a Christian, is not, however, solved. *Willehalm* is unfinished: the baptism of Rennewart, which would have been an obvious climax, is never reached; indeed, as the poem now stands, it is not even clear that Rennewart has survived the final battle. It may be that the poem is unfinished because Wolfram was embarrassed by the problem of Rennewart. On the one hand, he has earned the reward of baptism and betrothal to the Christian Aliz; on the other hand, he is a symbol of natural goodness—as is progressively realized by Gyburc and Willehalm—and this symbol would be spoilt by his baptism or marriage to a Christian. As it is, we are left with the question ringing in our ears: 'What difference does baptism make?'

Clearly the poet himself had some answer to this question. *Willehalm* opens with a prayer, in which Wolfram's confidence in God is based on the Christian's special relation to God. Baptism, by which he could call himself a Christian and so partake in Christ's name, was a token to him of special kinship; but there is a hint already, in the prologue, that God's providence is larger, is indeed immeasurable.

The problem of the heathen and their relation to Christians and to God is constantly being posed in *Willehalm* in different forms. Wolfram had scouted the popular theology of the Crusading movement. How characteristic he was in this we do not know; but he was certainly not alone, and the doubts he felt were one of the reasons why the Crusading movement fell into such rapid decline.

Wolfram's sympathy with the heathen was not due to any understanding of Islam, his account of which was wholly garbled. His sympathy sprang partly from the fact that men of his type were growing aware of the increasing contact between Muslims and Christians in Spain, in Sicily, in the Latin East, partly from his own determined, self-willed, even radical following out of tendencies in the twelfth-century theological schools. How much of formal theology he knew it is difficult to say; but it seems likely that he had rubbed shoulders with orthodox clerics. He came near to Pelagianism and near to universalism; but he showed only slight traces of the specific heresies of his day. It seems clear that he was (at least in intention) perfectly orthodox, but far from clerically minded. Chrétien's Grail had been a cup or a dish, symbol of the chalice of the Last Supper; Wolfram turned it into a stone, an Oriental talisman, and took it out of Church, so to speak. For whatever reason, churches and clergy are notable for their absence from his poems.

In his acute perceptiveness, his penetration, his theological understanding and his awareness of movements of thought, Wolfram was no doubt exceptional among the laymen of his day; he represents, not what most men thought, but the limit of what it was possible to think. Perhaps the hints of Pelagianism—the laymen's heresy *par excellence*—and the concern to find room for the good things of life in God's scheme, were more typical of lay thought. But the central interest of Wolfram is the attempt to find in the pursuits of a transformed chivalry and in Christian marriage a justification for the role of the lay warrior in a Christian world.

V · *The Christian Merchant*

The twelfth and thirteenth centuries were an age of increasing wealth in most European countries; and among the causes and the symptoms of this wealth were a rapid increase in the number of merchants and a development in the techniques of commerce. It was then that European capitalism had its rise, and then—if ever—that one might try to perceive a special relation between religious belief and rising capitalism. Unfortunately the material for such a study is lacking. We can deduce by plotting outbreaks of heresy on the map a link between heresy and trade routes; but it is not until the fourteenth century that we have any intimate evidence of the life and aspirations of a successful merchant.

Francesco di Marco Datini was born in or about 1335, and died in 1410.[8] At the mature age of fifteen he set off with a small sum of money to the great city of opportunity of the day, the crowded and stuffy capital of the Western Church and of Western finance, Avignon. He dwelt in Babylon for thirty years, and then returned, a rich man, to set up house in his home town, Prato near Florence, with his young Florentine wife. For most of their married life, however, they lived apart—he in Florence, she in Prato—and to this circumstance the historian owes a unique family correspondence. Neither was particularly well educated, but each could wield the pen to some purpose. From their letters emerges a vivid picture of two strong characters, and of the actuality of a medieval marriage.

Francesco was a man of strongly conventional turn of mind. Having made his pile, he thought he would marry, rear a family to enjoy his wealth, then gradually withdraw from business and do his share of good works before he died. None of these schemes turned out quite as he had expected. There is no hint of romance about the match; the husband expected to be director of all family concerns, to subject his wife, children, servants and slaves (for slaves were not uncommon in fourteenth-century Italy) to a moral discipline distinctly more strict than he himself adhered to. The wife was expected to bear children and to run the home; she was the housekeeper, her husband's bailiff; but she also had the privilage of intimacy with him, and if she managed him in the boudoir, that was his affair, so long as she did not parade her dominance in public. Margherita's letters are often shrewish; but she played her part in public well. Where she failed was that she could bear no children, and this was plainly the purpose for which Francesco had married her. But for all that there seems to have been a respect and an affection between them which matured in the last nine years of his life, when they were together more or less continuously; and although neither partner had conspicuously softened with age, their relationship was mellower. At the least, it had survived the crisis at which Francesco's attorney had written to him, 'Let not the many, many letters you write, to increase your bodily welfare and your riches in this world, make you lose your charity and love for the person to whom you are bound by God's laws. For your rough soul and your frozen heart need to be comforted.'[9]

The merchant of Prato accepted the normal beliefs of his age without question. He had little time in early life for religious observance, but in his heart he intended to treat God with the respect due to one's most powerful creditor. Like many men of affairs he was superstitious and quickly swayed by a striking sermon; as with most sermon-goers the impression rapidly faded. He took great pains to avoid usury; he took even greater pains to become rich; he admired and respected all the material symbols of wealth and power; invisible forces of good and evil he feared; he invited a cardinal to baptize one of the children of his illegitimate daughter, but subscribed to the conventional anti-clericalism of his more earnest friend the attorney; he left the bulk of his goods to feed and clothe the poor.

The Church condoned the acquisition of wealth so long as it was obtained without usury (by which it meant any overt lending of money at interest), and so long as the rich man was generous, especially to the poor—though it never quite forgot that 'it is easier for a camel to go through the eye of a needle, than for a rich man to enter into the kingdom of God.' The medieval Church had taken on itself the task of distributing charity so as to meet the needs of the poor; and, inadequate as its efforts no doubt were, they were not so haphazard or misdirected as has often been alleged. It was one of the main duties of a rich man's confessor to direct his spending on charity; to ensure that sufficient was spent to make some impression on local poverty and to prepare the rich man's soul for its encounter with the needle.

The Church's attitude to usury failed to take into account the new techniques of credit and banking developed above all by the papal bankers in the twelfth and thirteenth centuries; and certain methods of evading the rules were well known and generally practised. But the laws were not so irrelevant or so widely disregarded as has commonly been thought. Francesco, for instance, was extremely sensitive to them. He made money as he could; he had little positive vision of the benefit to society that might accrue from his wealth; but he accepted the limit set to his operations. Usury was immoral; it was also neither respectable nor safe. When he learned that his Spanish partners were engaging in borderline transactions (including a modest form of hire purchase), he was horrified.

Francesco found it very difficult to retire; the habit of anxious profit-making was too strong for him. 'I ruled myself ill and did not what I could and should,' he wrote when over sixty, '. . . in all this Lent I have heard only six sermons.'[10] His conscience was frequently stirred by his one intimate friend, his attorney Ser Lapo Mazzei, a younger and more attractive man. Mazzei's letters are a remarkable witness to the effect of private reading and long meditation on a pious, but practically minded and anti-clerical, layman. He spent most of his time looking after the affairs of a Florentine hospital; he was thus able to provide for his own living and look after the poor at the same time. He kept a copy of the *Fioretti*, the *Little Flowers* of St Francis, to remind him of the sanctity of holy poverty.

On Mazzei's advice, the merchant left most of his fortune to support the poor of Prato, and under Mazzei's firm direction he excluded the clerical hierarchy from the administration of his will (thanks to the good work of his relations and colleagues and the city fathers of Prato, his foundation still survives). Mazzei liked to hear preachers who were mildly heretical, but neither he nor his friend was tempted to major heresy. What was characteristic of both of them, and of the society in which they lived, was a mild puritanism and a not-so-mild anti-clericalism. So far as Francesco was concerned, this was combined with a meticulous attention to the formal observance of religion. He spoke his mind freely about clerics and monks; but he fasted and went to mass and confession regularly; his ledgers were inscribed with the Ten Commandments, and many pages have the words 'In the name of God and of profit' at their head; a strange mixture perhaps, but wholly characteristic of Francesco and his age. Material prosperity and its pursuit occupied most of his waking hours, and he needed Ser Lapo at his elbow to remind him of God. Yet he was extremely reluctant to exclude the Church from his will, lest he lose valuable prayers. In the end he accepted by implication Ser Lapo's view that to give everything to the poor and avoid the danger of clerical chicanery and embezzlement mattered more than masses and ceremonies. But he wanted the masses too; and so we take leave of the merchant of Prato, excluding

E

the Church from the administration of his fortune, but calling no less than five Franciscan friars to help him in his sickness; a strange mixture of conflicting assumptions, as most men are.

VI · *From Middle Ages to Renaissance*

The basic doctrines of the reformers of the fourteenth century or of the sixteenth century bore a strong generic similarity to those of the Petrobrusians in the early twelfth century; even the Anabaptist demand for adult baptism was anticipated. But the world in which the later movements took place was a very different world from that of the early twelfth century, and the intellectual milieu of the Reformers' theology was profoundly different from that of Peter of Bruis. If we ask the question, how the lay world of the twelfth century had been most strikingly transformed by the events and the pressures of the three centuries which followed, one historian might emphasize the growth of anti-clericalism and of antagonism to the state-like nature of the official Church; another might counter with the growth of material possessions, with growing desire for material rather than spiritual gain, and the wider choice of occupation that went with it; a third might emphasize the presence of new ideas—contact with Islam, renewed contact with ancient paganism—which invited disquieting reflection on the monopoly hitherto enjoyed by the Catholic faith; a fourth might place his emphasis on the growth of lay education, on the larger lay element in the universities and the professions, on the enlarged opportunity for lay speculation and lay influence on learning and thought. No doubt there are many other aspects of these centuries of change which could be singled out; and the sands of historical generalization are shifting and dangerous. But it seems appropriate to end this survey by a glimpse at each of these four points of view.

We can see signs of anti-clericalism in every age we have inspected: stirred by a sense of social cleavage and by Roman avarice in the twelfth century, by a sense of neglect and frustration in the thirteenth century, and by traditional enmity and suspicion in the fourteenth. There is no way of answering the question, Was it on the increase? Naturally one is inclined to suppose that it was; that the papacy, for instance, grew increasingly unpopular the more power it acquired, the more like a government it became; and especially when its energies were absorbed in the politics of Avignon and Italy. But in the nature of things this can be no more than supposition; and it can equally be argued that on countless laymen the papacy, though accepted as a distant authority, had never made any direct impression. To the merchant of Prato and his like the official hierarchy of the Church meant little, until they became so grand that they could correspond with cardinals. It is not clear that Francesco would have resisted a reformation or that Ser Lapo would have objected to one; but neither was likely to set one in motion. Francesco lived through most of the Great Schism and knew the eminent Cardinal d'Ailly; but there is no evidence that he knew or cared much for the issues involved. His elder contemporary William Langland, the author of *Piers Plowman* and a cleric in minor orders, expressed open contempt for the pope and the college of cardinals in an England rejoicing in the anti-papal Statutes of Provisors and Praemunire. But Langland was no Wyclifite; he was orthodox in intention, yet cared nothing for ecclesiastical organization. It may well be that such insouciance played a larger part than militant anti-clericalism in preparing the ground for the Reformation.

The merchant of Prato thought little about the issues of the Schism because he was immersed, most of the time, in affairs. There can be no question that wealth and its outward symbols had a more precise and pervading significance for the men of the fourteenth century than they had for those of the eleventh. This was inevitable; many of the symbols had simply not existed in the eleventh century. But it is not the same thing to stigmatize the last centuries of the Middle Ages as 'materialistic'. Whether such judgments can be made of a whole age is open to doubt; and material prosperity, then as always, worked both ways. The rise of living standards in the Church and the world in the eleventh and twelfth centuries stimulated the new emphasis on asceticism among the highly popular new monastic Orders. Growing mercantile wealth in the early thirteenth century stirred a merchant's son in Assisi to found the cult of Holy Poverty, which was to be the subject of violent and fundamental controversy in the fourteenth century. And we have seen that it was precisely in the towns, chief centres of growing wealth, that the heretical or quasi-heretical movements flourished, so many of which laid special emphasis on the dangers of wealth and material prosperity. In the end, growing material prosperity tends to give man a firmer control of his environment, and to reduce his sense of insecurity and superstitious dependence on unseen powers. Of this, however, there was no sign in the later Middle Ages. Recurrent plague in particular brought the fear of death close to men's minds with a new urgency. The merchant of Prato himself joined in one of those strange flagellant processions with which men strove to avert God's anger and to stop the plague.

None the less, even if to talk of growing materialism is to simplify unduly, it is clear that the fifteenth century was an age in which men were prepared to specialize, to divide their minds into compartments, to let their left hand ignore what their right hand was doing. It is this that seems to account for a difference between the humanism of the fifteenth century and the humanism of the twelfth. In earlier days men like Abelard or John of Salisbury, in their different ways, had attempted to integrate pagan thought and the inspiration of the classics with a Christian theology and outlook; this was no longer felt to be necessary. The pagan classics were admired more in isolation, or at least without an overt attempt being made by many of their devotees to reconcile the classics and the Fathers. Partly this grew from the increasing specialization of the schools in the later Middle Ages; this led to the divorce of theology, for instance, from philosophy, which began with the influx of Greek and Arab thought in the twelfth and thirteenth centuries, and was developed, after the heroic efforts at synthesis of St Thomas and others, by the philosophical scepticism of Ockham and his followers. Partly, too, this divorce was due to the growing number of laymen among the learned of the fifteenth century. This was especially true of Italy, where the learned layman was no novelty; but both as scholar and as patron, the layman was a key figure in the Italian renaissance. One finds a reflection of this everywhere in Europe; but before 1500 it is, in many parts, a pale reflection. In England, for instance, the patron of learning who was deeply influenced by the Italian renaissance was a rarity—Humphrey, Duke of Gloucester, and John Tiptoft, Earl of Worcester, were notable exceptions; but educated laymen were now common, in the legal profession, among the merchants and small gentry, in the civil service; and then as earlier they were to provide fertile ground for the spread of heresy. The renaissance was slow to impinge on England; but in many ways learning was becoming secularized, in practice if not in theory, and in England as elsewhere ideas of worldly authority were becoming secularized too: the ground was prepared for the Erastianism which played so large a part in the history of Europe in the sixteenth century.

At the root of many of the movements of the eleventh and twelfth centuries lay a book—the Bible, the Rule of St Benedict, Justinian's *Corpus*. This happened in an even more dramatic way in the renaissance of the fifteenth century. The power of a renaissance is conditioned in the first instance by the number of educated men who can understand its message and appreciate its values. Education was more widespread in the fifteenth century than in the twelfth; above all, it affected a larger cross-section of the community. Although the Church (or rather the Churches) retained great power in the universities of Europe until very recent times, laymen began to play their part in them in the later Middle Ages, especially in Italy. The old framework of clerical learning and lay ignorance no longer corresponded to the facts; Thomas More, lawyer and humanist, took his place beside Erasmus the regular canon and Colet the secular priest. The layman's role was changing.

In the eleventh and twelfth centuries men looked with new eyes at the Bible and were led to question the organization of the Church and the world as they knew it. In the fifteenth and sixteenth centuries like causes had like consequences; but this time the would-be reformers were able to hold their own against the power of the organized Church, and so the sixteenth century witnessed the Reformation.

NOTES

1. C. R. Cheney, *From Becket to Langton* (Manchester, 1956), pp. 155-6, where the texts from Deuteronomy and Gratian are also cited.

2. Recent study of this is briefly summarized by A. Frugoni in *XIe Congrès International des Sciences Historiques : Résumés des Communications* (Stockholm, 1960), pp. 119-20.

3. See p. 98. Professor Southern has emphasized that a distinction was sometimes drawn between being God's deputy and the vicar of the human Christ. But both ideas could be included in the phrase 'vicar of Christ'—and were so included by the twelfth- and thirteenth-century popes.

4. The title of a recent and interesting book by Norman Cohn (London, 1957).

5. R. B. Brooke, *Early Franciscan Government*, p. 203.

6. In writing this account of Wolfram, I have had generous help from Mr Hugh Sacker of University College, London, on whose 'The Tolerance Idea in Wolfram's *Willehalm*' (unpublished Doctoral Thesis, Frankfurt-am-Main, 1955) my account of Willehalm is based. The most readily available accounts of Wolfram in English are by Otto Springer in *Arthurian Literature in the Middle Ages*, ed. R. S. Loomis (London, 1959), pp. 218-50 (with bibliography, p. 218 n.), and by M. F. Richey, *Studies of Wolfram von Eschenbach* (Edinburgh, 1957). More valuable for our purpose are the writings of J. Schwietering (summarized in *Die deutsche Dichtung des Mittelalters* [1941], pp. 160-83).

7. The point has been disputed, like so much in the interpretation of Parzival; but this remains the most probable view.

8. He has recently been brought to life in a fascinating biography by Iris Origo, *The Merchant of Prato* (London, 1957).

9. Origo, p. 174.

10. Origo, p. 155.

BIBLIOGRAPHY

General

R. W. Southern, *The Making of the Middle Ages* (London, 1953).
J. Huizinga, *The Waning of the Middle Ages* (London, 1924).
C. Dawson, *Mediaeval Religion* (London, 1934) and *Medieval Essays* (London, 1953).
H. Grundmann, *Religiöse Bewegungen im Mittelalter* (2nd ed., Hildesheim, 1961).

On medieval heresy

A. Borst, *Die Katharer* (Stuttgart, 1953).
N. Cohn, *The Pursuit of the Millennium* (London, 1957).
S. Runciman, *The Medieval Manichee* (Cambridge, 1947).
J. Guiraud, *Histoire de l'Inquisition au Moyen-Age* (vols I, II, Paris, 1935–8).
H. Maisonneuve, *Études sur les origines de l'Inquisition* (2nd ed., Paris, 1960).

On St Francis of Assisi

P. Sabatier, *Vie de S. François d'Assise* (Paris, 1893–4).
R. B. Brooke, *Early Franciscan Government* (London, 1959).

On the medieval attitude to the poor

B. Tierney, *Medieval Poor Law* (Berkeley and Los Angeles, 1959).

On the fourteenth and fifteenth centuries (in England)

B. L. Manning, *The People's Faith in the time of Wyclif* (Cambridge, 1919).
H. S. Bennett, *The Pastons and their England* (Cambridge, 1922).

For Wolfram von Eschenbach and the Merchant of Prato, see above, p. 133, nn. 6 and 8.

5

E. Gordon Rupp

THE AGE OF THE REFORMATION
1500–1648

Introduction

THAT the layman has no mere walk-on part in the drama of the Reformation is self-evident. But why? Shall we seek the reasons in history—amid events, persons, social pressures? Or shall we study theology, the ideas of theologians, controlling, and in part conditioned by, events, ideas which begin as utterances from pulpit or pen, but which swiftly filter down into the clichés and evangelical jargon of ordinary men? Or shall we turn, as did Luther, Zwingli, Calvin themselves, to Holy Scripture and ask what neglected biblical truths were rediscovered, what new perceptions made? A sound method will make use of all three approaches, but the phrase 'Christian History' gives the overall term of reference. It is another method than that of confessional theology: we are not simply to list what the leading Reformers said about laymen (they being themselves clergy), alloting space to them in due proportion to the place of their descendants in the ecumenical scale. Theological ideas take root in history, but why some wither away and others bear fruit depends in part on the nature of the historical soil. We shall try to select some of the significant ideas, as near to the point of historic emergence as possible, and illustrate as widely as possible their echoes in succeeding years, and see where and how they were made flesh in the new apparatus of piety, discipline or worship. We can only murmur the question, 'What is a layman?' and may not stay for an answer. Yet it is something which the Reformation itself poses for us. Is not that eminent sixteenth-century figure, the leading layman, himself a kind of ecclesiastical person, one who has, to use the jargon of sport, forfeited his amateur status? Again, the Reformation owed much to ex-priests, and to ex-religious. But what virtue is there in that 'ex-'? Not to argue about the indelibility of Holy Orders once received, did a Bucer, a Pellicanus, a Lambert, Luther himself, rub off an ingrained professionalism which must have been as evident as that of a Guards officer or naval captain when he retires from active life? One suspects that those truculent English Reformers, Robert Barnes and John Hooper, were recognizable parson types for all that they went abroad in merchant dress. Andrew Karlstadt might renounce his D.D. and style himself 'a new kind of layman' (*ain neuwer laie*) but his argument about 'This is my body' (1524) is typical of a medieval theologian[1] and obviously different from the man-in-the-street, common-sense, use of the same argument by the layman, John Lascelles,[2] gentleman of the court of Henry VIII. That Nicholas Storch, weaver of Zwickau, and the famous peasant preacher, the Bauer von Wördth, could be widely suspect of being runaway clergy, points to confusion at this point.

I · The Layman as 'Leading Layman'

Three classes of eminent laymen may be mentioned: the lawyers, the merchants, the scholars. Not only did individual lawyers play a distinguished part in sixteenth-century history, Christopher Scheuerl in Nuremberg, Conrad Peutinger in Augsburg, Sir Thomas More in England, but this literate, professional class might on occasion—as in the England of Elizabeth I—achieve pivotal influence. Then there were the merchants, those rich men furnished with ability whose furniture and paintings were the wonder of the Swiss and German cities. Great families like the Fuggers and the Welsers—or like the London merchant, Humphrey Monmouth, who thought it greater piety to subsidize the exiled Tyndale than to pay for lights or obits, and who could attend a secret 'night schole' for Bible study. Such were the burghers who thronged in their hundreds the biblical expositions of Oecolampadius, Zwingli, Vadianus.

But the line between laity and clergy is most blurred among the humanists. Many of them seem to have taken orders simply for the money and lodgment. Surely the great Erasmus is the least clerical of all sixteenth-century clerics? It is not easy to discover whether Jacob Sturm in Strasburg, or Sir John Cheke in England were in orders, and it is almost irrelevant that they were. A bishop, John Fisher, writes to another cleric, Cuthbert Tunstall, but his discussion of MSS and of the importance of the Greek Fathers uses the same language and similar enthusiasm as a letter on the same theme from the layman Conrad Peutinger to his fellow-lawyer, the great Reuchlin.

II · The Layman as a Man

There is no such thing as 'laity' apart from real men and women, and it is worth while, before going on to talk of ideas, to remember some of these laymen.

Pre-eminent among the laymen of Berne (least clerical of all Swiss centres of reform) was the great artist, Nicholas Manuel (1484–1531),[3] who began by using his art, and his poetic and dramatic gifts, in the cause of reform: this part of his career reminds us of other artists— Albrecht Dürer, Lukas Cranach, Matthias Grünewald, the 'godless painters of Nuremberg'[4]—whose devotion to Protestantism, running counter as it did to the vested interests of their profession, points a question which the Marxist sociologists avoid. But Manuel became a statesman, and from 1524 onwards was more and more prominent in civic affairs, after 1528 the great spokesman of the pacific policy of Berne with the other Swiss cities. How different would the story of St Gall have been but for the figure of its greatest son, Joachim Vadianus[5] (1485–1551): poet, geographer, historian. Then, Town Physician—a reminder of those other eminent men of medicine: Otto Brunfels of Berne, Gereon Sailer of Augsburg, Henry VIII's physician Dr Butts, the heretic Michael Servetus. But Vadianus was also a lay theologian, perhaps the first to lecture with maps on the missionary journeys of St Paul. Finally, the honoured Burgomaster became a statesman, presiding over the great Disputation at Berne in 1528, and was hailed by Zwingli as the most eminent Christian layman in Switzerland. Here Vadianus is a type of other servants of cities and of kings: Councillors like Willibald Pirckheimer, Recorders like Peutinger and Lazarus Spengler of Nuremberg[6] and Stephan Roth of Zwickau: Mayors like Ulrich Rehlinger of Augsburg, or Jacob Sturm of Strasburg: kings' servants like Thomas Cromwell or Secretary Cecil in England or Chancellor Brück in Saxony.

Hans Sachs (1494–1576),[7] shoemaker and Master-singer of Nuremberg, points to another social setting. He links us with other artisan and craftsmen propagandists—with Clement Ziegler,[8] the market gardener of Strasburg, the bookseller Hans Huth, Pilgram Marbeck the engineer. By 1522 Sachs had collected some forty of Luther's writings, and was deeply versed in Scripture. From the publication of his 'Wittenberg

Nightingale' (1523) onwards, his poetic genius served the Lutheran Reformation in poems, polemic and an earnest moralism—while his hymns and his psalms remind us of the important role played in the Reformation by religious song.

By choosing a loyal Catholic, Sir Thomas More (1478–1536),[9] for our fourth type, we are reminded of the importance in this period not only of the Protestant, but of the Catholic laity. As a theologian and spiritual writer he reminds us of the Spaniard Juan de Valdés,[10] who caused a Cardinal to rub his eyes at the speed with which a courtier *'gentilhomo di spada e cappa'* could become an influential theologian. The Ursulines began in Italy as a lay movement, and both in Italy and Spain there were movements among devout gentlewomen.[11] We might recall, also, that the foundation of the future Jesuit Order was laid while Ignatius of Loyola was still a layman. But Sir Thomas More, as Lord Chancellor of England, may stand for Protestant temporal dignitaries too, for Hutten and Von Sickingen in Germany, for De l'Hôpital and Coligny in France, for Balneves and Maitland in Scotland, and at the opposite theological pole, for the gentleman Anabaptist, Eitelhans von Langenmantel, and the Silesian nobleman, Caspar Schwenckfeld.

III · The Laity and 'One Holy Christian People'— 'The Priesthood of All Believers'

Main elements of Luther's doctrine of the Church are to be found in his lectures on the Psalms (1513) and ante-date the struggle which began in 1517. None the less his thought matured and developed out of the fiery struggle with papalism and clericalism not simply in terms of medieval anti-clericalism, but as he explored the Holy Scriptures. In the doctrine of Justification in Romans and Galatians he found the clue to the unity and solidarity of all Christians, *Coram Deo*. 'There is neither priest nor layman, canon or vicar, rich or poor, Benedictine, Carthusian, Friar Minor, or Augustinian, for it is not a question of this or that status, degree, order', is his gloss on Gal. 3.28.[12] By baptism and through faith Christians are incorporated into the death and resurrection of Christ, and so into the one fundamental Christian estate. In the period of 1517–20 some of his finest writings expound this theme (the sermons on Baptism, on Brotherhoods, on the Lord's Supper, 'the Fourteen of Consolation').[13] In a letter to Spalatin in December 1519 he enunciated a view of a universal Christian priesthood which he published in the three great manifestoes of 1520.[14]

The fact that in later Protestantism this doctrine was perverted in an atomistic and naïvely anti-clerical sense should not blind us to its importance for Luther, and for other Reformers. Luther found his doctrine in such Scriptural passages as I Peter 2.5, 9; Rev. 1.6; 5.10; 20.6; Gal. 3.28; John 6.45. His references to it are more frequent than is sometimes suggested, and in later life such utterances as the famous Sermon at Torgau (1544)[15] show that it remained for him an important truth. Brunotte, in his careful summary of the evidence, compresses Luther's doctrine in four points:

1. Before God all Christians have the same standing, a priesthood in which we enter by baptism and through faith.
2. As a comrade and brother of Christ, each Christian is a priest and needs no mediator save Christ. He has access to the Word.
3. Each Christian is a priest and has an office of sacrifice, not the Mass, but the dedication of himself to the praise and obedience of God, and to bearing the Cross.
4. Each Christian has a duty to hand on the gospel which he himself has received.[16]

Those who turn to what John Calvin has to say about the same Scriptural passages in his great *Christian Institution* will find the same doctrine similarly expressed.[17]

The very interesting patristic handbook of the Reformers, the *Unio Dissidentium* (1527),[18] had great vogue in the Rhineland, in France and in England. In it there is a section entitled 'That All Christians are priests, kings and prophets—but not all are ministers of the Church', and this is supported by texts, mainly of the Greek Fathers, Origen, Cyril, Chrysostom, Eusebius. There are many and widespread echoes of this doctrine. In the Fraubrunner disputation in Switzerland (1522) the Catholic Dean flung it as a taunt—'Yes, you Greek-learning Grammarians, you are a fine royal priesthood!'[19]

In the English vestment controversy Nicholas Ridley neatly turned an argument of John Hooper:

> I do . . . count it no more an inconvenience, that some be called men of the clergy and some men of the laity, than in the University, that some be called 'scholars' and some 'men of the town' . . . but St Peter calleth all men priests. What then, pray you . . . will you gather that all men must have . . . one apparel?[20]

But it is John Knox who senses the revolutionary implications of the doctrine, in his great letter to the Commonalty of Scotland (1558):

I would ye should esteem the reformation and care of religion no less to appertain to you, because ye are no kings, rulers, judges, nobles nor in authority. Beloved brethren ye are God's creatures . . . and this is the point wherein I say, all man is equal.[21]

IV · The Laity and Civil Authority ('Obrigkeit')

It is Luther who first expounds the calling of the civil government. Karl Holl in a classic essay[22] analysed the grounds of Luther's *Appeal to the Christian Nobility of the German Nation* (1520). It was made in an emergency situation, in which the spiritual authorities had refused self-amendment. Luther then appeals to the rulers of Germany on the ground of the common priesthood of all Christians, and he asks them to intervene because theirs is the God-given office of maintaining peace and order. In the Swiss and German cities, where the 'godly magistrate' was the many-headed counterpart of the 'godly prince', there was also an empirical, emergency background. The magistracy, the machinery of civic and guild government, was the only means of achieving swift reform, in face of the stubborn vested interest of the bishops and cathedral chapters and religious orders.

It was natural that the magistrate or prince should enter the spiritual vacuum (*Ritter*) left by the expulsion of the spiritual arm from whole areas of jurisdiction (marriage law, public morals, church property). In England the Crown claimed to be Supreme Head or Governor of the Church, not as claiming *potestas ordinis*[23] but that *potestas jurisdictionis* which had belonged to the Pope (and so the layman Thomas Cromwell presided over the clerical assemblies and carried through the Dissolution of the Monasteries). There was of course a 'no-man's-land'; here was the seed of future tension, and by plugging into ancient sources of political power the Reformers were storing up trouble. We can find a hint of this in Luther's comments on the 'Instructions for the Visitation of Saxony' (1527–8).[24] The way was opening by which the temporal ruler might become first '*praecipuum membrum ecclesiae*' and then '*summus episcopus*' in Lutheran lands.

'Let every soul be subject to the higher powers.' Rom. 13.1 had long been the classical text for Christian obedience. It remained so for the Reformers. Luther begins his important tract *Von Weltlicher Obrigkeit* (1523)[25] with it, though it is in polarity with Acts 5.29, 'We must obey God rather than men', as he made clear when Duke George of Saxony tried to prohibit the new German Bible. The same orientation will be found in the massive expositions of the office of lay, civil government in the *Common Places* of Wolfgang Musculus[26] and Peter Martyr,[27] and in the *Christian Institution* of John Calvin (which reaches its majestic close with a reference to Acts 5.29).[28] Even Thomas Müntzer could not ignore Romans 13, though he turned it upside down in his fiery *Fürstenpredigt* (1524),[29] calling on the Saxon rulers to use their sword for the extirpation of the ungodly.

In the Swiss and German cities there were important discussions about the relation of the *jus reformandi* and the magistrates (notably in Strasburg and in Augsburg). But it is Ulrich Zwingli who conceded most to the lay power. His combination of civic patriotism and religious zeal led him to think of Zurich as a prophetic community, and to the view that without the Christian magistrate the commonwealth is mutilated and incomplete. So in Zürich the city councils regulated preaching, public morals, church attendance and, in the name of the whole church, excommunication.[30]

There were therefore affinities between the Zürich of Zwingli and of Bullinger and the England of Elizabeth I.[31] But though her Reformers might learn gratefully from abroad, Elizabeth was in fact consolidating the practice of her Tudor predecessors (including Mary) when she directed ecclesiastical policy, and laid new responsibilities on the lay churchwardens and justices of the peace. The Elizabethan House of Commons, especially in her last years, with its bumbling and truculent Puritanism, its eagerness to discuss and vote upon theological and liturgical matters, is one of the most startling examples of lay intervention in affairs of religion.[32]

That Zwingli conceded so much to the magistracy was noted with uneasiness by some of his friends, among them his devoted ally, Oecolampadius. In a great oration *On the Power of Excommunication* (1529)[33] he distinguished between the pastoral discipline of the Church, which is remedial, and that of the magistracy, which is punitive. But he was not clerically minded, and he sought to remedy affairs by allowing the Church to appoint 'lay overseers'. Though his blue-print was not fully worked out, Bucer followed him by introducing in Strasburg the lay *Kirchenpfleger*.[34] But it was John Calvin in Geneva who made this a mighty instrument of Christian discipline. On the one hand, he insisted that the Church must keep discipline in its own hands, hence his running fight with the Syndics in the matter of excommunication. On the other, the lay elder should become a safeguard against clericalism by keeping watch on the ministers.[35] Luther develops profoundly

in this and other writings the duties of lay Christians in the world, as
in his later writings he speaks of the three hierarchies of domestic,
ecclesiastical, political life. Our calling is the providential place where
we love God and our neighbour and play our part in the eschatologically
bounded war against Satan.[36] These callings are the means whereby
God exercises his care over all his children and gives them his good gifts:

> For what is all our work in the field, in the garden, in the home, whether
> we make war, or rule in government, towards God but child's play,
> through which God gives his gifts to field and house and the rest. They
> are the masks (*larvae*) through which he will remain hidden and yet do all
> things. . . .[37]

William Tyndale echoed this teaching in a striking passage from his
Lutheran *Wicked Mammon* (1527):

> Thou that ministerest in the kitchen, and art but a kitchen page . . .
> knowest that God hath put thee in that office . . . if thou compare deed
> and deed, there is a difference betwixt washing of dishes and preaching of
> the Word of God: but as touching to please God, none at all . . . let every-
> man, whether brewer, tailor, victualler, merchant or husbandman refer his
> craft and occupation unto the commonwealth and serve his brethren as he
> would do Christ himself.[38]

Bucer also stressed what has been called 'the gospel of hard work'
and in the *Unio Dissidentium* there is a section '*De Labore Manuum*'.
This doctrine of calling became an important element in Calvinism,
and the English Calvinist and Puritan William Perkins summarized a
century of Protestant teaching in his *Treatise of the Vocations*.[39]

V · *The Laity and the Congregation ('Gemeinde')*

For Martin Luther there is an important relation between the Word
and the People of God, for the gospel creates the Church as it is given
by God through preaching and the sacraments. Symbols of the restored
unity of all Christians are the restoration of communion to the laity
under both kinds, and the turning of the Mass into a communion of the
faithful. In 1523 Luther affirmed the right of a Christian congregation,
in defined circumstances, to depose a preacher and to call another who
would preach the gospel (at Orlamünde, Karlstadt went further in the
direction of what might be called 'congregationalism').[40] Luther's
liturgical reforms, and the promulgation in 1526 of an order for a German Mass, had, as he says in the Preface, the needs of the simple layman

in mind. In this document[41] he hints at the possibility of more private assemblies, where 'those who mean to be real Christians' might meet in houses for prayer, worship, sacraments, discipline, a paragraph whose import has been much debated but which may foreshadow Bucer's *Gemeinschaften* in Strasburg. But Luther was deeply concerned with the Christian people as a believing worshipping community and some of his most splendid creative works, the Bible, the catechisms, his liturgy and hymns, are directed towards the needs of the laity.

Here the Bible was of paramount importance. Erasmus was a great pioneer, for though he wrote for the educated and in Latin his new version of Scripture and his bold advocacy of a vernacular Bible were deeply influential:

> I wish that the ploughman may sing parts of them at his plough, that the weaver may warble them at his shuttle, that the traveller may with their narratives beguile the weariness of the way.[42]

To an age not very familiar with them, his *Paraphrases* brought home the gospel stories with new freshness, and in the English translation, chained in churches in 1548, men came face to face with the 'philosophy of Christ', that most unclerical of all leaders of religion. The influence was swift and deep. Urbanus Rhegius could write to Erasmus in 1522:

> Recently I heard a matron who was able to discuss the relation between Law and Gospel in the Epistle to the Romans more learnedly than many of our great doctors . . . thus hast thou recalled the whole world to the philosophy of Christ.[43]

Luther's German Bible, the Swiss Zürich Bible and the English Bibles bred a new biblical theology among lay people. In 1537 Bishop Edward Foxe told the English convocation:

> The lay people do now know the holy scripture better than many of us, and the Germans have made the text of the Bible so plain and easy with the Hebrew and the Greek that now many things be better understood without any glosses at all than by all the commentaries of the doctors.[44]

It worked at all levels in a society. Queen Anne Boleyn and her ladies read Tyndale's New Testament secretly at court. When in 1543 the English Bible became legal in Scotland, John Knox told ironically how

> it might have been seen lying upon almost every gentleman's table: they would chop their familiars on the cheek with it, and say, 'This hath lain under my bed foot these ten years . . . how often have I been in danger for this book, and stolen from my wife at midnight to read upon it.'[45]

Ironically enough, in this very year the Bible in England was forbidden for common people, and Robert Williams, a Gloucestershire shepherd, wrote bitterly in the fly-leaf of a learned work:

> This book I bought when the New Testament was abrogated that shepherds might not read it. Pray God amend that blindness.[46]

There were those, like the 'fresh young tailor' Porter, who read aloud to his unlettered companions from the Great Bible chained in St Paul's in London. In houses, barns, mills, forests, the radical sectaries read, learned by heart, passed on copies of the Scriptures in which their leaders, like the English Lollard Thomas Man, or the German Anabaptist Hans Huth, were saturated. A Catholic historian has these striking words about the humble tradesmen and artisan martyrs of the reign of Mary:

> Through their habitual frequentation of the Bible, these people have for themselves become transformed into scriptural figures, and all the drama of their lives has itself become transformed into a scriptural event, itself a continuation of the sacred story.[47]

As with the Bible, so with the new forms of worship. The illiterate, or those familiar only with some local dialect, might sneer, as did the men of Devon and Cornwall, that the new liturgy was 'but a Christmas Game'. But it was a creative achievement when Thomas Müntzer and Archbishop Cranmer turned the choir offices of Mattins and Vespers into congregational services in the vernacular. The new Lutheran liturgies and those of the reformed Churches, simplified, biblically orientated, in a tongue understood by the people, must have had for many the effect of putting on a pair of spectacles, as what had been remote, blurred, half-understood, now came close to them in sharp, intelligible focus.

It was no doubt eccentricity when Thomas Müntzer's[48] in the main conservative, choral rite enjoined that the words of the consecration should be pronounced by all the congregation, but the other Protestant liturgies were concerned to emphasize the wholeness of the worshipping congregation, the unity of minister and people. Here the psalms and hymns were of great importance. It has been said of Martin Bucer that for him the Church is built round the hymn,[49] and he produced in Strasburg in 1542 one of the loveliest of Reformation hymn books. The noble hymns and fine psalm translations of Luther, Sachs, Müntzer and others could not be confined within church walls, but were noised abroad, as men sang in their thousands round Paul's Cross in London, or in the streets of Paris and Geneva, and sometimes joyous, sometimes fierce, always confident, they penetrated the camp and battlefield, some like '*Eyn' feste Burg*' to count as much as a dozen cannon or a troop of horse.

That the laity, and especially the young, should be instructed[50] was an important item on the Protestant agenda. If we have not yet mentioned the schoolmaster it is because this was a largely clerical profession; but teachers like Jean Sturm, Thomas Platter, Oswald Myconius, Hans Denck, Sebastian Castellio meet us at every turn in the story. Luther and Melanchthon, Calvin and Beza, John Knox and Alexander Melville have their important place in the history of education. The catechisms of the Reformation period, of which Luther's lovely Children's Catechism was a pioneer, remind us of the instruction of the young in church and at home. Family religion where, in Robert Burns's phrase, 'the priestlike father read the sacred page' to his household, was of great importance. In 1524 Karlstadt had stressed this responsibility of the Christian parent:

> The father (*Hausvater*) has greater authority to order the worship of God in his house than any pope or bishop, yea, than the whole congregation.[51]

John Knox drew an important corollary from the Priesthood of Believers:

> Ye be in your own houses bishops and kings . . . let there be worship of God morning and evening.[52]

The Edwardian Reformers and the Elizabethan authorities in England issued forms for family morning and evening prayer. The order of the day of Martin Bucer's household in Cambridge has fascinatingly survived, and is the counterpart of innumerable godly Protestant and Puritan homes. New Primers, prayer books, Bibles, a new kind of simple, practical devotional literature arose to take the place of that rich devotional literature of the later Middle Ages.

VI · The Layman as Woman

We might suppose that the Reformation lessened the importance of women in the Church, for there were no more nuns or anchoresses. And it is true that John Knox's *Blast of the Trumpet* was no manifesto of feminism, though it would never have been blown had the author not discerned a militant femininity upon the walls of Jericho. For indeed the sixteenth century continued the tradition of Joan of Arc and the Lady Margaret Tudor, as we realize by a glance at such *grandes dames* as Anne Askew, the Lady Jane Grey, the Duchess of Suffolk in England, Marguerite of Navarre in France, Francesca Hernandez[53] in Spain, St Angela Merici in Italy, Marguerite Blaurer in Germany, and the Anabaptist gentlewoman, Helena von Freyburg.[54] In Strasburg, women sectaries dreamed dreams and saw visions in the authentic tradition of St Hildegard of Bingen and Elizabeth of Schönau. Some of them preached like that wife of the architect of Our Lady's Church in Zwickau of whom the authorities wrote despairingly 'the woman simply cannot be silent', or Argula von Grumbach[55] who movingly wrote that she had tried to obey the Pauline injunction, but because no man would preach the Gospel she was constrained to do so.

One new figure must be mentioned, the parson's wife. If it is true that half the names in the English *Dictionary of National Biography* are those of sons of the manse and vicarage, then their founding mothers must share the honours. The sharp wisdom of Katherine Luther, the organizing philanthropy of Mrs Matthew Zell, the cheerful common sense of the second Mrs Bucer began a great succession which has deeply enriched the world.

VII · The Layman as Martyr

Although many clergy suffered, an overall picture of the persecution of Protestants in the sixteenth century, including the Anabaptists, shows that the great majority of martyrs were laymen and women, many of them of humble station. This lay witness unto death is important— for though there were those, and not a few, who found that the new godliness was profitable, there were others who were obedient under torture and at the stake to a faith which had always stressed that the true Church is 'under the Cross'. Their sturdiness bred a different temper from late medieval heresy with its abjurations and evasions.

In the sixteenth century hitherto inarticulate levels of society became vocal, found new means of competence and autonomy.[56] The new forms of Christian instruction, not least the availability of the vernacular Bibles, became themselves a vehicle of lay education. Some of the most interesting evidence comes from the radicals and Anabaptists among the artisans and peasantry. In this field a great deal of work remains to be done, and if they can refrain from being doctrinaire, the church historians and sociologists have much to tell one another.

If the question be asked, 'What did this mean to the ordinary layman?'—there can be no simple answer. For as we have indicated, there is no average lay type: there is a layman who is a peasant, a craftsman, a merchant, an artist, a statesman, a prince—each looking at his own cross-section of his own world in a culture whose structure was complex.

A more pertinent and even more difficult question is why the Reformation did not maintain this new emphasis on Christian solidarity and on the initiative of the laity, why in this, as in other fields, it seems to have gone off half-cock. When we ask why, having originally expressed the same scriptural principles, one great Church becomes a *Pastorenkirche* and another breeds a Christian radicalism, the answer must be sought in history itself rather than in theology, and with regard not to one doctrine, but to the wholeness of the theological pattern and that mysterious imponderable which we discern but can with difficulty analyse, the 'ethos' of a great communion. We need to remember that the 'laity' were not a great, dominant theme of debate—the real dog-fight was about the ministry, and it was carried on by clerics in the main. It is surprising how seldom the words 'lay', 'laic', 'laity' even appear in the great indices to the theological compendia of which Calvin's *Christian Institution* is supreme. It would be an over-simplification to say that the Protestant Reformation consists of a clerical reformation superimposed on an anti-clerical revolution, the first still mainly controlled by clergy,[57] of the new kind, the second led by laymen.

It would need immense learning, and vaster charity, to strike a balance and estimate the gains and losses, comparing the Protestant layman with the Catholic, of the Middle Ages and of the Counter-reformation. The layman lost, for the most part, his pictures and his windows; his beads and Primers; his processions, candles, pilgrimages, his feasts and fasts. But he gained his Bible, his catechism, his Prayer Book, his hymns; he had worship in which he could share with intelligent awareness (though many must have listened passively as formerly they had looked passively).

In varying degrees he found open new responsibilities in the life of the Church, and could feel that the amendment of Christendom was his own responsibility where something real depended on his vote and voice, his initiative. And in whatever state of society it pleased God to call him, there he would work out his salvation. There were those who looked hard at these things, and turned with distaste and fresh loyalty to the old religion, which was also changing. But multitudes there were who found in the new frame of piety, worship and devotion a plain man's pathway to heaven, light and truth to bring them nearer to God's holy hill.

NOTES

1. *Was gesagt ist: 'sich gelassen', Andres Bodenstein von Carolstat, ain neuwer laie* (1523). See also the eucharistic dialogue 'Von dem . . . Missbrauch des Sakraments' in which a layman, Petrus, participates, and especially 'at last the laymen have come into their Christian liberty' (*Schriften* [ed. Hertzsch] II, p. 13).

2. A. G. Dickens, *Lollards and Protestants in the Diocese of York. 1509–58* (Oxford, 1959), p. 32.

3. For literature on Manuel see K. Guggisberg, *Bernische Kirchengeschichte* (Bern, 1958).

4. Th. Kolde, *Der 'gottlose Maler' von Nürnberg* (1902); W. Peuckert, *Sebastian Franck* (1943), p. 79.

5. W. Näf, *Vadian* (St Gall, 2 vols 1944, 1957).

6. Von Schubert, *L. Spengler und die Reformation in Nürnberg* (1938).

7. T. G. Bishop, 'Hans Sachs and the Reformation' (Leeds Univ. Diss.).

8. R. Peter, 'Le Maraîcher Clement Ziegler', *Rev. d'hist. et de phil. rel.* (1954), pp. 255–82; Rott, *Quellen zur Ges. der Täufer* VII, Elsass I (1960), pp. 8 ff.

9. R. W. Chambers, *Sir Thomas More* (London, 1935); H. A. Mason, *Humanism and Poetry in the Early Tudor Period* (London, 1959).

10. For Valdès, A. M. Mergal in the second part of Library of Christian Classics, vol. XXV (1957).

11. *The New Cambridge Modern History*, vol. II, ch. 9 (H. O. Evennett), pp. 289 ff.

12. Luther (*Weimarer Ausgabe*) 57, p. 28.15 ff.

13. *Works of Martin Luther* (Phil. ed.) I, pp. 49 ff., 103 ff.; II, pp. 9 ff.

14. Luther, *W.A.* (Briefe) I, p. 595.26 ff.; *W.A.* 6, pp. 407 ff., 649 ff.; *W.A.* 7, pp. 27 ff.

15. *Luther's Works* (American ed. 1960), vol. 51, pp. 331 ff.

16. W. Brunotte, *Das geistliche Amt bei Luther* (Berlin, 1959), pp. 133 ff.

17. *The Institution of the Christian Religion*, Bk 3.3.42; Bk 2.15.6; Bk 4.18.17.

18. *Unio dissidentium libellus . . . per Hermannum Bodium* (1527—and many later editions). Author unknown. The attribution by Herminjard and Droz to Martin Bucer is improbable. See E. Droz in *Aspects de la propagande religieuse* (ed. Meylan, Geneva, 1957), p. 39; also W. G. Moore, *La Réforme allemande et la littérature française* (Strasburg, 1930), pp. 157 ff.; J. Foxe, *Acts and Monuments* (ed. Pratt) IV, pp. 667, 685, 764, etc.

19. Guggisberg, *Bern. Kirchenges.*, p. 68.

20. J. Bradford, *Works* (Parker Soc. ed.) II, p. 386.

21. J. Knox, *Works* (ed. Laing) IV, p. 526; for similar sentiments in W. Tyndale see Parker Soc. ed. I, p. 258 and III, p. 158.

22. K. Holl, *Gesammelte Aufsätze I: Luther* (Tübingen, 1921), pp. 332 ff.

23. But see the interesting question circulated among the English bishops in 1540. 'Whether if it fortuned a Christian Prince learned, to conquer certain dominions of infidels, having nothing but temporal learned men with him, it be defended by God's law that he

and they should preach and teach the Word of God there or no? And also constitute and make priests or no?' All were agreed that they might preach in such circumstances, but there was division whether they might ordain and administer sacraments.

24. K. Holl, *ibid.*, pp. 366 ff. Holl's interpretation is open to criticism here.

25. *W.M.L.* 3, pp. 231 ff.; *W.A.* 11, pp. 229 ff.

26. W. Musculus, *Commonplaces* (ET 1561), fol. 546 ff.

27. Peter Martyr, *Commonplaces* (ET 1583) IV, pp. 226 ff.

28. *Institution of Christian Religion*, Bk 4.20.

29. *Thomas Müntzer's politische Schriften*, ed. Hinrichs (Halle, 1950). There is an English translation in G. H. Williams, *Spiritual and Anabaptist Writers* (Library of Christian Classics, vol. XXV, 1957), pp. 47 ff.

30. O. Farner, *Huldrych Zwingli*, vol. 4 (1960); R. Ley, *Kirchenzucht bei Zwingli* (Zurich, 1948).

31. H. Kressner, *Schweizer Ursprünge des anglikanischen Staatskirchentums* (Gütersloh, 1953): exaggerated but interesting.

32. On this the works of Sir J. E. Neale, especially *Elizabeth and her Parliaments, 1584–1603* (London, 1957).

33. E. Staehelin, *Das theologische Lebenswerk Oecolampadius* (1939), pp. 511 ff.; also *Akten und Briefe O.'s* vol. 2 (1934). On this problem in Lambert of Avignon, see G. Müller, *Lambert von Avignon* (Marburg, 1956), ch. 2.

34. A. Lang, *Puritanismus und Pietismus* (Neukirchen, 1941), pp. 22 ff. H. Strohl, *Pensée de la Réforme* (Paris, 1951).

35. J. Knox, *Works* II, pp. 233 ff.

36. G. Wingren, *The Christian's Calling* (ET: Edinburgh, 1958).

37. *W.A.* 31.1, p. 436.7.

38. W. Tyndale, *Doctrinal Treatises* (Parker Soc. ed.), pp. 101–3.

39. L. B. Wright, *Middle Class Culture in Elizabethan England* (Cornell Univ. Press, 1958), ch. 6.

40. *W.A.* 11, pp. 406 ff.; *W.M.L.* 4, pp. 73 ff.

41. *W.A.* 19, pp. 144 ff.; *W.M.L.* 6, pp. 172 ff.

42. Erasmus, *Werke* (ed. Holborn) I, pp. 142, 202 ff.

43. *Erasmi Epistolae* (ed. P. S. Allen), vol. 5, p. 3.

44. J. Foxe, *Acts and Monuments* (ed. Pratt) V, p. 382.

45. E. Whiteley, *Plain Mr Knox* (London, 1960), p. 21.

46. J. F. Mozley, *Coverdale and his Bibles* (London, 1953), pp. 265, 284.

47. P. Hughes, *The Reformation in England* II (London, 1953), p. 275.

48. Müntzer's liturgical writings will be found in the collections of Sehling and Richter. See also J. O. Mehl, *Thomas Müntzer's liturgische Schriften* (Jena, 1940).

49. Van der Poll, *Martin Bucer's Liturgical Ideas* (Assen, 1954), pp. 13 ff.

50. Cf. Grindal, 'Injunctions for the Laity' (*Remains*, Parker Soc. ed., pp. 132 ff.).

51. 'Von dem Sabbat' (1524): *Schriften* I, p. 42.

52. Whiteley, p. 151.

53. M. Bataillon, *Erasme en Espagne* (Paris, 1937), pp. 190 ff.

54. Roth, *Reformationsgeschichte Augsburgs*, vol. 2 (1904), pp. 410 ff.

55. 'Wie ain Christliche Fraw des Adels in Bayern durch iren in Götlicher Schrift wolgegrundten Sentbrieffe . . .' (1523). I owe this reference to Dr T. Borgen.

56. P. Peachey, *Soziale Herkunft der Wiedertäufer* (1954); N. Birnbaum, 'Social Structure and the Reformation' (Harvard Diss. 1957); 'The Zwinglian Reformation in Zürich', *Past*

and Present, April 1959; E. Trocmé, 'Une révolution mal conduite', *Rev. d'hist. et de phil. rel.*, Nr. 2 (1959), pp. 160 ff.

57. The Protestant clergy were aware of the danger of a new lay tyranny. The magistrates were also sensitive to the danger of a new Protestant clericalism. This emerges sharply in the attempt in Basel, 1538, of the University to bring the clergy under their jurisdiction; cf. the contemptuous reference of the Rector to the Reformers Myconius and Grynaeus—'Ecclesiam —hoc est sacrificulos[!] aliquot—magistratui non subijiciendos strenue contendunt' (*Die Amerbachkorrespondenz*, vol. 5 [Basel, 1959], p. 172.15).

6

Martin Schmidt

THE CONTINENT OF EUROPE
1648–1800

Introduction

THE age of orthodoxy, which followed on the first living period of the Reformation, wears a double aspect.

On the one hand, it maintained the new positions which Luther and Calvin and their colleagues had won for cleric and layman, for office-bearer and for voluntary worker alike. The task of bringing about a new established order demanded the extensive co-operation of the lay orders with the clergy. Indeed, without their co-operation in thought and deed, the organization of the Protestant movement in regular and institutional form could never have been brought about.

On the other hand, when we consider the extent and variety of the openings afforded by the Reformation to the laity in the service of the Church, this second period is marked by retreat and not by advance. Over the early days of the Reformation breathes the spring freshness of the new and original discovery of the Word of God. Over the second period blows the harsh autumn wind, after the harvest has been toilfully gathered in the midst of peril and stormy weather.

It could hardly have been otherwise. The demands of the time were theological. On the one hand, and permanently, there was the need for the defence of the Protestant position against the skill and vigour of the Counter-reformation. Energies were exhausted in the controversies between Lutheran and Reformed as to the right interpretation of the Evangelical faith. It has to be noted as curious that hardly a glance was cast beyond the English Channel to that world of Anglicanism, where similar problems were finding completely different solutions. England and the Continent lived in almost complete isolation from one another, until the eighteenth century, the 'century of the English', changed the situation.

The natural consequence of all this was that the scales came to be heavily weighted on the side of the theologians. It is perhaps to this period that we should look for a change in the idea of the distinction between minister and layman in the Church. This now rests not on ordination but on education; the pastor is the qualified professional, the man of extensive learning, in contrast to the lay folk who are necessarily amateurs, possessed of only limited and random scraps of knowledge.

So the lay folk retired in this period into the background. Yet this is far from meaning that the layman had no part at all to play in the new world of the Reformation and its sequel.

First and foremost we encounter the godly princes, whom Melanchthon had described as the outstanding members (*membra praecipua*) of the flock. In the Middle Ages one of the responsibilities of the ruler was *cura religionis*, care for the spiritual welfare of his people; this was now developed to a degree never seen or imagined before.

I · The Lutheran World

The earlier period could show a number of outstanding rulers of the new type. We may think of Maurice of Saxony (1521–53) and Ottheinrich of the Palatinate (1502–59). The seventeenth century was not lacking in men of similar calibre, both on the local and on the larger scene, though in the latter case Christian ideals tended to be mingled with factors of a very different kind.

Of the Christian ruler on the imperial scale by far the most brilliant specimen in this period was Gustavus Adolphus, King of Sweden (1594–1632) and champion of German Protestantism in the Thirty Years War. The young King was the son of a German mother and the husband of a German wife, and was surrounded at his court by German nobles. He was profoundly convinced of the truth of the Christian faith in its Evangelical Lutheran form. It was therefore natural that he should feel himself called to stand up in defence of the threatened Protestant cause; equally natural that it seemed to him no disadvantage that fulfilment of this obligation coincided with the setting up of a great empire on the Baltic Sea, and conferred on his country and his house a position of unequalled authority in world politics. The shrewd popular understanding of a countryman, paternal authority, delight in the exercise of responsibility, a wide understanding of political realities, and military prowess were in him combined, without any sense of contradiction, with stalwart Lutheran faith. His prayers in time of war show how deeply and how unselfconsciously he regarded himself as the saviour of the Church of God. After his landing in Pomerania, his prayer for a favourable wind for the following troops runs as follows:

> that I may carry on thy holy work; for thou knowest that this expedition and my intent have been planned and taken in hand not for my honour, but only for thine, and that comfort and help may be brought to thy poor oppressed Church.

On his general and successor, Count Bernhard of Weimar (1604–39), history must pass the same slightly ambiguous verdict. He was the leader of that militant minority among the princes which was determined to set limits to that autocracy which the Roman Catholic Hapsburgs were attempting to establish at the expense of the smaller princedoms. This autocracy was repugnant to his sense of history and to his loyalty to tradition as well as to his Evangelical conviction. Bernhard was primarily a fighting man; yet he must not be judged as a mere *condottiere*, willing to sell his sword to any master. In him we see the typical activity of the Protestant layman of that time, making use of those political and military tools that were available to his hand.

After the horrors of the war, there was great need of virtuous rulers to serve as the fathers of their people, and to build up something out of the ruins of the time. And the history of the Lutheran world offers a classical example of such a ruler—Ernest the Pious of Saxe-Gotha (1601–75). He was the brother of Bernhard of Weimar, to whom we have just referred. In 1640 he succeeded to the throne of his Thuringian principality, and spent the next thirty-five years trying to make of it a model state.

The crown of his achievements was the reorganization of education and of the life of the Church. Immediately after his accession he set in motion a thorough visitation of Church and school. In the course of this he succeeded in developing what became the most famous educational system of the age, and one which was imitated by many other German states. Luther's basic principle of wide popular education, which had temporarily been set aside in favour of Melanchthon's plans for the higher education of an élite, was brought back to honour. Education was made compulsory between the ages of five and twelve; textbooks were cheap; and it was said that peasants in Thuringia were better educated than nobles and burghers in other parts of Germany. The High School at Gotha and the University of Jena were also objects of the paternal care of Ernest the Pious. Among later students of the High School was August Hermann Francke, the famous pietist of Halle, who found there the inspiration for his life-work.

The counterpart of all this was the renewal of the Church in the form of a vast teaching mission. What Ernest planned was a kind of continuous preparation for Confirmation, of which death alone was to be the end. He expected his peasants to be as well-instructed as parsons; when he discovered that some of them did not really understand the last seven articles of the Augsburg Confession, he had these separately printed, and insisted that the clergy were to give special instruction in them. And learning was to be matched with life. Ernest laid great stress on the observance of the Sabbath; dancing, skittles and cards were sternly forbidden—we find here something of the spirit of Puritanism in England and of Precisianism in Holland. The Duke kept a list of all the clergy and teachers of his territory, and was liable from time to time to appear unannounced in the territory of one and another of them. In the upbringing of his own eighteen children he set an example to all his subjects.

But Ernest was much more than a faithful ruler of his own subjects. He felt a deep sense of responsibility for the whole Protestant cause in the world. Taking up an idea which had been put forward by Nicolaus Hunnius (1585–1643) in his work *Consultatio*—a plan for reconciling and ending the religious and doctrinal controversies among Protestants —the Duke wished to bring into existence a 'college', which should serve as a central point of consultation in all matters of theological controversy. The *rabies theologorum* was too strong for him, and he had no success with his plan; it is of interest that he recognized the central role of theology in the settlement of such religious disputes.

His glance ranged even beyond Germany, and led him to seek to help the oppressed Lutherans of Austria, Silesia, Hungary and Transylvania, where the Counter-reformation was specially strong and vindictive. And he even had ideas of trying to introduce the pure Lutheran faith into Abyssinia. (Job Ludolf had returned from that country in 1652, and published his Ethiopic grammar in 1661.) In him we see something of the same universal spirit that breathes in men of the stamp of John Amos Comenius, August Hermann Francke, and Gottfried Wilhelm von Leibniz.

A ruler of this stamp needs efficient lay colleagues around him.

Among the colleagues whom Ernest trusted one stands out as a notable example of lay piety and deserves separate mention—Veit Ludwig von Seckendorf (1626–92). This distinguished lawyer, who in the end rose to be Chancellor of the state, left behind him two works on politics which outlived their author, the 'State of the German Ruler' (*Deutscher Fürstenstaat*), and the 'Christian State' (*Christenstaat*). But what has principally secured him his niche of fame is his great historical work on Lutheranism, *Commentarius historicus et apologeticus de Lutheranismo*, which appeared in 1692. For the compilation of this outstanding work Seckendorf was able to use the immense collection of books and archives gathered by his master; his learning was so comprehensive that this work is indispensable today, and the student who believes himself to have made an original discovery finds all too often that Seckendorf has been there before him.

These men were the great men. What did life look like to the little men, the simple Protestant laymen? The fortunately preserved diary of Ludwig Kleinhempel, the master-coppersmith of Annaberg in the Erzgebirge (1612–92) gives us a glimpse into this other world, restricted of course to the limited knowledge of the man whose autobiography is thus set out before us. The picture it presents is that of family life entirely subordinated to the will of God. Attendance at church on Sunday is taken for granted, and each Sunday is noted in terms of the traditional gospel for the day. The disasters of the Thirty Years War, with occupation by troops now of one side, now of the other, with demands for the payment of tribute, rapine, battles, accompanied by famine, pestilence and exile, beat in waves upon the life of the individual as of the town. When at last peace is signed, the recorded thanksgiving comes from the very depths of the heart. The inarticulate writer bitterly laments the death of his wife at the birth of their first child, but grief is irradiated by submission to the will of God, and by the hope of the resurrection. As a craftsman it is his pride to produce sterling work, and he mentions with pleasure that his father had turned out bells for church steeples as well as brewing-pans, kettles and saucepans. As a citizen Kleinhempel rose to be overseer of one quarter of the town. Every advance in life, and also every reverse, is accepted as a gift from the hand of God.

When we speak of laymen, it is important not to forget the part that women have played in the life of the Church. For the earlier part of our period we can point to one startling, and not very attractive, example of lay devotion in the ruling class of the land. Sophie, Duchess of Albertine

Saxony (1561–1622), had been brought up in the strictest tenets of Lutheran orthodoxy and made it her life-work to see that these were observed in all their starkness, with no yielding to the compromises of Melanchthon or the errors of Calvin. Her weak husband fell under evil (i.e Calvinistic) influences; but after his early death, the duchy was quickly brought back to the true way. Such rigid harshness is hardly intelligible to us today; it has to be understood against the background of the times, and of those embittered religious controversies in which both sides felt that the salvation of men's souls was at stake.

But this was not the only kind of witness borne by women in that age of orthodoxy. It is possible to point to other women, of the same high station in life, who gave far more appropriate expression to their faith—as the writers of Christian hymns. The original impulse is seen in the simple and artless compositions of lay people. Then the plastic arts and music took hold of these simplicities and glorified them. The great century of Church music, which begins with Heinrich Schütz (1585–1672) and finds its apogee in Johann Sebastian Bach (1685–1750) and Georg Friedrich Handel (1685–1759), is one of the noblest examples of Christian lay service that is recorded anywhere in the history of the Church.

II · The Reformed Tradition

Calvinism, from its very beginnings, strikes a new note in Christian history, and the contribution of its lay people in the service of the Church is different from that which is to be found elsewhere. To start with, here there was no organization of the Church in close alliance with the government of the ruler and under his ultimate control; in the Reformed cities, the Reformer worked everything out in consultation with the city elders, and in almost every case it was the voice of the Reformer that was the deciding factor. This was one marked difference from Lutheranism. But what more than anything else gave its special colour and quality to the Reformed tradition was the closely articulated organization of the congregation as such. Here there was not just one ministry—that of the man ordained to preach the word and to minister the sacraments, a pattern which could not fail to be reminiscent of the priest of the Middle Ages—but at least four: preaching ministers, elders, teachers and deacons. In Lutheran Churches, it was always possible to feel that the minister, the holder of all ecclesiastical authority (*plenitudo potestatis*), stood in the sharpest contrast to the lay people, who had no rights and were there simply to listen to sermons and to receive the sacrament; and that the old medieval distinction between priest and laymen was in fact maintained unimpaired. In the Reformed Churches, it was not the minister but the congregation itself which was felt to be the incorporation of the Church. Lutheranism could be understood as the Christianity of the Middle Ages with some slight modifications; Calvinism presented itself as primitive Christianity, though not in as radical a sense as that of the Anabaptists. In the area of the Reformed tradition, the ruler who is the father of his people and the great shepherd of the Church is almost unknown. We shall encounter here far fewer striking personalities than in the Lutheran Churches. Lay activity is not so much the activity of the individual as the corporate witness of a community—and in times of persecution of a very close-knit community.

Far more than in the lands where the Lutherans enjoyed the protection of their rulers, the Reformed Churches—in France, in Holland, and elsewhere—were exposed to the bitterest enmity of the Counter-reformation and to most savage persecution. It is typical that the most outstanding lay leader of the Huguenots, Gaspard de Coligny, Admiral of France, was also one of the victims of the massacre of St Bartholomew in 1572. This had its dangers. From the time of Coligny onwards, the laity of the Reformed tradition possessed a certain political and militant character, which fitted them well to play a part on the political stage and to undertake responsibility in the affairs of the nation. But there was a darker side to this. There was always the danger of choosing unsuitable weapons, of making false calculations, and of relying on factors that have nothing to do with Christian faith. Yet this was only one side of the picture. The period of the persecutions yields a great many instances of faithfulness and heroic constancy in face of the fiendish cruelties of the Counter-reformation—summed up in the simple and effective formula *Résistez*. And Calvin in Geneva had made for ever the inalienable compact between humanism and the Reformation, between scholarship and faith. In the great century of France, the seventeenth, French Protestantism was to show what resources of intellectual vigour were in it in the heirs of such political philosophers and jurists as Jean Bodin (1530–96), François Hotman (1524–90) and Hubert de Languet (1515–81). It was men such as these who laid the foundation for the political thinking of France in the eighteenth century, and created the link between Calvinism and democracy which has remained part of its heritage until the present day.

We shall find this association between faith and learning running through the whole history of lay witness in the lands of the Reformed Churches; and no figure is more characteristic of them (though perhaps unequalled by others in intellectual power) than Hugo Grotius (1583–1645). Grotius was one of a group of polymaths (his older contemporary Justus Lipsius [1547–1606] was another), who to an astonishing degree made themselves masters of the whole range of the intellectual pursuits of man, and combined with their Christian convictions based on the Bible, insights and convictions drawn from the ancient world, especially from the schools of the Stoics. As Christians they would no doubt have said that it was always the Bible which was the determining influence. In the case of Grotius, the second Erasmus, it is possible to maintain without fear of contradiction that basic Christian conviction was by far the strongest influence in all his thinking.

Grotius was well acquainted with the internal strife over doctrines that racked the Calvinist Churches, and reached its culminating point in the Synod of Dort (1618–19). He was repelled by the rigidity and narrowness of the orthodox point of view, and for this very reason found himself driven to seek a better and more convincing Christian position. This was to find literary expression in his book *On the Truth of the Christian Religion* (*De Veritate religionis Christianae*, 1627). It was to find practical expression in his ceaseless activity in the cause of unity in the faith. In him the humanist scholar and the Christian of Reformed conviction are seen in operation together when he undertakes as one of his principal works a comprehensive exposition of the Christian Scriptures. No longer a Calvinist, Grotius must be reckoned the most distinguished of the Arminians. His work did not pass unnoticed; from an early date it exercised a profound influence on other Reformed laymen of inclinations similar to his.

A clear example of this influence can be seen in the outstanding burgomaster of Basel, Johann Rudolf Wettstein (1594–1666), who was one of the defenders of the independence of the Swiss Confederacy in the negotiations which led to the peace of Westphalia (1648). On the one hand Wettstein worked, in the tradition of the old Reformed orthodoxy, for the close co-operation of Church and State in the ordering of the Christian life. The Constitution of the Church of Basel, which was accepted by the city council in 1660 as a revision of that of 1595, is a notable example of the guaranteeing, by the authority of the state, of Christian standards of conduct in Church, school and family life. In another direction, Wettstein was deeply engaged in the movement for the unity of Christendom; and, as he grew older, became more and more committed to that separation between law and politics on the one hand and Church on the other, which is characteristic of the modern world. He passed on ideas of this kind to his son Johann Rudolf Wettstein (1614–84), who was led by such convictions into conflict with the one-sided orthodoxy of the Church and theological outlook of Basel. In his early years the younger Wettstein had studied his theology, but only half-heartedly; classical philosophy was the real love of his life; and in his public actions he felt himself to be the defender of the cause of the laity.

We saw that in the Lutheran world one of the most notable manifestations of the lay spirit was the expression of the Christian faith in music. On the Calvinistic side there is little of the kind to record. Here the creative expression comes through the art of the painter. It was in the Netherlands that this pictorial representation of the biblical material developed; and in this field Rembrandt (1606–69) stands head and shoulders above all others. Rembrandt had astonishing accuracy of observation, and the gift of profound reflection on his own personal experiences. His work shows accurate acquaintance with the text of Scripture, and a notable gift for seizing on the really important features of the scene that he is planning to depict. He can then translate the whole into living movement that makes its immediate appeal to the eye, and draws the beholder into itself. Any sketch, however brief, of the developments of lay service in this period which did not take seriously the contribution of Rembrandt would be grievously defective.

It is true that, as we said, the period of orthodoxy was one in which the theologian and the cleric were dominant. But this is not to be taken as meaning that the laity were completely disarmed, or reduced to the status of mere 'yes-men' in all the affairs of the Church. Our brief survey has shown that, even in that rigid and formal epoch, the Christian service of the laity could manifest itself as an original creative force, and could find the appropriate forms for its own exercise.

As far as organization is concerned, naturally the central figure is the ruler as father of his people. But in others too we find a new interest in political life, a new readiness to accept responsibility for various forms of service in the world, which are also among the fruits of the Reformation. The Reformers took a rather dim view of the world as the scene of the conflict between God and Satan. The world is defiled by sin. The task of the ruler is to guard it against complete dissolution, to keep it in being, until it can enter into the final deliverance which God has reserved until the last day. To the ruler is committed a task which no one else can undertake. He is the visible expression of the will of God to preserve and to maintain the world that he has created. But this rather pessimistic view has also its positive side. The responsibility of the ruler to carry out the will of God means participation, although not directly, in the whole work of the creation. The creation can, then, once again be regarded as the garden which it is man's business to care for and to tend. It was this concept which gave its character, not only to the work and outlook of the ruler, but also to those of the other men who held office in the state and in public life. Here the Reformation gave clear proof of its validity as the inspiration for the service of the Christian layman in the world.

We have written at some length of the development of lay activity in the Lutheran and Reformed Churches in the period of orthodoxy, since what happened there was basic to the developments that followed in later times. But the working of this leaven was in course of time to be seen in many other directions.

III · *A Lutheran Laymen's Church*

History cannot be reduced to formulas and is full of exceptions. It is surprising to learn that Lutheranism in the period of orthodoxy produced a Church composed entirely of laymen, and that this Church was able to maintain itself through the early period of Pietism up to 1734. This was the peasants' Church in the mountainous district of Salzburg.

The preaching of the Reformation in this area began as early as 1519, when the Archbishop of that time was not unfavourable to the new ideas. By 1527 he had changed his mind, and began to persecute the dissidents; but the gospel in its Lutheran form had taken deep root among these people and could not be eradicated. For two hundred years the Protestant community remained an unchanging feature of the local scene—without ordained ministers, without churches, without regular sacraments, hidden away in the remote mountain valleys. Each new archbishop had to reckon with this body, and the treatment accorded to them varied from time to time. They knew every kind of experience, from silent toleration of their existence to sudden threats, the despoiling of their goods and expulsion. The little helpless flock refused to be dismayed. Some fell away in time of trial, but the majority stood firm, and in fact the number of Protestants grew.

In the years before the Thirty Years War the inhabitants of the Pongau left the Roman Catholic churches empty, and attended Protestant worship in distant Schladming, a village in Styria, where such worship was permitted. At times they outwardly gave way and allowed their children to be baptized in the Roman Catholic Church; but they hardly ever attended Mass, and held their own house-services, at which the Bible was expounded by simple peasants, and those Lutheran books were read which they had inherited from their fathers or had managed to smuggle in. The end of the war in 1648 secured for them certain minimum rights. But 1685 brought further heavy persecution and the expulsion of a large number of Protestants from their valleys. It was at this time that Joseph Schaitberger (1658–1733), the miner and later woodworker, who was for years to be the heart and soul of the movement, came forward as the leader of the Protestants. He, too, after long imprisonment, was expelled from his home; but first he wrote what became the classic hymn of the exiles, and then from his new home near Nuremberg did everything that could possibly be done to care for those who had remained behind and now had to live outwardly as Roman Catholics.

From 1702 onwards he sent out his 'Evangelical Epistles'. In twenty-four booklets he drew up a manual of Christian piety for the simple man such as had never before been written. These booklets contained an account of the differences between the Roman Catholic and the Protestant faiths, questions to serve as an appendix to Luther's Shorter Catechism, a brief account of the development of the Protestant movement in Salzburg, meditations and counsels for the Christian's life of suffering, thoughts for a deathbed, admonitions to penitence, and finally a conversation with a mystically inclined Pietist, who thought that all religions were good, provided only that piety came from the heart. This is, all in all, a sober, impressive delineation of the Christian faith, which to a large extent threw the layman on his own resources, and which was very well adapted to his practical needs. The effects of this work were lasting. When, after the final act of expulsion in 1732, the last Protestants from Salzburg became members of congregations in Germany, or found refuge as English citizens in Georgia, they astonished the pastors, whose services they had at last been able to secure, by their knowledge of the Bible, and their more than merely verbal acquaintance with Luther's Catechism.

The impression left by Schaitberger on the mind is rather like that of Christian David, the Moravian carpenter, who in 1722 led the

F

oppressed Bohemian brethren to Herrnhut, and thereby laid the foundation for that Church of Zinzendorf, in which in a new and special way the layman was to come into his own. The laymen's Church in Salzburg reveals the inner strength orthodox Lutheranism could display, even in a situation of affliction and peril; the strength was there, it only needed to be called into activity. Of course, such orthodoxy did not have the opportunity to display itself in such a wide-ranging political and military activity as the Protestantism of Holland and France. Its characteristics were purity of devotion to the Church, loyalty to the Evangelical understanding of the faith, the spirit of self-sacrifice, and the cheerful endurance of suffering.

IV · *Mysticism and Pietism*

As we have seen, in the orthodox Churches, whether of Lutheran or Reformed persuasion, the task of the lay people was to work out the forms and institutions in which the life of these Churches was to be carried forward, and to take a responsible share in making the new organization work. Ideally this should have meant the co-operation of clergy and laity, working together with different means to the same ends. But the transition from the dynamism of revolution and of the fluid situation to established forms and orders always leaves the champions of the earlier period dissatisfied. There are certain values of the spiritual life that cannot be canalized into any forms, but rather live on in the guise of protests. In the period of orthodoxy this function of protest was taken over by those who are usually known in Germany as 'spiritualists', a word which may perhaps be best represented in English by 'sectaries'. They were the champions of a consecrated Christian life over against an excessive emphasis on purity of doctrine; and the chosen advocates of the laity against the dominance of the clerics.

During the Thirty Years War, the clearest voice on the side of the sectaries was that of the Brandenburgian pastor Joachim Beatke (1601–1666), who in 1640 published a work called *Sacerdotium*, which closely followed the lines of Luther's Latin tract *De Instituendis Ministris* of 1523. The opening sentence of the book says clearly what it is all about: 'All those who have been baptized into Jesus Christ / and live in his otherworldly kingdom / whether they be peasants / burghers / noblemen / are alike spiritual men and priests / provided they hold fast to the covenant of baptism / are faithful to their rebirth / and truly and diligently exercise their office of spiritual priesthood.' This is directly in the line of Luther's thought. Priesthood is based on the sacrament of baptism, which reduces to insignificance all other distinctions among men.

As Batke worked out his thesis, one of the differences which in practice he reduced to nothing was that between minister and layman. There is now really no difference between the two. Beatke still believed himself to be working along the lines of Luther's thought. What he failed to notice was that Luther, with his doctrine of the two realms, or two types of government, had accepted the world as one of the spheres of God's operation, and had done justice to the diversity of the functions of the various members of which Paul spoke in Romans 12 and I Corinthians 12. All this Beatke has given up; and it is therefore impossible for him to grasp what the vocation of the Christian layman as such really is.

Among the many remarkable laymen whom this movement produced, special mention must be made of the lawyer, Ernst Christoph Hochmann von Hochenau (1670–1721). At his conversion, which took place in 1693, he became convinced that the true Christian must separate himself decisively from the world. But for him the world was to be found also in the Church; the Church, too, is Babylon, and its pastors are of Babylon, not of God. Since they preach out of books and not out of the immediate experience of the Spirit, it is impossible that they should proclaim the truth. Thus the conflict was set with the order in Church and State that had become sacrosanct under Lutheran orthodoxy. Inevitably von Hochenau developed into a social revolutionary with Christian principles. He was convinced that the true Church of the Spirit and of true consecration to Christ, of genuine love and brotherhood, must come into being and win all men to itself. Wherever he went, he made himself unloved, indeed unendurable; and in every single one of his enterprises he failed. And yet he was not for that reason insignificant. He was the first to develop ideas which were to be taken up by other men in the nineteenth century—men like Richard Rothe (1799–1867) and Christoph Hoffmann (1818–55), who believed it to be their vocation to bring into being new types of Christian community, in which the antithesis of Church and State would be transcended, and in which brotherly love and the holy Spirit of God would be the sole driving forces.

Another layman whose contribution to church history was of lasting importance was Justinian von Weltz (1621–68). This nobleman from Austria was led, by his criticisms of the tame orthodoxy of his time, to the decisive conviction that missionary work is to be carried on among the heathen. It is to him we owe it that the challenge to Christian missionary work was not entirely silent in the Protestant world of his time. The challenge was heard by the Pietists, and in the following century was put into effect by A. H. Francke and his disciples Ziegenbalg and Plütschau, the first Protestant missionaries to India (1706). Von Weltz went out to Surinam as a pioneer missionary, and found there an early and a lonely grave. But his witness was not lost. It was his glory to have shown that the true following of Christ is to be found not in the cultivation of personal piety in the narrow circle of Christian friends, but in carrying the message of the Gospel out into the wide world beyond. He enlarged the idea of 'the Christian society', so that it became the idea of 'the Christian society as mission'.

One of the most remarkable features of this 'spiritualist' tradition was the scope it gave for the exercise of the gifts and witness of women. It was helped in this direction by its comparative independence of the ordained ministry and of the formal exercises of the Church, and its emphasis on personal and intimate conversation, in which there was no restriction on the participation and activity of women. It would be possible to make a list of at least a dozen very notable women of that time, among them Antoinette Bourignon (1616–80), authoress of *The Light of the World; a Most True Relation of a Pilgrimess Travelling Towards Eternity*, and Jane Leade (1623–1704) of the Philadelphian Societies. We must limit ourselves to a brief sketch of two of these remarkable ladies.

Anna Maria van Schurman (1607–78) was one of the outstanding blue-stockings of the age. In addition to Latin, German and French, which it was taken for granted that every educated person would learn, she was able to master Greek, Hebrew, Aramaic, Arabic, Coptic, Italian and English; as she was equally distinguished in mathematics, history and art, it is not surprising that she came to be known as 'the tenth muse'. In spite of these triumphs she remained humble and entirely free from vanity. For a time there was a danger that her love for learning might displace her love for Christ; but she experienced a second awakening under the influence of Jean de Labadie (1610–74), and from then on her only wish was to belong completely to God and Christ. In old age, she withdrew from circulation all her learned works in order to seek after the one thing that is needful. The outward sign of this surrender was her joining the 'house-church' conducted by de Labadie.

In order to give herself completely to learning and religion Anna Maria van Schurman had accepted the unmarried state. Johanna Eleonora von Merlau (1642–1724) found her vocation in marriage to a theologian five years her junior, Johann Wilhelm Petersen. Husband and wife together produced a whole series of works, in which their main purpose was to establish the hope of a thousand years of peace on earth, before the final day of judgment and the end of human history. Such apocalyptic hopes have never failed in the Christian Churches; but it was the Petersens who brought the concept back into vogue in the modern world, and there is hardly a limit to the influence that their ideas exercised. We can find traces of them in the great hopes and plans of Leibniz, in the Enlightenment as represented by Lessing, in the German idealism of Fichte and Hegel, and even in the far-flung optimism of Karl Marx and his followers.

So, in this tradition of mystical spiritualism, women, both unmarried and married, made their unique contribution, without which the development of the movement would have been very different from what it was. Each bore witness according to her natural gifts and to the situation in which God had placed her; and each manifested in her work the peculiarly feminine gift of spontaneity.

Our examples have, naturally, been drawn mostly from people of eminence and status in the world. But it is not to be supposed that the movement was limited to such people as these. There is no period in church history in which we have so much knowledge of quite simple people—artisans, peasants, servants, girls and even children. Those with no special talents served according to their capacity, and bore witness to the truth recorded in the Bible that God chooses the weak things of the world, and makes his praises to abound from the mouth of babes and sucklings. In the great pietistic collections of biographies, such as Gottfried Arnold's *Lives of the Believers* (1700) or Johann Heinrich Reitz's *History of the Twice-born*, the majority of the lives are those of very simple people. Here we learn of men like Hans Engelbrecht the clothier of Brunswick (1599–1642), who was called through visions to preach the gospel of repentance to a number of ministers; of Johannes Thaus the merchant of Husum, who in 1681 healed a number of sick people through the power of prayer; or of the other merchant Georg Frese of Hamburg, who in 1665–6 was used for the conversion of ungodly men in prison. These, and countless others like them, give evidence of a real movement of the Spirit of God among the people.

V · Pietism

Pietism follows on the lines already laid down by mystical 'spiritualism'. In the earliest of pietist writings, the *Pia Desideria* of Philip Jakob Spener (1675), one of the points desired is the elimination of 'the monopoly of the spiritual order'. Spener is thinking of the self-satisfied conceit of the orthodox clergy over their position as ministers and their learning. Preaching alone will never bring the gospel home to people in the way in which they need it. Pastor and layman must work together, each supplementing the imperfections of the other. The position of the pastor is that of 'director and elder brother'.

It was part of Spener's greatness that he saw the work of the Christian layman not simply in participation in pious meetings, 'conventicles', but also in his faithfulness in his calling in the world. Spener, like Luther before him, recognized the three different areas of human life— the clerical (*hierarchicus*), the public (*politicus*) and the private (*oeconomicus*). In the *Pia Desideria* he analysed the duties of the Christian man as he finds himself in each of these three areas. There is a certain naïveté in Spener's approach; he thinks that with the regeneration of all men through the Holy Spirit all the problems of public life will find a ready solution; he does not see as clearly as Luther the continuing power of sin even in the Christian, and the need that Christians and non-Christians should learn to live together in a world which is increasingly falling under the dominion of secularization.

The second great figure of German Pietism, August Hermann Francke (1663–1727), was the creator of the gigantic complex of buildings and charitable works that centred in the Orphanage at Halle. Francke had in early years attracted attention and disapproval by inviting women and artisans to his discussion classes on the Bible. Himself an ordained pastor, he was skilful in calling out the gifts of laymen, and attaching them to himself as his indispensable collaborators in his great work.

One of these lay helpers of Francke is so characteristic of Pietism on its practical side as to deserve special mention. Georg Heinrich Neubauer (1666–1726) had started out on the study of theology; in early years he was won for Pietism by Francke's discussion classes on the Bible; and thenceforward devoted himself to the service of his Master, not in the ordained ministry, but as secretary, builder and accountant. Neubauer had the gifts of the business man; he was the great administrator of the Orphanage at Halle. It was under his hand that the great succession of buildings grew; nothing, however small, escaped his attention, and the provision of a reliable water-supply was one of his more notable achievements. And all these exacting tasks he carried out on so minute a salary that he was dependent on the gifts of friends for his very clothes. Without him Francke's work would not have been possible. His was a nature that was ready at all times to pour itself out in self-forgetful and exhausting service. He was quite content to live out his life in the shadow of another and greater man. Alongside Neubauer stood Heinrich Julius Elers (1667–1728), the head of the printing department, and Christian Friedrich Richter (1676–1711), doctor, research worker, writer of spiritual books, and composer of some of the best pietistic hymns in the German hymn book.

Of all the lay theologians with whom we have to deal none ranks higher than Count Nikolaus Ludwig von Zinzendorf und Pottendorf (1700–60). Halle had laid in him the foundation of a deeply Christian and responsible spirit. The coming of the refugees from Moravia, the Bohemian Brethren led by Christian David, gave him the opportunity to bring into existence a real lay fellowship of Christians.

Christian David the carpenter (1691–1751), who with his own hands felled the first tree for the new settlement at Herrnhut, was himself a lay theologian of unusual character. He had grown up in Roman Catholic surroundings; but an evangelical conversion settled his destiny for life. Independently he wandered off to distant places as a missionary; and his meeting with the Danish missionary Hans Egede in Greenland introduced him to that Pauline doctrine of justification by faith, which he was later so emphatically to present to John Wesley, during the latter's stay at Herrnhut in 1738. The development of the Herrnhut community was the fruit of a prolonged, and not seldom strained, dialogue between the old Moravian traditions represented by Christian David, and the early Christian principles, the inspired intuitions, and the constantly shifting plans of the highly gifted Count. But throughout one principle stood fast—that of the Church of lay churchmen. Here joiners and masons, bakers and cobblers were ordained as bishops, and sent off as missionaries in foreign parts, often earning their passage by helping as temporary seamen by the way. Here, with at times some exaggeration, to be a Christian was understood as meaning to be a man, a layman, as near as possible to the example of those fishermen, shepherds and tax-gatherers by whom the gospel was first preached.

We are naturally reminded of the groups of Christians in the mountain valleys of Salzburg. Here too living Christian communities came into being and maintained themselves, without regular pastors or ministers with theological training. There was certainly a difference between the two. Zinzendorf in a peculiar way united in his own person the two streams of the Reformation. On the one hand, he was the ruler, the *membrum praecipuum* of the Church after the pattern of Melanchthon—it could not be otherwise when he was the patron and protector of the flock. On the other hand he took seriously the pietistic inheritance; and this led him to seek to renew the spirit of primitive Christianity, to work out new forms for Christian living which were out of accord with the general standards and practice of his day, but were so far in touch with reality as to produce genuine communities, of which the dominant characteristics were the fellowship of the strong with the weak, brotherly love and consideration, mutual understanding and helpfulness.

Of the notable women whom we meet in pietistic circles, certainly the most outstanding is Erdmuth Dorothea, the first wife of Count Zinzendorf (1700–56). From the first day their marriage was that of twin souls, each committed as a warrior on behalf of the sovereignty of God in Jesus Christ. She had been brought up in a pious family, in which all the streams of mysticism and pietism flowed together; but at the same time she received such practical training in the handling of the realities of life as was later to stand her in very good stead. In the early days of Herrnhut she was far from being completely in sympathy with the plans and ideals of her husband. Her aristocratic temper found it hard to submit to the discipline of the groups organized for mutual spiritual care, in which it was necessary to meet on terms of equality those who were not her social equals, and for the love of Christ to abandon every claim to worldly superiority. And she knew too well the character of her husband—his capacity for spinning glorious plans without any serious reckoning with the difficulties involved, and his tendency suddenly to drop some treasured project in favour of some new idea that had suddenly occurred to him. She seems at times to have poured much water into the wine of his high-flying dreams and plans. But from 1727 Dorothea was completely committed to the work of Herrnhut; and she found her special vocation as the manager of its economic life. During the long absence of Zinzendorf in America in 1741–3, the guidance of the brotherhoods in Europe fell almost entirely into her hands.

But life was not easy for her. In the end she became disillusioned with her eccentric husband, and exhausted with the cares which seemed to have no end. She is a good example of a wife who wore herself out in service to her husband's work, who was prepared to go to the utmost limits in self-denial, in diligence, in renunciation and patience; a true servant of the Lord—yet one who was not able to endure suffering without complaint.

Conclusion

The 'spiritualist' movement had laid great stress on the spiritual priesthood of all believers. Pietism accepted this principle, and carried it further in the sense that the layman was expected to have such a deep and comprehensive knowledge of the truths of the gospel that the great distance between the layman and the pastor with his complete training in theology was notably reduced. And, in strange contrast with this development, theologians and pastors of this period devoted themselves to professions and fields of activity that are generally supposed to be the preserve of the laity. Spener was not only an ordained minister; he was also an expert in heraldry, and had a knowledge, perhaps unequalled in his time, of the coats of arms of the nobility. August Hermann Francke was as much organizer and promoter as preacher of the gospel. Friedrich Christoph Oetinger studied chemistry and was owner of a mine. Johann Konrad Dippel (1673–1734), the last great figure of the spiritualist tradition, was a physician and chemist, as well as a writer of theological treatises. Here we encounter the spirit of the Enlightenment, which reduced the prestige of the profession of the clergy, and at the same time exalted the layman, not so much in the Church as in the world of human society.

Pietism was successful both in raising the esteem in which the laity were held, and also in opening out before the layman almost unlimited fields for activity. The possibilities of action which orthodoxy had developed within the institutional framework of the Church remained in existence and had to be maintained. Now that new and dynamic activities opened up, the possibilities of lay action were naturally doubled. And so we find both types—the great outstanding lay personality stands side by side with the ordinary layman, who is present as a member of that new fellowship of the children of God, which is made up of those who have passed through the experience of conversion. It is easy to understand why the age of pietism is the classic period of the activity and service of the Protestant layman in the Church.

7

Peter Meinhold

MODERN EUROPE
1800–1962

Introduction

THE emancipation of the layman began in the period of the Reformation. From the middle of the nineteenth century onwards, the significance of the layman in all the Churches in Europe increased in such a way as to bring to full flowering all that had been present in germ in the Reformation. This is true not only of the Protestant Churches, but in equal measure of the Roman Catholic Church. At the same time we must reckon with the fact that this development of the laity did not take place only within the walls of the Church; the process was going on also outside the Church, in part in hostility towards the Church, and in deliberately chosen liberation from the Church.

Moreover, if we are rightly to understand the lay movement, and its great creative achievements in every department of human life, we must take account of the fact that what we here have to do with is not succession, in the sense of a series of distinct and clearly marked stages of development, but parallel developments, which we shall find occurring contemporaneously in a variety of Churches. Thus, for instance, we shall encounter in the nineteenth-century secularism, 'laicism', a movement in favour of emancipation from the Church, directed against a certain kind of clericalism, or perhaps we should rather say a certain clerical domination of the world. But, in the world of the Roman Catholic Church, this is accompanied in the same period by the beginnings of a new self-consciousness of the laity within the framework of the life of the Church. This, in its turn, is balanced almost evenly by similar developments in almost all the Churches of the Protestant world. But here too we see the beginnings of an uprising of lay folk who have liberated themselves from all their old loyalty to the Church, and who are bent on a new ordering of the world in complete independence of ecclesiastical leadership. Then, this is matched in the Protestant Churches by new developments in the service of lay people in the Church; and this steadily increases until what it amounts to is a recovery of the responsibility and the ministry of the laity in the life of the Church.

For this reason, it is impossible to treat of the development which has here been indicated in relation to this or that Church, this or that country, in isolation. For the same phenomena are to be observed emerging at the same time in every Church and in every country. The problem we are dealing with breaks all the bounds of the confessional divisions of the Church; our concern must be with the development of the lay movement, and with the position of the lay people, in the Churches of modern Europe as a whole. We start with the assumption that modern Europe began to come into being somewhere about the middle of the nineteenth century. We shall set out the course of the development in five sections; and these will make clear the extent to which the character of a lay movement was in every case determined by the attitude which it took up in relation to the Church. The sections are as follows:

1. The secularization of the world as a form of conflict with the Church.
2. The new ordering of the world in total independence of the Church.
3. Service to the world as an overflow from the life of the Church.
4. The ministry of the layman in the conflict of the Church with the world.
5. The transformation in the layman's own understanding of his calling.

I · Secularism and the Church

It was in France that the resolution of the lay people to liberate themselves from the Roman Catholic Church first came to tangible expression. This resolve arose from the insights which inspired the French Revolution and determined the attitude which it took up towards the Church. Here the Church was regarded as a spiritual and political power, which after the pattern of the medieval Church had extended its domination over every part of the life of man, and the aim of which was absolutely to secure the authority of the clergy over all others and at every point. People had come to be convinced that this clerical domination made wholly impossible any free development in education, in the sciences, in art, in economic or political life. But the aim was not simply liberation from ecclesiastical tutelage; it went much further, and demanded total liberation from all the presuppositions of the Christian faith, in order to be free to carry out in practical terms the reordering of all these various realms of human life, on the basis of those natural and objective principles which were found to be valid within the sphere of each of them, and on nothing else. Secularism, then, takes on the form of a conflict with the Church, at the same time as it sets itself to carry through a new ordering in freedom of every area of human life.

The first field in which this opposition became fully manifest was that of the schools, of education and of the sciences. The decisive battles, with victory on the side of the secularists, were fought out in France, where from the beginning of the century there had been in existence a strong anti-clerical movement of thought, which was bent on the complete secularization of the life of men. The first great victory in the political field was won, when in the so-called 'Third Republic' this movement came to power through its alliance with the radical party. The decisive step was the Education Act of 30th October 1886, which secularized all the schools supported by the state, that is to say, excluded every trace of ecclesiastical influence from the schools, and brought into existence the *École laïque*, the school without religion. Such a school stood in sharp contrast to the church school, since here not only freedom of conscience, but the freedom of the teacher to teach according to his convictions was safeguarded against any attempt to control it on the basis of a Christian understanding of truth. The intellectual position on which this movement was based has for this reason come to be known as *laïcisme*, for which the nearest English equivalent is perhaps 'secularism'.* The appearance of this set of convictions on the political stage and its claim to be the determining factor in the whole ordering of public life naturally provoked a violent series of conflicts. One evidence of this was the complete separation of Church and State in France, which was achieved in 1905. The Church was reduced to the status of a private corporation. The financial help which had previously been given to church schools was now entirely withdrawn.

As far as the state was concerned, secularism meant an attitude of complete neutrality, or rather a refusal to be drawn into any religious questions. The principle which had been accepted for the schools was

---

* For convenience we have sometimes reproduced the French word in the English form *laicism* (Tr.).

now extended to higher education and to the work of the universities. Here too the supreme influence was that of secularism. A secularism which was hostile to the Church and resolutely refused to lift its eyes beyond the immediate concerns of this world had in course of time extended its influence, and penetrated ever more deeply into every part of public life. This development was most notable in France; but similar things were happening in other countries also, and especially in Belgium.

Secularism, as we have seen, is based on certain general convictions, which involve an attitude of total hostility towards the Church and the Christian faith. But in France, another term has come to be adopted for that attitude of neutrality in all religious questions which is now expected of the government. This term is *laïcité*. This attitude, which guarantees the complete neutrality of the state in all religious questions, is now firmly rooted in the French Constitution. The Constitution of 1954, as well as that of 1946, accepted the principle of non-intervention (*laïcité*); but the original hostility towards Church and religion has been entirely dropped. It is taken for granted that the state is neutral in all matters of religion; but it does not regard the work of the Church with the same relentless hostility as in time past. The state schools, of course, as before are schools without religion. But it is open to the Church, if it wishes, to establish its own confessional schools.

From the time of the *Syllabus Errorum* onwards, the Roman Catholic Church has steadily attacked secularism. In the Papal Encyclical *Quas Primas* of 11th December 1925, secularism is condemned as the denial of the sovereignty of Christ over the nations and of the right of the Church to carry out its ministry of teaching, as a perilous subordination of the Church to the State, and as the introduction of the completely secularized and godless state. Here secularism is understood as a set of convictions which must lead to the development of a completely non-religious culture in a completely non-religious state. In such a state the Church can exist only as a private corporation.

The term *laïcisme* is not commonly used in Germany. But closely parallel developments were to be observed in Germany after 1918, and here too the aim was the banishment of religion from the schools, and indeed the secularization of the whole of public life. In Germany these purposes were not crowned with success. The separation between Church and State was not carried through in the same radical way as in France, and attempts to banish all religious training and instruction from the schools were defeated. There can, however, be no doubt that in Hitler's 'Third Reich' secularism, though on a rather different intellectual basis from that which we have so far been describing, did meet with a very great measure of success. For National Socialism, too, was concerned only with this world and its affairs; it too fought to expel the Church from public life, and to establish culture on a purely secular and this-worldly basis.

It was only through the fearful experiences of the two world wars that men were brought to realize that a culture which has cut itself free from every tie with religion and is interested only in values within the world of time and space simply has not the strength to check the tendency to abandon every standard of human decency, of which we have such fearful evidence in the 'Third Reich' and in other completely secularized states. It was only then that men became aware of the gigantic dangers that are inseparable from secularism. This movement has not really brought about a liberation of the lay people; it has served only as the basis for the claim to a totally irresponsible independence, in which man himself is the sole and only measure and standard of behaviour. It is easy to understand why in the more recent developments less and less stress has been laid on the anti-Christian and anti-religious elements in secularism, and it has gradually been transformed into a movement which demands no more than the neutrality and independence of the State in all religious affairs. So, in contemporary France, the old *laïcisme* has been transformed into the new *laïcité*, and in this form has struck deep roots into the French Constitution. Understood in this sense, it determines the attitude which the State is to take up in those areas in which religion and politics meet. But it has come adrift from those intellectual and theoretical convictions on which it was originally based.

II · A New and Independent World

A most important new understanding of the term 'layman' and of the activity of lay people in the Church and in the world began to take shape in Germany in the middle of the nineteenth century. In 1848–9 Richard Rothe published his celebrated *Christian Ethics*, in which he developed the idea that the Church is a historically conditioned stage, through which mankind has to pass on its way to 'Christendom'. On Rothe's view, the Church has now completed its task. Its place is henceforth to be taken by the State, which will be able to undertake responsibility for the Christianization and the moral education of the world on a far wider scale than was ever possible for the Church. Rothe held the opinion that the time has come in which the ordained minister must retire gracefully into the background, and that all the social work which has in the past been called into being by the Church must now become the responsibility of the lay people. The clergy are specifically the teachers of the Christian religion. But the building of the kingdom of God, which Rothe understands as a great ethical reality within the world, must from now on be undertaken by the laity.

The Church has played a great part in the history of the world, but its role is no longer primary; it has found its successor in the State, which is also to be recognized as an ethical community, and which must now take up the task of building the kingdom of God in the sense which has just been described. And, as Rothe understands things, naturally the principal part in carrying out this new function of the state will fall to the lay people.

This will naturally result in a process of identification with the world; by this is meant the putting off of that ecclesiastical form, which Christian faith inevitably had to adopt at its first entering into the world; and with this a process of secularization, which on the deepest levels corresponds to that development in the history of Christianity which first came to open expression in the Reformation. Rothe is fully convinced that what in times past was specifically the work of the Church is now really being carried on outside the Church. 'Today we can no longer look for Christian saints within the Church.' It is sometimes possible to find such saints even in the ranks of the ordained clergy—Rothe makes particular reference to Oberlin—but in such cases we find that the man is working in the main by means that are very far from ecclesiastical. Rothe directs attention to the fact that not only Pietism with its widely extended social work, but also Wichern, and the whole movement which he had called into being through the foundation of his 'Rough House' and the development of the 'Inner Mission',* operated outside the ordinary channels of ecclesiastical life. So we are driven to the conclusion that today the true labourer of the Church wears 'the layman's coat under the churchman's robe'.

These views of Rothe attracted very wide attention. It is impossible for us to assess them correctly, unless we bear two considerations in mind. In the first place, the idea of the replacement of the Church by

---

* *Innere Mission* cannot really be translated into English. 'Home Missions' gives quite the wrong idea; it seems better simply to keep the term 'Inner Mission' for this particular phenomenon, though the phrase is not really English (Tr.).

the state does involve, as Rothe has stated the issue, a complete identification of Christendom with the world; but this is a principle which
Rothe finds already present in the incarnation of God. This event, so
central to Christian faith, is interpreted by Rothe in an idealistic sense.
According to him, the incarnation of God means the complete and un-
restricted entry of God into the life of mankind, in such a way that
mankind as a whole eventually becomes identical with the Redeemer.
In the substitution of the state for the Church this process of incarnation reaches its highest point, indeed its consummation. The Redeemer
has now in the fullest possible sense entered into the life of mankind,
since mankind, at its present level of moral education, has become
capable of participating in the work of building the kingdom of God.

The other central principle which determined Rothe's ideas is to be
found in his understanding of the Reformation. His new principle, he
maintained, had actually come to light in the Reformation itself in so
far as it eliminated Christian faith as that had been previously understood. Contemporaries understood the Reformation as an improvement, as a reform of the Church; but in reality it reduced the Church
to a position of insignificance, as no more than a temporary help in a
situation of emergency. In the Reformation the Church achieved its
own deliverance 'into the world of the purely ethical', in order to set
up in that world 'the standard of Christianity for all future times'.

This involves a completely new understanding of the situation of the
layman. What Rothe means can be understood in the light of the three
following affirmations:

1. The kingdom of God is here interpreted as an entity, which without dependence on supernatural or other-worldly dimensions comes to
be actualized in the field of the purely ethical. If the kingdom of God
is apprehended in this way, it is clear that the building of it cannot be
a task to be carried out only by Christians outside the limits of the
Church.

2. The service which the layman is to carry on in the world is to be
Christian without making use of that name. He is to serve, without
maintaining any living connection with the Church, on the basis only
of his Christian self-consciousness as a member of the Church. He has
reached a kind of maturity conferred on him by his Christian self-
consciousness as a civilized being in a civilized society.

3. The ethical principles of Christianity can be expressed in action,
even in detachment from Christian faith as such. The ethical-in-
itself is so completely identified with the kingdom of God that the

ethical-in-itself can be put into effect by powers outside the Church, and by men who are not Christians. Such activity is just as much co-operation in the building of the kingdom of God as any work that is carried on within the limits of the Church.

These principles formed the basis for a type of lay activity within the Protestant Churches, grounded on the belief that the building of the kingdom of God can be promoted by ethical and social action. The culmination of this activity is without doubt to be found in the social legislation of Bismarck. It was from his understanding of the idea of a Christian state that Bismarck was led to tackle the task of social reform, in the conviction that this is a task which is incumbent on the state as an ethical institution. Bismarck clearly expressed the view that this activity of the state in the fields of social reform, education, and general welfare, is a task that is laid upon it by the very inmost nature of its being. In this connection it is not our concern to set out in detail the contents of this legislation, or the manner in which it was carried into effect. What is of decisive importance are the basic principles or assumptions which underlay this legislation. These, it is clear, were a concept of the kingdom of God, and an understanding of the responsibility of the layman, in precisely the sense in which Rothe had developed these ideas. And work carried out beyond the limits of these fields is recognized as being equally a realization of the kingdom of God, and of ethical value fully equal to that of the work carried on within the Christian sphere. Decisive also for the understanding of this kind of work is the conviction that it really is work for lay people, since the layman, free from the narrow and restricted presuppositions of the ordained minister, will be able, better and with less prejudice than one who is specifically a churchman, to serve on the basis of those needs which are objectively present in each situation, and on nothing else. Here we are face to face with the idea of a new ordering of the world, which is to be carried out in complete independence of the Church. We are reminded at many points of the kind of activity promoted by the spirit of 'laicism' in France; though the point of view in Germany was free from that hostility to the Church which, as we saw, was one of the characteristic features of the movement as it developed in France.

It is in this sense that the *Kulturkampf* (the battle between Church and State in Germany) also is to be understood. At the time of its occurrence, this was regarded as a struggle against the reactionary attitude of the Church, and was related to the tendencies of secularism elsewhere, in so far as one of its aims was the restriction of the influence of the Church on the State, on education and on society. In the eyes of Bismarck it was a struggle on the part of the State to maintain its own integrity over against the influence of the Church, and a struggle to maintain the rights of the monarchy over against claims made in the name of Christianity. It is to be noted that this view was based on a very narrow understanding of culture—this seems to have been taken to be more or less synonymous with material civilization and technical progress. The *Kulturkampf* is also evidence of the immense secularization of life that had set in, and that together with its consequences had made great progress not only in German regions such as Bavaria and Prussia, but also in other European countries, such as Austria and Switzerland. In so far as the aim in these various conflicts was to defend the rights and liberties of the lay folk against the clergy, the *Kulturkampf* can be taken as the expression of a world in which the layman is to be in sole control; and this, in its turn, is identical with secularism in its purest form.

To sum up, this second form of lay activity in Europe, the intellectual foundations of which are to be found in the work of Richard Rothe, is directed towards a new ordering of the world in total independence of the Church; but this can be achieved only in association with that understanding of culture, Church and kingdom of God which is typical of the movement; all these three great realities are interpreted in terms of ethical categories and nothing else.

III · *New Ideas of Service to the World*

At the time when Richard Rothe was defending secularization (in the sense of that identification of the Church with the world which was to be regarded as the culmination of the process of its incarnation in the world) and associated with it the idea of a new type of layman who has outgrown the leading-strings of the Church, a new and quite different understanding of the layman and his work was then springing into life within the Protestant Churches. The special feature of this was that it ascribed to the layman a special part in that service which the Church is called to render to the world, and attributed to him a particular function which he alone can fulfil.

This new interpretation of the status of the layman is to be found first in Johann Hinrich Wichern, and later in Theodor Fliedner.

In 1833 Wichern had started out on a systematically planned work of reclamation among the neglected young people in the slums of Hamburg. He was guided in his work here by the apprehension that Christian ethical principles are not primarily concerned with the individual in his isolation. Christian life is literally impossible, if the atmosphere in which it has to be lived is so conditioned that the moral principles of the gospel simply cannot be put into effect, and that the very existence of the Christian as Christian is imperilled.

In the second place, Wichern was inspired by the conviction that it is the business of the Church to seek out precisely those groups that have been excluded from the privileges of society and neglected by it, in order to save the lost—a term which Wichern understood in the sociological no less than in the theological sense. But the Church cannot fulfil this function, unless it takes its stand firmly on the side of the lost. And this is in particular the task of the Christian, whose calling it is at all times to give a good account of himself as the representative of the Church in the world.

On the basis of these convictions Wichern arrived at a new understanding of the responsibility of the layman, which was to be of the highest importance for the work of the Protestant Churches in Germany. The layman of whom Wichern is thinking takes his stand as a servant of the Church. He is distinguished from the minister by the fact that he is not ordained, is not burdened with the responsibilities of pastoral care, of the administration of the sacraments and .preaching, and does not undertake the offices of teacher and shepherd in one particular congregation. It is his peculiar function to manifest his solidarity with the lost world as a 'brother', and so to advance into regions and to work among groups of the population, with which the Church as such no longer finds itself in a position to make contact.

It was out of his own work of reclamation that Wichern developed his general understanding of the lay folk as the representatives of the people of God in the world. The 'Inner Mission' is the unique attempt to challenge the lay people of Christendom to take up this new form of service in the world and to the world. Use has been made of every kind of means for charitable work that are at its disposal. It has expressed itself in training institutions and welfare homes, in hospitals and in homes for the aged, in the development of a new kind of popular Christian literature, and in the free activity of unions of various kinds, to meet the ever-changing needs of the time. In actual fact, Wichern succeeded, through this understanding of the responsibility of the whole people of God for service to the world, in bringing into being a new activity of the lay people, and in bringing home both to the Church and to individual Christians a sense of that responsibility, which they had largely forgotten, to make the gospel heard and to make it effective in the world.

Our second figure is Theodor Fliedner. Following up various earlier attempts, which can be traced in the Rhineland before his time, Fliedner at Kaiserswerth developed ideas similar to those of Wichern, in regard to the possibilities for the work of women in the Church. Wichern developed the idea of brotherhood as the principle for the service of men in the world. Here at Kaiserswerth we meet the idea of a sisterhood, which should also carry out its work of ministry in the world. As early as 1818 Amélie Sieveking had conceived the idea of a sisterhood in the Protestant Churches, the members of which would carry out their work of ministry in the world, but would be closely linked to one another in the fellowship of a sisterhood. No doubt these ideas had their origin in the example of the Roman Catholic orders for women; but here everything has been thought through afresh in the light of the gospel. The sisterhood is not to be thought of as a religious order the aim of which is the perfection of the devotional life of the individual; it is to be consciously directed to service in the world; this service is to be understood as the exaltation of that love which meets us in the sacrifice of Christ, in order to awaken faith and love in circles which at present are entirely alienated from the Church. This activity of the sisters, directed as it should be principally to the poor, the old, children and sick persons, should be in itself a form of proclamation of the gospel; it should break through all hindering 'proprieties', and perform its ministry to the world in perfect freedom.

In this way Theodor Fliedner was led to re-create the office of deaconess. The ministry of women was to be the means through which the life that draws its strength from the Church should become visible in the world; but at the same time the women engaged in this service should be held together in the sisterhood, and should come to regard the Mother-house as their own home. Fliedner thus opened up for women an immense field of service. We must not, however, forget that the emancipation of women and the opening up of new fields of enterprise for them was by no means the object for which all this work was undertaken; the aim of these activities of women was that in them the love of Christ should become visibly manifest. For this reason Fliedner was all the time opening up new fields of endeavour—in social work, particularly in prisons and in the care of discharged prisoners; in

schools for little children and for young people; in the work of education, and of places of refuge for the helpless.

But, as with Wichern, the development of all these new forms of
service for men and women did not aim at the opening up of new professions in which they could engage; the considered intention was the
renewal of the service of the lay people of the Church, who should find
in the exercise of the office of deacon or deaconess their regular sphere
of activity. It was therefore quite logical that Wichern and Fliedner
brought into being special training institutions, both for deacons and
for deaconesses, in which these new forces that were to be available for
the service of the Church might receive the right kind of preparation
for their work.

This renewal of the idea of the diaconate gave a decisive impulse in
favour of a new activity of lay people in the Church. This idea of service,
in total independence of and freedom from the State and in close relation to the Church, found its clearest expression in the views and ideas
of Wilhelm Löhe, who in rather a similar way took up and developed
the principle of *diakonia*, Christian service in the world. Here we find,
with special emphasis, the thought of service which goes out from the
Church into the world. But Löhe is not entirely free from the spell of
the nineteenth-century understanding of the kingdom of God; we find
at one moment that the activities in service of the sisters are understood
as the work of the Church going forth from itself into the world; at
other times this work is regarded as one form of the actualization of the
kingdom of God upon earth. Similar points of view are to be met with
even in Wichern and Fliedner; but in both of them the kingdom of God
is still understood in its eschatological significance. The service of lay
people in the world is, therefore, primarily a visible representation of
the message of Christ, an attestation of the love of God, surrender of
man's life to God, in the likeness of that sacrifice which Christ has
offered on our behalf.

Thus it was a combination of the most diverse motives which led,
in the world of the Protestant Churches, to the recovery of the diaconate as an ecclesiastical ministry, with its activity directed outwards
towards the world. It is clear that a new understanding of the Church
itself, especially in regard to its relationship to the world, was implied in
these new discoveries. The layman is no longer that individual who is
negatively defined as 'not belonging to the clergy', and to whom the
ministrations of the clergy are particularly directed; now he is positively the representative of the people of God in the world; he is that

member of the Church through whom alone the Church can carry out those special tasks that are laid upon it in the world. It is further required that the Church as a whole shall recognize this service as a necessary part of its own existence, and accept the vocation of working for its accomplishment.

So here we have a third concept of the laity to set beside the idea of the secularization of the world, undertaken in the spirit of hostility to the Church, and that other understanding of the layman as the man who will set himself to work to reorder the world in complete independence of the Church. The very basis of this concept is a fresh recognition of the vocation of the Church to undertake service in the world. It is, of course, true that in accordance with the structure of society in the nineteenth century this work was actually carried into effect through independent societies. But that was no more than the outward garb, under which such work could be carried out in accordance with the sociological relationships of one particular century. And it was precisely for this reason that it was able, on a very large scale, to catch the imagination of Church people, and of the world of the laity. We must not overlook the fact that by it the laity were stimulated to activity in a new way, of which the full results were to be seen only at a very much later date, when it had led to the foundation or maintenance of all kinds of institutions in connection with the Church—to the development of hospitals, schools, training homes, centres for the care of the neglected, the sick and the old. We grasp the full significance of this many-sided work only when we recall that its effect was to open out many new fields of activity for the state as well as for the Church. Such active participation of lay people in service as grew out of the work of the 'Inner Mission' has exercised a quite appreciable influence on the whole social activity of the state. Before the end of the nineteenth century, the Church as represented by its lay people had become unmistakably recognizable as the great inspirer of the activity of the state in all the fields of welfare, education and social improvement. This raises the problem of the secularization of the work undertaken by the Church, as it passes over into the hands of those who are not connected with the Church, and comes to be carried out on presuppositions entirely different from those of the Christian faith. But this falls outside the subject assigned to this chapter.

IV · The Layman and the Church in Conflict

The conclusions we have so far reached regarding the recovery of the 'diaconate' of the Church as that ministry through which the Church makes its presence felt in the world are valid in roughly the same degree for all the European Churches. Naturally there are variations, and forms are related to the structure of each Church; but all have experienced a quickening of the work of the laity, which has found appropriate expression in home missions and foreign missions, in charitable work, in student movements, in the YMCA, in all kinds of societies for men and women, not to mention the unions of working men and artisans. All those efforts have been of great importance, and have stirred particularly the young people to active work in connection with the Church. On the other hand it has to be admitted that the congregations as a whole took up in general an entirely passive attitude; and lay activity of the kind that we have been describing was regarded as a reserved occupation for small numbers of Christians who had undergone a specially deep conversion, or were specially active in the affairs of the Church.

The situation in the Free Churches was notably different from that in the state, or 'People's', Churches. There, even in earlier times, much greater activity on the part of the lay people had been the rule. Such lay service, however, was understood not so much as that service that *the Church* is called to render to the world, as that form of activity which it is self-evident that every individual Christian must carry on in the world as a testimony to the love of God and the lordship of Christ. It was only as a result of a number of new experiences that Christians were led to understand that there is a special vocation of the layman, the basis of which is precisely the truth that the obligation to serve in the world rests upon him not as a Christian individual, but as a member of the fellowship of the Church. But before this new idea of the layman as the man who is called to serve as the representative of the Church in its confrontation with the world could be accepted, a deeper theological appraisal of the situation had to be carried through; for this lay service of the Church in the world is rightly understood only as service which is carried on by those who themselves are in the world, and in a certain measure stand in opposition to the world.

Thus, one of the first questions that had to be reconsidered was the nature of the mission of the Christian congregation to the world. To put it in another way, the question was this—how far is the Christian congregation which after Sunday morning service becomes 'the congregation sent forth into the world', able to make plain to the world the nature of the experience that has come to it in its act of worship? It is this challenge to the congregation that the formula 'the congregation after church service' is intended to describe. It is meant to draw attention to the nature of Christian service in a world all the co-ordinates of which have so completely changed. The members of the congregation cannot play a simply passive role in all the situations of everyday life; it is precisely in those situations of everyday life and in every area of human life that they are to serve as the representatives of the Church. It is recognized that in the person of its lay people the Church is as a matter of fact present in every area of human activity. So the Church is actually there—in offices and factories, in government offices and in places where political decisions are made, in industrial towns and in the countryside—literally in the midst of every profession carried on by men and of every conceivable kind of human activity. Whether the Church is effectively there or is not there depends on whether the laity genuinely represent it—that is to say, bear witness to its reality, and so make the world aware of its presence.

Once this is recognized, it is clear that the lay folk have a part of quite extraordinary importance to play in the life of the Church. Without the layman, the Church has literally no place in the world of today. What he bears witness to is the sovereignty of God in everyday life, not simply as a power which determines his own personal attitudes and actions, but as a power which is the controlling force in history; for he points to the Church, through which God continuously carries on and brings to its completion his work for the redemption of the world.

It was for this reason that we said that there is a work for the layman to do in the world, and in some measure in opposition to the world. Thus, the Second Assembly of the World Council of Churches at Evanston in 1954 was right in expressing the conviction that today the battle of faith and unbelief is being fought out, not only in the relationships between the nations, but in every relationship of human life. We are of the opinion that in this battle of faith and unbelief, the layman is called to an office which makes him the representative of the Church in the world; and he is called to exercise his office in relation to the world in such a way that the eager striving of God to win the world back to himself is going forward through him.

In the light of this understanding it is now possible to offer a new definition of the work that the layman is called to carry on. It corre-

sponds closely to the structure of society in our day. Wherever the layman is, he is a member of the people of God. But it is not possible for
him to live as such, unless he is so aware of his own status as a member
of the Church that what becomes effective through him is the presence
of the Church in the area of life which is accessible to him, and this in
its turn reveals to the world the work that God is carrying on for its
redemption. So the layman in his sphere is called to carry on just the
same struggle as is carried on by the Church as a whole in the world
and in opposition to the world. In just the same way as the whole
Church, the individual Christian is exposed to the dangers of confor-
mity to the world. He may succumb to the influences of the world, if
he tries to fight God's battles with the weapons and the methods of
the world. He may fall into the error of not using things simply as
instruments by means of which the work proper to the Church can be
carried on, but of regarding them as objectives, of which the Church
must secure control in order to safeguard its own position in the world.
So, precisely because he is the representative of the people of God in
the world, he will say to himself very firmly that every modern technical device, and the presence of Christians in all the infinitely varied
professions of men, are simply opportunities afforded him to use these
things to point to the reality of that lordship of God over the world, in
which alone the salvation of the world is to be found.

It must, however, be recognized that today it is almost impossible
for the individual Christian to fulfil his ministry as an individual. He
can carry out his duties as a member of the people of God only when he
is aware that there is a unity of witness, a unity of service of all the
Christians in the world. It is hardly possible for the individual to be
fully aware of the immensely complicated nature of the Church's task
today, and to know the answers to all the problems that arise out of its
situation, if the Church as a whole does not point out to him the ways
that have to be followed, and provide him with the answers.

The task which the layman has to carry out in Europe today is a task
of the Church and for the Church; and so we are justified in saying
that the layman too has his office, his ministry in and for the Church.
We have no intention whatever of pitting ecclesiastical office and lay
ministry against one another; each must be seen in close and continuous relation to the other. The layman, as a member of the people
of God at work in the world, cannot maintain his own position in the
world, and cannot make the world aware of his position as a member of
the Church, unless he bears in mind that obligation which at all times

rests upon him to recognize that his life in the world is only a different aspect of that particular office which has been entrusted to him in the Church.

There is as yet no agreement as to the kinds of office which should be open to the layman in the light of this new understanding. The nature of particular forms of lay ministry that ought to be developed is still a subject for discussion.

In the brotherhoods and sisterhoods, which have been reorganized in almost all the Churches, the service of the Church to the world is beginning to take on new forms. In these communities, which cannot be regarded simply as an extension into our own time of the service of the Church to the world as that was understood in the nineteenth century, the new understanding of the work of the layman is beginning to take shape. These fellowships are not now thought of as separate societies which exist alongside the Church. We may rather say that, in their daily services, they share in the common life of the Church. They make it plain that the Church itself is a brotherhood; they plan their work in the world as service to the world. They wrestle on behalf of the world in order to bring the world itself under the sovereignty of God. Here the lay movement has worked out for itself a new and characteristic expression, which at the same time leaves its impress on its manner of life in the world.

Another notable form of lay service is to be found in the Evangelical Academies in Germany, in so far as they provide the point of meeting, in which sections of the population which have so far lived in isolation from one another can be brought together, and so led to a new mutual understanding. In a special way it is a concern of the Evangelical Academies to make plain the responsibility of the Church in relation to the life of the nation, and the share of responsibility that the lay people must accept for the development of public life. One of the essential tasks of such institutions is to meet contemporary man in the realm of the questions that are raised for him by everyday life, to help him to find a solution of his problems in the light of the gospel, and to make plain the unity of life in the freedom of the faith through intellectual mastery of those problems by which modern man is perplexed.

Another new development of lay work has taken the form of 'Christian stewardship'. This idea originated in the American Churches; but it has quickly made itself at home in all the Churches. In this connection the Lutheran Churches have particularly developed the idea that all man's gifts and possessions are given to him by God alone; he cannot therefore dispose of them as he pleases, as though they were his own property; his relationship to them must be that of trusteeship. For this reason, in American Lutheranism the idea of stewardship is very closely linked to the obligation to bear witness; this finds expression in the contemporary slogan—'Testify or die; this is the great alternative which is set before the Churches today.' The reference here is to the activity of the lay people in the world outside the Church, in which the idea of stewardship has taken on a certain special character of its own.

Since the Second World War lay service through the associations of Protestant men and women has undergone great development. On the men's side, the basic principle has been the recognition of the three great areas of the farmers and peasants, the artisans, and the factory workers as specialized fields of service; in each the aim has been to bring these great classes into a new and living relationship with their Church. Correspondingly, Protestant work for women through women's organizations has occupied itself very intensively with the urgent questions of the present time—the problems of marriage, of motherhood, of the family and of education.

It must not be forgotten that there is another sphere in which the ministry of the laity can be exercised in the Church. It is not enough that the layman should take part in body and in spirit in the worship of the Church. He may be called to exercise that positive ministry which the Church recognizes alongside the regular ministry of its ordained servants. We refer to the task of giving religious instruction, and to the exercise of certain liturgical functions, such as are associated with the office of lector or catechist. The decisive importance of such lay ministries in times of crisis and distress can be clearly seen today in those areas in which the Church lives under such constraint that it cannot staff itself adequately with ordained ministers, or arrange for the work of the ministry to be carried on in regular and orderly fashion.

We have now reached the end of this rapid glance at various forms of lay ministry today; and must make an attempt to summarize the change that has taken place in the form of lay service in the Church, in its connection with the parallel changes in the understanding of the nature of the Church and of the service that the Church is called upon to render. The layman today has a certain definite understanding of his status and his task; here we become aware of the change that has taken place. But, on the other hand, basic to this development is the change that has taken place in the Church's own understanding of its nature and function.

V · A New Understanding of the Church

If we take a look at the activity of lay people in the Churches of the continent of Europe today, it is so many-sided that it is impossible to present it from a single point of view. We are concerned with a number of parallel developments, all centring in a changing understanding of the nature and function of the lay people, which began to take shape about the middle of the nineteenth century and has continued into the earlier decades of the twentieth.

One cardinal feature of this new understanding is that it has felt itself to be in radical opposition to the clergy, to those who are specifically charged with the ministry of the Church. From the clerical point of view, the laity is that body of people on which the clergy are to act —the whole activity of the clergy is directed towards this body. Apart from the clergy the laity have no special function of their own to fulfil in the Church.

The movement, of which we have used the French word 'laicism', grew up by reaction against this clerical point of view. Its aim was to free itself from the leading-strings and the tutelage of the clergy, and to order the world anew by making the fullest possible use of all those modern technical achievements through which the progress of civilization is secured. The Church, very one-sidedly, was regarded as hopelessly bound to an outworn view of the world, to superannuated patterns of society, and to reactionary ideas in politics. The domination of the Church must be broken. It is the task of the lay people, who have grown to a new maturity, in total independence of the Church to undertake the secularization of the world, especially in the fields of the schools and education, and of the separation of Church and State.

Contemporaneously also in the nineteenth century another view of the laity grew up which did recognize the opposition between the laity and the ordained leadership, but was not actuated by the same radical hostility towards the Church as the movement called 'laicism'. The layman here regards himself as the Christian who has attained inner freedom from the Church, whose business it is to bring to full fruition in every area of moral and social existence those tasks which the Church exists to perform. The layman brings to effect on weekdays what the

Church teaches on Sundays. The true Christian is not, then, the man who goes to church, but the man who proves his worth in the world of every day, and there perfectly shoulders his moral responsibilities. The worshipping company of Christians in church, and the Christians who take responsibility in the world of every day, are regarded as two separate bodies, which are not held together by any essential link.

A third understanding of the position of the layman, and one that is full of promise for the future, also begins to appear in the course of the nineteenth century. The basis of this is recognition of the fact that there is a service which the lay people are called to render to the world, but that this can be fulfilled only through the inspiration that comes from the life of fellowship in the Church. Out of this grows a revival of the 'diaconate' of the Church, its organization for the ministry of service, which corresponds to the changes that have taken place in the structure of the world. The task of the layman is to represent to the world in general the saving and serving love of God, and so to bring back to God the world that has become alienated from him. This leads on to a new understanding of the nature of the laity, which opens up to the laity again certain genuinely ecclesiastical functions in the service of the Church. And now the Church itself is seen in a new light, in relation to its mission to the world and with the world.

In the most recent period of all, this new understanding of the laity has led on to a third insight; here the shattering experiences of the Second World War, and the experiences of the younger Churches have made a decisive contribution. The insight in question is this—it is out of date to regard the ordained ministry of the Church and the lay people as two mutually exclusive bodies. The layman is to be regarded as being, in the full sense of the word, a member of the people of God, to the maintenance of which every ministry of the Church is directed, and without which no ministry can have any separate existence of its own. As such, the layman is the representative of the Church in the world. Ordained ministry and lay folk, Sunday and weekday, the Church assembled for worship and 'the Church after worship' stand to one another always and necessarily in the relationship of the two poles of an ellipse. At no time can the one exist without the other. The word 'Church' is to be understood as covering both; and the Church is present in the world inasmuch as the lay people make its presence a felt reality in every area of the life of man. This is the particular function of the layman, his share in the ministry of the Church. This lays upon the layman certain definite tasks; and in the carrying out of these he is called to co-operate with the ministry of the Church in the narrower sense of that term.

So here a further step has been taken in the layman's understanding of his position, in relation to the special tasks which he is called to fulfil as a member of the Church.

In certain areas those ideas of the nineteenth century which found their expression in 'laicism' are still in operation. The difference between the two centuries lies in the fact that today 'laicism' is balanced by a massive lay movement from the side of the Church. This movement does not set before itself as its goal a new ordering of the world in opposition to the Church, or in freedom from the Church in a supposed autonomy or independence. On the contrary, its understanding of its new task is this—the work of the laity in the world is directed towards making an effective reality in that world the presence of the Church, through which God's own struggle for the redemption of the world is going forward to its completion.

BIBLIOGRAPHY

Evangelisches Kirchen Lexikon II, 1024; *Lexikon für Theologie und Kirche*[2] VI, 733–42, 750–1; *Die Religion in Geschichte und Gegenwart*[3] IV, 203–6, 210.

G. Weill, *Histoire de l'idée laïque en France au XIXe siècle* (Paris, 1925; 2nd ed. 1929).

E. Maquin, *Laïcisme et laïcité* (1930).

J. R. Mott, *Liberating the Lay Forces of Christianity* (New York and London, 1932).

W. von Loewenich, *Der moderne Katholizismus* (1955), pp. 128 ff.

G. Rahner, 'Über das Laienapostolat', *Gesammelte Schriften zur Theologie* II (1955), pp. 339–78.

R. Reimond, *Evolution de la Notion de Laïcité* (1958), pp. 71 ff.

H. Kraemer, *A Theology of the Laity* (London, 1958).

Laici in Ecclesia, ed. Department on the Laity (World Council of Churches, 1961): an ecumenical bibliography.

E. Hegel, in *Staatslexikon*[6] V, 213–17.

Yves Congar, *Lay People in the Church—A Study for a Theology of the Laity* (London, 1957).

8

Stephen Neill

BRITAIN
1600–1780

I

IT has become a commonplace of historians that the Reformation was in large measure the layman's reformation. In a manner unknown since the early centuries the layman now came forward to take up responsibility in the life of the Church, to exercise his rights, and to find a field for service. This was as true in Britain as in other countries of the West; but the developments show at every point a certain sturdy British independence, and do not follow precisely the lines of any continental pattern.

From the time of the great Acts of Parliament in the 1530's, there could be no doubt that the English king could and did exercise immense influence and authority in the affairs of the English Church. But this is not in itself to be regarded as a reassertion of the rights of the laity. Henry VIII certainly did not regard himself as a layman; he was not a priest, and laid no claim to priestly office, but he was the Christian prince, holding directly from God a special office and authority, which he was to exercise in that single Christian community, which under one aspect was state or people, and under another aspect was Church. All the official documents of the English Church bear witness to this understanding of the situation.

The sixteenth century passed into the seventeenth. The English crown passed into the hands of a man who regarded himself as singularly well equipped to exercise his office in relation to the Church. James I was certainly the most learned monarch of his time, and took a real delight in learned discourse with other learned men—a fancy which is pleasantly represented in the pages of Scott's *Fortunes of Nigel*.

There is no trace of originality in his theological writings, and the king must be judged to have been a pedant rather than a scholar. But throughout his reign he was profoundly interested in the affairs of the Church, which he had taken as his Church, and on which to a considerable extent he relied for the support of his throne.

Charles I had not inherited any of his father's zeal for learning. He was a simple, godly, virtuous man, with a sincere affection for the Church and regard for its ordinances. The last act of his life was to listen to the morning service for the day, as he sat waiting to be led out to execution. Bishop Juxon had read as the lesson Matthew 27: the king thanked him for having read a passage so consoling at such a time, but the bishop explained that he had not chosen it specially; it stood in the lectionary for the day, 30th January 1649. Charles's misfortune was his shy remoteness from his people and from their thoughts and feelings, a somewhat petulant obstinacy that was unwilling to listen to advice when advice was most needed, and the conviction that it was not possible for the king to do wrong. It was this that led him to his doom and the Church to temporary disaster. But one of the acutest of modern historians, Bishop Mandell Creighton, always maintained that Anglicans were right in regarding the king as a martyr; if he had been willing to sell England to the Presbyterians, he might well have been able to make a bargain that would have saved his life; it was loyalty to the Church of England as he had known and revered it which made the disasters that had come on him irrevocable.

So close an association between the royal family and the Church was not to be known again for nearly eighty years. Charles II had other interests, and Dutch William was too much occupied with his continental projects ever to understand much of the life of the Church of which Providence had so strangely made him supreme governor. Queen Anne was a devoted churchwoman, but of limited intelligence. The true successor of Henry VIII and James I was Queen Caroline, the wife of George II (1663–1737). This amiable German princess had a deep interest in all things intellectual and religious. The correspondent of Leibniz, she believed that there was nothing the female intellect was incapable of grasping—it is not quite certain that all her correspondents shared her view. Her conversation parties were famous; and among those who enjoyed or endured them were the best theological minds of that not very creative age. Her husband was quite prepared to leave to her the management of affairs in which he was not much interested, and for a number of years a woman was the bishop-maker of England.

It must be said that she used her opportunities well and wisely; most of the bishops of the day who were eminent for learning owed a good deal to her; to mention none other, it was in response to her dying request that George II raised to the episcopate the greatest of Anglican thinkers, Joseph Butler.[1]

It was part of the wisdom of Henry VIII that he saw to it that all his reforming designs were passed through Parliament; and what Parliament has once decided, only Parliament can alter. To most men in the England of the sixteenth century this seemed eminently reasonable; in a matter of such moment to the whole life of the kingdom, it was good that the Great Assembly of the nation should have something to say. Hooker was no doubt expressing the general opinion when he wrote:

> The Parliament of England, together with the Convocation annexed thereunto, is that whereupon the very essence of all government within this kingdom doth depend; it is even the body of the whole realm; it consisteth of the king, and of all that within the land are subject unto him: for they are all there present, either in person or by such as they voluntarily have derived their very personal right unto. The Parliament is a court not so merely temporal as if it might meddle with nothing but leather and wool. When all which the wisdom of all sorts can do is done for the devising of laws in the Church, it is the general consent of all that giveth them the form and vigour of laws.[2]

Hooker held the view that the Convocation of the clergy should take the initiative in making laws for the Church; but it seemed to him most undesirable that this law-making should be regarded as a function of the clergy alone:

> Till it be proved that some special law of Christ hath for ever annexed to the clergy alone the power to make ecclesiastical laws, we are to hold it a thing most consonant with equity that no ecclesiastical law be made in a Christian commonwealth without consent as well of the laity as of the clergy, but least of all without consent of the highest power.

The British Parliament today is a highly miscellaneous collection of citizens. It has included Christians of a great variety of confessions, Jews, atheists, communists, a Parsi and so forth—hardly a suitable body to decide on matters of intricate theology or liturgical decorum. In the seventeenth century none of these absurdities existed. All members of Parliament were members of the national Church, though some of them were very ill-satisfied with that Church as it then was, and thought that they knew exactly how it should be further reformed.

G

Indeed one of the major troubles of the reign of Queen Elizabeth was that both the Queen and the Puritan members of her faithful Commons were sure that they knew exactly the will of God for England—but they knew it in strangely diverse ways. What is plain in the seventeenth no less than in the sixteenth century is that the members of Parliament took with extreme seriousness their position as Christian legislators, as indeed they did until after the middle of the nineteenth century. One of the most remarkable manifestations of this spirit were the corporate communions for members of Parliament held a number of times in the first half of the seventeenth century, with the clear understanding that every member without fail would be present to pray for the heavenly wisdom without which even the secular affairs of men cannot be well ordered.

The first of the solemn Communions of the House of Commons was held on Palm Sunday 1614 in the historic church of St Margaret close to Westminster Abbey (the Abbey was thought to be dangerously high church, and the proposal to hold the service there was later modified in favour of the parish church). Seven years later, a similar proposal was made by Sir James Perrott, member for Haverfordwest in Wales:

> *Sir James Perrott* moveth for a Communion of all the Members of the House—Out of many parts of the Kingdom—A Means of Reconciliation, and so of Concord in Counsel of those who dwell near; and of those more remote, to know their Religion.—This is touchstone to try their faith. *A Jove Principium*, according to His Majesty's late speech in Star Chamber —A Blessing by it upon all other consultations.—All then to take it.[3]

There is no need to doubt the sincerity of the members of the House, as they fulfilled their duty and trooped into St Margaret's Church that chilly February morning, where Dr Ussher, later to be Archbishop of Armagh and a great ecumenist of his day, kept them until well after lunch-time with 'a long and drie sermon'. But ere long it became apparent that the dragooning of members into attendance, and the use of the most sacred mysteries of the Church as a kind of added test of loyalty, could in some circumstances come nearer to profanation than to reverence; and, though attendance at worship on solemn occasions has always been one of the privileges of membership of the House, in later times that service has rarely, if ever, taken the form of the Holy Communion.

These grave legislators no doubt regarded themselves as the de-fenders of the Church; as good a case could be made out for regarding them as its destroyers. For the basic fact about this seventeenth-century Church was that it was very poor. Henry VIII, with his dissolution of the monasteries, had taught the lay lords to poke greedy fingers into the treasures of the Church. The lesson had not been lost upon his thrifty and at times parsimonious daughter. Elizabeth is not to be too severely blamed; she had limited resources of her own, the government simply had to be carried on, and the temptation to drive hard bargains with the Church and so progressively to relieve it of its supposedly super-fluous wealth could hardly be resisted. Where the Queen so boldly entered it was hardly to be expected that courtiers would bashfully hold back. Laymen managed by one means and another to acquire a great proportion of the resources on which the Church depended for the maintenance of its life. 'Impropriations' were the favourite method; the layman acquired possession of the income of a benefice; by far the greater share he retained for himself, to help him to carry out his no doubt extremely important functions; he paid a pittance to some priest to keep going the necessary ecclesiastical functions in the parish of which the layman was in fact the legal owner.

Having gained this stranglehold on the life of the Church, the laymen proceeded to aim at the impossible. They demanded an educated and preaching ministry, having in the meantime reduced the income of the clergy so low that it was almost impossible to expect any educated and promising man to enter so base and servile a career. For the subser-vience expected of the clergy by their lay masters was indeed pitiful. The matter was put convincingly by the generally temperate Chilling-worth:

> Consider in what a miserable state the Church must be . . . when those to whom you have committed your souls in trust . . . shall through want and penury be rendered so heartless and low-spirited that for fear of your anger, and danger of starving, they shall not dare to interrupt and hinder you, when you run headlong in the paths that lead you to destruc-tion; when, out of faintheartedness, they shall not dare to take notice, no, not of the most scandalous sins of their patrons; but, which is worst, be the most forward officious parasites to soothe them in their crimes.[4]

Having so far depressed the status of the ordinary parochial clergy, some of the godly laymen who were inclined to the Puritan outlook endeavoured to redress the balance by establishing lectureships in a number of parishes, or alternatively to acquire the impropriations and to use them for the appointment of ministers of their own persuasion. One of the most notable of such endeavours was carried out for a number of years by the body known as the Feoffees for Impropriations. But it did not at all suit the Crown and the authorities that laymen of this stamp should be enabled in this way to secure the control of an increasing number of pulpits for the dissemination of their own not very popular views and doctrines. The Feoffees were brought before the Exchequer Court and suppressed; as the judge pertinently remarked, the danger was that they would draw to themselves 'the principal dependence of the clergy . . . in such measure and on such conditions as they should fancy, thereby introducing many novelties of dangerous consequence, both in Church and in commonwealth'.

Archbishop Laud was shrewd enough to see that, without economic independence, the Church could not play the role which he believed that it ought to play in the life of the nation. One method of restoring this independence would have been to recover the impropriations; but the time had passed when this would be possible. Even that sound churchman Edward Hyde, later Lord Clarendon, recognized that good principle cannot always be put into effect:

> He must depart too much from his natural understanding who believes it probable that all that hath been taken from the Church in previous ages will be restored to it in this or those which shall succeed, to the ruin of those many thousand families which enjoy the alienations, though they do not think it was with justice and piety aliened.

If it was not possible to restore the economic position of the clergy, another method favoured by Laud for the restoration of their credit was that of appointing them as justices of the peace, where they would sit on an equality with their more aristocratic and well-lined neighbours. But this had the contrary effect to what was intended:

> The inferior clergy took more upon them than they had used to do, and did not live towards their neighbours of quality or their patrons themselves, with that civility and condescension they had used to do; which disposed them likewise to withdrawing their good countenance and good neighbourhood from them.

Once again Clarendon is our authority. The attempt to bring the Church back into independence of the laymen had failed; by reaction everything was swept away in the torrent of the revolutionary era.

It is true that the Church was restored with the coming again of Charles II in 1661; but what was restored was not the Church as it had been. Lay control in many ways became absolute. Elizabeth had worked on the principle that she had two systems of government to work with,

the civil in Parliament, and the clerical in the Convocations; the right
of Parliament to interfere in matters of religion was strictly controlled
by the royal prerogative. But from 1661 the Convocations came to
count for less and less, and finally ceased to meet; they were in abeyance
from 1717 to 1851. The Church courts lost ground at every point
before the civil courts of the land. Convention was observed, in that the
revised Prayer Book of 1661 was sent up from the Church to Parliament; but it is from the Act of Uniformity passed by Parliament in that
year that the Prayer Book receives its authority, and without the
authority of Parliament no change can be made in it, as was demonstrated with crushing clarity in 1927 and 1928, when the House of
Commons twice rejected a Prayer Book which had received at least a
large measure of approval of the Church.

The position had come to be exactly that which Lord Hardwick, in
a legal judgment put forth in 1731, clearly and uncompromisingly
declared it to be:

> The constant uniform practice ever since the Reformation . . . has been
> that when any material ordinances or regulations have been made to bind
> the laity as well as clergy in matters ecclesiastical, they have been either
> enacted or confirmed by Parliament; of this proposition the several Acts
> of Uniformity are so many proofs, for by these the whole doctrine and
> worship, the very rites and ceremonies of the church and literal form of
> public prayers are prescribed and established.

The Church of England, though happily not any other part of the
Anglican Communion, is a Church that has fallen completely under lay
control. The control is not generally very exactly or tyrannously exercised; but this does not alter the fact; the victory of the laymen in the
seventeenth century was almost complete, and the consequences of it
endure till the present time.

II

If we turn from legislators to more ordinary men, nothing in that
most religious age is more remarkable than the zeal for theological study
and serious religious thought manifested by outstanding men of every
party and of none. Space permits the mention of five only, out of a
much larger number who could be cited.

The capacious mind of Mr Secretary Milton (1608–74) had room
for almost every kind of human knowledge; his organ tongue for noble
and sapient utterance on many things. But he was never more at home

than when debating with himself and attempting to probe the deepest mysteries of God's ordering of the world. This is evident not only from *Paradise Lost*, with its expressed intent to justify the ways of God to man; Milton was the author also of a prose exposition of the Christian faith,[5] in which the independence of his thinking led him into judgments and opinions which would not have won him the favour of the orthodoxy of his own, or indeed of any other, age.

English literature would be much poorer without Sir Thomas Browne (1605–82), most lovable and godly of physicians, the splendour of whose eloquence at its best falls little if at all short of Milton's own. Browne has been admirably and sympathetically characterized by another lay theologian of a later date, Professor Basil Willey:

> Perhaps no writer is more truly representative of the double-faced age in which he lived, an age half-scientific and half-magical, half-sceptical and half-credulous, looking back in one direction to Mandeville, and forward to Newton. At one moment a Baconian experimentalist and herald of the new world, at another Browne is discoursing of cockatrices and unicorns and mermaids in a tone which implies that though part of him is incredulous, the world is still incalculable enough to contain such marvels. . . . An essay by a provincial doctor on cinerary urns—which today would be a dull paper read to a local archaeological society—could also be in De Quincey's words, an impassioned requiem breathing from the pomps of earth and from the sanctities of the grave.[6]

This is finely and well said. Browne, too, might not squeeze through every needle's eye of orthodoxy; yet this is a humble and godly man who speaks to us, and one who has knowledge both of time and eternity:

> We whose generations are ordained in this setting part of time, are providentially taken off from such imaginations; and being necessitated to eye the remaining particle of futurity, are naturally constituted unto thoughts of the next world, and cannot excusably decline the consideration of that duration, which makes pyramids pillars of snow and all that's past a moment.

Few characters of that troubled time are more attractive than Lucius Cary, Viscount Falkland (1610–49); we have the great good fortune to have detailed accounts of him from the pen of Clarendon who had known and loved him. Falkland was of that moderate party which began by opposing the king, but ended by taking his side against what seemed to them the floods of thoughtless disorder. According to Clarendon, Falkland had diligently studied the controversies and exactly read all, or the choicest, of the Greek and Latin Fathers, and had a memory so stupendous that he remembered, on all occasions, whatsoever he read. But he was of so charitable a disposition that, in disputations with those of other than the Anglican form of the Christian faith, he would never permit anything of temper or bitterness to intrude. His prodigious parts of learning and knowledge, his inimitable sweetness and delight in conversation, his flowing and obliging humanity and goodness to mankind, and his primitive simplicity and integrity of life, made him dearly beloved by a large circle of friends. His early death at the battle of Newbury in 1643 was a sad loss to the kingdom and the Church.

In John Evelyn (1620–1706) we meet a lay Christian of yet another type—learned without brilliance, pious without excess, thoughtful, dignified and courteous. Evelyn was much what every educated Englishman imagines himself to be, or wishes that he could be. We know him well from his diary, a book valued for many reasons, not least because it gives us a picture of an Anglican living steadfastly and hopefully through the dark days of the Commonwealth, when his religion was proscribed and the way of worship to which he was accustomed was forbidden. Evelyn helps us to understand why Anglicanism has proved so persistent a form of the Christian faith. This Church too has its lovers; and those who love it are often of the type of John Evelyn.

Of the sublime genius of Isaac Newton (1642–1777) many have written in sundry places and diverse manners. The late Lord Keynes left on record his opinion that Newton had in a higher degree than any other man of whom we have record the faculty of long and concentrated thought on a particular problem. But it is evident from Newton's writings, in many passages, that this calm and lucid intellect was possessed not only by scientific integrity but also by a simple and earnest religious faith. It is now known that Newton held Socinian views, and being an honest man could not bring himself to accept ordination in the Church of England, the usual condition in those days for the holding of an academic post at Cambridge.[7] Yet for all his unorthodoxy, Newton was an intense and ardent student of the Holy Scriptures, and in his later years spent much time in speculations on the books of Daniel and Revelation, of a kind that would not earn him high marks in a modern theological examination. This point was not lost on Voltaire, who commented somewhat acidly on the decay of a great intellect that results from too close a preoccupation with religion.

III

So far we have spoken generally of laymen as laymen. Now it is time to consider the part played by laymen in the life and organization of the various Churches.

We may start with the Presbyterians, who in the early years of the civil war made a vigorous and nearly successful bid to secure control of the national Church of England, and to fashion it nearer to the heart's desire. What the sunnier clime of England looked on coldly the *ingenium perfervidum Scotorum* welcomed with alacrity; and the historian is left debating which is the more marvellous phenomenon— that Presbyterianism should have so little hold in England, or that Episcopalianism should have so little hold in Scotland.

Mr Calvin held that, of the various offices noted in the New Testament as belonging to the Church, those which were of more than local relevance were not intended to endure beyond the earliest age of the Church:

> According to this interpretation, which appears to me consonant both to the words and the meaning of Paul, those three functions [*sc*. apostles, prophets and evangelists] were not instituted in the Church to be perpetual, but only to endure so long as Churches were to be formed where none previously existed. . . . The office I nevertheless call extraordinary, because it has no place in churches duly constituted.

For this view Calvin adduced nothing that could be called evidence; but naturally, in Churches where his word is accepted as only on a slightly lower level of inspiration than that of the Scriptures themselves, his view has been accepted, and no place found for full-time ministries other than the local ministry of pastors and teachers. Whereas Lutherans have generally held that no particular form of the ministry and the order of the Church is to be found revealed in the Scriptures, all these things being of human choice and order rather than of divine inspiration, Calvinists have generally held that everything necessary to the order of the Church has been revealed in Scripture and is therefore unalterable. There is a scriptural pattern of the Church, and this is at all times to be followed. When the good Calvinist read the Scriptures, not unnaturally the pattern of the Church which he found there was neither the episcopal nor the congregational.

In his presbyterian pattern, Calvin did make a place for the layman, which was of the greatest significance for the future. Of the various ministries other than those of the word and sacraments of which traces are to be found in the apostolic writings, two which Calvin selected as having permanent validity were that called by St Paul 'government' (I Cor. 12.28), and the care of the poor:

> By these governors I understand seniors selected from the people to unite with the bishops in pronouncing censures and exercising discipline. . . . From the beginning therefore each church had its senate, composed of pious, grave and venerable men, in whom was lodged the power of correcting faults. . . . Moreover experience shows that this arrangement was not confined to one age, and therefore we are to regard the office of government as necessary for all ages.

Under the system approved by Calvin, therefore, in every parish the pastor was to be assisted by a group of ruling elders, responsible with him for the discipline of the Church. The exact status of the ruling elder is a little difficult to define. For he is ordained to his office; and it might therefore be thought doubtful whether he should find a place in a book on the laity. On the other hand, he is not ordained to the ministry of the word and sacraments; he is not dependent on the Church for his living and has another secular calling in which the greater part of his time is spent. He may perhaps be rightly regarded as a layman set apart for certain special functions within the Church. It is perhaps not stretching a point very far to include him in this survey. In Scotland, where the Calvinistic system came to be adopted in its fulness, the laity, through the elders, had a place on every level of the Church's administration, up to the General Assembly itself. This produced an interest in the affairs of the Church, a sense of responsibility and participation in great decisions, such as have rarely been equalled under other systems of church government. The layman is not merely a hearer of the word; he can aspire to exercise his influence on the whole life of the Church, in his own parish and beyond it.

It was not a church historian but a secular historian, Dr G. M. Trevelyan, who has paid the most glowing tribute to the effects on Scottish life and character of the Shorter Catechism, and of the kind of church life of which it was the expression. With minds disciplined and sharpened by the Scriptures and the interpretation of them in sermon and catechism, with what at the time was probably the best system of national education in the world, with an austere uprightness of character nurtured by an earnest though somewhat narrow understanding of the Bible, with the regular practice of family devotion in which the head of the family played his part as priest and minister of the word, Scotland produced generation after generation of lay folk well instructed, zealous and occasionally fanatical. The rapidly growing prosperity of the country was in part due to the fact that the banks could make loans without demanding security; the austere integrity of the Lowland farmer was itself the security that the loan would be repaid.

A different development, but one equally momentous, was to be found among the sectaries or separatists. While the Presbyterians on the whole had been prepared in the matter of the reformation of the Church to 'tarry for the magistrate', the extremer wing of the Puritans demanded reformation 'without tarrying for anie'. In this extremer wing, a clear concept of the gathered Church prevailed. 'The true planted and rightly gathered Church of Christ is a company of faithful people, separated from the heathens and unbelievers of the land, gathered in the name of Christ.' In this fellowship none is above and none is below, but all are equal in the sight of God and of Christ. All true believers were to be held 'ecclesiastical and spiritual', and we 'know not what you mean by your old popish term of laymen'.

At no point was this sense of Christian equality more notably displayed than in the choice and ordering of the pastor or preaching elder. There was no distinction of order between preacher and people, but only one of function. The choice of the pastor was to be

> by the holy and free election of the Lord's free and holy people; and that according to the Lord's ordinance humbling themselves by fasting and prayer before the Lord, craving the direction of his Holy Spirit for the trial and approving of their gifts.

Ordination was to be by the laying on of hands, but this was to be understood as the laying on of the hands of the congregation, and not necessarily of those who were already ministers: 'thus hath everyone of the people interest in the election and ordination of their officers.' This ordination was specifically to the care of one congregation, and ordination signified the pastoral relationship between that congregation and that pastor. If a pastor moved from one area to another, the ordination would naturally be repeated, before he undertook the charge of another Christian fellowship. This strict independent rule was not, however, very long continued, and before long it became a common practice to invite ordained preachers from other congregations to conduct the ordination of a newly elected pastor.

Here the laity had come fully into their rights; for they were a holy people and a royal priesthood; and responsibility for all the affairs of Independent Churches, both spiritual and temporal, was shared by people and pastor. This was a true and good understanding of the great principle of the priesthood of all believers. This phrase has constantly been used as the excuse for secularizing the concept of the Church by denying the existence within it of any kind of priesthood at all. In these small Independent groups, the purpose, often to a great extent realized, was to glorify the Church by making it holy in every part, and by recognizing that the gift of the Holy Spirit would be given to the least as well as to the greatest in the membership. In every church meeting, all felt that they had come together under the guidance of the Holy Spirit to transact business of great moment in the life of the Church. The word of the Holy Spirit might be given to any one among the members; and then it was the duty of all to listen with reverence and to accept what was authenticated as the Spirit's word.

The development of this Independent polity had consequences which were perhaps even more important for the life of the state than for that of the Church. It was not a very long step to ask whether the equality which was recognized in the assembly of the faithful ought not in some way to be recognized also in the common life of men. Independency in Christian conviction tended to be allied to radical views in politics. It is perhaps in this direction that the Independents made the greatest contribution of all to the history of the world. There are those who trace to these at the time insignificant people the beginnings of genuinely democratic thinking in England. If this view can be maintained, it may explain why in Britain, in contrast to France and in part to America, democracy has always been so closely linked to a Christian understanding of men and the state. When men were convinced that the believer, however simple and ignorant, was capable of taking responsibility for the gravest decisions affecting the Church and congregation, it was perhaps not difficult to suppose that in another setting the same man might be capable of exercising a judgment in those great matters that concern the state. Colonel Rainsborough was not alone in recalling that the poorest he in England hath a life to live no less than the richest he; and that perhaps he would be well occupied in taking some responsibility for the kind of society in which he was to lead that life.

One of the excellences of the Independents was that they were genuinely independent, and none of them can be taken as in every way typical of what was a rather ill-defined and nebulous movement. But for many purposes a study of the career of John Lilburne (1614–57) will prove highly rewarding. Lilburne was a man born for trouble as the sparks fly upward. A Puritan, he knew nothing of the gloom that is usually associated with the term. The historian of the civil war tells us that his clothes were gay and sparkish, as far as his narrow means allowed. He was possessed of a ready wit; under the Commonwealth, when bear-baiting and other such sports were forbidden, the London populace took something of the same pleasure in following the controversies of Lilburne with his foes as they had formerly enjoyed in these rougher sports. But, in more serious vein, the historian remarks that, 'if he was a demagogue, he was also a saint.'[8]

Lilburne was filled with a passion for freedom and righteousness. He had first been a protester in the dark days of Laud, and in 1638 by order of the Star Chamber had been whipped from the Fleet to Westminster. Later he turned from religion to politics, though he would have been the first to deny that this involved any turning, and came out on behalf of freedom for the ordinary man, for more democratic government of the city of London, and for greater honesty in commercial affairs. *England's Birthright* appeared in 1645. This was followed in 1646 by *The Just Man's Justification* and *The Freeman's Freedom Vindicated*; the latter, published when he was already in Newgate in trouble for the former, was a violent attack on the House of Lords as the oppressors of the common people. When summoned before the Lords, Lilburne kept his hat on his head, refused to kneel, stopped his ears against his accusers, and then retaliated with a loud and denunciatory speech. It is not surprising that the Lords committed him to the Tower for seven years, fined him two thousand pounds, and ordered that he was to be kept *incommunicado*, an order which naturally was not obeyed.

And their lordships had failed to reckon with the more ruthless sex. Lilburne's wife was worthy of her husband. She accused the Lords of putting man and wife asunder, an action directly contrary to the law of God which they claimed to be maintaining. They were not prepared to go so far as to let Mr Lilburne out; they did relent so far as to let Mrs Lilburne in, whenever she wished to see her husband.[9]

Lilburne is a joy to us, as he was to his contemporaries, or rather to some of them. But it would be a grave mistake to regard him as a mountebank. He was sometimes muddle-headed and always passionate; but he was a man of deep and sincere Christian conviction, who through that conviction had been led to see clearly many things that others were not to see for many years after his death. He was a true confessor in the cause both of Christian and of secular liberty.

It must not be supposed that in the established Church, more hierarchically disposed than the others, there was no lay participation or activity. In fact there was a great deal.

There was first the strange Anglican mystery of patronage, some aspects of which we have already considered earlier in this chapter. This relic of the Middle Ages and the *Eigenkirche*, when the local landlord built the church, appointed the priest and supplied the land on which he was to live, survives to the present day. Owing to the accident that in England the advowson, the right to present a priest to a 'living', is a legal form of property that can change hands, the patron of a parish may be almost anyone—the Crown, a distant college in Oxford or Cambridge, the rector of a neighbouring parish, the local squire or squiress; Roman Catholics are not excluded, though they cannot under the law of the land exercise the right of appointment. This means that a large number of laymen had a considerable and immediate interest in the affairs of the Church. With the rise in the value of property and in the esteem of the country clergy in the eighteenth century, it became quite a common thing for the younger sons of good family to 'enter the Church' in the expectation of later holding the family living. Edmund Bertram of *Mansfield Park*, the perfect type of the clerical younger son, belongs to a period slightly later than that of this chapter; but Miss Austen lived in a conservative world, and reflects many of the usages of an earlier time. Probably not all country squires were as zealous in the care of their neighbours, and as well up in theology, or at least in sermons, as Sir Roger de Coverley; but here again is the perfect type of the upright, hearty, sincere Anglican layman, concerned as much for the welfare of the Church as for the protection of foxes in his neighbourhood.

Nor must it be forgotten that in those days the ecclesiastical parish was also the unit of local administration, a situation which has been so much altered by the developments in local self-government in the nineteenth century that it is very difficult for us to think ourselves back into it. The vestry was a body of no small importance. The churchwardens had many duties to attend to, and one of them at least was ordinarily chosen by the votes of the freemen of the parish. The parish clerk had statutory rights as well as duties. And even the parish constable should not be forgotten; perhaps Master Dogberry was not the most estimable of men; but he had his place in a society in which the distinction between 'church' and 'society' was far less clearly drawn than it is today. In those days at least seventy per cent of the population lived in small villages, where everyone knew everyone else; a very considerable proportion of the population must have been in some way engaged in the service of the Church, which does not of course mean that everyone of those so engaged was a devoted and sincere Christian.

On the whole this system of the establishment and of the close association of Church and State seems to have suited Englishmen well. Edmund Burke may not have been far from the mark when towards the end of the eighteenth century, in his *Reflections on the Revolution* in France, he defines the attitude of the ordinary Englishman to his Church in the following terms:

> The majority of the people of England, far from thinking a religious national establishment unlawful, hardly think it lawful to be without one. . . . This principle runs through the whole system of their polity. They do not consider their Church Establishment as convenient, but as essential to their State. Not as a thing heterogeneous and separable— something added for an accommodation—what they may either keep or lay aside according to their temporary ideas of convenience. They consider it as the foundation of their whole constitution, with which, and with every part of which it holds an indissoluble union. Church and State are ideas inseparable in their minds, and scarcely is the one ever mentioned without mentioning the other.

But not all were quite so enthusiastic as Mr Burke; and, though the eighteenth-century Church has been somewhat rescued from the dark shades into which it had been cast by the unfavourable judgment of later ages, there were many who did not find it attractive, and who were driven in their search for vital religion to find a home outside it. The greatest religious movement of the eighteenth century in England was undoubtedly the Methodist movement. In this, as in most great movements, there was an element of paradox. Methodism was in principle a highly clerical movement. It was founded by two good Anglican high churchmen, and the constitution with which John Wesley left it allowed hardly any place at all for the energies of laymen in the direction of the movement's policy and the settlement of its affairs. It was the opinion of many, during the reign of the Reverend Jabez Bunting (1779–1858), that Rome was not the only city which had its Vatican and its Pope. Nevertheless by force of circumstances Wesley was led to become the creator of one of the greatest organizations for the employment of the lay forces of the Church that has ever existed. Opinions

will differ to the end of time as to whether he was well advised in the
various steps which he took to supply his societies with ordained
ministers. There can hardly be anything but approval for the planned
use of laymen in the service of the cause. The lay preacher was given
the fullest opportunity to exercise such gifts of prophecy as he might
possess. And he was expected to qualify himself, not only by enthusiasm
but also by long-continued and serious study for the exercise of his
calling. Perhaps the Methodist local preacher or circuit rider was seen
in his full glory and heroism on the far side of the Atlantic. But to this
day he has continued to serve, and not rarely to make the Anglican lay
reader look like a pale imitation. Even more important, perhaps, because of the numbers involved, was the development of the class
meeting. To be a good Methodist class leader demands knowledge,
tact, humility and deep spiritual insight. It is not to be supposed that
all class leaders at all times have displayed all these gifts; the astonishing
thing is that so many have displayed so many of them for so much of
the time. Here was a calling of the layman into responsible activity in
the Church on a scale that had hardly ever been before. It has rightly
been said that, when the class meeting flourishes, Methodism flourishes
with it; when the class meeting declines, Methodism is on the wane.

With all the excellence of this organization, and the service that it
rendered to true religion, it must not be forgotten that this service was
rendered within the walls of Zion, and that both local preacher and class
leader were in danger of becoming ecclesiastical laymen of the kind in
whom this survey is not specially interested. It is time to turn to the
Christian layman in the world and in society.

IV

The Evangelical movement has always to a large extent been a layman's movement, and laymen have always been among its most notable
figures. Wesley started with the poor; it was not long before he had
supporters in a very different class of society.

A place all alone must be found for the divine Selína, Countess of
Huntingdon (1707–91), of whom Macaulay so truly remarked that, if
she had been a Roman Catholic, she would certainly by now have been
canonized and remembered as the foundress of some great religious
order. But saints are not always easy people to live with, and some of
her friends and admirers at times found the Countess a little difficult.
Living at a time when lords were lords and ladies were ladies, she found

it difficult to realize that she could not have her way in everything. It seemed to her natural to use some of her great wealth to build chapels and to appoint to minister in them clergymen of whose sound evangelical principles she was convinced. It was less obvious to her that, if these chapels were supposed to be in some way connected with the Church of the land, some respect must be paid in them to the order of that Church and its established ways. Not perhaps quite understanding all that was involved, Selina wrote sadly, 'I am to be cast out of the Church now, only for what I have been doing these forty years—speaking and living for Jesus Christ.' It is easy to see at this lapse of time that there was on one side some unnecessary stiffness in the interpretation of the law, and on the other some failure to regard the rights of the law, as law, to be obeyed. But it is sad that in the end it came to a separation; against her will the Countess found herself a dissenter, the foundress of the small group which still exists under the name 'the Countess of Huntingdon's Connection'.

Sad, because of the real value of the work that Selina had done. That was an age in which, in the delightful words of the biographer of Wilberforce, the spreading of the gospel among the higher classes of the nation 'was a work which could be hardly committed to the hands of any ecclesiastic; while it required for its proper execution the full devotion of rank, influence, and talents of the highest order'. The Countess certainly drew to the hearing of the gospel many in the very highest ranks of society, including it is alleged even some of the bishops. Not that all of them enjoyed what they heard. It was after one of Whitefield's sermons that the Duchess of Buckingham penned her famous outburst, that 'it is monstrous to be told that you have a heart as sinful as the common wretches that crawl on the earth' and that she was amazed that Lady Huntingdon could 'relish sentiments so much at variance with high rank and good breeding'. Even more violent, apparently, were the reactions of Lady Suffolk to a sermon which she believed to have been preached directly for her benefit.

Another man of high rank whose name constantly appears in the Christian records of the eighteenth century is the second Earl of Dartmouth (1731–1801), who appears to have undergone conversion in 1756. It was of this nobleman that the Christian poet William Cowper, another notable lay witness of this period, wrote that 'he wears a coronet and prays'. Dartmouth held a number of important posts in the government, including the Secretaryship for American affairs, and also that of steward to the royal household. Much less flamboyant than

Selina, he used his wealth unobtrusively in the service of countless good causes; and, in a time when it was difficult for a clergyman of pronounced Evangelical views to obtain any kind of preferment, he helped a number of ordained men to suitable cures, and a number of candidates for the ministry to find bishops who would ordain them. The most illustrious of those whom he helped was probably John Newton, the ex-slaver and writer of many hymns. His name is suitably commemorated in the famous college in New Hampshire, which, in spite of some disagreements before and after the year 1776, still bears his name.

Most of the service rendered by these lay men and women was rendered in the Church or on its fringes. It could not be otherwise at a time when Church and nation were practically synonymous. There could be no witness outside the Church, unless this found expression in an interest in foreign missions, at a time when everyone in the country stood in some relationship to the Church and was well aware of that relationship. And, till the middle of the eighteenth century, this was the situation in England. The Church might and did gravely neglect its duties. Many folk might be lax in the performance of their duties and the observance of the Christian law. But to mention only one point at which the Church touched the lives of most people in the country, at that time and for long afterwards, there was no way of getting married except by a priest of the Church of England. Even Roman Catholics could not withdraw themselves from this requirement, though no doubt they repaired later to their own church for a second ceremony. It was taken for granted that every child would be baptized, except of course those born in the restricted circles of the Jews.

But this idyllic situation was changing. The industrial revolution was on its way, bringing with it a rapid increase in population and a shift of the population from the country to the town, with resultant dislocation of the old ways of society, and new kinds of misery and degradation. For the first time for a thousand years the hold of the Church on the nation began to weaken, and the signs of the post-Christian period, now so familiar to us, were beginning to appear. The Church was still organized on medieval lines. It was a Church of village-dwellers, or of town-dwellers who were never very far, except in London, from the village background. It paid dear for the support of the state in the crippling limitations which made it legally impossible for the Church to reorganize itself to meet the new day, limitations some of which still remain, and which were hardly touched until Bishop Blomfield's 'ungovernable passion for business' got to work on them when a third of the nineteenth century had already passed.

This meant that something like a proletariat was growing up in Britain. There were whole areas where the voice of the Church was not heard; it was only in the nineteenth century that the Methodist movement, and that almost exclusively in its 'Primitive' form, for a time presented itself as the proletarian Church. There were whole classes of people in dire need of help for whom the Church, if by that is meant the ordained clergy and the Church in its existing organization, was wholly unable to do all that was needed. It is at this point of history that we meet memorably and notably the Christian layman who was driven by the compassion of Christ to work outside the Church in the unchurched world, to bring the Church and the gospel back to the areas from which they had been excluded.

It was providential that the Evangelical revival had broken on England just at the time when the need was beginning to grow serious. Piety, indeed, was not limited to any one class, and Christian generosity knows no limits of party or tradition. But Evangelicalism gave to those who had come under its influence a clearly and consciously held, though sometimes rather narrow, Christian faith, a profound seriousness and sense of responsibility, dynamic vigour in action, and a certain freedom from convention, which made them willing to walk in new paths undeterred by criticism and opposition. Three examples may serve to make clear the nature of the new kind of service which Christian laymen were beginning to render.

Robert Raikes (1735–1811), a wealthy Evangelical layman of Gloucester, became unawares the father of the Sunday School movement. As soon as children were able to work at all, they were sent to work long hours every day through the week, and then left with nothing whatever to do on Sundays. In their rags they would hardly have been welcome in the Churches. Naturally they had no other occupation than to get into mischief. The Evangelical leader William Romaine wrote in 1784 that

> the Lord's day has hitherto been prostituted to bad purposes. Farmers and other inhabitants of the towns and villages complain that they receive more injury in their property on the Sabbath than all the week besides; this in a great measure proceeds from the lawless state of the younger class who are allowed to run wild on that day freed from all restraint.

With the simplicity of genius, Raikes with the help of his parish priest set to work to provide some better employment for these neglected children. Four respectable women were hired to serve as teachers, and as a start ninety children were collected to study under them. It is to be noted that these schools were not Sunday schools in the later sense of the term, schools given up wholly to religious instruction. They were to provide for the children the elementary education which was denied them on the other days of the week. School was on Sunday morning from 10 o'clock till noon, then again from 1 p.m. till the hour of Evensong, to which the children were conducted by their teachers. But this was not yet the end of their day—they returned once again to school to learn the church catechism by heart, a task which continued until 5.30, when they were at length sent home.

A pleasant picture of the work of the schools comes from the pen of Raikes himself in 1794:

> Twenty is the number allotted to each teacher, the sexes being kept separate. The twenty are divided into four classes. The children who show any superiority in attainments are placed as leaders of the several classes, and are employed in teaching the others their letters, or in hearing them read in a low whisper. . . . Their attending the service of the Church once a day has seemed to me sufficient; for their time may be spent more profitably, perhaps, in receiving instruction than in being present at a long discourse, which their minds are not yet able to comprehend; but people may think differently on this matter.[10]

One point of great importance must be noted in passing. So great a work could not be the sole concern of a single man; it was inevitable that before long a society should be formed to aid and augment the work, and the Sunday School Society (1786) was one of the first of those voluntary societies which were the most characteristic feature of Christian life in England in the nineteenth century.

The second character in our gallery of servants must be Hannah More. This remarkable woman (1745–1833) had moved in the highest society in London, and had been widely recognized as a blue-stocking. Her book, *Thoughts on the Importance of the Manners of the Great*, published anonymously in 1788, had an enormous vogue. Gradually her way of life became more serious and more deeply Christian; and, in search of a quieter life, she built a house at Cowslip Green in Somersetshire, not far from Bristol. Here her attention was drawn to the terrible moral and spiritual destitution of the people. With the help of her sister she started a number of schools, set up clubs for women, introduced such useful arts as spinning for the women, taught the gospel to young and old alike, and produced something like a social and cultural revolution in one of the most backward parts of England.

Such charitable work would today be harshly criticized as paternalistic. It is quite true that Hannah More was a wealthy and influential woman. She did not foresee the revolutions that were still far below the horizon, and would have been horrified if she could have had an inkling of them. But all this work was directed by a deep love for Christ, carried out in the closest possible association with a Church which had not shown itself skilled in meeting the needs of poor and humble people; and its aim was not to pauperize the poor but to raise them to a situation in which they could more fully respect themselves. The clubs were not free; women who joined them had to pay a subscription of three half-pence a week, quite a considerable sum, when the extreme poverty of the poor in those days is taken into account.

The third, and perhaps the most typical in the galaxy, is Granville Sharp (1735–1813). He specially deserves our mention, as belonging to that elect class of laymen who have refused to be ordained because they were convinced that they could better serve God in the lay capacity than in the ordained life. Sharp's greatest glory is his championship of the slaves. His attention having been drawn to the plight of an African slave, whose master was trying to recover possession of him, Sharp, unaided by any powerful forces in society, fought the case from court to court, until finally he obtained the ever memorable decision of Lord Mansfield, issued on 22nd June, 1772, that slavery cannot exist in England, and that as soon as a slave sets foot on its soil he is *ipso facto* free. Inevitably, when the Society for the Abolition of Slavery was formed in 1787, Granville Sharp was chosen as its first chairman, and Bishop Beilby Porteus of London spoke no more than the truth when he said:

> It ought to be remembered in justice to one no less remarkable for his modesty than for his learning and piety—Granville Sharp—that the first publication which drew the attention of the country to the horrors of the African slave trade came from his pen.

Granville Sharp had not in early life been associated with Evangelicals—both his father and his brother were Archdeacons, and his grandfather had been Archbishop of York; as we have seen, in those early days Evangelicals did not fly so high. The inspiration for his devotion to the Christian cause came from that solid, undemonstrative Anglican piety, which never failed throughout the eighteenth century; but he was drawn more and more into association with Evangelicals through like-minded devotion to similar causes, and it was on them that he could principally rely for help. As Sir James Stephen has picturesquely expressed it, Sharp sat on his office stool at the Ordnance Office 'with a soul as distended as that of a Paladin bestriding his warhorse'; cruelty or injustice anywhere was certain to find in him a sworn foe. He was not as fortunate in all his enterprises as in the affair of slavery. In later years, he once secured an interview with Charles James Fox, with the intention of convincing that not very Christian statesman that Napoleon was in fact the little horn spoken of by Daniel the prophet. Mr Fox showed himself courteous but perplexed; and, as they came away, Sharp remarked to his young companion, 'Upon my soul, Sir, I believe that he had never so much as heard of the Little Horn.' He was probably right.[11]

Once again it is right to draw attention to the formation of the society. Almost all great movements and reforms owe their origin to the vision and passion of some individual who was not willing that all things should continue to be as they had been from the foundation of the world. But visions transform themselves into realities only through the work of many willing hands. The society is indispensable. The Church should be its own society. But this is not always practicable, either because the Church has lost its zeal, or because in a world in which there are many denominations the support of them all is needed if the victory is to be won over some great evil. We have seen the formation of two societies for the promotion of Christian aims. The nineteenth century was to be the great period of the religious and philanthropic society, and the formation of such societies for every conceivable purpose, including the prevention of premature burial, was a great Evangelical hobby. We have not dealt in this chapter with the life and work of William Wilberforce, since his greatest achievements fall within the period of the following chapter. But in 1800 Wilberforce was already thirty-nine years old; and this pillar and founder of so many societies had already tried his prentice hand at the formation of a society for the Reform of Manners (the manners, be it noted, of the rich and not of the poor). The century which had opened with the foundation of the Society for Promoting Christian Knowledge, with its splendid work for education in all its forms, with the Charity School Movement, which secured the support and approval of such laymen as Joseph Addison and Richard Steele, and the Society for the Propagation of the Gospel in Foreign Parts, ended auspiciously with the foundation in 1799 of the Church Missionary Society for Africa and the

East. The eyes of the Church of England and of its laymen were beginning to be lifted up beyond the narrow horizons of the British Isles.

We have watched some of the brilliant stars of the eighteenth century in their courses—and that century was rich beyond most others in individuals of note, if not of genius. But perhaps before the chapter ends we should turn back to some who, from the Christian point of view, were less notable, yet perhaps for that reason all the more representative of the British layman in his attitude to and service of the Church.

If it is possible for one man to represent a century, it might be argued that the most representative Englishman of the eighteenth century was Samuel Johnson (1709–84). Johnson was gloriously full of prejudices and eccentricities. Yet his character stands out in massive grandeur, in sterling integrity based on the musings of a capacious intellect and on a profound faith in the verities of the Christian religion. And Johnson was very much a layman; a faithful member of the Church, sitting regularly in the gallery of St Clement's Church, the friend of many clergymen, but critical of sermons preached without passion. He deserves the eulogy written by Dr Relton:

> A man of profound personal religious character and devotion, deeply attached to his personal Saviour, while his moral judgments and his actions are marked by a noble heroism and a continued testifying to truth and righteousness in an age which, judged by its secular literature, was none too sensitive.[12]

Nothing about Johnson is more interesting than his friends. And two of them, by sheer contrast, show up very different aspects of the eighteenth-century layman. James Boswell (1740–95) was far from being a wholly estimable character, and the best thing we know about him is that Johnson seems really to have cared for him. Boswell could combine thoughtful and apparently reverent attention to sermons with an immediate indulgence in debauchery, his inclinations to which he seems to have been entirely unable to control, and of which he has left us such painfully minute descriptions in his recently recovered and published London diary. And yet for all his weaknesses, the Christian faith would not let him alone; he knew himself to be the heir of a great Christian tradition, and from this he could not dissociate himself. And, at the opposite pole, we encounter Sir Joshua Reynolds (1723–92), a man who impressed himself on all his acquaintance by the extraordinary sweetness and purity of his character, excellences that seemed to come to him naturally, and not as with most men through a long process of training and self-discipline. Reynolds too would be a Christian layman, but he would find the sphere for the exercise of his Christian witness in his art; not that Sir Joshua ever stooped to the production of that very ambiguous commodity, religious art; it was his aim to reflect in the purity and perfection of his art his understanding of the majesty of God, and of the glory that is revealed in the beauty both of man and of nature. What united him to Johnson was this quality of integrity—in words for one, in lines and colours for the other; but for both surely a means and manner of the lay service of God in the world.

It is impossible to sum up in a line either the British character or the British understanding of Christianity. Moderation can all too easily become a synonym for mediocrity. Yet a certain continuity can be traced between the seventeenth century, in which religion was quite evidently the centre of the passionate concern of a great many people, and the eighteenth, when religion tended to flow in quieter channels, sometimes so quiet as to seem to have gone entirely to sleep. In both we find variety and originality, purpose, passion and achievement; and in the very century that most decried and disliked enthusiasm, we find some of the most adventurous, passionate and effective laymen that have been seen in the history of the Church to the present day.

NOTES

1. To most English readers Caroline is likely to be familiar from the picture of her given in Scott's *Heart of Midlothian*.

2. Hooker, *Laws of Ecclesiastical Polity*, Bk VIII, ch. 11.

3. Quoted in Charles Smyth, *Church and Parish* (London, 1955), p. 12.

4. *Works* III, pp. 201-2, quoted in C. Hill, *Economic Problems of the Church* (Oxford, 1956), pp. 219-20.

5. The *De Doctrina Christiana*, which was not published till 1825, fortunately perhaps for its author.

6. Basil Willey, *The Seventeenth-Century Background* (London, 1950), pp. 41-3.

7. Newton was fortunate in holding the Lucasian professorship of Mathematics, one of the few posts for which this condition did not hold.

8. C. V. Wedgwood, *The King's War, 1641-1647* (London, 1958), p. 518.

9. C. V. Wedgwood, *op. cit.*, pp. 581-2.

10. R. Raikes, *Gloucestershire Tracts*, 14.

11. The anecdote is recorded by the young companion, Sir James Stephen, in his incomparable *Essays in Ecclesiastical Biography*.

12. Overton and Relton, *A History of the English Church* (ed. Stephens and Hunt) VII (London, 1906), p. 286.

9

F. C. Mather

THE BRITISH LAYMAN IN MODERN TIMES
1780–1962

Introduction

THE beginning of modern times may be variously dated in accordance with what the writer deems to be the most important criteria of the world in which he lives. But if we may assume that the distinguishing features of modern England are an industrial economy, an urban civilization and a form of government which is at once democratic and bureaucratic there is much to be said in favour of regarding the year 1780 as an approximate turning-point. It was in the seventeen-eighties that Britain embarked upon the process of industrialization which has turned the average Englishman from a countryman into a town-dweller; then also that the Younger Pitt began the post-war reconstruction from which modern administration has proceeded, whilst the years 1779–80 witnessed an outburst of radical agitation which foreshadowed the parliamentary reforms of the nineteenth century. The historian J. R. Green did not lack justification when he wrote in 1880: 'The England that is about us dates from the American War.'[1]

I · Clapham, Hackney and the 'Primitives'

By a curious coincidence, round about 1780 also occurred the release of a vast quantity of spiritual energy channelled mainly though not exclusively through laymen. It would be misleading to suggest that what happened then was a radical break with the past. For, as Dr Norman Sykes has pointed out, the eighteenth century as a whole 'witnessed a steady and progressive laicization of religion'.[2] The

Methodist revival which depended heavily upon the work of laymen began as early as the seventeen-forties and forms a link in an almost unbroken chain of lay endeavour stretching back to the religious societies of the reigns of William III and Anne. Nevertheless there was at least a very striking reinforcement of the lay contribution to Christian work in Britain in the last quarter of the eighteenth century. This was to be seen partly in the growth of Methodism, which was accelerated after about 1778, partly in developments within the old lay-centred Nonconformist Churches, which took on a new lease of life from that time onwards and added to their already extensive openings for lay service by increasing greatly the number of their lay preachers.[3] There was also, however, a lay revival extending to the Established Church, one which expressed itself principally through societies and committees for religious and humanitarian purposes. The Naval and Military Society for circulating the Scriptures among soldiers and sailors founded in 1780 was one of the first of a crop of such ventures which multiplied during the next half-century. Wilberforce's societies for the abolition of the slave trade and for the reformation of manners, the Church Missionary Society established in 1799 and the Incorporated Church Building Society launched in 1818 were simply a few among many. Pusey, writing in 1838 with Tractarian contempt of the religion of his time, spoke of 'societies taking the initiative for every purpose under the sun . . . and the ultimate end of these societies is to obtain acts of parliament.' 'Societies', he added, 'are our Episcopacy, and newspapers our rules of faith.'[4]

These organizations derived their strength from two brotherhoods of Christians, each living in a particular locality and sharing a common theological outlook. The first, the Evangelical 'Clapham Sect', was almost exclusively lay. Among its principal members were William Wilberforce, the eminent House of Commons man, Zachary Macaulay, the Africa merchant, James Stephen, the Scottish lawyer, and Henry Thornton, the banker. There was, however, a High Church counterpart of the Clapham Sect commonly known as the 'Hackney Phalanx', and in this also laymen took the lead. The movement was in existence as early as about the year 1789, when William Stevens, the London hosier who had written tracts on theology, joined with J. A. Park, the barrister, and the Rev. Dr Gaskin in a voluntary committee to work for the repeal of the penal legislation which oppressed the Episcopal Church of Scotland.[5] In 1800 a club was founded in Stevens's honour under the name of Nobody's Club. Its president was Sir Richard

Richards, who afterwards became a judge.[6] At a subsequent date
leadership among the active High Churchmen of Hackney passed from
William Stevens to Joshua Watson, a rich wine merchant who retired
from his business in 1814 at the early age of forty-three to give his full
attention to the work of the Church. He and other laymen took the
initiative in the establishment of the Incorporated Church Building
Society in 1818. He, also, was a founding father of the National Society
for Promoting the Education of the Poor in the Principles of the
Established Church, which he afterwards ran as treasurer.[7]

When full allowance has been made for the activity of the Clapham
Sect and Hackney Phalanx, it is scarcely too much to claim that the
reforming influence in the Established Church between 1780 and 1830
was lay rather than clerical. It was an influence, moreover, which
tended to promote not a mere ecclesiastical regeneration narrowly conceived but the application of Christian standards to public affairs. For
the men who worked through the religious societies accepted no rigid
separation of the secular and the spiritual. The Clapham Sect fought
the battle against the slave trade and slavery for nearly fifty years, and
still found time to spare for upholding reforming influences at home.
Penal reforms, opposition to the press-gang and the game laws, and
even the early experiments in factory legislation benefited from its
support, whilst its campaigns against drunkenness, cruel sports and
duelling tended ultimately to raise the moral tone of society. As a by-
product of their reforms the Claphamites bequeathed to posterity
improved methods of political organization and propaganda which
helped to make government more responsive to the pressure of public
opinion.[8] Thus unwittingly they prepared the way for the achievement
of the democracy which we now enjoy. Meanwhile at Hackney Christian energy was displayed in promoting popular education and in
relieving famine victims in Germany after the battle of Leipzig.

The flaw in this pattern of Christian lay witness in society was the
restricted social outreach of the movements through which it was trans-
mitted. Drawing their support mainly from the upper stratum of the
middle class—City merchants, bankers, nabobs and successful lawyers
—the Clapham Sect and Hackney Phalanx were both well placed to
influence the governing aristocracy, with whom they shared a common
culture and a common Anglican religion. 'Clapham' also succeeded, by
virtue of its lack of denominational narrowness, in striking up a political
alliance with the wider middle class which was largely Nonconformist.
Where it failed lamentably, however, was in its relations with the

workers. For Wilberforce and his associates, though sympathetic towards the poor, shared the prejudices of their order against working-
class movements. Fearful of revolution, they supported the repressive
measures of Pitt and Sidmouth, and were convinced by the teachings of
the Classical Economists that neither trade-unionism nor state paternalism could cure the ills of English society in the gloomy aftermath of the
Napoleonic Wars. Their reward was the implacable and often quite
unreasoning hatred of the popular leaders. Cobbett defined paradise in
terms of the absence of Wilberforce; and the latter was obliged to put
his London house into a state of defence during the Corn Bill riots of
1815.[9]

If the industrial workers and their movements were largely insulated
by political differences from the influence of 'Clapham' and 'Hackney',
they experienced their own lay revival in the rise of Methodism. No
Christian body relied more upon the laity than did Methodism.
Methodist pulpits were of necessity manned by laymen, as Wesley was
unable to induce more than a small minority of the Anglican clergy to
follow him in his evangelistic work. Other laymen served as stewards
and trustees, and, through the class-meeting system, lay persons
assumed responsibility for the recruitment of members and the pastoral
oversight of their fellows.

By no means all Methodists were working men. Bishop E. R. Wickham's
survey of religion in Sheffield reveals that in the eighteen-twenties all
the churches in the town, including those of the Methodists, were predominantly middle-class affairs.[10] On the other hand there is contemporary evidence that in some areas and trades a strong working-class
participation in Methodism persisted in the early nineteenth century.
One commentator writing in 1823 remarked that the great mass of the
weavers were 'deeply imbued with the doctrines of Methodism'.[11] The
working-class component was particularly strong in Primitive Methodism, and in regions where that sect enjoyed widespread support labour
movements assumed a strong Nonconformist colouring. Primitive
Methodist local preachers were prominent among the leaders of the
strikes of the miners of Northumberland and Durham in 1831-2 and
again in 1844. At meetings of the turn-outs they underlaid their
speeches with large quotations of Scripture, and strikers attended
weekly prayer meetings to pray for the success of their enterprise. In
Staffordshire too, another stronghold of the Primitives, prayer meetings
were held in the pits.[12] The influence which Primitive Methodism
exerted upon labour movements was partly the result of the lay-centred

organization which that denomination shared with the rest of Methodism. By using working men as class-leaders and local preachers
Methodism trained them for responsible office in their other communal
activities. Perhaps also the extensive openings for lay service attracted
to the Methodist churches the natural extravert who would also tend to
be a leader in his trade-union, co-operative society or reform association. Something more is required, however, to explain why the Methodist lay preacher took his Bible with him when he went into politics or
into industry, why he infused the spirit of Methodism into his secular
pursuits. He did so because he sensed, in a rough-and-ready fashion
perhaps, the relevance of his religion to his craft. At its worst this perception degenerated into a crude moral certainty which identified the
workers with the Israelites in bondage and the employers with 'the
Pharaohs who oppressed them'. 'Who were their opponents?' declaimed
a speaker at a miners' demonstration in 1832. 'They were only an arm
of flesh, whilst with them was the arm of the living God.'[13] At his best
the Primitive Methodist trade-unionist showed a firm grasp of Christian responsibility for the affairs of this world, exhorting masters and
men to join in prayer to God for guidance in their disputes and
earnestly restraining his followers from resort to violence in the pursuit
of their quarrels.[14]

By the eighteen-thirties the first phase in the modern lay revival was
over. Both Clapham Sect and Hackney Phalanx were moribund, and
the growth of Evangelical Nonconformity measured in terms of the
provision of accommodation was slowing down.[15] The early renaissance
had achieved a high degree of Christian involvement in the secular
order, but this had severe limitations in respect of the industrial working
class. The efforts of the Primitive Methodists, assisted here and there
by some of the older Dissenters, notably the Baptists,[16] to penetrate
labour movements could be no more than moderately successful in
maintaining a Christian influence over those activities. Especially was
this so when the Wesleyans, by far the largest of the Methodist
denominations, dominated by a cautious ministerial oligarchy, used
every means at their command to restrain their followers from participating in radical movements. It is not surprising, therefore, that by
the eighteen-thirties large masses of the working people had found their
leaders in men like Robert Owen, Julian Harney and Feargus O'Con-
nor, who displayed a marked hostility, if not always to Christianity
itself (as they conceived it), at least to the organized Churches. Meanwhile, in great towns like Sheffield a state of unprecedented spiritual

destitution had come to prevail, with not one family in twenty among the artisan class in the habit of visiting either church or chapel.[17] That was the problem which the Christian denominations of England at the beginning of Queen Victoria's reign inherited from their predecessors, and signs were not wanting that they were at last profoundly disturbed by it.

It was not until about 1850 that the second stage in the lay movement in the various English Churches began to unfold, though the changes which then occurred were germinating in the two preceding decades. What happened then was of a threefold character and the strands were inextricably interwoven. There was a marked shift towards greater lay participation in the government, worship and evangelistic mission of the Churches. There was a reappraisal of the attitudes of the several Christian denominations towards social questions, bringing those bodies into closer contact with middle- and working-class aspirations. Finally there was a growing theological awareness of the importance of the Church as the Body of Christ and of the role of the laity within the body. These changes which spanned the second half of the nineteenth century and the early years of the twentieth cut right across denominational barriers and furnished yet another example of the growing together of the Churches which was to issue forth in the twentieth century in the ecumenical movement.

II · Lay Participation in the Life of the Churches

In Methodism the process by which the layman's part in the government of his Church was extended was stormy but for all that absolutely sure. Although laymen carried immense responsibility as local preachers, class-leaders, trustees, etc., in all branches of Methodism, their control of church government was at first severely restricted in the main Wesleyan body by the pretensions and powers of a professional ministry which had grown out of Wesley's corps of itinerant preachers. Conference, the supreme legislative body of the Connexion, was a purely clerical assembly, and even in the localities the authority of the pastor over his flock was very considerable. In particular, the Superintendent Minister had immense power in the selection of class-leaders and the administration of discipline. This exalted power of the ordained ministry was resented, however, by Wesleyan laymen, most of whom, being drawn from the middle class, were becoming habituated to self-government in consequence of the reform of parliament in 1832 and the reconstitution of the municipal corporations in 1835. They found leadership in a number of ministers who adopted a lower view of ministerial prerogative than that upheld by Jabez Bunting, the President of the Conference. Bunting believed, with some justification, that he was maintaining the tradition handed down by John Wesley in insisting upon a distinctive *episkopē* residing in the pastorate.[18] The friction was intensified by Bunting's high-handed and inquisitorial methods. Opposition to him mounted steadily in the 'thirties and 'forties of the nineteenth century and came to a head in the years 1849–57 when 100,000 members quitted the Wesleyan body. A sizeable minority of these formed themselves into a new Methodist denomination, the United Methodist Free Churches, in which circuit independence and the rights of the laity were greater than in the parent Church. Even in Wesleyanism, however, striking changes occurred in the second half of the century. Little by little the responsibility of the minister for the admission and expulsion of members was taken away, and in 1878 laymen were admitted to Conference to share equally with the pastorate in matters of policy and finance.

These developments within and without the Wesleyan Connexion were closely paralleled by a significant deepening of the Methodist contribution to Liberal politics and labour movements at a time when these two forms of activity were closer together than they were to be in the twentieth century. The rebels against the authority of Jabez Bunting and the Wesleyan Conference sympathized with the liberal causes of their day, and the United Methodist Free Churches which they eventually formed were solidly Liberal in politics during the second half of the nineteenth century.[19] The Wesleyans remained more mixed politically and more fearful of associating themselves as a body with party politics. Nevertheless, between the middle 'sixties and the middle 'eighties Liberalism, from being a minority opinion, became the predominant political tendency among them;[20] and Wesleyanism, which in contrast with Primitive Methodism had contributed practically nothing to the trade-union movement earlier in the century, threw up a few labour leaders. Henry Broadhurst, the organizer of the stonemasons, and Ben Pickard, the leader of the miners of West Yorkshire, were two notable examples taken from the last quarter of the nineteenth century.[21] The connection between Liberalism and laymen's rights was illustrated in Wesleyan Methodism by the career of Hugh Price Hughes, one of the most influential ministers in the denomination at the close of the century. Hughes rejoiced greatly in the admission of the laity to Synod and

Conference, and was also the exponent of a Liberal political faith which had, as one of its most notable features, an ardour for social reform.[22]

The Methodists were not alone in gravitating towards the Liberal party during the second half of the nineteenth century. That tendency was perceptible throughout Nonconformity, and its importance in national history was enhanced by the fact that the Free Churches (and to a lesser extent the Church of England) were being renewed spiritually and strengthened numerically by a second Evangelical awakening. In 1859 a religious revival originating in Canada swept into the British Isles, and from that time forward down to the eve of the First World War the tide of religious enthusiasm was sustained by successive waves of evangelical fervour, of which the Welsh revival of 1905 was perhaps the last. The movement deserves a place in its own right in the history of the laity in Britain. For though different in character from the Wesleyan revival of the eighteenth century, relying more upon the tactics of the 'big meeting' and the popular preacher and less on the careful shepherding of souls through classes and class-leaders, this new spiritual renaissance depended extensively, in its own distinctive way, on the work of laymen. Lay evangelists were among its leading heralds. Some were of good birth like Hay Macdowall Grant, the Scottish laird, and Brownlow North (grand-nephew of Lord North, the Prime Minister) who was converted at the age of forty-five after a life of dissolute frivolity. Others were working men like Richard Weaver who began work as a coal-miner at the age of seven, and William Carter, a master chimney-sweep.[23]

Although the second Evangelical awakening added much to the strength of Nonconformity, it was itself essentially an undenominational enterprise. Unlike the earlier revival led by the Wesleys which was Anglican in intention if not always in result, it was based upon the principle, reaffirmed in the twentieth century in the Billy Graham crusade, that one was led first to Christ and decided afterwards one's denominational allegiance. It resulted, moreover, in an efflorescence of unsectarian philanthropy in which laymen figured prominently. Dr Barnardo's homes, the first of which was established in 1870, Sailors' Rests in the great ports founded by Reginald Radcliffe the Revival preacher, and movements for the reclamation of prostitutes, criminals and alcoholics were among the products of the awakening.[24] Politics, too, sustained a Christian influence. For Keir Hardie, the leader of the I.L.P., of whom it was later said that 'he made the Parliamentary

Labour Party more of a Church than a merely political body',[25] was converted under the ministry of D. L. Moody.[26]

The Established Church was affected less than the Free Churches by the second Evangelical awakening. Nevertheless Anglicanism underwent, during the second half of the nineteenth century, its own lay revival, a movement which resulted in making the laity of the Church of England more active both in the internal organization and working of their Church and in the leavening of society. The revival was many-sided and was a product of many dissimilar influences.

The Oxford Movement, too often dismissed as a clericalist reaction, had its contribution to make in the form of sisterhoods for women and guilds for men. The emergence of the laywoman as a major contributor to the work of the Church is the religious aspect of that great social development of the nineteenth and early twentieth centuries, the emancipation of women. Moreover, it was in the Churches that some of the most important precedents of the emancipating movement were established. The Quakers had a tradition, dating back to the seventeenth century, of employing women to preach, to visit the sick and to administer funds.[27] In this they were exceptional; but during the first two decades of the nineteenth century two new Christian denominations, the Bible Christians and the Primitive Methodists, which made extensive use of women preachers, came into existence.[28] The revival of the religious orders in the Church of England, which began as early as 1841 at the instigation of the Tractarian fathers, Newman and Pusey, was a further important extension of the sphere of women's usefulness a decade or more before the feminist movement formally took shape. The earliest communities were all for women. Sisterhoods were established at Regent's Park in 1845, at Devonport in 1848, at Wantage in 1849 and at Clewer in 1852. These were conventual organizations living under strict religious rules, but their members withdrew from the world for the purpose of serving it in many practical ways. By running colleges for sailor boys, industrial schools, lodging-houses for poor families, and 'rescue' homes for prostitutes, the sisterhoods supplied a channel through which the energies of middle- and upper-class women who were growing exceedingly restive under the restraints of home life could be applied to the benefit of society.[29] As the nineteenth century advanced, the Churches provided many other openings for women's service. Deaconesses were introduced into the Church of England in 1861, the example being followed by the Methodists and the Church of Scotland in 1888,[30] and from the eighteen-seventies onwards feminine religious organizations such as the Mothers' Union, the Girls' Friendly Society and the YWCA sprang up in quick succession, whilst the newly founded Salvation Army provided unique opportunities for women in evangelistic work.

By that time, however, there were many secular outlets for feminine energy. The religious communities set up by the Tractarians had done pioneer work when such openings were few. Nor, indeed, was that their only contribution to the creation of an active laity. The sisterhood of St John the Baptist at Clewer became the nucleus of a larger body of associates who were men and women pursuing their own secular vocations but bound together by a solemn undertaking entered into upon admission, and by a rule of daily prayer and regular communion. Associates were expected to undertake works of mercy individually and collectively. The branch which was founded in the parish of St Alban, Holborn, in 1867 gave a weekly meat dinner to twelve poor and sick children of the locality. But, unlike the various humanitarian and philanthropic societies which existed to further a specific social purpose, the association was based upon the principle of collecting together the workers first and then helping them to find out what their work was as well as to learn how to do it. Augustus Arthur, secretary of the Clewer sisterhood, defined this as 'getting up . . . the human steam first of all, and then carefully directing it into the right channels, so as to tell with full force upon the social machine.'[31]

If the Oxford Movement enhanced the role of laymen in the Established Church, so in a different manner did resistance to the Anglo-Catholic revival which the Movement initiated. For the all-too-frequent ritual prosecutions of the 'seventies and 'eighties placed a great deal of responsibility for regulating the Church's worship in the hands of lawyers. Dean Church told the Commission on Ecclesiastical Courts in 1883 that 'there had been more questions of Church law ruled by the courts, say, for the last fifty years, than almost any time since the Reformation.'[32] He emphasized the danger of binding Anglicanism to a 'case-made theology' produced in the courts.[33]

But the main extensions of the role of laymen in the Established Church of England during the second half of the nineteenth century originated neither in the advanced churchmanship of the Tractarians and their 'Ritualist' successors nor in the bigotry of their ultra-Protestant antagonists. They arose rather from the thoughtful endeavours of more moderate churchmen to adapt the establishment to the changed conditions in which it had to operate in the nineteenth century. Three

H

great events in national history following one another in rapid succession—the repeal of the Test and Corporation Acts in 1828, Roman
Catholic emancipation in 1829 and the passing of the Reform Bill in
1832—had overthrown the old eighteenth-century constitution in
Church and State, leaving the Church of England still legally established but shorn of her most important civil privileges and exposed, in
the country and in the Commons, to an opposition unprecedented in
fury since the days of the Long Parliament.[34] Plans for confiscating her
endowments and applying them to general educational purposes were
openly discussed by Radicals. Faced with this situation, discerning and
level-headed churchmen like Charles James Blomfield, Bishop of
London, and Sir Robert Peel, the Prime Minister, set about the task
of rendering the Church more efficient with a view to establishing it
once again in the hearts of the people. New dioceses were created,
new churches built and the revenues of the Church of England were
diverted from sinecures to the maintenance of hard-working parish
priests in the districts where they were most sorely needed. These
reforms, however, which found their focus in the permanent Ecclesiastical Commission set up in 1836, were able to make but little headway
against the great spiritual destitution prevailing in the great towns, and
the religious census of 1851 administered a further severe shock to
ecclesiastical consciences by revealing that in the country as a whole
only about $7\frac{1}{4}$ million persons out of a total of $12\frac{1}{2}$ million possible
churchgoers attended any kind of Sunday service. Of these, moreover,
scarcely more than a half were Anglicans.[35] Furthermore, during the
eighteen-fifties political Nonconformity had been gaining in strength
and cohesion, and by the end of the decade the Church of England
again felt itself to be threatened.[36]

It was in response to this situation that the first important steps were
taken during the 'sixties to create new machinery and offices through
which laymen might participate, officially and with full ecclesiastical
recognition, in the life and government of the Church. The immediate
threat from the activities of the Liberation Society in the House of
Commons was countered by the formation of Church Defence Associations. Henry Hoare, a distinguished Anglican layman, founded a
London Church Institution, with branches in the provinces and its own
newspaper, to influence public opinion in the constituencies in favour
of the Church.[37] The Church Defence Associations were ephemeral
bodies, but out of them grew the Church Congresses which met
annually between 1861 and 1913 and provided a forum in which laymen

and clergymen met to discuss a wide range of problems affecting the well-being of the Church.

One of the chief concerns reflected in the early debates of the Congresses was the desire to win back for the Church of England the lower middle and working classes which had been alienated either to Nonconformity or to non-attendance at any place of worship. Two solutions of this problem were repeatedly under discussion. One was to introduce suitable laymen into a permanent diaconate which would perform evangelistic and pastoral work among the poor. The other was to revive, for the same purpose, the office of Reader which had existed in the Church in the reign of Elizabeth I and had afterwards died out. Bishop Blomfield had suggested in 1851: 'We want some persons, deacons or lay-teachers, who will hunt out the poor at their own homes on Sundays, the only day on which they are to be met with there.'[38] And when the proposals were mooted in the Church Congresses in the eighteen-sixties, their champions argued further that their adoption was necessary in order to create Christian work for middle- and lower-class laymen. 'It is certain', maintained Professor Harold Browne, 'that . . . unless you can enlist the energies of the middle classes you cannot retain them in, or rather restore them to, our communion.'[39] The Rev. F. C. Massingberd hinted that some who had become Wesleyan local preachers would have preferred to work within the Anglican communion could a place have been found for their talents.[40]

The bishops rejected the plan of a permanent diaconate but decided in favour of instituting Readers, following a lead from the colonial churches.[41] Accordingly in 1866 the Bishop of Bristol and Gloucester admitted the first of the modern Lay Readers in this country to his office by prayer and delivery of the New Testament.[42] The number grew until at the end of the nineteenth century more than 2,000 held licences in the provinces of Canterbury and York.[43] The earliest Readers did not usually officiate in church. Their pulpit was the mission chapel or schoolroom and their work more like that of a Salvation Army captain than that of an Anglican Lay Reader in our own day, as the following description given to the Church Congress of 1875 by Colonel Bagnall, High Sheriff of Staffordshire, who had been licensed by the Bishop of Lichfield, will testify: 'We read the morning and evening Prayer, and we preach, I am glad to say, not to empty chairs. . . . But we do not preach within the walls of the mission chapel only, for unfortunately there are many people who will not come within the chapels if nothing is done outside to bring them in; and so we go forth singing hymns from "Hymns: Ancient and Modern", and in this way gather our congregations.'[44] Gradually, however, and against strong opposition from many conservative churchmen, clerical and lay, Readers began to take their place in the services of the parish church. In 1891 Frederick Temple, then Bishop of London, created in his diocese the special office of Diocesan Reader which carried with it the privilege of preaching in church at evening service, and admitted to it seventeen laymen of superior education or special experience. Among them was Dr Eugene Stock, editorial secretary of the Church Missionary Society.[45] With the growing shortage of priests during the twentieth century, all Readers have had to assume a heavy responsibility for the conduct of the regular public worship of the Church.[46] This has changed somewhat the character of their office. From being an auxiliary ministry charged with a specific function which the clergy could not easily perform, they have tended to become substitutes for the clergy in the conduct of morning and evening prayer. No doubt this has enriched the Church's pulpits with a variety of experience, but it has also meant that the pastoral and evangelizing work for which Readers were originally intended has largely gone by default.

The creation of special institutions for the representation of laymen in the government of the Church of England had to await the growth among churchmen of a feeling of being distinct from the nation. For while Church and State were regarded as integral parts of the same Christian commonwealth, as Burke emphatically insisted in 1792,[47] the voice of the laity could be conceived as being adequately expressed through such organs of the community as parliament and the parish vestry. In the middle years of the nineteenth century, however, when Protestant Dissenters were gaining rapidly in political importance and successfully resisting attempts to tax them for ecclesiastical purposes through church rates and to assert an Anglican influence over national projects for elementary education, many leading supporters of the Established Church came to think of that Church in less than national terms. In the debates of the eighteen-fifties on church rates, Samuel Wilberforce, for example, affirmed his willingness to surrender the rates 'if in exchange we could get the inestimable privilege of declaring who are and who are not members of the Church'.[48] Not unnaturally, therefore, from the eighteen-sixties onwards a movement for the provision of representation for an Anglican laity narrower in scope than the people of England gathered force. At first the organs which were created lacked statutory recognition. Parochial church councils estab-

lished on a voluntary basis by the goodwill of the incumbent existed in
the eighteen-seventies.[49] In 1864 the first diocesan conference met.[50]
In 1886 and 1892 the Convocations of Canterbury and York respectively set up Houses of Laymen,[51] and in 1903 the institution of the
Representative Church Council united laity and clergy of both provinces
in a single assembly.[52] As the nineteenth century drew to its close, however, there was a growing demand for a system of lay representation
which was more official in character and depended less upon the grace and
favour of the clergy. In the late eighteen-nineties Charles Gore headed
a campaign for the establishment, with full diocesan sanction, of parish
councils which would ultimately be granted legal status.[53] This movement eventually achieved a limited success in the Enabling Act of 1919,
which set up the Church Assembly, with its elective House of Laymen,
to prepare ecclesiastical measures for Parliament, and prescribed that
parochial church councils should be formed in every parish. It cannot
be said, however, that the arrangements then authorized have fully
satisfied the demand for lay representation in the Church of England,
and today the admission of laymen into the Convocations is being
strongly urged as necessary to promote full synodical government.

The more the Church of England explored the possibility of extending the sphere of usefulness of her laity, the more her understanding of
the nature of the Church Catholic deepened, the more she became
aware of the meaning of the Pauline assurance: 'Ye are the body of
Christ and members in particular.' Speakers in the Church Congresses
of the later nineteenth century drew heavily upon this doctrine to
justify practical measures affecting the rights and duties of the laity.
G. W. E. Russell, for example, speaking in 1899 on the contribution
which laymen might make to church services and parochial administration, quoted Canon Moberly's Bampton Lectures of 1868 on *The
Administration of the Holy Spirit in the Body of Christ*, in which it was
argued that, although the ordained ministry was the official organ for
publicly uttering divine truth, it performed that function as the mouthpiece of the entire 'Spirit-Bearing Body' to which God had entrusted
that truth.[54] At the same Congress Charles Gore maintained that lay
members of the Body shared the Kingship of the Head, and had, therefore, the right to a say in church government. 'Every boy or girl who
was confirmed according to ancient usage', he said, 'was anointed upon
the forehead with the holy oil, for a reminder, as medieval authorities
tell us, that each member was to wear the diadem of the kingship as well
as the dignity of priesthood.'[55] In more recent times efforts have been

made to express liturgically the truth of the laity's share in the collective priesthood of the Body. The parish communion movement, with its emphasis on the importance of the communion of the people in contradistinction to the non-communicating High Mass, has been one of the most important of these. In some parishes, moreover, the offertory in the Eucharist is made to appear a real oblation of the people by selecting members of the congregation to bring the bread and the wine up to the altar at the appropriate moment.

III · The Laity of the Church in Social Action

Whilst some churchmen were working out the implications of the doctrine of the mystical body of Christ in the sphere of church government and by the employment of Readers, others were helping the Anglican Church to witness more effectively in society by formulating a new social philosophy which would bring the Church into contact with labour movements. Christian Socialism, the movement which they inaugurated, came into being in 1848 in consequence of the desire of a group of Anglican clergy and laymen to furnish the working classes, long alienated from the Church, with a Christian alternative to their secular hopes of social regeneration which had been discredited by the collapse of Chartism. Its ideal was an alliance of parsons, educated laymen and working men to actualize the Kingdom of God by transforming the basis of society. In this movement laymen played an indispensable part, one which furnishes an almost ideal example of the role of the Christian laity in society. On the one hand the layman is seen informing the Church of the world's problems. For, as Maurice Reckitt has shown, F. D. Maurice, whose capacious theology provided the intellectual basis of the cause, was first made aware of the needs and temper of the working classes of the time by a young barrister of Lincoln's Inn, J. M. F. Ludlow, who had experience of mixing with workers on a footing of equality in a guild of French Protestants for the relief of distress.[56]

But laymen supplied Christian Socialism with more than the information on which it fed; they also furnished the links with the working-class leaders and organizations of the time, and saved the movement from the fate of being purely academic or, at most, helpful to the working classes in a paternalist sense. Again Ludlow was indispensable. It was he who contributed to Christian Socialism its democratic impulse, 'a faith not only in the people's cause but in the people themselves'.[57]

Kingsley, the priest, with his appeal to the workmen of England to trust the working clergy of England 'who know what your rights are, better than you know yourselves, had little of this.[58] To Ludlow more than anyone else was due the fact that the early Christian Socialist experiments should have taken the form of trade associations of working men, beginning with the Tailors' Working Association of 1850. Other laymen too, not all of them fully committed to Christian orthodoxy, took their place in the movement, contributing experience and organizing ability. These included Lloyd Jones the Owenite, and Walter Cooper the Chartist workman.[59]

The early co-operative experiments sponsored by the Christian Socialists failed signally within a year or two of their inception, but the link between Church and people which the leaders had forged was maintained long afterwards by the witness of devoted laymen. Ludlow, Thomas Hughes and E. V. Neale, who belonged to Christian Socialism in its early phase, were connected with working-class causes to the end of their careers. Hughes became the trusted legal adviser of trade-unionism,[60] pleading its cause before the Royal Commission of 1867; Neale performed lifelong service to the co-operative movement as honorary secretary of the Co-operative Union, and it was said of him that the co-operative movement was his monument.[61] Other laymen who came into contact with Christian Socialism in its later stages and translated its principles into the sphere of political and social action were George Lansbury, who rose through the trade-union world to Cabinet rank in a Labour government, and Albert Mansbridge who founded the Workers' Educational Association in 1903. Mansbridge was an Anglican Lay Reader and a fervent admirer of Charles Gore, then in the Christian Social Union phase of his career. He acknowledged in his autobiography that the Church of England had been one of the three great formative influences of his life.[62] Through men such as these the Established Church came to play its part, alongside Methodism which had been long in the field, in infusing working-class movements with a Christian leaven.

It was not until well into the twentieth century that working men took their place in the forefront of the British political arena. A generation earlier, however, the witness of several distinguished laymen drawn from a more favoured social background came together to make the Victorian era a golden age of Christian statesmanship. Among the contributors to this result Gladstone stands pre-eminent. His latest biographer wrote of him that no statesman in modern times 'has been in a position to dedicate such an extraordinary combination of qualities so unreservedly and effectively, on so grand a scale and for so long a period, to the task of giving effect in politics to the Christian religion'.[63] The desire to realize on earth the spirit of the Christian ethic was for Gladstone the mainspring of political action and the form which such action took was not a little influenced by the religious movements of his time. The Oxford Movement, for example, by reminding the Church to which he belonged of its Catholic and European heritage, drew him away from the insularity of outlook common among nineteenth-century Englishmen, and deepened the European sympathies which were to mould so powerfully the policies which, as Prime Minister, he was later to pursue.

Gladstone was indeed unique in the intensity of his self-conscious preoccupation with the task of building the Kingdom of God on earth. No less commendable, however, for being less obtrusive was the Christian motivation of the work of the great Victorian Conservative statesman, Lord Salisbury, who derived from his religion not only a guiding principle, to respond to the will of God as he understood it, but also a strong fear of presumption. To one who remarked to him that it was a noble wish to get good done in the world he replied: 'Yes, but not by you—never by you—never allow yourself to believe that for an instant.'[64] To be able to seek the guidance of God without equating one's judgments with the will of God is a major part of Christian wisdom. If Salisbury's diplomacy was superior to Gladstone's, the difference was in no small measure due to the greater depth of the former's grasp of the truth that he was dealing with a providential ordering of things which worked outside himself as well as within him. Gladstone and Salisbury, however, were both sons of the Church of England, and in different ways their careers reflect the increased vitality which was surging through the veins of the Establishment as the reign of Queen Victoria ran its course.

The revival of Anglicanism as a social force during the second half of the nineteenth century pales into insignificance, however, beside the general loss of influence by the Christian Churches in the first half of the twentieth. One of the clearest manifestations of this has been the weakening of the Nonconformist contribution to public life, strikingly illustrated in Sheffield, where five Congregationalists held the office of Lord Mayor in the first nineteen years of the century but only two Free Churchmen altogether in the following twenty years.[65] The alliance between religious dissent and the forces transforming society which was strong in Victorian England has since broken down and leadership among the industrial workers has become increasingly secularized. Part of the explanation lies in the displacement of the Liberal party and the moderate New Model unions, with which Non-conformity was closely associated, by the Labour party and an industrial unionism which was more favourably disposed towards Socialism. For the new developments in the British 'left', with their class-conscious appeal to the interests of the workers, could not hope to command the wholehearted allegiance of denominations which were mixed socially both in their leadership and in their rank and file. There is evidence, in fact, drawn from south-west Wales, that both churches and chapels have responded to these socially divisive changes by holding themselves aloof from the discussion of political issues.[66]

In large measure, however, the waning political influence of Dissent must be ascribed to the general decline in religious observance which set in even before 1900 in the metropolis and was reflected in the Free Churches after about 1910 by falling membership statistics and a tailing-off in chapel building.[67] We are not concerned here with the decline of the churches in order to bewail it, nor is there space to undertake the more useful task of rational inquiry into its causes. What must be noted, however, is that the recession of belief has itself prompted new lay initiatives, many of them ecumenical in character, reflecting and assisting the growing unity among the Churches which has been the most heartening feature of Christian history in the twentieth century. For it has come to be realized with increased conviction that only through a fully active laity can the Christian faith make any real impression upon the contemporary world. One of the boldest of recent experiments has been the Industrial Mission in the diocese of Sheffield, which was launched in 1944. It employs missioners to discover potential leaders among the workers and managers of the great steelworks, and sets out to train such men, once they have been discovered, to spread unobtrusively among their fellows the Christian approach to the problems of living and working. What is projected is not indoctrination—the use of the laity to propagate an authoritatively determined code of social ethics—but rather the stimulation of laymen to think out for themselves, if possible in conjunction with their workmates who are not committed Christians, the right answer to the practical questions of life. A senior manager may convene fellow-managers for a study of their common problems and interests; a lad may organize a meeting for other apprentices.[68] The idea that the Church should incite and encourage her lay members to work out their problems for themselves, in the light of both the Christian understanding of the nature of man and an expert knowledge of the facts, was an important feature also of the Christian Frontier movement and the Frontier Council formed in 1942. The Frontier movement has been concerned with man's duty to obey God in all the social groups and natural relationships in which by God's ordinance and the necessities of historical existence he finds himself. Its sphere of interest has included politics, international, national and local, industry and commerce, scientific research, education generally, the arts, the family and the professions. It has endeavoured to work out the implications of the belief that in all these walks of life men are called to glorify and obey God and to serve their neighbours. The Christian Frontier Council has promoted the formation of specialist groups to work intensively and continuously at particular subjects, and the fruits of the thinking which it has stimulated have been seen in various publications. One of these[69] grew out of the deliberations of a group of university teachers and administrators jointly sponsored by the Council and the Student Christian Movement; another[70] was the outcome of discussion by a Frontier group of doctors.

IV · The Laity as the Church in Diaspora

With these developments the lay revival in British Protestantism has entered a new and significant phase. In the nineteenth century all too often the layman was thought of merely as an instrument of evangelization. The phrase 'lay agency', which was frequently on the lips of ecclesiastical reformers in the eighteen-sixties, conveys clearly and unmistakably that view. More recently, however, we have come to see that the task of Christians, whether clerical or lay, is not to do something for the Church but to be the Church. The peculiar privilege of lay Christians is to be the Church in *diaspora*, the Church dispersed throughout the world in every social class and every just vocation. The House Church experiment as conducted by Canon Southcott, formerly of Leeds and now Provost of Southwark, is a way of expressing through forms of worship this conception of the Church's nature. In it the parish meets for worship, not only generally in the parish church but in smaller groups in private houses, so that the very centre of the Church's life, her corporate offering of praise and thanksgiving, is set in close proximity to the world of everyday affairs in which the worshippers move.

The experiment of House Churches has spread from Leeds to many parts of the British Isles. In Scotland the experiment has been tried in old-established parish churches and in new housing estates in Glasgow, Greenock, Edinburgh and Aberdeen. By being thus dispersed in the homes of her laity, the parish church is more effectively earthed in its locality, better equipped to cope with the problems of a secularized world. Canon Southcott describes the variety of uses to which the Church in the House may be put: 'We have discovered that the Church in the diocese, the Church in the parish, needs the Church writ smaller, the House Church. The parish communion of the people of God on Sunday in the parish church demands the house communion in the people's homes on weekday. The parish meeting of the people of God in the parish hall needs the intensive house meeting in people's homes. The parish church for "the whole" needs the house communion for the sick and elderly. Public baptism of the people of God quarterly on a Sunday needs the Extensive House Church in homes of lapsed and the outsider. The parish Confirmation annually in the parish church needs the house confirmation classes. Sunday evening worship in the parish church needs the house services. Children's work and instruction in the parish church needs the house school.'[71] Moreover, by meeting in private houses members of the Church recall the atmosphere of apostolic times when, 'breaking bread from house to house', Christians 'did eat their meat with gladness and singleness of heart' (Acts 2.46).

During the last one hundred and eighty years, as we have seen, Great Britain has experienced an important lay revival, which has unfolded itself in three successive stages. The first, which ended about 1830, was practical. The second, which occupied the second half of the nineteenth century, was ecclesiastical and theological, mainly concerned with realizing the Pauline doctrine of the Body of Christ by fitting laymen into the Church's internal structure. During the twentieth century, however, a third phase has opened, not less theological, in some respects more profoundly so, but more ecumenical in character and more firmly focused upon the Church's mission to society. Secular events have affected the process in all its phases. Thus, for example, the growing emphasis on representative government profoundly influenced the struggle for laymen's rights in Methodism in the middle years of the nineteenth century and was not without effect upon the movement for lay representation in the Church of England.[72] Perhaps the most powerful secular influence, however, has been the growth of an industrial and urban civilization. On the one hand the city, with its huge accumulations of viable wealth available for philanthropy and its highly organized business life tending to promote the spirit of association, has provided the means of lay activism. Clapham and Hackney, two of the earliest manifestations of the modern lay renaissance in Britain, were strongly supported by City men. On the other, industrialization has supplied the challenge to lay endeavour, by divorcing the people from organized Christianity and by building up a secular culture indifferent if not hostile to religion. The Churches in Britain are still far from having solved these problems, but the steps which they have taken have in the past few years helped them to understand, perhaps better and more fully than ever before, the nature of the laity, and of its vocation to serve God at all times and in all places to his glory.

NOTES

1. J. R. Green, *History of the English People* (1886), IV, p. 272.

2. N. Sykes, *Church and State in England in the Eighteenth Century*, p. 379.

3. N. J. Smelser, *Social Change in the Industrial Revolution*, p. 69; E. R. Wickham, *Church and People in an Industrial City*, pp. 46-8; R. W. Dale, *History of English Congregationalism* (1907), p. 593.

4. Quoted from Olive J. Brose, *Church and Parliament: The Reshaping of the Church of England*, p. 146. I am indebted to Dr G. F. A. Best of the University of Edinburgh for calling my attention to the importance of the seventeen-eighties as marking the beginning of a religious and philanthropic revival which was largely conducted by laymen.

5. *Gentleman's Magazine* LXXVII (1) (1807), pp. 174-5.

6. *Dictionary of National Biography* 48, p. 218.

7. A. B. Webster, *Joshua Watson: The Story of a Layman, 1771-1855*, pp. 62-3; ch. 3 *passim*.

8. E. M. Howse, *Saints in Politics*, pp. 180-2.

9. R. Coupland, *Wilberforce* (1945), pp. 337, 349.

10. Wickham, *op. cit.*, pp. 70-5.

11. Quoted from Smelser, *op. cit.*, p. 71.

12. R. F. Wearmouth, *Some Working Class Movements of the Nineteenth Century*, sec. 3, ch. 4 *passim*.

13. *Ibid.*, p. 302.

14. *Ibid.*, p. 301.

15. 'Census Report of 1851-3 on Religious Worship', *English Historical Documents XII* (*1*), *1833-74*, ed. G. M. Young and W. D. Handcock, p. 382.

16. A. T. Patterson, *Radical Leicester: A History of Leicester 1780-1850* (Leicester, 1954), p. 302; see also Wickham, *op. cit.*, pp. 61-6, for the affinity of Radical Dissenters and the artisan class in Sheffield in the late eighteenth century.

17. *Ibid.*, p. 92.

18. John Kent, *Jabez Bunting: the Last Wesleyan*, ch. 2.

19. Wickham, *op. cit.*, p. 123.

20. Maldwyn Edwards, *Methodism and England*, pp. 167–8.

21. R. F. Wearmouth, *Methodism and the Struggle of the Working Class, 1850–1900*, pp. 172–4. Even in the first half of the nineteenth century some Wesleyans became trade-union leaders, notably the Tolpuddle martyrs, but this was very exceptional before the eighteen-fifties. E. J. Hobsbawm, 'Methodism and the Threat of Revolution in Britain', *History Today*, February 1957.

22. Edwards, *op. cit.*, ch. 9.

23. J. Edwin Orr, *The Second Evangelical Awakening in Britain*, pp. 234–8.

24. *Ibid.*, pp. 211, 214 and 235.

25. Quoted from R. F. Wearmouth, *The Social and Political Influence of Methodism in the Twentieth Century*, p. 178.

26. Orr, *op. cit.*, p. 264.

27. Arnold Lloyd, *Quaker Social History, 1669–1738* (1950), ch. 8.

28. In 1819 the Bible Christians employed fourteen women evangelists with their sixteen male travelling preachers. C. J. Davey: *The Methodist Story* (1955), pp. 74–6. For the use of women preachers by the Primitive Methodists see *ibid.*, p. 112.

29. F. W. Cornish, *A History of the English Church* (ed. Stephens and Hunt), *The Nineteenth Century* (1910), Part II, ch. 4.

30. *The Oxford Dictionary of the Christian Church*, ed. F. L. Cross, article 'Deaconess'.

31. *The Official Report of the Church Congress held in 1868*, pp. 204–6.

32. B. A. Smith, *Dean Church. The Anglican Response to Newman* (1958), p. 190.

33. *Ibid.*, p. 195.

34. For a new assessment of the ecclesiastical significance of these reforms see G. F. A. Best, 'The Constitutional Revolution, 1828–32, and its Consequences for the Established Church', *Theology*, June 1959. Also Olive Brose, *Church and Parliament; The Reshaping of the Church of England, 1828–60*, chapters 1 and 2.

35. *English Historical Documents XII (1), 1833–74*, pp. 385–6.

36. Throughout the eighteen-fifties the Liberation Society, known first as the Anti-State-Church Association, made steady progress in numbers, finance and organization. Establishing its own Whip and in 1853 its own parliamentary committee, it scored notable successes in procuring the admission of Dissenters to the degrees of Oxford University and in winning over a majority in the Commons to support the abolition of Church Rates. In 1859 its founder Edward Miall delivered a speech at Manchester affirming the ultimate intention of disestablishing and disendowing the Church of England. For this information I am indebted to an unpublished thesis on 'The Rise of Combative Dissent, 1832–1859' presented to the University of Southampton by B. J. Mason.

37. *Rept. Ch. Congress, 1862*, pp. 167–8; *1863*, p. 85.

38. A. Blomfield, *Memoir of C. J. Blomfield* (1863), II, p. 169.

39. *Rept. Ch. Congress, 1862*, p. 53.

40. *Ibid.*, p. 62.

41. It was reported as early as 1862 that there were Readers in the diocese of Newfoundland: *ibid.*, p. 59.

42. *Oxford Dictionary of Christian Church*, article 'Lay Reader'; for particulars of the ceremony of admission see W. S. Williams, *A History of the Reader Movement in the Church of England* (privately printed, 1932), p. 4.

43. 2,375 in 1903. *Report of the Joint Committee of the Convocation of Canterbury on Readers and Subdeacons, 1904*, pp. 39–40.

44. *Rept. Ch. Congress, 1875*, p. 335.

45. W. S. Williams, *A Brief History of Readers and their Work in the Diocese of London, 1866–1926* (privately printed, 1927), p. 34.

46. Canon T. G. King, Hon. Secretary, Central Readers' Board, has kindly supplied me with the information that at present at least one hundred thousand services of Morning and Evening Prayer with sermon are taken each year by Readers in the provinces of Canterbury and York.

47. E. Burke, 'Speech on the Petition of the Unitarians', 11th May 1792, quoted in Norman Sykes, *Church and State in England in the Eighteenth Century*, p. 379.

48. Brose, *op. cit.*, p. 212. Other examples quoted in this work reflect a shift among Anglicans from a national to a pluralist position.

49. An Evangelical clergyman, the Rev. J. W. Bardsley, told the Church Congress in Stoke-on-Trent in 1875: 'Parish councils—I would not be without mine for any consideration': *Rept. Ch. Congress, 1875*, p. 332.

50. F. Makower, *The Constitutional History and Constitution of the Church of England*, p. 381.

51. Cornish, *op. cit.* II, pp. 325–7.

52. G. K. Bell, *Randall Davidson* (1935), pp. 402–3.

53. In 1898 Gore edited a volume of *Essays on Church Reform* in which appeared contributions dealing with the position of the laity in the Early Church and in the branches of the Anglican Communion outside England and one which stated the case for parochial church councils. In the following year he spoke at length at the Church Congress in favour of the latter: *Rept. Ch. Congress, 1899*, pp. 63–7.

54. *Ibid.*, pp. 54–7.

55. *Ibid.*, p. 64.

56. M. B. Reckitt, *Maurice to Temple: A Century of the Social Movement in the Church of England*, p. 19.

57. *Ibid.*, p. 14.

58. *Charles Kingsley: His Letters and Memories of His Life*, ed. by his wife (1877), I, p. 156.

59. Reckitt, *op. cit.*, pp. 89–90.

60. Guy Kendall, *Charles Kingsley and His Ideas*, p. 66.

61. Reckitt, *op. cit.*, pp. 95–6.

62. A. Mansbridge, *The Trodden Road*, p. 47.

63. Philip Magnus, *Gladstone: A Biography* (1954), pp. 440–1.

64. A. L. Kennedy, *Salisbury, 1830–1903: Portrait of a Statesman* (1953), p. 357.

65. E. A. Payne, *The Free Church Tradition in the Life of England* (1944 ed.), p. 128.

66. T. Brennan, E. W. Cooney and H. Pollins, *Social Change in South-West Wales*, pp. 131–45.

67. Wickham, *op. cit.*, ch. 5.

68. *Ibid.*, pp. 252–3.

69. Walter Moberley, *The Crisis in the University*.

70. *The Doctor's Profession*, The Christian Frontier Council.

71. E. W. Southcott, 'The House Church in Halton, Leeds', *Bulletin of the Department of the Laity, World Council of Churches, April 1957*.

72. Charles Gore told the Congress of 1899: 'In an age when all government is representative, it is impossible that in the highest department of our life we can acquiesce in a government in which we can take no part and exercise no constitutional influence' *Rept. Ch. Congress, 1899*, p. 67.

BIBLIOGRAPHY

T. Brennan, E. W. Cooney and H. Pollins, *Social Change in South-West Wales* (London, 1954).

O. J. Brose, *Church and Parliament: The Reshaping of the Church of England, 1828–1860* (London, 1959).

Church Congresses, 1861–1913, Annual Reports of.

F. W. Cornish, *A History of the English Church* (ed. Stephens and Hunt), vol. 8 (London, 1910).

M. Edwards, *Methodism and England* (London, 1944).

E. J. Hobsbawm, 'Methodism and the Threat of Revolution in Britain', *History Today*, February 1957.

E. M. Howse, *Saints in Politics* (London, 1953).

J. Kent, *Jabez Bunting: the Last Wesleyan* (London, 1955).

F. Makower, *The Constitutional History and Constitution of the Church of England* (London, 1895).

A. Mansbridge, *The Trodden Road* (London, 1940).

J. E. Orr, *The Second Evangelical Awakening in Britain* (London, 1949).

Readers and Subdeacons, Report of the Joint Committee of the Convocation of Canterbury on, 1904.

M. B. Reckitt, *Maurice to Temple: A Century of the Social Movement in the Church of England* (London, 1947).

N. J. Smelser, *Social Change in the Industrial Revolution* (London, 1959).

N. Sykes, *Church and State in England in the Eighteenth Century* (Cambridge, 1934).

R. F. Wearmouth, *Some Working Class Movements of the Nineteenth Century* (London, 1948).

—, *Methodism and the Struggle of the Working Classes, 1850–1900* (Leicester, 1954).

—, *The Social and Political Influence of Methodism in the Twentieth Century* (London, 1957).

A. B. Webster, *Joshua Watson: The Story of a Layman, 1771–1855* (London, 1954).

E. R. Wickham, *Church and People in an Industrial City* (London, 1957).

W. S. Williams, *A History of the Reader Movement in the Church of England* (privately printed, 1932).

—, *A Brief History of Readers and their Work in the Diocese of London, 1866–1926* (privately printed, 1927).

10

Howard Grimes

THE UNITED STATES
1800–1962

Introduction

FROM its beginning organized Christianity in the United States has been characterized by great diversity, a fact which was intensified in the nineteenth century by the multiplication of denominations. Thus the selection of data for a discussion is not easy, and only major lines of development can be noted. Primary attention is given to those Churches which, either by virtue of their early transplantation or their origin in America, are most representative of American patterns. The Lutheran bodies are not considered, nor is any attention given to Roman Catholicism or Eastern Orthodoxy. Although 'modern times' is understood to mean the nineteenth and twentieth centuries, aspects of the Colonial period are so crucial in understanding later developments that brief comments are made about that period.

I · The Colonial Period

Laymen assumed considerable control in the religious life of the Protestant colonies in America from earliest times, a situation which is most obvious in New England where the 'holy experiment' of a Christian commonwealth was most completely envisioned. Although the seeds of democracy were present in the Puritan experiment, it was not a plan whereby 'the people should rule but that they should be ruled by the specially elect of God'.[1] The elect did not hesitate to exercise churchly as well as political functions, as Elder Brewster did prior to the arrival of the first ordained minister in Plymouth Colony. As in many other instances necessity played a significant role in the impetus for lay leadership, as did political factors also. Yet it must be remembered that, as is pointed out in another chapter of this book, Puritanism was considerably lay-centred, and Separatism, out of which emerged the Baptist movement, was radically so oriented.

Nor was it only in New England that this lay control emerged. In Virginia the Vestries of the Anglican churches assumed such powers in relation to the clergy that the Archbishop of Canterbury is reported as expressing surprise, in 1697, that clergymen might 'be removed like domestic servants by a vote of the Vestry'.[2] An early eighteenth-century source described the situation in these words: '. . . the Vestries, legally chosen by the parishioners, have ever since the first settling of the country presented their own ministers and the Governor as ordinary might institute and induct them.'[3] Here too necessity was a factor, leading one historian to conclude that 'if the services of the Church were to be maintained it was necessary for the laymen to take entire charge not only of the management of property but also of the worship as well.'[4]

The lay-centred tendencies were intensified as the more radical Protestant groups were established. Roger Williams's insistence on religious freedom led to the founding of Rhode Island in 1636 and gave impetus to the beginning of the Baptist movement. Shortly thereafter the Quakers began migrating to America, at first finding refuge in Rhode Island, later settling in the colony charted by William Penn in 1681. Pennsylvania became the most pluralistic of the American colonies in the next century, thus forming the pattern for religious liberty stated in the Bill of Rights.

By the beginning of the eighteenth century, American church life had developed along the lines which flowered in the following century. Although the established church pattern continued in New England and the south, the independence of the laity also persisted. For example, Anglicans so feared the dangers of episcopal interference that they prevented the establishing of a resident episcopacy until after the Protestant Episcopal Church was formed in 1789.

In the meantime another group, the Presbyterians, was beginning to assert its influence. In the seventeenth century (and even later), Presbyterians and Congregationalists had scarcely been recognizable from one another, differing primarily on whether the congregation should ordain (Congregationalists) or other ministers (Presbyterian). From the establishing of the first presbytery in 1706, the Presbyterians became an increasing factor in American church life. It was in this group, for example, that the first Great Awakening arose. In some sense a continuation of the impetus for reform which had led many of the colonists to America, the result of the revival was to encourage the trend towards the minimizing of form and order in the church. Further, it led to an increase in the number of Presbyterians and Baptists and began the growth of the Methodists (though the Methodist Church was not organized until 1784). The enthusiasm among laymen which the revival engendered was to have continuing consequences in the future towards increasing the lay character of American Christianity.

II · *The Growth of Lay Influence*

Increasingly in the second half of the eighteenth century, the spirit of democracy developed. One cannot understand either the character of American democracy or its effect on the Churches without taking into account the pervading influence of the frontier up to about 1900. The frontier, beginning with the eastern seaboard in the seventeenth century and advancing steadily westward for more than two centuries, provided an area where restraints were minimal and where individualism and its consequent freedom were necessary, a place to which the Easterner who became dissatisfied with the growing restrictions of civilization could always move. As a recent writer has put it, it was not that democratic ideas were bred on the frontier: '. . . the American wilderness simply provided a congenial atmosphere for the well-established movement toward democracy.'[5] Under such conditions, where resident clergymen were more often absent than present, the necessity for as well as the belief in lay participation in the Church was intensified.

Another significant element in American democracy which affected the Churches was the separation of Church and State, a situation which led to the structuring of what had already been partly established, the principle of voluntaryism. The covenant emphasis in Congregationalism and Presbyterianism and the presence of the more radical groups provided the basis for the principle. With the eventual disestablishment of all Churches, it became necessary for members to assume responsibility for the total life of the Church, including its financial undergirding. A nineteenth-century commentator described this principle for his European readers: 'Thus have the Americans been trained to exercise the same energy, self-reliance, and enterprise in the cause of religion which they exhibit in other affairs.'[6] A recent interpreter of the spirit of American Christianity places the voluntaryistic principle first in his analysis, concluding that 'this utter dependence of the church upon the current support of its members for its very life has produced a strong sense of personal responsibility at the heart of American churchmanship.'[7]

In this atmosphere the 'Free Churches', discussed in another chapter of this book, flourished. The Mennonites had migrated in substantial numbers in the late seventeenth and early eighteenth centuries, and the Brethren came to Pennsylvania at William Penn's invitation between 1719 and 1729. The Dunkers, the Ephrata Society, and similar groups also came to the new world in the eighteenth century. Even more influential than these transplanted groups, however, were the more or less indigenous ones which grew out of the radical Reformation.

From the mid-eighteenth century onwards, the Baptists were one of the most influential in this regard. As the population moved westward, so moved the Baptists, their lack of concern for form fitting them for the rugged life of the frontier. 'The typical Baptist preacher of the early frontier', writes William Warren Sweet, 'came from the ranks of the people, among whom he lived and worked. He was a farmer and worked on the land five or six days a week, except when he was called upon to hold weekday meetings or funerals.'[8] A contemporary source gives the number of Baptists as almost one million by 1851.[9]

A second group which flourished on the frontier was the Methodists. Although formed into a Church only in 1784, growth was rapid and by 1851 their number is listed as 1,250,000.[10] Although its government was episcopal in form, its generous use of lay preachers, exhorters, and class-leaders; its system of circuit riders; and its 'democratic' theology (modified Arminianism) made their appeal to the frontier. Its adaptation to the frontier was so complete that it was separated almost completely from its Anglican parentage, being converted into a 'Free Church' in everything but church government.

A third group, indigenous to American soil, was the Disciples of Christ movement. Dating its origin from 1809 when Thomas Campbell served as counsellor to a group of twenty-one ministers who drew up a 'Declaration and Address' on the state of the Church, the movement was formally organized in 1830. Its extreme lay-centredness, to be described later, fitted it for the frontier so that its growth, too, was rapid.

An experience which affected these and other Churches was the outbreak of revivalism again on a large scale in the early years of the century. Leading eventually to the 'camp meeting' (where many of the participants camped for the duration of the revival), the character and affect of this movement were not unlike its earlier counterpart. One modern writer has described the situation in these words:

> The legacies of the circuit riders endured long after the spread of settlement and education made their calling obsolete. They had spread the potent, pervasive, democratic and irresistible Arminian theology up and down the West, and it was to be the hallmark of revival preaching ever after. Because their lack of education made them laymen in all but name, they had proved by their work that laymen could be the backbone of evangelism, and the revivalists who came after them were for the most part innocent of formal theological training, though they might acquire degrees of divinity in the course of their labors.[11]

These forces—and others—led to a distinctive kind of laicized Christianity which Sidney Mead has described as follows:

> Throughout the long hard process of institutional adaptation to the exigencies of a new world during which traditional churches and sects were metamorphosed into denominations and a kind of congregationalism came to prevail in every group as lay influence burgeoned, the spiritual and ideological apprehension of the faith itself was transformed from one primarily ritualistic and sacerdotal to one primarily evangelical. . . .[12]

It might be added that the Church under democracy was always in danger of ceasing to be the 'congregation under God' and becoming the 'congregation as self-governing', and a kind of laicization with secular overtones was a constant threat.

III · The Nineteenth Century

In previous sections some of the major influences in the development of the American understanding of the laity have been considered. We turn now to an account of how these forces eventuated in specific action in the life of the Churches and of the nation.

Church Polity. Three types of church government are common to American life: the episcopal, the congregational, and the presbyterian. The data to be presented indicate that in all three the laity came to a position of considerable influence as American church polity developed.

1. The Protestant Episcopal Church is an example of the first type. Because of the developments in Anglicanism in pre-revolutionary times, it is not surprising that when the constitution of the newly

formed Protestant Episcopal Church was adopted in 1789, it contained a provision for lay representation in the General Convention. Although no formal provision was made for Vestries until 1904, the plan which had existed in the Colonial period had been continued, and Canon 13 as now stated is 'simply a restatement of what had been before recognized as law'.[13] This canon provides that the 'Vestry shall be agents and legal representatives of the Parish in all matters concerning its corporate property and the relations of the Parish and its Clergy.'[14]

A further provision for lay participation is the 'lay reader', the layman who, under certain conditions, conducts public worship. Although the early canons on the lay reader concerned only candidates for Holy Orders, the General Convention of 1871 extended this provision to lay communicants for certain services, and in 1883 the number of such services was expanded, including the right, with special licence, to deliver 'addresses, instructions, and exhortations in vacant Parishes, Congregations, or Missions'.[15] The number of lay readers increased from 2,015 in 1900 to 7,750 in 1952,[16] and to 15,044 in 1960.

The Methodist Church is also episcopally governed in the United States, though its wide use of laymen and its extensive accommodation to the frontier were not always consistent with its polity. It is not surprising, then, that its laymen were dissatisfied with their lack of representation in its governing bodies beyond the local congregation and engaged in a long and at times vitriolic controversy to obtain it. After several secessions and much bickering, with clergy and laity supporting both sides, both branches of Episcopal Methodist granted laity rights in the 1870's, these rights being gradually extended in subsequent years so as to provide equal representation in both the annual and general conferences. A reading of the arguments, many of which are extant, leads to the conclusion that political rather than theological reasons were most often utilized, and thus those who won were no doubt right but probably for the wrong reasons.

2. By 1850 approximately one-third of the total membership of the American churches was in the Free Churches (not including Methodist).[17] In all of these, by their very nature, laymen had a significant share in church government.

None is more radically lay-centred than the Society of Friends. As a modern *Manual* puts it, 'All Friends have a ministry in the meeting of worship. . . .'[18] Likewise all members are participants in the monthly meeting for business, which elects the officers of the group. 'Ministers' are recorded, but this is only the recognition of those who have a gift for ministry and carries with it no special prerogatives except those accorded to ordained ministers by the state.

The Disciples of Christ (recently redesignated 'Christian Churches') is also radically lay-centred by its tradition. Both Thomas and Alexander Campbell (its founders) 'insisted upon the right of laymen to exhort, to teach, and, on occasion, to preach'.[19] The younger Campbell —Alexander—was bitter in his criticism of the Protestant clergy, insisting that there had arisen 'a Protestant priesthood which stood between the people and the Bible'.[20] He referred even to Baptist ministers (with whose Church the movement was associated for some fifteen years) as 'Bishop'. The minister was regarded 'as simply a special worker chosen by a congregation to have oversight of one voluntary society, who, when he leaves that society, has no office in any other in consequence of his being an officer in that.'[21] Any believer was (and still is) authorized to administer Holy Communion. Although there has been considerable self-examination within recent decades about some of these practices, they have remained essentially the same.

The Baptist churches have also been essentially lay-controlled since their beginning. Three principles contained in a church manual of 1867 are indicative of this fact: 'That the governmental power is in the hands of the people. . . . The right of a majority of the members of a church to rule, in accordance with the law of Christ. . . . That the power of a church cannot be transferred or alienated, and that church action is final.'[22] As a later manual puts it, 'The Church . . . acts as a pure democracy, every member having a voice and all equal with each other.'[23] Clergymen 'derive their authority to preach and administer the ordinances *from Christ, through his churches.*' Pastors 'should be elected by the church'.[24]

3. The Presbyterian Churches represent a position somewhere in between the two extremes, but have developed a system of lay representation which extends to all levels of church government. The provision for 'assistants', or 'ruling elders', in local churches dates in the United States from 1714.[25] The ruling elders (together with the deacons for some functions), all of whom are laymen, are to govern the church as representatives of the people, though the congregation as a whole retains many prerogatives. To be sure, the ministry (or 'teaching eldership') is not the same as the ruling eldership, and the pastor is amenable to the presbytery, not the congregation. The presbytery has a lay representative from each session, and the synods and the General Assembly also include equal clerical and lay representation.

In these three types, both the degree to which laymen exercise control and the way in which it is done vary, but the significant fact is that they all involve lay participation, which, when not originally provided, was fought for until granted. How much of this was due to political reasons and how much to an understanding of the Church is problematical, but the facts of the matter stand.

Interior Church Movements. It is not in church government alone that laymen have come into a share of the life of the Church in America. There have also been 'lay movements' within the Churches, most of them developing in the nineteenth century, which point to this larger participation. One of the earliest and most far-reaching of these is the Sunday school movement.

Although begun by Robert Raikes in 1780 in England as a school held on Sunday for poor children, the Sunday school was changed, perhaps partly in response to the secularization of public education in America, so as to become the major teaching agency of the Church. From the first it was a lay enterprise, both in control and teaching. As late as 1818, the New York Sunday School Union Society decried the lack of clerical support and concluded that the New York schools had 'been left entirely to lay instruction'.[26] As the Churches incorporated Sunday schools into their regular work in the 1820's, more clerical leadership was provided, but they were, and continue to be, one of the most authentic lay ventures in American Protestantism.

A second manifestation of lay concern is found in the various youth movements. The earliest were student Christian groups at Yale and Harvard in the eighteenth century. The student movement spread in subsequent years, and in the 1860's the Young Men's Christian Association was organized for young men, and later the Young Women's Christian Association for young women. The early 'Y' movement in the United States, as in England, provided opportunities for Christian lay study and activity.

The organized Churches followed somewhat later in providing groups for young people, with the interdenominational Christian Endeavor Society being formed in 1881. Many of the denominations followed soon after with their own organizations, for study, fellowship and service. Student Christian groups, both denominational and interdenominational, increased in the later nineteenth and early twentieth centuries.

A third manifestation of this demand for a larger share in the work of the Church is to be found in the women's movement. Local 'missionary societies' had come into existence in the early years of the century, and a women's auxiliary to the Missionary Society of the Methodist Episcopal Church was organized in 1819. In the 1860's and 70's, separate groups began in many of the Churches, such groups often being organized against the wishes of the men.

A fourth movement, never very strong, was the men's Brotherhood Movement. 'The antecedents of this emphasis on masculinity in religion', writes one historian, 'began with the Theodore Roosevelt impetus, which features virile leadership by men. Just as missionary and other societies for women mothered and accompanied the movement for women's rights, the "Laymen's Missionary Movement" [interdenominational] was the offspring of an era of men's self-consciousness in religion.'27 Thus, in addition to denominational groups, the Laymen's Missionary Movement, organized in 1906, provided an outlet for the concerns of men. Within more recent years the trend has been towards a more formal organization of men's work, with the Disciples of Christ creating the Department of Laymen's Organizations in 1944, and the Methodist Church organizing a separate Board of Lay Activities, first in the southern branch in 1914, later in the united Church in 1939.

In these and in similar ways, then, laymen expressed their concern for implementing their faith. However superficial some of the efforts may have been, they are of no slight importance for the story of the layman in the American Churches.

Women's Position. In most of the material presented thus far, the term lay*man* in the specific rather than the general sense is the appropriate one. This is not true with respect to the Sunday school, of course, in which women engaged as teachers from the first. Although women had also served in various ways in relation to charity, by and large they were reluctantly accepted into the organized life of the Churches.

The notable exception is the Society of Friends, where from its inception the equal ministry of women and men was accepted. Yet, in another Church almost as fully lay-centred, the Disciples of Christ, they had little place until the formation of the Women's Board of Missions in 1874. In the Methodist movement women such as Barbara Heck gave leadership in the early days in America, but it was 1898 in the southern branch before they could serve as Sunday school superintendents, with laity rights beyond the local church being extended to women in the northern group in 1900 but in the southern only in 1918. Women are accepted into church councils in varying degrees even today, with the Protestant Episcopal Church rejecting proposals to include them as members of the General Convention in both 1925 and 1955.

It should not be forgotten, of course, that in the larger conception of Christian vocation women have played a crucial place in the transmission of the Christian faith. As Kathleen Bliss puts it, 'If social conditions or church restrictions prevent her from such activities, she retreats into her base—the home—and there she is the transmitter of culture from one generation to another, the inculcator of morals and the teacher of faith.'[28]

Church and World. The previous statement leads us to a larger conception of lay activity than we have been considering, namely, the work of both men and women in the larger culture: home, business life, market-place, the political areas, and the like. The importance of this larger view none can deny; the facts are not easy to come by, however, and major research must still be done before this phase of the story can be told adequately. Further, H. R. Weber's evaluation of the American churches in this century, to the effect that they are too much concerned with what happens within the walls of a building, is probably a just criticism of American Christianity in earlier periods also.[29]

There are exceptions, of course. The earliest major social movement in American national life was the Anti-slavery Movement. Church leaders, lay and clerical, presented no united front on the matter, and the Churches *as organized* played a less important part than Christian clergy and laity within non-church movements. The Quakers were among the first and most steadfast in providing this leadership. John Woolman, beginning in the 1740's, led the opposition to slavery, and so solid had this become by around 1776 that it was thenceforth the official position of the Quaker group. Later leaders among the Friends included Lucretia Mott, John Greenleaf Whittier (the poet), Benjamin Lundy, and many others.

Laymen from other groups followed the Quaker lead: Presbyterians included the Tappans, wealthy merchants of New York, and James Birney, from Alabama. The Congregationalist Wendell Phillips and others also provided leadership. William Lloyd Garrison, the leader of the extremists, has been likened to an Old Testament prophet.

Somewhat later the temperance movement attracted leadership of both men and women from the Churches. Local protests had been made in the early years of the century, while Frances Willard became the acknowledged leader in post-Civil War days.

Timothy L. Smith has recently shown how both the opposition to slavery and other forms of social reform were influenced by the revival and holiness movements of the mid-nineteenth century. He concludes by pointing towards the later 'social gospel' movement when he writes: 'Not Darwinian philosophy or the new sociology but the nearness men felt to God in the mid-century awakenings catalyzed the Kingdom ideology whose elements Edward Beecher had weighed out in 1835.'[30] Yet there is evidence to indicate that this movement was probably too clerically dominated, that the clergy failed to take the laity along in their thinking. How fully statesmen and other national leaders have seen themselves as acting Christianly, or how much they were led to act on Christian motivations, it is difficult to say. Yet this was probably one factor entering into the social revolution which has occurred in American life beginning with Theodore Roosevelt and continuing especially under Franklin D. Roosevelt.

Nor is it only in the broad area of political and social reform that the result of lay Christian activity can be seen. However narrowly conceived the image of the 'Christian business man' in American life may be, their sincerity in principle cannot be denied, and their number is probably greater than is generally believed. The philanthropy which has characterized American life and the setting up of foundations for educational and charitable purposes must also be seen as partly motivated from Christian concern. In the field of education also, the work of Christian laymen may be discerned. Although the general pattern has been for clergymen to be presidents of church-related colleges, this has not always been the case, and certainly in lower echelons of administration and among the faculties there are outstanding examples of Christian laymanship. In benevolent and social service enterprises the same factor can be seen at work.

The dream of a Christian nation may have proved to be naïve and unrealizable, but the contribution of Christian laymen, both men and women, to the development of American life cannot be denied.

IV · The Twentieth Century

Those conditions which had their origin in the Colonial period and flowered in the nineteenth century still persist to a great extent in American church life. The amount of lay activity within the Church is staggering, especially in the south, the mid-west, and the south-west, where Protestantism is still growing and dynamic. Yet the situation has also shown considerable change, and to this we now turn.

Henry Steele Commager's recent appraisal of the changing role of the Church in American culture is not without foundation. It has, he writes, 'largely forfeited its moral function and assumed, instead, a secular one—that of serving as a social organization'.[31] This judgment points to an increasing tendency within recent years for the Church to be thought of primarily as an institution, with the clergyman as a professional—a specialist in religion—and the layman as a kind of 'helper' to the specialist, serving in a multitude of ways within the institution. Indeed it may be said that the major Protestant Churches have assumed many of the characteristics of 'established' Churches, closely allied with the culture, and that the increase in the number and membership of the newer Free Churches is partly in protest against this situation.

These newer 'Free Churches', often referred to in America as 'sects', are in many ways nearer the nineteenth-century image of the lay-centred church than are now many of those which flourished in that century. In many of the newer groups, there is little line of demarcation between clergy and laity, their educational standards for the former often being non-existent. There is a kind of community within their congregations which no longer exists to that degree in the more established Churches. The disinherited of society find in them an acceptance which they no longer receive from the older denominations. They remain less institutionalized, more lay-centred, and less professionally oriented than the major groups.

One manifestation of change in the more established groups is the expansion of the 'programmes' of local churches and the burgeoning of national boards and agencies to support such programmes. The concept of the 'seven-day-a-week programme' became increasingly popular in the period following World War I, with a multiplication of 'activities' —recreation, sports, dramatic clubs, hobby and craft groups, social affairs, 'family nights' and the like. Concurrently, with the increased secularization of public education, the Churches have developed their educational programmes, adding various forms of weekday activities. Adult education has also greatly expanded. In such a situation many laymen must be *used* in order to keep the programme going.

The accompanying expansion of national boards and agencies has led such agencies to conceive of their task partly as one of promotion. Pressure is exerted through channels to see that local churches carry out the interests of a particular agency. Although Churches with a more centralized form of government (such as the Methodist) succumb to this trend more easily than the more congregational, a recent study of the American Baptist Convention indicates that this group has not been spared,[32] and this would appear to be the case in most instances.

All of this has led to the growth of the administrative responsibilities of church leadership, both lay and clerical. In a study of the ministry made by Dr Samuel Blizzard, it was discovered that his ministerial respondents spent on the average two-fifths of their working day on administration, with more time spent in stenographic work than in sermon preparation.[33] Much of the administrative work consists in directing the 'army of lay workers' who carry on the programme of the local church, along with additional time which he must spend in denominational and interdenominational concerns. There is almost no time left for the Church to be the Church!

The growth of the specialized ministries has also added to the complexities of the picture. Directors of Christian Education in local churches first began to be employed in the 1920's, and since then student workers on college campuses, administrators for local churches, directors of evangelism, directors of recreational activities, ministers of music, beyond-the-local church administrators, interdenominational executives and the like have been added. Such employees may be either clergy or laymen, but in either case their status tends to be thought of in professional terms, not clerical. These are the 'clericalized laity', to use Hendrik Kraemer's term.[34]

Such developments have not, on the whole, increased the understanding of the Church as the *laos tou theou*, for these professionals, though laymen according to traditional definitions, are serving in capacities once delegated either to the ordained clergyman or to the non-professional layman. They have increased the tendency in American Protestantism which has existed to some extent all along which blurs the distinction between the ordained and the unordained. On the other hand, they have increased the hierarchical conception of church membership, with three classes now existing: the ordained clergyman, the full-time but unordained church worker, and the ordinary church member, whose services are needed to carry out plans made by the first two classes.

This growing professionalism has affected directly the American Churches' image of the laity. Although the danger of American Protestantism has seldom been *clericalism, professionalism* has arisen in its place. The temptation is then for the 'ordinary' layman to leave the work of the Church to the professionals.

Accompanying the institutionalization of the Church there has also developed a superficiality about church life, a failure on the part of many laymen as well as clergymen to understand the deeper dimensions of the Christian gospel. The greatest temptation of the American Churches has been to fall victim to what Richard Niebuhr calls the 'Christ *of* culture' motif in the relation of Church and world,[35] to an identification of the Judaeo-Christian tradition with the 'American Way of Life' (Herberg), to the growth of 'folk religion' (Eckardt) or 'religion-in-general' (Marty).[36] The American Church, concludes H. R. Weber, 'Instead of being "the salt of the earth" . . . easily becomes a "religious country-club".'[37]

Out of this type of 'piety' have come many lay-sponsored and usually non-denominational groups which are fearful and suspicious of movements and individuals within the Church concerned with social and ethical issues. Such groups may support the retention of segregation, the purging of the Churches of alleged Communistic tendencies, and opposition to any form of social liberalism (which is usually identified with Communism). They may begin by showing concern for alleged Communist infiltration or being opposed to integration, but they often show their true colours by revealing that they are also anti-Catholic and anti-Semitic. Many also reveal themselves to be anti-clerical rather than pro-laity. Churches have in good faith put power in the hands of laymen but have not provided for them the kind of undergirding faith which directs the power in Christian channels, and now the Churches are being threatened by this undisciplined lay power. The fact that these laymen are often substantial contributors to the Church and its educational and social institutions is a complicating factor.

Fortunately these are not the only developments within American Protestantism, however, for in the period primarily since World War II new signs of lay vitality and concern have appeared. There is a growing dissatisfaction among a minority for the superficiality which has been far too common. Unlike the more popular movements (such as the 'peace of mind' school), these stirrings receive little notice and as yet affect only a small group. But they are important beginnings of renewal.

The most common pattern which has emerged is the small, concerned group within the congregation, either for study or fellowship and prayer. Although they ante-date World War II as a manifestation within the Student Movement, their growth in local parishes has been since the war. They follow various patterns both in character and origin. In some instances the pastor is responsible for their beginning, while in others a few laymen initiate such a study group. The pattern of the adult Sunday school class meeting on Sunday morning serves as the structure for some; others meet on Sunday evening or weekdays or nights. The pastor may be the leader, or laymen may assume the initiative, often rotating the leadership. Usually some specific printed material is used as the basis for study, and each member is expected to do outside study.

One such experience is described by the pastor in whose congregation the movement arose:

> We had been in Aldersgate Church a few months when a young couple with very little church background joined that church. The whole family, father and mother and three children, were baptized one Sunday morning. Shortly after joining the church they said, 'We don't know anything about Christianity, but we'd like to learn about our faith. Can you help us?' This seemed to be the opening we had waited for. We found two other couples and two or three other individuals, and we began to meet twice a month at night in the homes of the people who were in the group.
>
> We studied the Gospels; we discussed; we prayed together. The group went along without much organization, and we watched the friendships of those within the group begin to deepen. We were in one another's homes; we were talking about things that mattered. No matter how academically I would start the discussion, the people would invariably bring it down to their daily lives where they needed help. We began to see that this experience was providing real Christian fellowship, more fellowship in Christ than any other group or work going on in our church.[38]

In another church a small group consisting of both college professors and non-college graduates began meeting on Sunday morning before worship, providing their own leadership. In still another the pastor regularly offers a course in Biblical Theology on week-nights in which he has engaged almost half of his congregation over a number of years. In yet another a group of a dozen or so met on Sunday evenings in each other's homes, with the pastor present part of the time and with no formal leadership. In a student centre near a state university campus a 'Guild of Lay Theologians' is under way, the purpose of which is to provide theological education for students in order that they may more effectively witness in the campus organizations to which they belong. Further examples are described in a book edited by John L. Casteel, *Spiritual Renewal Through Personal Groups.*[39] Such groups are burgeoning all across the United States in congregations.

A second manifestation of lay renewal is found in the development of the conference centre, much like the 'academies' of Europe. The movement has a history extending back to the camp meetings of the nineteenth century. The first such centre was established at Lake Chautauqua, New York, in 1874, at first as a training centre for Sunday school workers but later as a cultural and religious educational centre. In the early years of this century the conference centre for young people developed, and in the period since about 1930 the summer conference has been one of the most useful phases of youth work. Since World War II more and more regional denominational agencies have developed their own camp and conference centres, at first principally for youth meetings. Increasingly, however, adults have utilized the facilities for retreats, leadership training enterprises, and other meetings. Although the more common pattern is still the training enterprise or the youth conference, the number of adult study conferences for laymen in general has steadily increased.

Other centres have developed primarily for adults, with the emphasis on fellowship, prayer and study. Over a quarter of a century ago the Quakers established Pendle Hill, at Wallingford, Pennsylvania, as a year-round study centre, 'bringing to meditation and study the Christians of many denominations and also many foreign students of differing faiths during their stay in the United States.'[40] Kirkridge, near Bangor, Maine, was begun in 1942. A residential centre was initiated by the Episcopal Church at Parishfield, Brighton, Michigan, in 1948, and is open to all denominations. The United Church of Canada has established four lay training centres: the Prairie Christian Training Centre at Fort Qu'Appelle, Saskatchewan; the Five Oaks Christian Workers Centre at Paris, Ontario; the Atlantic Christian Training Centre at Tatamagouche, Nova Scotia; and the Christian Leadership Training School at Naramata, British Columbia.

In 1952 an unusual experiment was begun in Austin, Texas, as a resident community for students at the University of Texas. Non-credit theological study is provided for the residents. In 1959 a new phase of the venture was launched, directed towards both clergy and laity in local parishes. Called the 'Laos House', it conducts short courses 'to meet the needs of an increasing number of persons both inside and outside the Church who are seeking a theological education adequate to their desire for intellectual honesty and integrity'.[41]

Yet another centre is Yokefellow House, in Richmond, Indiana, begun in 1956, where two-day and one-week institutes are held as a means of 'reformation *within* the Church that brings to the nominal member a new commitment and understanding of his participation in the Christian community'.[42]

So many of these centres have been established recently that no complete listing is available. Margaret Frakes lists twenty-two of a varied character,[43] and yet her list does not include the experimental work being done by the United Lutheran Church nor a centre established by the Episcopal Diocese of the state of Oklahoma at Fern Mountain, near Muskogee, Oklahoma. Franklin Littell lists several others not on her list.[44]

Although not, strictly speaking, a lay enterprise, a third manifestation in American church life is sufficiently near our primary concern that it may be mentioned briefly, namely, parish renewal. The best known of the experimental parishes is the East Harlem Protestant Parish, begun in the mid-forties in one of the worse slum areas of New York City. It has consistently emphasized the unstructured approach to church life, often operating out of small store buildings and seeking to meet the people of the community in terms of their own needs. The Church of the Saviour, in Washington, D.C., is also an unusual development, emphasizing as it does full participation of the entire congregation in the total life of the parish and continued small group study. The Judson Memorial Church in New York City may also be cited.

It seems only fair to say, however, that Protestantism has generally been reluctant to discard conventional forms of congregational life, even in those areas of both country and city where the Church is badly failing. Creative work has been done on a small scale through the 'larger parish' (the joining of several small congregations into one parish) and 'group ministry' (the providing of a team ministry for the several congregations) plans in rural areas. Not much has occurred of a significant nature by way of the renewal of the church in the inner city.

V · The Future and the Past

Serious questions have been raised concerning much of the American Churches' understanding of the laity and the work currently being carried on by laymen. It is too much church-centred, too little world-centred. Too much of what the Church now does is to *use* laymen rather than helping the laity be the Church in the world.

To raise such questions, however, is to minimize neither the heritage of American Protestantism nor the current signs of renewal. The heritage provides a structure in which laymen are recognized and given an opportunity to be an active part of the Church. The continued insistence that church membership places upon both clergy and laity certain requirements and the vast reservoir of enthusiasm and vitality which exist among the laity provide the basis upon which a more adequate understanding can be built. Current signs of renewal indicate that an awakening is already under way.

If this heritage can be re-evaluated; if there can be, even for a minority, an increased understanding in depth of the meaning and message of the Church; if there can be a growing appreciation of the meaning of Christian vocation as living Christianly in all of life—and there is evidence that these *do* exist to some extent—then there is hope for the future. It may be that God will be able to use both the structures of the past and those which are emerging in American church life as channels through which he can do his work of renewal in the latter half of the twentieth century.

NOTES

1. James Truslow Adams, *The March of Democracy: A History of the United States*, vol. I: *The Rise of the Union* (New York: Charles Scribner's Sons, 1932, 1933), p. 36.

2. Quoted by Elizabeth H. Davidson, 'The Establishment of the English Church in Continental American Colonies', *Historical Papers of the Trinity College Historical Society*, Series XX (Durham, North Carolina: Duke University Press, 1936), p. 19.

3. *Papers Relating to the History of the Church in Virginia, A.D. 1650–1776*, ed. Williams Stevens Perry (privately printed, 1870), pp. 197–8.

4. Daniel D. Addison, 'The Growth of the Layman's Power in the Episcopal Church', *Papers of the American Society of Church History*, Second Series, vol. III, ed. William Walker Rockwell (London and New York: G. P. Putnam's Sons, The Knickerbocker Press, 1912), p. 67.

5. Ray Allen Bullington, *Westward Expansion* (New York: The Macmillan Company, 1949), p. 745.

6. Robert Baird, *Religion in America* . . . (New York: Harper & Brothers, 1844), p. 132; see also pp. 131–8.

7. Ronald E. Osborn, *The Spirit of American Christianity*, p. 54. See also H. R. Weber, 'A Greenhorn's Impression of the People of God in North America', *The Ecumenical Review* IX (April 1957), pp. 265–78.

8. William Warren Sweet, *Religion on the American Frontier: The Baptists, 1783–1830— A Collection of Source Material*, p. 36; see also pp. 17, 40–1.

9. R. Baird, *The Progress and Prospects of Christianity in the United States of America* . . . (London: Partridge and Oakey, 1841), p. 20.

10. *Loc. cit.*

11. Bernard W. Weisberger, *They Gathered at the River: The Story of the Great Revivalists and their Impact upon Religion in America* (Boston and Toronto: Little, Brown and Company, 1958), pp. 49–50.

I

12. 'The Rise of the Evangelical Conception of the Ministry in America (1607–1850)', *The Ministry in Historical Perspectives*, ed. Richard Niebuhr and Daniel D. Williams, p. 219.

13. Edwin Augustine White and Jackson A. Dykman, *Annotated Constitution and Canons for the Government of the Protestant Episcopal Church in the United States of America*, revised edition (Greenwich, Connecticut: The Seabury Press, 1954), p. 328; see also pp. 7–8.

14. *Ibid.*, p. 327.

15. *Ibid.*, pp. 246, 248 and *passim*.

16. Walter Herbert Stowe, *More Lay Readers than Clergy: A Study of the Office of Lay Reader in the History of the Church* (Church Historical Society Publications, No. 42, 1954), p. 26.

17. R. Baird, *The Progress and Prospects of Christianity*, p. 20.

18. *Faith and Practice of the Philadelphia Yearly Meeting of the Religious Society of Friends: A Book of Christian Discipline, 1955* (Philadelphia, Pa.: 1515 Cherry Street), pp. 17, 189; see also pp. 45–6, 61.

19. Winfred Ernest Garrison and Alfred T. DeGroot, *The Disciples of Christ: A History*, pp. 157–8.

20. *Ibid.*, p. 177.

21. *Ibid.*, p. 341.

22. J. M. Pendleton, *Church Manual Designed for the Use of Baptist Churches* (Philadelphia: American Baptist Publication Society, 1867), pp. 102–3.

23. F. M. McConnell, *McConnell's Manual for Baptist Churches* (Philadelphia: The Judson Press, 1926), p. 83.

24. Pendleton, *op. cit.*, p. 65 (itals. his); McConnell, *op. cit.*, p. 85.

25. Samuel J. Baird, *A Collection of the Acts, Deliverances, and Testimonies of the Supreme Judicatory of the Presbyterian Church* . . . (Philadelphia: Presbyterian Board of Publication, 1855), p. 65; see also Charles Hodge, *Discussion in Church Polity* . . . (New York: Charles Scribner's Sons, 1878) and Eugene Carson Blake, ed., *Presbyterian Law for the Local Church: A Handbook for Church Officers and Members*, rev. 1956 (Division of Publication for the Board of Christian Education of the Presbyterian Church in the United States of America, 1953, 1956).

26. 'The Second Annual Report of the New-York Sunday School Union Society, Presented on the 12th of May, 1818', *The Sunday School Repository* II:50 (June 1818).

27. Garrison and DeGroot, *op. cit.*, p. 427.

28. *The Service and Status of Women in the Churches* (London: SCM Press, 1952), p. 13.

29. Weber, *op. cit.*, p. 269.

30. *Revivalism and Social Reform in Mid-Nineteenth Century America* (New York and Nashville: Abingdon Press, 1957), p. 237 and *passim*.

31. *The American Mind: An Interpretation of American Thought and Character since the 1880's* (New Haven: Yale University Press, 1950), p. 426.

32. Paul M. Harrison, *Authority and Power in the Free Church Tradition: A Social Case History of the American Baptist Convention* (Princeton, New Jersey: Princeton University Press, 1959), esp. ch. 6.

33. Samuel W. Blizzard, 'The Minister's Dilemma', *The Christian Century* LXXII: 508–10 (25th April 1956).

34. Hendrik Kraemer, *A Theology of the Laity* (Philadelphia and London: Westminster Press and Lutterworth Press, 1958), pp. 165–6.

35. *Christ and Culture* (New York: Harper & Brothers, 1959), ch. 3.

36. The three analyses from which these terms are taken are: Will Herberg, *Protestant-Catholic-Jew: An Essay in American Religious Sociology* (Garden City, New York, 1956); A. Roy Eckardt, *The Surge of Piety in America: An Appraisal* (New York: Association Press, 1958); and Martin E. Marty, *The New Shape of American Religion*.

37. Weber, *op. cit.*, p. 269.

38. Robert A. Raines, *New Life in the Church*, p. 84.

39. Published by Association Press, 1957.

40. 'Laity Trends in North America', published by the World Council of Churches as part of its 'Laity Packet'.

41. From a leaflet published by the Christian Faith and Life Community, 'The Laic Theological Studies', available from the Director, the Rev. W. Jack Lewis, 2503 Rio Grande, Austin, Texas, USA.

42. From a leaflet published by the Yokefellow House; further information may be secured from the Director, Samuel Emerick, 228 College Avenue, Richmond, Indiana, USA.

43. Margaret Frakes, *Bridges to Understanding: The 'Academy Movement' in Europe and North America*, pp. 128–9 and ch. 6.

44. Franklin Hamlin Littell, *The German Phoenix: Men and Movements in the Church in Germany*, ch. 6, esp. pp. 157–65.

BIBLIOGRAPHY

Jerald C. Brauer, *Protestantism in America: A Narrative History* (Philadelphia: Westminster Press, 1953).

Howard Brinton, *Friends for 300 Years: The History and Beliefs of the Society of Friends Since George Fox Started the Quaker Movement* (New York: Harper & Brothers, 1952).

Howard Cameron, *Methodism and Society in Historical Perspective: Methodism and Society*, vol. I (New York and Nashville: Abingdon Press, 1961).

John L. Casteel (ed.), *Spiritual Renewal through Personal Groups* (New York: Association Press, 1957).

Margaret Frakes, *Bridges to Understanding: The 'Academy' Movement in Europe and North America* (Philadelphia: Muhlenberg Press, 1960).

Winfred Garrison and Alfred T. DeGroot, *The Disciples of Christ: A History* (St Louis, Missouri: Christian Board of Publication, 1948).

Winthrop S. Hudson, *The Great Tradition of the American Churches* (New York: Harper & Brothers, 1953).

Franklin H. Littell, *The Free Church* (Boston: Beacon Press, 1957).

—, *The German Phoenix: Men and Movements in the Church in Germany* (Garden City, New York: Doubleday & Company, Inc., 1960), ch. 6.

William Wilson Manross, *A History of the American Episcopal Church* (New York: Morehouse-Gorham Co., 1935, 1950).

Martin E. Marty, *The New Shape of American Religion* (New York: Harper & Brothers, 1959).

Perry Miller, *Errand into the Wilderness* (Cambridge, Massachusetts: The Belknap Press of Harvard University Press, 1956).

James Hastings Nichols, *Democracy and the Churches* (Philadelphia: Westminster Press, 1951).

Richard Niebuhr and Daniel D. Williams (ed.), *The Ministry in Historical Perspectives* (New York: Harper & Brothers, 1956).

— (in collaboration with Daniel Day Williams and James M. Gustafson), *The Purpose of the Church and Its Ministry: Reflections on the Aims of Theological Education* (New York: Harper & Brothers, 1956).

Ronald E. Osborn, *The Spirit of American Christianity* (New York: Harper & Brothers, 1958).

Robert A. Raines, *New Life in the Church* (New York: Harper & Brothers, 1961).

Anson Phelps Stokes, *Church and State in the United States*, three vols (New York: Harper & Brothers, 1953).

William Warren Sweet, *The American Churches: An Interpretation* (New York and Nashville: Abingdon-Cokesbury Press, 1948).

—, *Religion in Colonial America* (New York: Charles Scribner's Sons, 1942).

—, *Religion on the American Frontier*, vol. 1: *Baptists, 1783-1830—A Collection of Source Materials* (New York: Henry Holt & Co., 1931).

—, *Religion on the American Frontier*, vol. 2: *Presbyterians, 1783-1840—A Collection of Source Materials* (New York: Harper & Brothers, 1936).

Leonard J. Trinterud, *The Forming of an American Tradition: A Reexamination of Colonial Presbyterianism* (Philadelphia: Westminster Press, 1959).

George W. Webber, *God's Colony in Man's World* (New York and Nashville: Abingdon Press, 1960).

Gunnar Westin (tr. Virgil A. Olson), *The Free Church Through the Ages* (Nashville, Tennessee: Broadman Press, 1954, 1958).

11

Franklin H. Littell

THE RADICAL REFORMATION

Introduction: The Movement of Restitution

WITHIN recent years there has been growing attention to a major 'fault-line' in Protestant ranks, distinguishing those of European state-church type from the Free Churches which have come to strength in Great Britain and to predominance in America and among the Younger Churches. To the earliest representatives of the free church type, in the sixteenth and seventeenth centuries, the terms 'Left Wing of the Reformation', 'Radical Reformation' or 'Restitution' are more and more frequently applied.

Today it is clear that the 'Left Wing of the Reformation' numbered many men and movements whose attacks on Christendom were as varied in style and kind as were its defenders' excuses for it. The main groupings which may now be discerned in the radical Reformation of the sixteenth century, groupings which are also found in the religious pattern of the Commonwealth Period in England (1640–60), were these:

1. Religious revolutionaries ('Maccabean Christians' like Thomas Müntzer, Bernt Rothmann, the Fifth Monarchy men);

2. Anti-Trinitarians, both individuals and groups (Michael Servetus, Adam Pastor, the Polish Minor Church);

3. Spiritualizers (*Spiritualisten*) opposed to 'institutionalized religion' like Caspar Schwenckfeld, Sebastian Franck, Johannes Bünderlin;

4. Biblical restitutionists (Swiss Brethren, South German Brethren, Hutterites, Mennonites, Congregationalists, Baptists, Quakers).

The predominant note in the radical Reformation was that of the 'Restitution of the True Church' before the Great Church 'fell into apostasy'. To make a clear distinction, it might be well to speak of those in the sixteenth century to whom the key word was *reformatio* and to distinguish carefully from them those to whom the key word was *restitutio*. That a quite different view of church history is involved should be clear. A new periodization was introduced by the restitutionists; the ages of the Church as given by Orosius and Augustine are replaced by the following scheme: (*a*) the Early Church ('the Golden Age of Christianity'); (*b*) the Fall (occurring about the time of Constantine, but continuing as a condition through the 'dark ages'); (*c*) the Restitution (by the Anabaptists dated by their own movement; by later men like William Penn and Alexander Campbell dated by Luther and Zwingli—who were supposed, however, not to have carried out their own purposes to a consistent conclusion, thereby making a later completion by Quakers or Disciples necessary). The technical English term for this view of Christian history is 'Primitivism'.[1] The Early Church was the 'True Church'. 'Early Church' becomes a normative concept. The programme for the faithful is to restore the simple, inspired, non-dogmatic, brotherly community of the apostles and martyrs before 'the bishops went over to the world'.

For the Anti-Trinitarians before the Sozzini—as for New England Unitarianism before Transcendentalism—the programme was to get back behind the Fall to the simple, ethical, uncrystallized, true faith. The 'Fall' occurred with the enforcement of Trinitarian formulas after Nicaea (325). For the Spiritualizers, rise of the monarchial episcopate reinforced by apostolic succession marked the fall: pomp replaced apostolic simplicity, pride of position replaced the simple brotherhood of the disciples, the demands of the institution dried up the wellsprings of the Spirit. The 'Fall' was marked by the rise of institutionalism. By the biblical restitutionists, the 'Fall' was dated by the union of Church and State under Constantine: it was then that the suffering band of apostles and martyrs became the persecuting official religion. The hierarchy now administered where once the Holy Spirit had ruled. The simple, ethical faith of the True Church was replaced by greed, corruption, and pride of place. The leaders of the institution became like the leaders of the Gentiles against whom Jesus had spoken (Matt. 20.25). The most power-conscious of all was that persecutor who claimed the title '*servus servorum*', but by his conduct identified himself with the Anti-Christ.

Our concern here is with those men and movements who strove to restore a 'True Church' on the basis of the New Testament ordinances, in imitation of the Early Church. No further attention will be given to the other types in the 'Left Wing', although they have their followings even today. Nor will time be taken to show the influence which the Anabaptists had on the state-church Reformation in Hesse, Strasburg, Geneva and other areas, although this has now been amply documented. Our purpose is to show the way in which a restitutionist church view affected the attitude to the laity.

It is true that the 'laity', in Scriptural parlance, is the whole body of the Church. To speak of 'laity' as 'non-clergy' is to accept as normative the definition which grew up during the centuries when, for all practical purposes, the professionals were the Church. Nevertheless, because of this long separation of 'the religious' from the whole Israel of God, the reassertion of the integrity and authority of the ordinary communicant or member slips easily into an anti-clerical posture. The fault lies, however, not with those who reassert New Testament standards but with those who desire to continue the image of the 'good layman' as one who is an obedient subject—docile, servile and silent. The restitutionists proposed, and yet propose, that the 'good layman' should become again what he was in the Early Church: *the carrier of the faith.*

Such offices as are reconstituted in their congregations in imitation of the Early Church are, like those of the primitive congregations, strictly functional in character. The Hutterites had only the *'Diener am Wort'* (the servant of the Word) and *'Diener der Notdurft'* (the servant of those that are in need) (Acts 6.1–6). Every Christian man, by the ordination of his baptism, is called to witness. On him, and not solely on 'the religious', the *consilia perfectionis* are binding. This led, in the four branches of the Anabaptist movement (Swiss Brethren, South German Brethren, Hutterites, Mennonites), to the enforcement of rules for the whole membership which previously had been applied only to 'the religious': e.g., non-resistance, apostolic simplicity of life, avoidance of evil, avoidance of the oath, avoidance of the magistrate's office. In addition, separation from the 'spirit of the times' (*kosmos*) showed itself in enlargement of the 'peace testimony', adoption of the 'hat testimony' (Quakers), plain clothes and other peculiar customs. The entire community was put under the disciplines of discipleship, and not just a small minority admired and obeyed by the rest. It has sometimes wrongly been said that the Anabaptists, Baptists, Quakers, Mennonites, Brethren and like groups have no true doctrine of ordination and frequently no clergy at all. A more perceptive over-simplification would be to say *not that they have no clergy but that they have no laity.*

At least in their classical periods the restitutionist movements have had no laity of the sort that Christendom, until the coming of the 'post-Christian era', counted by the million.

I · Restitution Principles of Church Government

One of the evidences of the 'Fall' repeatedly noted by restitutionist groups has been the rise of sectarian parties and names. The restitution of the True Church involved also the recovery of the lost unity of Christian brethren. It is one of the ironies of Christian history that many new Churches and sects should have had their start in the determination of certain groups to remove themselves from existing parties and unite all Christians on a platform of primitive Christianity. The Anabaptists began as such, denying affiliation with papal, Lutheran or Zwinglian parties and claiming only the names 'Brethren' and 'Christians'. Among the radical Puritans the same theme reappeared. With the break-up of the colonial state-churches in America, many of the movements of mass evangelism were also restitutionist in church type and looked for church reunion to come in the new era of voluntaryism. The movement founded by James O'Kelly (1757–1826), which in 1931 combined with the Congregational churches, used only the name 'Christians'. That founded by Thomas Campbell and Alexander his son (1788–1866), and the movement led by Barton W. Stone (1772–1844) which joined forces with the Campbells in 1832, sought fellowship for years with the Baptists and Presbyterians, and welcomed into the groups of 'Christians' and 'Disciples' all those who sought a return to the original foundation and practice of the Early Church. Today this movement, split in 1906 over the matter of musical instruments in the church, includes two of the largest Protestant bodies in the USA: the Disciples of Christ (Christian Churches) and the Churches of Christ. In the restitutionist ecclesiology, the restoration of the True Church in the New Age was to be accompanied by an end of sectarianism and the return of primitive unity. According to the restitutionists, the Church was in fact one until prideful leaders appeared and suppressed the ministry of the whole people.

According to the restitutionists, sectarianism arose as a result of pride and ambition on the part of worldly men. In the simple brotherhood of the Early Church, where all shared in responsibility and authority, there was no occasion for such division and sectarian strife. 'The variety of this world, of the irreligiousness of the religions of it', remained an abiding concern to William Penn (1644–1718), and a standing proof that the established Churches had apostatized. The source of that unbrotherliness and the occasion of division was identified with the fall of the Church, when the Church began to follow the leadership-principle of the Gentiles rather than to preserve the simple life of the democracy of the spirit. This opinion was prevalent also among the Baptists of England and America. The autonomy of the single congregation was maintained not only to prevent the dangers of a centralized bureaucracy; primarily, it was stressed because at this level the faith and initiative of the frequently inarticulate non-professional could find proper expression and hearing. The Congregationalists, better educated, were also restitutionists, in their view of the renewal of lay initiative and control in the Churches. John Wise (1652–1725), author of the famous *Vindication* of the Congregational church order, argued that the New Testament was the Magna Carta of the Churches and that division, universal apostasy and desolation had followed the abandonment of the 'old Constitution of the Christian Churches'. Democracy was the highest form of government, and it was this form of government which Christ established among his people. '. . . He must needs be presumed to have made choice of that government as should least expose his people to hazard, either from the fraud, or arbitrary measures of particular men.'[2] The Restitution of the True Church restored authority to the whole people and removed the occasion of division.

Both Wise, the outstanding defender of thorough-going Congregationalism in early New England, and John Owen (1616–83), the principal apologist for Congregational polity in England, were radical restitutionists. Wise began his tract by dividing all Christian history into three periods:

> The first division contains the first three hundred years of Christianity, which may be accounted the most refined and purest time. . . .
> The second grand division of time, contains the space of the next twelve hundred years, downward, more or less: within which circuit is included the commencement, and progress of a direful apostasy, both as to worship, and government in the Churches . . . the Christian World became a Notorious Apostate.[3]

The third period, that of the Restitution, began with the great Reformers but was not successfully completed. But what they began in the general priesthood had been carried through in New England. In his

Restitution platform, a major plank was the reassertion of the 'Prerogatives, or Peculiar Immunities of the Laity' (Chapter IV). Voting, electing officers, deposing, approbating ordination and censures of members were all in the competence of the full membership.

John Owen, in *The True Nature of a Gospel Church and Its Government* (1689), also argued the case for a restoration of lay responsibility and authority. Christ alone was the head of those covenanted together in a voluntary religious society, and under him all church government and discipline were maintained by those acting for all the faithful.

> . . . as this whole church-power is committed unto the whole church by Christ, so that all are called unto the peculiar exercise of any part of it, by virtue of office-authority, do receive that authority from him by the only way of the communication of it—namely by his word and Spirit, through the ministry of the church. . . .

As for a voice in church government, the individual believer 'hath a right and title radically and originally unto. . . .'

> The church is a *voluntary society*. Persons otherwise absolutely free, as unto all the rules, laws and ends of such a society, do of their own wills and free choice coalesce into it. This is the original of churches. . . . It is gathered into this society merely by the authority of Christ.

Just as there could be no promiscuous membership of a whole population in the Church, so the integrity of its discipline could only be maintained among those who had freely and properly submitted to the rule of the brethren. The state-church practice denied the New Testament pattern and rested on a false base:

> A power of excommunication at random, towards all that those who exercise it can extend force unto, hath no foundation in the light of nature or authority of Scripture; and it would be ridiculous in any corporation to disenfranchise such as never belonged to it, who were never members of it. . . . They must be *members of that church* by which the sentence is to be pronounced against them; and this, as we have proved before, they cannot be without their consent. One church cannot excommunicate the members of another. . . .[4]

For both Wise and Owen, as representative Congregationalists, the power of the keys rested with the whole membership. This position they shared with the Anabaptists, the Baptists, the Quakers, and other restitutionist groups both then and now.

Church discipline, among the restitutionists, was based on Matt. 18.15–19. The responsibility of maintaining standards of entrance and of continued membership belong to all those who shared in the ordination of baptism. The keys of Peter to loose and to bind, as well as the key of David to unlock Scripture, belonged to the whole body of believers. The ordinance of the ban was described by Balthasar Hübmaier as follows:

Leonard: What is fraternal discipline?

John: When one sees his brother sin, he should go to him in love and admonish him fraternally and privately to leave off such sin. If he does leave off, his soul is won. If he does not, then two or three witnesses should be taken, and he may be admonished before them a second time. If he yields, it is well—if not, the church should hear of it. He is brought before her and admonished a third time. If he leaves off his sin the church has won his soul.

Leonard: Where does the church get its authority?

John: From Christ's command, given in Matt. xviii. 18, John xx. 23.

Leonard: By what right may one brother use his authority over another?

John: By the baptismal vow, which subjects everyone to the church and all its members, according to the word of Christ.

Leonard: Suppose the admonished sinner will not correct his course?

John: Then the church has the power and right to exclude and excommunicate him, as a perjurer and apostate.

Leonard: What is excommunication?

John: It is exclusion and separation to such an extent that no fellowship is held with such a person by Christians, whether in speaking, eating, drinking, grinding, baking, or in any other way, but he is treated as a heathen and a publican, who is bound and delivered over to Satan. He is to be avoided and shunned, lest the entire visible church be evil spoken of, disgraced and dishonoured by his company, and corrupted by his example, instead of being startled and made afraid by his punishment, so that they will mortify their sins. For as truly as God lives what the Church admits or excludes on earth is admitted or excluded above.

Leonard: On what are the grounds for exclusion?

John: Unwillingness to be reconciled with one's brother, or to abstain from sin. . . .[5]

The attitude to discipline and to ordination, as well as other matters, followed logically from the initial premise. The minister or theologian held his office, and it was an honoured one, in trust from the whole Church. Radical Puritanism brought not the debasement of the ministry but the elevation of the laity. To quote Peter Taylor Forsyth,

Independency erased the distinction between the theologian and the layman more completely than any other. No church was so little a church of its ministers, influential as these were. It was influence they had, and not power. The priesthood of all believers here first became practical and effective for church life . . . the voluntary principle became the whole principle of English Nonconformity.[6]

The ordinary member of the congregation shared the priesthood and by it the responsibility for an active initiative and standard of witness in the Church.

Such a view of the role of the member produced a quite different personality-type from the docile subject of an earlier period. The extraordinary qualities of the laity in the early Free Churches was a matter of constant comment (and contempt) on the part of those who believed that commoners should keep their appointed silent stations in society *and* in the Church. And indeed some of the activities of radical Reformers in the Churches of the establishments were unusual and embarrassing. They appeared to be always appealing decisions, as it were, from the duly constituted authorities to a 'higher court'. They denied that decision rested exclusively with the ordained or theologically schooled, and claimed *Sitzerrecht*, i.e., their own right to sit in judgment on the meaning of Scripture under the guidance of the Spirit (I Cor. 2.13, 15 f.). They openly challenged the decisions rendered by 'duly constituted' church authorities. Anabaptists, Independents and Quakers were trying to prove this principle by such odd behaviour, even though it often resulted in ejection or incarceration.

One of the first recorded instances of such appeal to another level occurred during the debate between Ulrich Zwingli and the Anabaptist leaders at Zurich. During the Second Disputation it became clear that Zwingli intended to refer the programme of reformation back to the Town Council, while the representative of the Catholic party wanted the university faculties circularized for opinions (*Gutachten*). Simon Stumpf took the floor to argue that the decision had already been taken, in the meetings for Bible study and prayer where earnest Christians had considered and reached a mind on these matters. 'The Spirit of God decides. And, if my Lords intend to recognize and maintain a position which is against the judgment of God, then I will pray Christ for his Spirit and teach and act against it.'[7] This incident has been used repeatedly by state-churchmen to demonstrate that the Swiss Brethren were 'enthusiasts' and individualists like the Zwickau prophets, and that such behaviour denies the reality of the Church. But that was not the direction of Stumpf's plea. He was arguing that decisions on such matters are made by brethren who follow the pattern of apostolic decision-making, that is, by the Holy Spirit in the midst of his people.[8] Such decisions cannot be referred outside the congregation, outside the setting of full participation by all those who live in the Church under the guidance of God the Holy Spirit. What the Anabaptist was trying to say was that the decision had been properly reached in the Church, with Bible study and common prayer and discussion on the part of all duly concerned. The Holy Spirit had decided, and the proper report would be, 'it seemed good to the Holy Spirit and to us' (Acts 15.28). And now Master Ulrich proposed to refer the decision back to the Town Council, a body without proper authority in matters of the faith! The Swiss Brethren were not *Schwärmer* ('Enthusiasts'), but free churchmen.

During the decades when the episcopal, presbyterial and congregational parties were struggling for the yet-undetermined control of the Church of England, the same type of appeal was brought forward on occasion. Sometimes a radical Puritan would simply stand up in the midst of the sermon or service and challenge the preacher's interpretation of the Word of God. This might be done by a brief address or by use of a series of proof-texts. In either case, the point was not so much to confront one inflexible opinion with another unyielding standpoint as it was to precipitate a discussion. We miss the whole point unless we see this clearly. The view of the Church which lay behind such conduct was, of course, restitutionist. Decisions involving all believers, appeals to witness which committed all members, could not be handed down from the pulpit. Preaching could enliven and inform the mind of the membership, but it was no substitute for it. The concern was dialogue, not dogmatics.

A clue to the peculiar actions of the restitutionists may be found by regarding the complaints of the conservatives. They objected to the radicals' 'principle of mutability': i.e., the latter could not be pinned to a fixed position from which they could not be moved, like most of the controversialists. The reason stands out: the radicals believed that in the process of a full and fair discussion something could be learned which was apparent to none of the participants at the beginning. Their experience in the intimate give and take of lay Christian groups, in which they saw the restitution of the simple fellowship of the Early Church, had convinced them that proper decisions could only be reached in the Church by sharing the conscientious judgment of all concerned. This was the only way in which 'the sense of the meeting' could be reached. In demanding a discussion, the radical Puritans were not primarily maintaining a fixed dogmatic position: they were insisting on a certain style of decision-making in the Church. That which made them disturbing to their opponents, who stood to fixed positions set in synods and assemblies, was precisely their willingness to change their stand if persuaded by sound argument based on the Scriptures.

No one stated the restitutionists' view of church government more winsomely than Menno Simons (1496–1561), in writing the introduction to his 'Meditation on the Twenty-fifth Psalm' (*c*. 1537):

> Then if I err in some things, which by the grace of God I hope is not the case, I pray everyone for the Lord's sake, lest I be put to shame, that if anyone has stronger and more convincing truth he through brotherly exhortation and instruction might assist me. I desire with my heart to accept it if he is right. Deal with me according to the intention of the Spirit and Word of Christ.[9]

The appeal of Menno that he be met with Christian charity was treated with contempt: he lived out his ministry harried by both governments and state-churches. But the process of decision-making for which he stood has become standard procedure in the Free Churches which flourished in Great Britain and came to fruition in the Free Churches of America and the Younger Churches of Asia and Africa. In those areas, even religious bodies which once had a totally different structure of power and decision have learned to listen as well as speak to those who sit in the pews and gather at the Lord's table.

II · *Restitution Principles and Missionary Work*

The church membership produced by the Restitution was not only sensitive to its prerogatives and responsibilities but also contributed greatly to the launching of the modern missionary movement.[10] In world Christianity today, at least since the 1938 *Statistical and Interpretative Survey of World Missions* (edited for the International Missionary Council by Joseph I. Parker), it is widely recognized that the Free Churches and other radical restitutionist groups are carrying the main load at the growing edge of the Christian movement. What is not sufficiently recognized is that this is a logical result of a church-view which made every baptized person a missioner—a reading of the layman's role which was vigorously denied by the Protestant state-churches on theological, historical and administrative grounds.

During the sixteenth century the claims of the Great Commission (Matt. 28.19–20; Mark 16.15–16) were, it would seem, officially denied by the Protestant state-churches, although the Jesuits and other Roman Catholic Orders had carried the gospel to the distant parts of the world. In evangelism at home, Lutherans, Calvinists and Anglicans reserved the work of evangelism and witness to those who had been given the authority to preach by the civil authorities. 'First, the Apostles preached the gospel to the whole world in their time; secondly, the Commission was exhausted.' The heathen outside Christendom are under the judgment of God because their fathers rejected the faith when it was offered them. The missioner's *Amt* was a matter of personal privilege with the apostles, but it is now controlled by the church order and system of civil appointment: '. . . whoever preaches without an appointment, that one is an enthusiast (*Schwärmer*).'[11] It took over a century before the theologians of the state-churches realized the significance of the discovery of America. For the discovery of tribes across the broad water meant that there were those who had never had the opportunity to hear the gospel and accept or reject it. It took over two centuries before the Pietist movement of renewal made the mission of the Church again the responsibility of those lay members who would accept the yoke.

Among the restitutionists, however, the Great Commission was held binding on all members of the covenant. The rule applied to both men and women: among the restitutionists, women too were speakers and missioners. The most significant Protestant missionary effort of the sixteenth century was that carried by the Hutterite colonies of Moravia.[12] Not just fervent eschatology, but the discipline of the membership, sustained the work. Of course certain *Vorsteher* (outstanding members) came to authority in the colonies. But the Great Commission was held to be binding upon every baptized believer. And from 1530 to 1573, when the Jesuit Counter-Reformation destroyed the Hutterite villages and brought to an end the golden period of the movement, the Hutterites sent *Sendboten* (envoys) all over the known world. Apostles suffered imprisonment and the death penalty in such distant centres of Christendom as Krakau, Salonica and Aachen.

Modern missions came into their own among the Continental establishments with the rise of Pietism. Only comparatively recently have some of the Continental Churches as a whole accepted the burden of the Christian mission. For a long time the missionary societies founded as a result of Pietist initiative functioned as voluntary societies on the margins of normal church life. In contrast, missionary work in the world of the restitutionists was carried by whole Churches. The Quakers were among the first to travel to distant points proclaiming the word. When missionary societies were founded among the Free Churches they became the expression of efforts of the total membership.

The founder of organized missionary effort in England was a Baptist, William Carey (1761–1834). Carey, beginning as an unlettered cobbler, became one of the greatest missionaries and translators in the history of the Church. Missionary work in America was founded by Samuel J. Mills (1783–1818), Congregationalist, whose efforts led to the founding of the American Board of Commissioners for Foreign Missions (1810), and Adoniram Judson (1788–1850), whose transfer to the Baptist cause led to the founding of the American Baptist Missionary Union (1814). These men were all restitutionists, men who believed that the standards of the Early Church were normative and that one of these standards was support of missionary work by the total membership. The base of missions was the commitment of the whole *Laos* to Christ and his mission.

Although for some time missions were opposed even among the young Free Churches in America, and an Anti-Missionary Union continued to function throughout much of the nineteenth century, today congregations from Maine to California have missionary allotments as part of their annual budgets. As might be expected, the American denominations which have been slowest to undertake independent missionary work have been the Episcopalian and Unitarian. The state-church status of Anglicanism during 175 years of colonial administration atrophied missionary concern on the part of the membership. And when the standing order split in New England, those who stood for 'Christendom'—the Unitarian Congregationalists—remained non-missionary. In contrast, those who had adopted the restitutionist view of church order—the Trinitarian Congregationalists—speedily developed a vigorous home and foreign missionary programme. It was the conviction of the restitutionists that the spread of the faith, like other dimensions of Christian statesmanship, was the responsibility of the total membership. In carrying through on this, they have made the carrier of the faith again the ordinary believing 'layman'. It is the small gifts of a multitude of concerned members in a multitude of congregations which today sustain the expansion of the Christian cause around the world. In the immediate future it may be the believing layman rather than the professional missionary who will carry the faith into large areas closed to traditional 'missions'.

III · *Restitution Principles and the Citizen*

There is a final dimension of the restitutionists' understanding of the layman's witness which deserves special attention: the effect on the body politic. This is one of the most difficult questions, for at first the Radicals of the Reformation appeared to be lacking in any sense of social and political responsibility. The Anabaptists, with their heightened eschatology and comparatively brief opportunity to develop, had no clear view of natural law. Their attitude to government was one of avoidance and restraint, for obvious reasons: the only governments they knew either slaughtered 'the faithful' or might be expected to persecute on the morrow. It was in the Commonwealth Period (1640–60), when Britain was ruled by restitutionists, that the general social and political significance of the position became clear.

Briefly stated, the lessons learned in the church meeting were 'secularized'; i.e., appropriated in the society at large. A. D. Lindsay and Daniel T. Jenkins have related the story with splendid sensitivity. The members trained to statesmanship in the simple democracy of the free church congregations became the type of citizens unwilling to submit blindly to arbitrary rulers. The concept of decent human relations and basic human rights cultivated among fellow-Christians was translated into the rights and responsibilities of fellow-citizens. The idea of a political compact based on consent grew out of the church covenant. Above all, the view that true and just decision can only be made when all concerned and subject to it shall have had their say was transferred from the congregations to the villages and hustings. However naïve and anti-historical the idea of the restitution may have been in its original form, the end result of the myth has been not only active laymen but active citizens.

He who was no longer content to be a passive object in religious affairs, but persisted in becoming a protagonist, was unwilling in the long run to be a docile and silent subject of monarchy and despots. When James I rejected the Puritans at Hampton Court (1604) with the ejaculation, 'No bishops, no king!', he was perceptive indeed. For the restitutionists' cause was not only the enlivenment of the total believing membership; it led inevitably and logically to the appearance of a new type of man in civil affairs as well, a man who was not a subject but a citizen.

NOTES

1. See the article of this title in *Weltkirchenlexikon*, ed. Franklin H. Littell and Hans Hermann Walz (Stuttgart: Kreuz-Verlag, 1960), cols. 1182–7.

2. John Wise, *A Vindication of the Government of New-England Churches . . . 1717* (Gainsville, Florida: Scholars' Facsimiles and Reprints, 1958), p. 62.

3. *Ibid.*, pp. 3–4, 5, 9.

4. John Owen, *The True Nature of a Gospel Church and Its Government . . . 1689* (London: James Clarke and Co., 1947), pp. 44–5, 61, 108, 114.

5. Henry C. Vedder, *Balthasar Hübmaier* (New York and London: J. P. Putnam's Sons, 1905), pp. 212–14.

6. Peter Taylor Forsyth, *Faith, Freedom, and the Future* (new edition, London: Independent Press, 1955), p. 324.

7. Cited in Heberle, 'Die Anfänge des Anabaptismus in der Schweiz', *Jahrbücher für Deutsche Theologie* (1858) III, p. 239.

8. See the writer's 'The Work of the Holy Spirit in Group Decisions', *The Mennonite Quarterly Review* XXXIV (1960) 2, pp. 75–96.

9. *The Complete Writings of Menno Simons (c. 1496–1561)* (Scottdale, Pa.: Herald Press, 1956), p. 65.

10. See the writer's 'The Free Church View of Missions' in *The Theology of the Christian Mission*, ed. G. H. Anderson (New York and London: McGraw-Hill and SCM Press, 1961); also 'Protestantism and the Great Commission', *Southwestern Journal of Theology* II (1959) 1, pp. 26–42.

11. *Gutachten* of the Wittenberg theological faculty, 1651, cited in Gustav Warneck, 'Mission unter den Heiden: 2, protestantische', *Realencyklopädie für prot. Theol. u. Kirche*[3] (1903), XIII, pp. 130–1.

12. See the biographical articles on the leading *Sendboten* (George Blaurock, Ulrich Stadler, Peter Ridemann, Peter Walpot) in Harold S. Bender *et al.*, *The Mennonite Encyclopedia* (Scottdale, Pa.: Mennonite Publishing House, 1955–9), 4 volumes.

ADDITIONAL BIBLIOGRAPHICAL SUGGESTIONS

Roland H. Bainton, 'The Left Wing of the Reformation', *The Journal of Religion* XXI (1941) 2, pp. 124–39.

Winthrop S. Hudson, *The Great Tradition of the American Churches* (New York: Harper & Co., 1953).

Daniel T. Jenkins, *Church Meeting and Democracy* (London: Independent Press, 1944).

A. D. Lindsay, *The Essentials of Democracy* (Philadelphia: University of Pennsylvania Press, 1929).

Franklin H. Littell, *The Anabaptist View of the Church: An Introduction to Sectarian Protestantism* (Boston: Beacon Press, 1958), 2nd edition.

—, 'The Claims of the Free Churches', *The Christian Century* LXVIII (1961) 14, pp. 417–19.

—, *The Free Church* (Boston: Beacon Press, 1957).

Ernest A. Payne, *The Free Church Tradition in the Life of England* (London: SCM Press, 1951), 3rd edition.

George Huntston Williams and Angel M. Mergal (ed.), *Spiritual and Anabaptist Writers* (Library of Christian Classics XXV—Philadelphia and London: Westminster Press and SCM Press, 1957).

A. S. P. Woodhouse (ed.), *Puritanism and Liberty* (London: J. N. Dent & Sons, 1938).

The reassessment of the Anabaptists has followed on the publication of primary sources in recent years. See the discussion of the publishing project in the introduction to *Quellen zur Geschichte der Wiedertäufer, I: Herzogtum Württemberg*, ed. G. Bossert (Leipzig: M. Heinsius Nachf., 1930), *Quellen und Forschungen zur Reformationsgeschichte* XIII; see also 'The Changing Reputation of the Anabaptists', ch. 5 in *The Anabaptist View of the Church* (Boston: Beacon Press, 1958), 2nd edition.

12

Vasil T. Istavridis

THE ORTHODOX WORLD

I · Preliminary Observations

1. Periods of church history

SEVERAL Orthodox church historians studying or writing in their own field are generally apt to divide their subject, with some minor differences, into three main parts:

Ancient church history (100–800)
Middle church history (800–1453)
Modern church history (1453 to the present)

The first period starts with the end of the apostolic age and has the Seventh Ecumenical Council of Nicaea (787) or the preliminaries to the Great Schism between East and West as concluding point. The fall of Constantinople (1453) constitutes a turning-point from the middle to the modern period, which extends to our own day. These periods are further divided into minor chronological sub-divisions. These periods correspond roughly with those of church history in general. One may say that Orthodox manuals of church history present no leaps and bounds in the study of Western Christendom as is usually done from the Western (mainly Protestant) side in the study of the Eastern Orthodox Church.

2. The Eastern Orthodox Church and world

The Orthodox Church is also known as Greek, Eastern Orthodox or Orthodox Catholic in comparison with the Latin, Western or Roman Catholic Church. In the first centuries of Christianity the term 'Orthodox' (from right belief) was used to denote the Catholic, Apostolic or Christian Church against the heresies. In the East its use became com-

mon since 843, the year which marks the victory of the Church over
the Iconoclasts: the first Sunday in Lent is celebrated as the Sunday of
Orthodoxy.[1] Up to the nineteenth century, the term 'Eastern' was
appropriate geographically. But today Orthodoxy has become a world-
wide phenomenon, owing to the migration of Orthodox to almost all
parts of the world.

Orthodoxy organically is composed of independent and self-govern-
ing ecclesiastical units called Patriarchates and Autocephalous Churches.
First among equals (*primus inter pares*), with some special rights, is the
Ecumenical Patriarch of Constantinople.

Besides the Eastern Orthodox, the existence of other ancient Eastern
Churches should be noted. Historically, these Churches, with ten to
fifteen million members, go back to the dogmatic discussions over the
one or the two natures of Christ. They are the Assyrians, the Armenians,
the Syrians, the Syrians of St Thomas in India, the Copts and the
Ethiopians. Some of them use in their official title the term 'Orthodox'.
They are usually known as the Lesser Eastern Churches. In the subject
with which we are dealing there is no substantial difference, either in
principle or in practice, between any of the Eastern Churches, including
the Orthodox and the Lesser Eastern Churches. No separate chapter or
section is given to these Churches, but note is taken of them at appropriate points.[2]

3. Continuity in Orthodoxy

According to Orthodox ecclesiology the One Church of the Symbol
of Faith has never ceased to exist in the Orthodox Church. Orthodoxy
lives in an unbroken historic continuity with the past through the
apostolic succession of its bishops, the transmission of the apostolic
faith, and the celebration of sacraments. This Church has seen no change
or reformation in the Western sense, and thus lives in an unbroken
stream of living tradition.

II · The Laity in the Orthodox World

1. Church organization

Within the Orthodox Church all baptized members belong to the
class of laity. In the sacrament of ordination, those who receive a special
charisma through the laying-on of hands by the bishops become clergymen, thus becoming entitled to the right and duty of church administration, sanctification of the faithful and preaching the Word of God.

Laymen are not inactive in the domain of church organization. The government of the Church is synodical. Every ecumenical council, which constitutes the highest authority of church organization, was convened by the Byzantine Emperor, who was present in some of its sessions, or represented by his delegates throughout all sessions.[3] Besides the state officials, other laymen, mostly theologians, were taking part in these synods. This also applies to the other forms of the synodical system. From contemporary historical accounts and the signatures appended to synodical decrees, the presence of laymen in the various synods of the Ecumenical Patriarchate before and after the fall of Constantinople is a well-attested fact. This state of affairs continued until the promulgation of the General Regulations (1860), which gave the administration of spiritual matters to a twelve-member synod of metropolitans and left the rest of a temporal character to the care of a mixed national council of metropolitans and laymen. From 1923 onwards the mixed national council ceased to exist.

In Russia, from the time of Peter the Great (1721) till 1917, the Church was subjected by the Emperor to lay control; but this is to be regarded as an exception in Orthodox life. A great number of laymen were members of the Great Church Council, 1917/18, which decided to use laymen in church organization. This principle was applied in the life of the Russian Orthodox Church of the Diaspora, and in the Church of Russia since the Great Council of January 1945.

The presence of a lay procurator, without any real executive power today, in the sessions of the Synod of the Church of Greece is thought of as representing the lay element in the organization of the Church through the State.

The different synodical committees which study and report on several matters to the synod of each Church include laymen.

Throughout the centuries, laymen were directly or indirectly taking part in the election and appointment of the clergy. The special church assemblies, which were called during the vacancies of the Ecumenical Patriarchate with the purpose of electing a new Patriarch, included laymen, from the time of the Byzantine Empire till 1923. Today this system is still the practice, in different degrees, in some Orthodox Churches, those of Alexandria, Antioch, Jerusalem, Russia, Serbia, Cyprus and Bulgaria.

Until some centuries ago laymen, as members of the synods of the Ecumenical Patriarchate, played a direct role in the election of bishops. On the other hand, the Orthodox faithful, in vacant episcopal sees, made indirect appeal to the Church through written petitions, making proposals for their candidates to the Patriarchate, or expressing their consent or disapproval after elections. Even today, the approval of the faithful during and after the elections of their bishops or their parish priests is sought. The opinion of the faithful in the ordination services is also expressed through their acclamation '*Axios*' ('he is worthy').

In each local parish an ecclesiastical committee, elected by its members or appointed by the bishop, takes care of the financial and other temporal affairs of their community.

The same situation exists, more or less, in the parish life of all the Lesser Eastern Churches. From the middle of the nineteenth century onwards the lay element enters more in the administration of general church affairs. In the Armenian Church, in the Patriarchate of Constantinople (since 1860) the creation of a National Assembly should be noted. A similar arrangement exists in the Syrian Church (since 1913/14), and the Coptic Church of Alexandria. The electoral assemblies of the highest dignitaries of the Armenian, Syrian and Coptic Churches include a high percentage of laymen compared with clergy.

2. State-Church relations

State and Church relations in the East followed a different course from the West. With the foundation of a new state, the man in command acquired a special position and played a great role in the life of the Church. The Emperor, a layman himself, had the task of protecting the Church and not interfering with its internal affairs. He, besides having the right to call an ecumenical council, was actively engaged in the work of preparing church legislation, either by approving the laws of the Church and thus giving them the status of a state law, or by directly issuing laws affecting the life of the Church. In practice the principle of not interfering with the internal affairs of the Church was not always kept. On several occasions we see the Christian prince directly participating in the theological debates and trying to force the Church to accept his personal views, especially at times when the Church was confronted by problems relating to heresies, schisms and the unity of the Church. In some instances, the Christian prince was forcing the patriarchs and bishops to resign, and after that filling the vacancies by men of his choice. After the fall of Constantinople, the Ottoman Emperor, although of Muslim faith, assumed some of the rights of the Byzantine Emperor in handling church affairs.

The ideal of a Christian prince as the protector of the Church was put into practice in Russia, where the Church followed Byzantine norms and traditions of ecclesiastical life. The state-Church system was also copied by the newly founded Balkan states of Greece, Serbia, Rumania and Bulgaria, and replaced by a free church situation, with recurring pressures and attacks against the Church, by the atheistic states. Today only in Greece and Finland are the Orthodox state Churches; the rest are in a free church situation, sometimes legally recognized by governments, or without any legal recognition. The free church situation is also that of the Orthodox living in the Diaspora, that is, outside the boundaries of their respective mother Churches, in western Europe, the Americas, Australia and eastern Asia. Some of the Orthodox Churches in the Diaspora continue to live in a dual form of State-Church relations, first, trying to set up in their new surroundings the original conditions which existed in the countries they came from, and secondly, trying to establish themselves as 'free churches' within their new environment.

Among the Lesser Eastern Churches the only one which does not live in a free church situation but functions as an established Church is the Church of Ethiopia.

3. *The catholicity of the Church* (sometimes expressed by the Russian word *sobornost*)

The catholicity of the Church means the universality of the Church and the inner unity of spirit and love connecting the separate local churches. In this way oneness and Orthodoxy become synonymous with the term catholicity. The Church, according to the image of the Body of Christ, which represents the essence of Orthodox ecclesiology, is a wholeness which keeps the right faith and in which each member is in full accord with the other by the bonds of love. This inner quality is the most precious element in Orthodoxy and its maintenance one of the most important duties of the entire Church.

Laymen, by their presence in the deliberations of the ecumenical councils, and their presence and signing of the decrees of the synods after the fall of Constantinople, were engaged in the work of definition and explanation of the dogmatic teaching of the Church. But the most decisive role of the laity is played in the work of verifying and certifying the dogmas of the Church. In this domain the laymen, as members of the Body of Christ, have not a passive but an active and decisive voice. Every baptized Christian is accepted to be a 'theologian' in the true sense of the word, and called to verify the genuine church conscience.

The expression of the church conscience, having nothing typically of an organic or administrative character by which to act as a higher authority, possesses nevertheless the power of certifying and authorizing even the dogmatic decrees of the ecumenical councils. It is an expression of the corporate will of the body of the Church. In the history of the Church the decrees of the ecumenical councils have been either authorized by the silent acceptance of the church conscience or rejected by the unanimous refusal of the clergy and the laity. An ecumenical council, therefore, which is accepted to be the highest authority in the Church, is retained or loses its value with the final voice of the Church as a whole. Classic examples of Synods rejected by the Church as a whole are the robber Synod of Ephesus (449), and the Synod of Florence (1439).

The laymen, alongside the clergy, as members of the Church, are entrusted with the keeping of the faith from any external or internal rift. This truth is expressed in the well-known Encyclical Letter of the Eastern Patriarchs (1848), according to which 'the guardian of Orthodoxy is the body of the Church, i.e., the members themselves.'[4]

Laymen in the Armenian Church have taken active part in the discussions over the questions of doctrine and discipline, and as members of the councils have signed their decrees.

4. *Worship*

Worship is an essential element of Orthodoxy and an empirical realization of its dogmatic teaching. Members of the Church, unable to read or not having a sufficient knowledge of Orthodox teaching, are schooled through worship in the dogmas of the faith. Although all sacraments and other sacramental acts make the composite parts of worship, its central act remains the Holy Eucharist.

The existing difference between clergy and laity is not a difference of rank or of power, but of members with various functions who serve the same Body, and this truth becomes evident in eucharistic worship.

The clergyman does not pray as a representative of the laity and instead of him, but serves in the sacraments and the holy worship and prays with and for the laity.[5]

The laymen also serve and participate in the celebration of the Holy Sacraments. In early times, the whole Church took part in church singing, which is being done today by church choirs, composed mainly of boys and men, or by mixed choirs. Today some church leaders make efforts to revive the old custom or at least make the participants in holy worship read aloud some prayers in common. In case of emergency, and in the spirit of 'economy', laymen may carry the holy elements, or perform the sacrament of baptism.

In the celebration of the Holy Eucharist the participation of the laity is necessary. According to the canons of the Church, the Holy Liturgy may not be performed in their absence. The Holy Eucharist is understood as the corporate worship of the whole Church inclusive of the lay people, wherein every member has his appropriate liturgy to perform. In the offering of the holy elements the priest prays for those who have offered them, and throughout the Liturgy he always uses the expression 'we' instead of 'I', as the officer who speaks in the name of the congregation and not of himself. Through the centuries, the Orthodox Church has never known an alienation of the laity from their liturgical functions during the celebration of the sacraments, of the kind which happened in the West. It has stood within the ancient liturgical tradition which is again being recaptured in the Western Churches through the present Liturgical Movement.

In a sacramental and dogmatical Church like the Orthodox, the existence of lay preachers and of priests who are not theologians is a paradox, which is well explained by the position given to the laity in the sacramental life of the Church. Laymen who are not graduates of theological schools, after receiving the permission and consent of the bishop, are being appointed preachers in the local churches. And the Church, in order to meet the shortage of clergy, ordains to the priesthood qualified laymen, graduates of secondary schools or without much education but fulfilling the requirements of the Canon Law and with a good ecclesiastical record.[6]

The Lesser Eastern Churches through their ancient liturgical traditions also keep the same liturgical spirit of the Church as a wholeness, including clergy and laity.

5. *The contribution of lay artists and writers to Orthodox life*

History has not preserved the names of many workers who have spent their whole lives in the service of the sacred arts. In the Orthodox world the ideal of the sacred arts—church architecture, church painting, and hymn writing—is to glorify God. These arts are used as vehicles bringing men from this world to eternity. So their servants, being aware of their smallness before the greatness of God, want to keep themselves in obscurity. A great number of them, besides the monks, belong to the class of laity. According to their understanding, what they were doing was the outcome of a sacred vocation. That is why before starting their work, as happens even today, they prepared themselves in life through prayer and fasting in seclusion. Through their efforts and understanding the dogmas of the Church were no longer barren abstractions but living expressions of daily religious life.

The Church of St Sophia and other Byzantine churches, the magnificent panel-icons, wall-paintings and mosaics being restored in several ancient Byzantine and post-Byzantine churches, the illuminated manuscripts, and the church hymns sung in the different services and feasts of the Church form an integral whole explaining how lay artists think to present in an external form the religious feelings of the different epochs.

Besides the work of these lay artists, the work of Orthodox writers in general is also of importance. It is interesting to see these secular writers showing a keen interest through their writings in the different aspects of church life, criticizing several unchristian servants of Christ, describing and painting with vivid colours other real Christian characters, religious, moral, and social themes and feasts of the Church. There are countless pieces of prose and poetry which have fed the religious needs of generations of Orthodox nations and served in moulding the piety of the common Orthodox people. In modern times the names of Zacharias Papantoniou and Demetrios Moraitidis are well known in Greece, and in Russia those of the great writers Dostoievsky and Count Tolstoi.

In the Lesser Eastern Churches Armenian literature mostly bears a predominantly religious character. In the last two centuries lay writers have defended religion against attacks from different sources.

6. *Saints, martyrs, confessors, monks*

The life of the Church is not limited only to this world. It covers this world as well as eternity. The Mystical Body of Christ includes the Church Militant on earth and the Church Triumphant in heaven. The Church Triumphant consists of the saints, those who have lived in this world a life of penitence and obedience to God's will, those who have departed in faith and love, enjoying the glory of God and tasting in advance eternal blessedness.

Sainthood is a category of Christian life reached through constant effort in this world and later acknowledged and venerated by the Church. Sainthood is not a state of life practised by a special ecclesiastical order or class. It is a path open to all members of the Body of Christ here on earth from whatever strata of society; clergy or lay people, men or women. Nor is it a state of life practised in the early centuries of the history of the Christian Church and later given up. Throughout the centuries sainthood found its expression through several channels of a life full of obedience to God. Saints are being officially recognized as such by the Church on a local or a universal level even today. In 1955, the Ecumenical Patriarchate officially recognized the Athonite monk Nicodemus (1748–1809) as a saint.

In the first three centuries of the Christian era, the saints were mainly those who, during the great persecutions of the Church, steadfastly kept their faith against the many tribulations brought on them by their persecutors, and at the end died for Christ. Those ending their lives in this way were called martyrs, and others who had undergone hardships for the faith but escaped death, confessors. State rules against the Christians were applied first to the leaders of the Church, the bishops, priests and other clergy. But many martyrs were laymen of all ages, even catechumens. Martyrs' wishes were held in high regard by the members of the Church, especially when, during their persecutions, the lapsed presented to the Church letters written by martyrs (before their death) urging the reacceptance of the lapsed into ecclesiastical communion. This was also done by the confessors, who in the first three centuries of Christianity formed an influential class within the Church. The Orthodox Church can show martyrs, both clergy and laymen, who have suffered death for the sake of their faith during persecutions in its long history.

With the end of the persecutions in the fourth century, the spirit of renunciation of this world takes another form with the appearance of monasticism, whose adherents fly into the deserts in order to perfect themselves. While in the first three centuries the majority of saints were martyrs, monasticism from then on came to the fore. Monasticism in the East had and still keeps its predominantly lay character. This reality is well described by Professor Florovsky in one of his articles.

Early Monasticism was not an ecclesiastical institution. It was precisely a spontaneous movement, a drive. And it was distinctively *a lay movement*. The taking of Holy Orders was definitely discouraged, except by order of the superiors, and even abbots were often laymen. In early times, secular priests from the vicinity were invited to conduct services for the community, or else the neighbouring church was attended on Sundays. The monastic state was clearly distinguished from the clerical. 'Priesthood' was a dignity and an authority, and as such was regarded as hardly compatible with the life of obedience and penitence, which was the core and the heart of monastic existence. Certain concessions were made, however, time and again, but rather reluctantly. On the whole, in the East monasticism has preserved its lay character till the present day. In the communities of the Mount Athos, this last remnant of the old monastic regime, only a few are in the Holy Orders, and most do not seek them, as a rule. This is highly significant. Monasticism cut across the basic distinction between clergy and laity in the Church. It was a peculiar order in its own right.[7]

The Orthodox folk look at the lives of the saints as examples to be followed. The accounts of their lives are read both in church and at home and form the basis of Orthodox popular piety.

7. *The Christian family*

Matrimony is accepted in the Orthodox Church as one of the seven sacraments. This means that the coming together of one man and one woman in marital union is not only a social or a worldly affair, but an ecclesiastical service, by which the grace of God is conveyed, sanctifying the union of man and wife. Parents within their families are servants of redemption. This is attained by the spirit of mutual helpfulness and assistance, by a life of partnership, by the procreation of children, their Christian nurture and upbringing. Through the procreation of children, parents offer members to the human race, but above all new members to the Church. Through the centuries the family has been a unit parallel to the Church working for the fulfilment of God's will on earth. There are examples of parents who by their life and example helped their children to become servants of redemption as clergy or encouraged their vocation to give up the world and spend a life of solitude and constant prayer in monasteries. But generally, the Orthodox family has played a great role in the preservation and in the handing on of the faith. This truth becomes self-evident if we take into consideration, especially after the Arab and Ottoman conquests, the existence of a non-Christian state, the scarcity of schools and of educated clergy, and the inability of the official Church to meet the needs of the Orthodox faithful in the realm of religious education. This becomes more obvious during the periods of external crises or tensions between states and Church. In the present, it has been again tested and continues to be so in the Orthodox Churches behind the Iron Curtain, where any religious education by the Church is forbidden. There, apart from regular preaching during the church services, which is constantly threatened, the Orthodox family is the only place where any teaching concerning the faith can take place. One may be rather pessimistic about the future of the Church under such circumstances. The differing statements of the Russian Orthodox leaders and of several visitors, clergy or laity, during recent years, do not give the real picture of the actual situation of Orthodoxy. But the emergence of the Church and its survival in those areas, after almost forty years of constant pressure, is a hopeful sign for the future.

Within any form of society, the Orthodox family, besides being a handmaid of the Church in the transmission of the faith, is a school of Orthodox living, piety and moral life. Parents who grow up within the bosom of the Church and in constant touch with her show an active interest not only in the physical but also the moral and spiritual development of their children. This is well expressed in a recently written book on the meaning of Orthodox matrimony and priesthood.

> Parents teach their children good manners in the Christian tradition, the first lessons of prayer and of both religious and social knowledge. They check their habits. They exercise care in knowing their children's playmates and friends. They examine the books of their children, read and even note the vocabularies their children use when talking to either the young or the old. They guide them to school and to church and check both progress and attendance. They help them to participate in the family prayers and direct them in preparing themselves properly by fasting and confession to receive the Lord worthily in the sacrament of the Holy Eucharist. They read for them and with them the Holy Bible and other religious books dealing with the lives of the saints and the duties of every Christian. They lead them to church and show them how to light their candles and venerate the icons of the saints and how to behave during the entire service.[8]

Nor should we forget family influence on social life. The spirit of love, of co-operation with others, of brotherhood, of work, is first shaped within family life, which constitutes the smallest unit.

No one today could deny that there are many non-Christian influences which attempt to upset the foundations of Orthodox family life, but for the Orthodox one fact remains clear, that the survival of Christianity depends on the survival of the Christian family.

8. *Philanthropy*

This, both individual and organized, is a very strong tradition from Byzantine times.

The Church, even in the most tragic moments of her existence, has tried, through all means accessible, to give material help to the poor, to care for the sick, prisoners of war, and generally for those in need. Churches or monasteries have founded many philanthropic institutions, such as orphanages, hospitals, houses for the old, etc. The Church fulfils this work mostly through the contributions of the Orthodox laity, which constitutes a sacrifice on the altar of love for the honour of Christ and for sustaining his suffering Body.

A regular feature of almost every Orthodox parish is the existence of a philanthropic society run, in most cases, by Orthodox women, although not excluding men. The existence of independent lay institutions with the same ideals should also be noted. These philanthropic organizations offer warm food to the poor, clothing, medical care, and scholarships to poor students. The tradition of such organizations goes back to the years after the fall of Constantinople, when there were several brotherhoods or guilds of craftsmen of the same profession, serving their members or offering on a wider level their material assistance to philanthropic aims. Those in Istanbul, founded and supported mostly by lay people, are particularly famous for their efficiency. The first hospital is mentioned in 1520. But hospitals in the modern sense were founded in the eighteenth century; for instance that by the guild of the grocers in 1753, the other for seamen in 1762 by the rich Greek George Spatharis Stavrakis, and the Greek hospital in Beyoglou. These hospitals in the beginning were independent, but since 1794 were merged under one administration. Since 1836, with the construction, through the generosity of rich Orthodox laymen, of new hospitals in Balikli outside the walls, all former hospitals have been moved to new sites, where they are still today run and supported by Orthodox people, serving without discrimination people of all faiths. Charitable institutions or individuals, again with the material help of Orthodox people, have in the present century founded clinics within the grounds of the parish churches, where the poor of different faiths find medical care and get their medicines free of charge. The same story may be repeated in relation to the history of the foundation of orphanages for boys and girls.

Women take an active part in the organized social and philanthropic Christian work. Some serve on a voluntary basis as sisters in orphanages, hospitals and other similar institutions. Today in some Orthodox Churches there is a tendency to revive the ancient order of deaconesses. The Greek Archdiocese of North and South America, under the jurisdiction of the Ecumenical Patriarchate, and the Church of Greece have taken active steps in this direction. Graduates of St Barbara's School for deaconesses already serve in this capacity in the Church of Greece. St Barbara's School has been in partial operation since 1957 and in full operation since 1959. It accepts women graduates of the Theological Schools of Athens and Thessalonike, and offers courses in New Testament, the history of deaconesses in the Orthodox Church, practical sociology, psychology, home economics and hygiene. Students at the same time do field work in hospitals, prisons, maternity wards, homes for the blind and for the old and centres of rehabilitation. This school belongs to the Home Mission (*Apostolike Diakonia*) of the Church of Greece, and has been founded through the support of the Church of Greece and the donations given through the World Council of Churches by other Churches from abroad, including the Protestant Episcopal Church in the USA and the Disciples of Christ.

A tradition of rich Greek Orthodox families, especially in the past, was to take under their care poor families, help to educate their children and assist in the dowries of the girls for their marriage. In this line is the custom of the present royal family of Greece, which opens bank accounts with substantial sums for girls of poor families.

Last but not the least is what mostly amateur theatrical or musical groups offer for the entertainment of those in hospitals or for the communities of orphanages and homes for the aged.

9. *Education*

Although education in Byzantium was divided into profane and sacred, it still had an ecclesiastical or theological character. From what we know, every child received his religious teaching from his father and was taught orthography in the local school. Those who could afford to, went to a secondary school, where grammar was the main subject, and to the university, where rhetoric and philosophy were chiefly taught. Theology formed a separate branch, studied not only by the clergy and monks, but by a few laymen as well. Theology was taught in the Patriarchal School or in schools connected with monasteries. It is commonly acknowledged that secular education was permeated by ecclesiastical and theological principles. This is mostly apparent in literature. According to Ehrhard, 'the entire Byzantine literature brings in itself a character essentially ecclesiastical and theological.'[9]

After the fall of Constantinople and until the nineteenth century education within the confines of the Ecumenical Patriarchate was chiefly ecclesiastical in character. This was also true, to a certain extent, in the Russian Church, but because the state was also interested in matters of education, Western secular and philosophical influence appeared earlier than the nineteenth century. In the Orthodox world there was no distinction for some centuries between secular and theological education. The programme of the schools in the vast geographic areas of the jurisdiction of the Ecumenical Patriarchate included religious and theological courses. Teachers were mainly clerics, but laymen were not lacking. Two types of school existed. Firstly, there were the lower or elementary schools, which were the grammar schools of the period and gave the children a basic education and prepared those who were to become clergy. The curriculum included reading, spelling and reading from religious books. Secondly, there were the higher schools, called gymnasia or academies, where grammar, sciences and theology were taught. These schools filled the gap caused by the lack of theological schools. The present Patriarchal School in Phanar was originally one of these schools. Graduates from these schools often went abroad in order to study at Western universities and qualified in various professions.

What has been said about the Byzantine literature can be repeated for the literary production of those years. Again 'as regards the quality of the literary production of the period, we must always bear in mind that its character is chiefly ecclesiastical'.[10]

Clergy and monks write not only on theology but on the ancient classics, rhetoric, philosophy and ethics as well. At the same time laymen in various professions write on different theological subjects. Physicians, philosophers or diplomats who are at the same time competent theologians are commonly found.

With the appearance of universities and theological schools in Russia, and later in the nineteenth century in the Ecumenical Patriarchate and the new national Churches, this picture changes. Secular teaching at all levels of education replaces the former Orthodox ecclesiastical education. It can be said that this brings a break in the Orthodox culture and the Orthodox mind; however, family life, together with religious instruction in the schools and the church, still maintains a strong link with the past in keeping this Orthodox ethos within the Orthodox Church.

Many of the intelligentsia leave the Church or become entirely secularized. It is interesting to see not only theologians but also theologically trained laymen supporting religious and moral principles. The names of Armenis Brailas, Demetrios Mavrokordatos, Ioannis Skaltsounis, Alexis Khomiakov, Nicolas Berdyaev are examples of this trend.

K

If we turn to the Orthodox theological schools we come across professors who are laymen. Some of the students and graduates of these schools remain laymen, serving the Church in different capacities. The student body includes women as well. According to some sources the Church of Greece has the highest percentage of women theologians.

Lay professors of theology, along with the clergy faculty members, give themselves to academic life, transmitting to their students their knowledge of the sacred science, enriching theology by their writings, and taking part in different theological conferences. Their contribution is more than that. They form the theological staff of the Church, they are members of several synodical committees, and are sent as delegates of their respective Churches to Union conferences, and to the many conferences and meetings of the ecumenical movement. According to a recent decision of the Church of Greece only lay theologians are sent as its delegates to the meetings and conferences of the World Council of Churches, and this for reasons of caution towards this Council, predominantly Protestant. Lay graduates in theology teach the religious courses in the gymnasia, preach in the churches, as has already been mentioned, occupy some secondary ecclesiastical posts, and occasionally turn to other professions. Lay women theologians teach also religious courses in secondary schools and are concerned with social, philanthropic and evangelistic work, mostly among women.

10. *Mission of the Church*

(*a*) **Internal.** Religious movements in several Orthodox Churches have seen an enormous growth, especially during the present century. In these movements the role played by the laity is highly significant. Some have the distinction of being founded by laity, in others lay people appear as co-founders and sustainers of the movements along with the official Church or individual clergymen.

As an example of this growth we can take the Church of Greece where we find religious movements as official church agencies or on a voluntary basis. But it should be noted that all missionary work in the Church of Greece owes its beginning to individual efforts, either by clergy or laymen. The origins of the present Home Mission are found in the nineteenth century.

Cosmas Flamiatos established his 'Philo-orthodox Society' and in 1849 sent his declaration 'Cosmas Flamiatos' voice Orthodox and important', which is the first document of this kind. He further formed around him a group of enthusiastic clergy, monks and laymen with the same ideals.

Apostolos Makrakis (1831–1905) in 1886 started his missionary work in Athens, preaching in the streets and the churches. He tried to bring a religious and moral awakening of Christians through publications (newspapers and books), political and religious clubs and a school. He had around him the future founders of the most important religious movements, such as Anaplassis and Zoe. He started to attack the hierarchy, founded a separate church and taught the trichotomy of man, consisting of a body, a soul and a spirit. The Church because of his schismatic tendencies and his heretical teaching condemned him. His followers little by little left him and returned to the Church. Today some Orthodox in America have rediscovered him and are attempting to rehabilitate him. They have formed the Orthodox Christian Educational Society, in Chicago, and are in process of translating and publishing his works into English.

K. Dialesmas, who left the Makrakist movement, founded in 1887 the society Anaplassis, which aimed at reforming and organizing society through Christianity. Co-workers of Dialesmas were Ioannis Skaltsounis, Michael Galanos, the priests George Makris, Panaretos Douligeris, Timotheos Anastassiou and Eusebius Matthopoulos, and the then students P. Trembelas and D. Panayotopoulos. With a central office in Athens and departments in other cities of Greece, these men, with the help of others, tried to strengthen the religious spirit through regular preaching, publications and the periodical *Anaplassis*. George Makris in 1896, within Anaplassis, established the first catechetical school in the Church of Greece. With the passing away of the first leaders, Anaplassis showed some signs of decline and the periodical ceased publication. Today Anaplassis is experiencing a period of revival under the presidency of Professor Rammos of the University of Athens, and the publication of the periodical was revived in 1953.

The brotherhood of theologians Zoe (1907) is the most important of all movements in the Church of Greece. It is a monastic community. But no one is forced to stay if he decides to have a family. Those who formed the first nucleus of Zoe were in the beginning connected with Makrakis and then with Anaplassis. The founder of the Zoe movement is Fr Eusebius Matthopoulos (1849–1929) who had as his collaborators the theologians D. Pharazoulis, P. Trembelas, D. Panayotopoulos, and others. The Zoe movement has worked through preaching, a liturgical life, the edition of the weekly *Zoe* (since 1911), the Bible and other publications, the Sunday schools, and other groups, summer camps, etc. The Zoe brotherhood in order to appeal to more people has organized, since 1930, several other co-operative movements which together form 'the co-operating Christian Societies of St Paul'. Some of these are the brotherhood of theologians Zoe, the 'Eusebeia' missionary sisterhood of Christian women, the Christian Union of professional men (which since 1938 has published the periodical *Aktines*, in 1946 edited the *Declaration*, and in 1950 in English the work *Towards a Christian Civilization*), the Christian Union of Educators (1947), the Christian Union of Working Youth (1946), the Student Christian Union (1933, 1945), and others. Recently a group left Zoe to form a new brotherhood called '*Ho Soter*' (1960).

Another movement similar to that of Zoe has created the Christian Orthodox Unions, which are connected with the name of Fr Marcos Tsactanis (1883–1924). His work starts officially with the year of his ordination (1913), and is oriented in two directions: the efforts to revive the work of preaching, and the establishment on firm bases of Sunday schools and the unity of Christians through Christian groups and unions. Fr Tsactanis, a married priest, established the first Sunday school on a permanent basis within the Church of Greece in 1913. In 1922 he founded the Christian Unions of Young Men and Girls, movements dedicated totally to the service of youth. After the death of Fr Marcos, Fr Angelos Nissiotis became president of the Unions; he still successfully acts in this capacity. In 1945 the Student Christian Association of Greece was founded within the framework of the Unions, whose honorary president is Professor P. Bratsiotis. Other means used by these movements are preaching, work in factories, summer camps, excursions and pilgrimages, social work, drama, children's choirs, etc.

The place accorded to the laymen in the above-mentioned most important movements is also given by the Home Mission (*Apostolike Diakonia*) of the Church of Greece which extends its work throughout all the dioceses. The Home Mission was founded by the Archbishop of Athens Chrysostomos Papadopoulos (1923–38), but its present enormous growth since 1947 is the result of reorganization by Professor Basil Vellas, who became its director. His successor until 1962 was Professor Andreas Phytrakis, again a layman, who put all his dynamic drive behind the many-sided work.

In other Orthodox Churches, besides the official sections on Home Missions, there are also religious movements, working with the blessing of the Church. These are mostly youth movements, found within almost all Orthodox churches outside the Iron Curtain. Of importance is the work of the Orthodox Youth Movement in Syria and Lebanon (1942), which tries to strengthen among its members and further among the Orthodox families the spirit of Orthodox living. This movement has organized Sunday schools, Bible classes, retreats and conferences. Some of its members studied theology and became priests. It has established Orthodox primary schools, colleges, and introduced again monasticism through the organization of monastic houses for men and women. It has shown interest in the work of publication.

Some Orthodox youth movements came together and established an organ of co-ordination between all movements, called Syndesmos. The beginnings of Syndesmos go back to 1948 when some Orthodox young people, meeting at the Ecumenical Institute of Bossey, discussed the ways and possibilities of co-operation amongst Orthodox youth movements. The fourth and most recent General Assembly of Syndesmos met in Thessalonike, Greece, from 4th to 7th September 1958, where progress in many aspects was recorded. Youth movements or student organizations from Cyprus, Finland, France, Germany, Great Britain, Greece, Japan, Korea, Syria and Lebanon are affiliated members. A quarterly *Syndesmos* was published regularly in English for some time.

Syndesmos and individual Orthodox youth movements give due attention to and participate in the work of the ecumenical movement. It can be said that most of the younger Orthodox participants in the World Council of Churches have come from these movements.[11]

Youth movements extending their work to many spheres of the religious and moral life are strong in the Coptic and the Syrian Orthodox in India Churches. In the latter Church the first movement was established in 1908 and today has grown immensely. Mention should also be made of the Martha Mariam Samjam (St Mary's Association), an organization entirely devoted to the service of women, with a central office and branches in almost every parish in the Church of Malabar.

(*b*) **External.** Orthodox churches have a great tradition of missionary work outside the Church. This work was well organized and practised during the Byzantine period from Byzantium and other Orthodox centres. Russia and the other Churches in the Balkans owe their existence to missions conducted by men sent from Constantinople. This work came to an end with the rise of the Ottoman Empire. On the other hand the Orthodox Church of Russia continued evangelization work in the vast areas of the north and the east, to Siberia, China, Korea, Japan and Alaska. Many laymen served this missionary work as evangelists, teachers, doctors and in other capacities. The Church of Russia was until the Communist Revolution engaged practically in evangelism in the areas towards the east. Subsequently almost all communications between the mother Church and the missionary fields ceased. Nevertheless, the newly formed Churches in China, Korea and Japan stood on their own, assumed their national and indigenous character and started missionary work among the non-Christians. In the Orthodox Church of Korea and Japan a number of conversions is regularly reported.

Missionary zeal is fostered in theological schools through courses on missions and related subjects. The subject of missions, internal and external, was on the agenda of the First Congress of Orthodox Theology held in Athens, 29th November to 6th December 1936, when some papers were read.

A paradoxical phenomenon of Orthodox missionary work in the present is the appearance of Orthodoxy in Uganda.[12] There, around the twenties of this century, a native named Reuben Sebanya, formerly an Anglican, took the name of Spartas and from his reading discovered Orthodoxy and wanted to establish it in his country. In 1932, an *episcopus vagans*, Daniel William Alexander, passed through Uganda and ordained two priests, one of them being Reuben Spartas, as Orthodox. When this irregularity became known, after the visit of a Greek Orthodox priest of the Patriarchate of Alexandria, Fr Nicodemus Sarichas in 1933, Reuben Spartas came into contact with Alexandria and for many years wanted the Patriarchate to receive him. The Patriarchate of Alexandria was in a delicate position towards the Church of England, with which this ecclesiastical affair was discussed. The only major request from the Anglican side seemed to be that Reuben Spartas avoid proselytizing among members of the Anglican Church. The Patriarchate of Alexandria in 1942 sent to Uganda the Metropolitan of Axoum, Nicolaos, who presented to the Patriarchate his report, a really illuminating document. In 1946 Reuben Spartas came to Alexandria and was named by the Patriarch 'Patriarchal Vicar in Uganda, Kenya and Tanganyika' and received the Holy Cross. In 1952 Patriarch Christophoros of Alexandria visited Uganda and other countries of Central Africa, thus officially bestowing his blessing upon the newly founded Orthodox Church of this area. Today, the number of the Orthodox in Uganda is increasing. Also the Metropolitan of Eirenopolis, Nicolaos, of the lately established diocese of Eastern Africa, has officially declared the Orthodox position, that in his diocese, as in the Orthodox Church, no proselytism is allowed among Christians of other denominations.

Some recent developments in the field of Orthodox missions can be seen in America, where in 1956 the Greek Orthodox Holy Cross Missionary Society was established in the Holy Cross Greek Orthodox Theological School, Brookline, Massachusetts. This society has helped the missionary Churches of Korea and Uganda materially, through scholarships and by preparing people to undertake missionary work. The Greek Orthodox Youth of America (GOYA) set up in August 1958 as a standing national project a Missions Study Committee which issues a news-sheet called *The Goyan Missionary*. The Fourth General Assembly of Syndesmos, held in 1958, decided to establish in the near future an International Missionary Society, with the immediate appointment of an Executive Committee with provisional headquarters in Athens. The Committee's tasks are:

(*a*) To cultivate a feeling of need for missions and arouse enthusiasm; (*b*) to propagate the idea of missions; (*c*) to study the past experience of Orthodox and non-Orthodox missionary bodies; (*d*) to study the character and form of this missionary organization; (*e*) to help the three Churches in Japan, Korea and Uganda. This Committee is trying to do its best in order to arouse enthusiasm for missions, through prayers, meetings, correspondence and publications. The Committee's bulletin *Poreuthentes* ('Go Ye') has been regularly published since 1959.

Active missionary work to those outside Christianity is carried on in the Churches of Syrian Orthodox at Malabar and in Ethiopia. Such missionary movements in the Church of Malabar are the Servants of the Cross (1924), the Evangelistic Associations of the East (1925), and the Christu Sishya Ashram (1933).

NOTES

1. Gennadios of Heliopolis, 'The terms "Orthodox and Orthodoxy",' *Orthodoxia*, 26 (1951), pp. 233–5 (in Greek).

2. L. W. Brown, *The Indian Christians of St Thomas. An account of the Ancient Syrian Church of Malabar* (Cambridge University Press, 1956); Yassa Hanna, 'The Place and Significance of the Congregation in Orthodoxy', *Student World* 51, No. 1 (1958), pp. 46–52; R. Janin, *Les Églises Orientales et les Rites Orientaux* (4th ed. Paris: Letouzey et Anne, 1955); Yassa'Abd' Al-Masih, *The Faith and Practices of the Coptic Church* (Alexandria, 1953); Malachia Ormanian, *The Church of Armenia*, 2nd ed. rev., transl. from the French by C. M. Gregory, ed. by Terenig Poladian (London: Mowbray, 1955); Korah Philipos, 'The Malabar Church: South India', *The Ecumenical Review* XI, No. 3 (April 1959),

pp. 300–6; *The Teaching of the Abyssinian Church*, transl. by the Rev. A. F. Matthew (London: Faith Press, 1936); Cardinal E. Tisserant-E. R. Hambye, S. J., *Eastern Christianity in India* (London, New York and Toronto: Longmans, Green & Co., 1957).

3. Francis Dvornik, *Emperors, Popes and General Councils* (Dumbarton Oaks Papers 6, 1951), pp. 1–23.

4. Hamilcar S. Alivisatos, *The Conscience of the Church* (Athens, 1954), pp. 31–4; Georges Florovsky, 'Sobornost: The Catholicity of the Church', *The Church of God*, ed. E. L. Mascall (London, SPCK, 1934), p. 71.

5. Jerome Kotsonis, *The Position of the Laity in the Ecclesiastical Body According to the Canon Law of the Eastern Orthodox Church*, p. 30 (in Greek).

6. See the chapter 'The History of a Country Parson', in Peter Hammond, *The Waters of Marah, The Present State of the Greek Church* (London: Rockliff, 1956), pp. 154–67.

7. 'Empire and Desert: Antinomies of Christian History', *The Greek Orthodox Theological Review* 3 (1957), p. 148.

8. Athenagoras Kokkinakis, *Parents and Priests as Servants of Redemption. An Interpretation of the Doctrines of the Eastern Orthodox Church on the Sacraments of Matrimony and Priesthood* (New York: Morehouse-Gorham Co., 1958), p. 19.

9. In Krumbacher, *Geschichte der byzantinischen Literatur*, 2nd ed. (Munich, 1897), p. 37.

10. Theodore H. Papadopoulos, *Studies and Documents Relating to the History of the Greek Church and People under Turkish Domination* (Brussels, 1952), p. 125.

11. Vasil T. Istavridis, 'The Orthodox Youth and the Ecumenical Movement', *The Greek Orthodox Theological Review* 2 (1956), pp. 81–8; Heikki Kirkinen, 'Reactions of Orthodox Students to Ecumenical Encounter', *Student World* 51, No. 1 (1958), pp. 26–33; Albert Laham, *Syndesmos and the Ecumenical Movement*. Report of the 4th General Assembly of Syndesmos . . ., pp. 20–3.

12. Theodore Nankyamas, 'Orthodoxy in Uganda', *Syndesmos*, Series 2, No. 5 (September 1957), pp. 12–15; Nicolaos of Axoum, *Triloghia Anamneseon apo ten Anatoliken Afriken* (Cairo, 1947).

BIBLIOGRAPHY

Nicholas Afanassiev, *The Service of the Laity in the Church* (Paris, 1955) (in Russian).

—, 'The Ministry of the Laity in the Church', *The Ecumenical Review* X, No. 3 (April 1958), pp. 255–63.

Panagiotis Bratsiotis, *Religious Movements in Greece since 1900* (Mytilene, 1951) (in Greek).

—, 'Die geistigen Strömungen und die religiösen Bewegungen in der Orthodoxen Kirche Griechenlands', *Die Kirchen der Welt*, ed. H. Harms et al., vol. I; *Die Orthodoxe Kirche in Griechischer Sicht*, ed. P. Bratsiotis (Stuttgart: Evangelisches Verlagswerk, 1959) 2, pp. 49–69.

Demetrios Constantelos, 'The Zoe Movement in Greece', *St Vladimir's Seminary Quarterly* 3 (1959), pp. 11–25.

Paul Evdokimov, 'An Orthodox Contribution. A Symposium on Holy Worldliness', *Laity*, No. 5 (June 1958), pp. 17–19.

Lev Gillet, 'Les Laïcs dans l'Histoire de l'Église', *Contacts* 11 (1959), pp. 158–63.

Basil Ioannidis, 'The Life of a Greek Orthodox Parish', *Laity*, No. 6 (December 1958), pp. 4–7.

Jerome Kotsonis, *The Position of the Laity in the Ecclesiastical Body according to the Canon Law of the Eastern Orthodox Church* (Athens, 1956) (in Greek).

—, 'Die Stellung der Laien innerhalb des kirchlichen Organismus', *Die Kirchen der Welt*, ed. H. Harms *et al.*, vol. I; *Die Orthodoxe Kirche in Griechischer Sicht*, ed. P. Bratsiotis (Stuttgart: Evangelisches Verlagswerk, 1959) 2, pp. 92–116.

Marcel Morcos, 'The Orthodox Youth Movement in Syria and the Lebanon', *Syndesmos*, Series 2, No. 7 (November 1958), pp. 10–13.

L. N. Pariskij, 'Die Rolle der Laien im Leben der Russischen Orthodoxen Kirche', *Kirche in der Zeit* (Jhrg. 1957) I, pp. 12–15.

Panagiotis Trembelas, *The Participation of the Laity in the Election of Bishops* (Athens, 1955) (in Greek).

—, *The Laymen in the Church* (Athens, 1958) (in Greek).

13

Jan Grootaers

THE ROMAN CATHOLIC CHURCH

*The wretched theologians! They have forgotten two things—
the laymen and the Holy Spirit.*

Cardinal Saliège

I · Introduction

IF we ponder for a moment the phrases quoted above from Cardinal
Salièges, we shall find in them a deeper meaning than that of a rather
rough witticism. If we wish to systematize the history of the Roman
Catholic Church in the simplest possible way, we might say that it is
the history of the tension between the *institutional* and the *prophetic*
elements in the Church. The history of the layman has been very
largely the history of the prophetic element, and the historians no less
than the theologians have been very much inclined to neglect this side
of the affair.

It is not altogether easy to define what we mean by the term 'layman'. Lay status can be defined in relation to, or in contrast with,
ordination to the priesthood; and this is in fact the definition given in
Canon Law as it is in force at the present time. But if we think of the
spiritual ideal of the layman as 'the Christian engaged in the life of the
world', the primary point would be the contrast with the monastic ideal
of withdrawal from the world. Yet again, if we look at the matter from
a mystical or inward point of view, every Christian, be he bishop or
monk or simple believer, is primarily a baptized person; all the baptized are bound together in a common obedience to the Saviour, which
admits of no distinctions; all, as members of the *laos*, the people of
God, are 'laymen'.

In this chapter, when we use the words 'laity' and 'layman', we shall
try to keep in mind both the essential aspects—(*a*) the layman has no

such share in the priestly authority of the Church as would entitle him to exercise it in public—he may take an active part in the public worship of the Church, but he is not authorized to read the liturgical prayers which constitute the assembly, still less to preside over the assembly; (*b*) the layman is the man who attempts to respond to the call of Christ to service in the world by exercising a vocation in 'worldly' things, primarily in the life of the family and in a profession.

In the period before the Council of Trent, the prophetic spirit constantly found expression in the religious Orders, which from time to time arose for the renewal of the Church. It is surprising to note how often the founder of an Order was a layman, and how many of the Orders were born and nurtured in lay surroundings. The early Benedictines (sixth century) were in reaction against the 'clericalism' of the Constantinian Church; as monks they did not ordinarily receive ordination to the priesthood. Francis of Assisi (thirteenth century) was the opponent of the institutional power of the Church, and of the decadence of 'feudal' monasticism, and strove, without success, to guard for the Order that he founded the character of a lay fellowship. And when in the sixteenth century Ignatius Loyola sets to work for the renewal of the whole Church, he incorporates much of the prophetic spirit that was to be found in certain groups of laymen in his time.

Many students of the work of the Jesuits in the second half of the sixteenth century have overlooked the fact that the clergy in a number of dioceses were hostile to them, while in a great many places they enjoyed the support of the laity. In a letter addressed by the Fuggers to Gregory XIII in 1572 regarding the arrival of the Jesuits in Augsburg, we read: 'We can assert that, with the exception of a few wretches, there is not in this city a single Catholic layman who does not regard the Jesuits as models of virtue, and who has not the highest regard for their solid piety . . . it is true that the clergy are not of the same opinion, but it is only too easy to understand the reason for their hostility.'[1]

It remains, however, the fact that all these great religious Orders in turn, one after the other, have become 'clericalized'; this means not only that the majority of their members have received ordination as priests, but that they have gradually become assimilated to the Church in its most highly institutional form, and have lost contact with the ordinary folk of the Church.

For all that, however, at the height of the seventeenth century the spiritual ideals most closely related to the needs of Christians living in the world, and most deeply concerned with the vocation of the layman as such—notably in the teaching of St François de Sales—were developed and spread abroad by Franciscans, Dominicans, Jesuits and Capuchins, who were in the closest contact with the largest number of believers. The teaching of Cardinal Bérulle, which laid greater stress on separation from the world, was more warmly received by the secular clergy, the Benedictines and the Premonstratensians.

It is important to remember the role of intermediaries played by these religious Orders, in which aspirations originally and characteristically lay had between the thirteenth and eighteenth centuries found more or less complete organic expression. From a sociological point of view a real comparison can be established between these religious Orders and the 'sects' to be found within the Protestant world.[2] In so far as the 'sectarian spirit' of the religious Orders, in reaction against the authoritarian attitude of bishops and clergy, sets them in opposition to the Church *as institution*, the lay folk are solidly behind them. But if this sectarianism is carried to the point of endangering the Church *as fellowship* (as when the Orders have tried to make themselves out to be the sole specialists in the way of holiness), lay folk will be inclined to rally to the Church, as the bearer of that message of salvation which is to be proclaimed to the world; and here they will feel themselves nearer to the secular clergy than to the religious.

Professor F. X. Arnold, in his book on the pastoral ministry today,[3] expresses regret that up to the present time no history of the inner life of the Church is available to us. Such a history would have to include the history of piety, of the pastoral ministry, of preaching and of the liturgical life. It is our judgment that it is within such a history of the inner life of the Church that the history of the layman should find its place. Enough has been said to indicate the difficulty of the task.

Let us start by indicating the sections which ought to find a place in this chapter, and have not been written. We ought to have been able to describe the part played by the layman in catechetical instruction—at times this has been of the very highest importance—in preaching—in the apostolic work of missions (a study of the first century of Spanish missions in America, and of the seventeenth-century Jesuit missions in China might yield surprising results)—in the development of the practices of piety. Here a complete survey of the history of frequent communion would be required.

It has not been possible to follow one single line of approach in every section of this chapter. For the seventeenth century we have taken up mainly the 'spirituality' of the layman in his family life and in his profession on the one hand, and on the other in the direct work of Christian witness. For the eighteenth, the main issue must be the great challenges and conflicts in the world of thought, and the contrast between the faith of loyal Christians and the worldly spirit of the higher clergy. In the nineteenth century, we observe a profound religious renewal, diffused by eminent laymen of many countries in many spheres of life. Nor must we forget that the great political crises, which have so extensively changed the relations between Church and State, have always exercised a profound influence on the attitudes taken up by the laymen in the Church. Inevitably, the outlook of the seventeenth century undergoes a complete change in the eighteenth; and further developments are to be noted in the nineteenth.

This chapter cannot claim to be more than a series of points of departure. If it stimulates others to take up some of the points that have here been no more than indicated, and to pursue research in an area which is rich in materials but has been very largely neglected, the purpose for which it has been written will have been excellently served.

II · The Sixteenth Century : the Humanists

We have noted a certain similarity between the Franciscan movement in the thirteenth century and the success of the Jesuits at the end of the sixteenth and during the seventeenth centuries. Now we must take note of an even more unexpected and highly instructive similarity between Francis of Assisi and Erasmus, as powerful forces working for the emancipation of the layman. Immense as are the differences between them, both men fought against the same abuses—the Pharisaism of the higher clergy, the ossification of the liturgy, the spiritual neglect of the simple folk. Both demanded a return to the radical simplicity of the message of the gospels.

For many of us it is a surprising experience to re-read some of the more famous of the writings of Erasmus with the needs of the lay folk in mind. To re-read—or perhaps to read for the first time; for, as has been truly said, Erasmus is more admired than read. In some of these works, we can see how the Catholic laymen of the sixteenth century set to work to understand their duty as Christians living in the life of the world; and these writings, through their fantastically high sales in almost every country in Europe, helped to crystallize opinions which had already been present in solution in the minds of men.

Erasmus has suffered from the attacks long made upon him by the Counter-reformation no less than by Protestantism, both movements having regarded him with suspicion and disdain. In the light of the basic studies carried out by a number of scholars (P. S. Allen, A. Renaudet, J. Huizinga and others), it is possible to read the writings of Erasmus with new eyes, and to appreciate the specifically Christian elements in works such as the *Manual of the Christian Soldier*, the *Praise of Folly*, and the *Familiar Colloquies*, which in comparison with his great scholarly achievements had generally been regarded as minor works.

In the preface to his famous edition of the New Testament (1516) Erasmus struck out one of those key-phrases which we must constantly bear in mind as we read him:

> Perhaps it is right to conceal the secrets of kings, but the mystery of Christ wishes to be spread abroad. My desire is that women should be able to read the Gospels and the Epistles of Saint Paul; that the weaver should be able to sing them at his work, and the traveller to beguile with them the tedium of his way. Baptism, the sacraments are common to all Christians; why should doctrinal principles be reserved for those who are called theologians and monks, who make up but a very small part of the Christian people? . . . All who are inspired and uplifted by the Spirit of Christ are in possession of the true theology, though they be only ditch-diggers or weavers.

Such words claim for the layman that place within the Church to which his aspirations were specially directed in that time of renewal. Let us take two aspects of the spiritual ideal as presented by Erasmus— the life of husband and wife in the family; and the life of the Christian in his profession.

The *Manual* teaches us that husband and wife will find the appropriate way to salvation not by trying to imitate a monkish type of piety, but in realizing to the full the meaning of the bond of marriage and of the duties of parents. If we consider the duties of each Christian in that state of life in which God has been pleased to set him, we find that Erasmus is of the opinion that a ruler who spends his time in prayer instead of properly administering the affairs of his subjects is no true Christian. Every Christian is called to Christian perfection; and this ideal is to be pursued just in that environment in which God has placed each man.[4]

We shall find even more striking examples in the *Colloquies*. Of the people who take part in the *Convivium Religiosum*, Eulales always carries

Paul's letters about with him; Chrysoglottus fights against superstitious practices; Timothy defends the right of the simple Christian to concern himself with theology; Eusebius apologizes for leaving the table, as he has to go and give spiritual counsels to a friend who is in danger of death. These are Christian laymen, as Erasmus sees them. The list could be very much prolonged by other examples.

If we are to understand the extent of the influence of these and other types, it must be remembered that the *Manual* was one of the most widely read books in the world. Hundreds of thousands of copies of the *Colloquies* and the *Adages* were sold. The *Colloquies* were reprinted no less than 130 times in 32 years, and at least one edition was of no less than 24,000 copies.[5] And to the effect of the original Latin we must add the effect of the many translations in the languages of the day.

We know of groups of humanists in various places who set themselves to live a truly Christian life on the Erasmian pattern, though we have less detail than we could wish as to the part actually played by laymen in this movement for Catholic reform. Let three names stand as representatives of all the others. First, and certainly greatest, is Sir Thomas More, the outstanding practical lawyer and Lord Chancellor of England, beheaded by order of King Henry VIII, whose witness was unmistakably that of a mature and enlightened Christian. More had lived at the centre of a highly educated family, and of a group of humanists, which included such men as John Clement, the translator of the Greek Fathers, and William Roper, son-in-law and first biographer of More, husband of that Meg More whose learning had been noted and praised by both Erasmus and Cardinal Pole. Juan Luis Vives, the Spanish humanist and teacher, was a friend of Erasmus and More. And notable in its originality is the figure of the Venetian Senator, Casparo Contarini, a lay Christian of profoundly mature Christian experience, at the same time deeply conscious of his responsibilities to the Church. It was only towards the end of his life that Contarini accepted functions in the Church which involved his ordination.

All this movement was very far from taking place merely on the fringe of the Church. Erasmus was on the best of terms with no less than five Popes; Paul III even offered him a cardinal's hat, which Erasmus was wise enough to refuse. And throughout the history of the sixteenth century we keep meeting the 'Erasmian cardinals'—men of the stamp of Pole and Contarini; of them Hauser and Renaudet have gone so far as to write:

The Erasmians, following up the thought of their master, were the first to prepare a carefully thought out plan of Catholic reform; until the very eve of the Council of Trent the Church had officially no plan for its own renewal other than that expressed in their formulae.[6]

The diet of Ratisbon and the arrival of John Calvin at Geneva (1541), the bull sanctioning the establishment of the Roman inquisition —these things were the passing-bell of the Erasmians in the Church. This does not lessen their importance. Half a century ago, P. Imbart de la Tour could go so far as to write:

> The Reformation did not break out at the moment when the Church had reached its lowest point of corruption, beyond hope of any possible improvement; on the contrary it came at a time at which the religious institution, like all other institutions, was repairing its ruins. It did not attack a society which had given itself up to immobility or death; it broke out in a Church which was very much alive, which was longing to be born anew, which had begun to be born anew.[7]

The attempts at reform, which are based on a return to the Gospels themselves, are evident in the projects for the reformation of the religious Orders, in the initiatives of countless bishops, and in those taken by lay members of the Church.

It appears to us that the religious revolution of the decades before Luther was, to a degree hitherto unsuspected, also a revolution carried out by laymen on behalf of laymen and a new affirmation by the laymen of the Roman Catholic Church of their position and standing within that Church.

III · The Tridentine Epoch

The second half of the sixteenth century saw the division of the Christian world into two armed and hostile camps; and this was an atmosphere most unfavourable to the spirit of humanism. Yet the spirit of Erasmus lived on, and sometimes in unexpected places. In spite of the decline of the Erasmian influence in the period 1540–50, the themes and the spiritual attitudes which owe their origin to the teaching of Erasmus were far more widespread in both the Catholic and the Protestant worlds than the historians of either confession have generally recognized.[8]

We must take note of the fact that laymen took little or no part in the Council of Trent, and that one of the effects of this Council was an increasing clericalization of the Church. But we must not unduly simplify. The Church was in a situation of great peril, and, in taking up a position of emphatic independence in relation to the temporal power of the secular arm, one of the legacies from the Christendom of the Middle Ages, and in limiting active participation in its work to the bishops, it was in fact simply going back to the traditions and practice of a much earlier time. And to a remarkable degree, in its first period, Trent 'owed a considerable part of its inspiration to the mutual inter-penetration of the world of the laity and the world of the clergy'.[9]

This was largely due to the actions of Pope Paul III, who took a whole group of laymen, and by appointing them as Cardinals, made them chief agents for the implementation of his desire for reform. We have already referred to Contarini. The English humanist Reginald Pole presided as legate over the early sessions of the Council in 1546— he was not ordained priest for another ten years, in fact two days before his consecration as Archbishop of Canterbury. The learned Italian Cervini (later Pope Marcellus II) was still a layman when appointed Cardinal in 1539. Angelo Massarelli was officially appointed Secretary of the Council, though according to some authorities eleven years were to pass before he was raised to the priesthood. Count Ludovico Nogarola, a friend of Contarini, drew up the reports of the theological discussions, and though a layman, preached on St Stephen's Day before the assembled legates and bishops. Finally we must mention Ercole Severoli, procurator-fiscal of the Council, and intimate friend of the leading participants in it.[10] This first period of the Council of Trent, when things were in the hands of 'those who were prepared to discuss things', more or less came to an end with the death of Paul III in 1549.

We may, perhaps, sum up the situation by saying that the Council of Trent took steps to free itself from the 'power of the laity' in the medieval sense of the term, i.e., from the political power of the states; but at the same time did attempt to a certain extent to associate laymen (members of the *laos*, the people of God) intimately with a great enter-prise of renewal and reorganization. It was in this sense that Henri Bremond was able to write that Christian humanism, purged of all the elements that had rendered it suspect, was able to sit triumphantly among the Fathers at the Council, and to leave its impress on some of the most notable of its decisions.[11]

Unfortunately, in the inflamed atmosphere of the wars of religion, some of the decisions of the Council were gravely distorted and others remained a dead letter. Let us note two instances in matters relating to the laity. The directives intended to secure greater participation of the laity in the fellowship of liturgical worship were simply disregarded; it was left for the twentieth century to rediscover the true function of the lay people 'about the altar of the Lord'. Professor F. X. Arnold notes that catechetical instruction, which had been planned in well-balanced form by the *Roman Catechism* of 1566, became disjointed and 'off-centre' in the very influential *Catechism* of Robert Bellarmine (1598) which to far too great an extent was taken up with the controversies against the Protestants.

IV · The Seventeenth Century

In this section our main concern will be with France in the seventeenth century. But it is important not to forget that there were other countries besides France in the Roman Catholic world, and that in each of them the renewal of the laity had followed upon the great renewal of the Church. We would like to know more for instance of Hippolyte Guarinoni (1571–1654), municipal physician of Hall in the Tyrol, and author of a work on the *Frightful Degeneration of the Human Race* (Ingolstadt, 1610). He is the typical Christian, active in his profession—social apostle, builder of churches, teacher of poor children, in fact the Austrian counterpart to the Baron de Renty, to whom we shall come later in this section of our chapter.[12]

Most of those to whom the spiritual renewal of France in the early years of the century was due were lay people, daily confronted by the problems of the world—ladies in high society, lawyers, members of the University, with some priests to whom the lay folk turned for spiritual counsel.

It is important to note that a great many of these had been trained in foreign schools of mystical devotion. A study of books on the spiritual life published between 1550 and 1610 reveals an astonishingly high proportion of French translations, including translations of Fathers of the Church; this is evidence that lay people who could not read Latin were actuated by a strong desire to study deeply questions relating to Christian life and doctrine. Bremond remarks that, before the time of François de Sales, 'we encounter hundreds of introductions to the life of devotion, written in French and addressed to the general public.'[13]

It is the spring of 1602. If we make our way to the salon of Madame Acarie, where Madame receives visitors almost every day, we shall meet the same old friends as assemble in another salon, that of Madame de Bérulle, but we shall find others also—François de Sales and Pierre de Bérulle, who are just beginning to come into prominence; Duval and Gallemand, doctors of the Sorbonne—and the servants of the house, for the doors of the salon were left open, in order that they might share in the conversation. We shall hear the guests deplore the corruption of the ancient monasteries, cry out for a thorough reform of the parochial clergy, and proclaim as necessary those great religious ideas that in recent times have sunk into oblivion.[14]

It was circles such as these, which without knowing it were genuinely prophetic, that were the source of most of the reforms by which the 'Great Century' of France is marked. Mgr Calvet, sketching rapidly the outline of the century, identifies the following types of lay Christian who are to be encountered in it: the plain man, deeply versed in devotion; militant Christians like the Marquis de Fénelon and Gaston de Renty; the charitable women grouped around St Vincent de Paul; and women of the world such as Madame de Sévigné, who while still living in the world are yet profoundly penetrated by the Christian spirit.

Midway between the beginning of the movement and its close we encounter François de Sales (1567–1622). His work is the very core of the study in which we are engaged; his influence extended so far in space and time that for the laymen of the Roman Catholic Church he was, and still is, one of the very greatest masters of the spiritual life. Moreover, the future Bishop of Geneva is the point of the encounter between the living Christianity of the great humanists and the seventeenth century; he is the creator of what, since Henri Bremond wrote his great work, has commonly been called 'devout humanism'.

The common opinion of the time, in disregard of the formal teaching of the Church, was that Christian perfection is something reserved for the clergy. It was the genius, and the work, of François de Sales to extirpate this tenacious prejudice, and to set in motion a return to the conviction of the Early Church that *holiness is obligatory for all Christians*. Christians are called to live in a world which is not really Christian, to exercise to the full their duties as men, and yet to remain completely Christian. Religion is to be integrated with life. The life of the layman in his family and in his profession is precisely the field in which he is to exercise the true vocation of the Christian in the world.

The effects of this new—and ancient—form of teaching were immense. Bremond, after extensive researches into the practice of private prayer, ends on the following note: 'It is beyond measure astonishing that, from the middle of the seventeenth to the end of the eighteenth century, these collections [of prayers] deliberately disregard the traditional distinction between the religious and the layman.' All this is very much in the spirit of the Bishop of Geneva, who advises that the Christian must be ready to 'pass directly from prayer to any kind of activity that your vocation or profession may require . . . the lawyer must be able to pass directly from prayer to the law court, the merchant to his business, the married woman to the duties imposed upon her by her marriage and to the cares of her household.'

We shall now take a rapid glance at some of these Christian lay people, and try to understand what their Christian faith meant to them as they lived their life in the world.

One of the most remarkable figures is Madame Acarie (1566–1618), who is perhaps better known as mystic than as laywoman, if such a distinction is permissible. Everyone knows more or less that it was Madame Acarie who introduced into France the Carmelites as reformed by St Teresa, and that she worked also for the reform of the Benedictine abbeys. It is sometimes forgotten, in part or altogether, that she was a most attentive and on occasion energetic wife, the accomplished mother of six children, and a housewife to whom a husband a little inclined to live in a world of his own imagination had handed over the whole weight of his domestic cares. She regarded the duties of her station as taking precedence over everything else; thus we find her hurriedly leaving a morning Mass before it came to an end in order not to keep her husband waiting for his breakfast.[15] There was hardly any limit to the influence that she exercised on the Church in France in the seventeenth century; and this, as the Abbé Bremond justly remarks, 'was paradoxical; for this lady continued to live with her husband and to bring up her children, and had no particle of that authority which the Church grants to abbesses, and other women who are "superiors" in the strict sense of that term.'

Gaston de Renty (1611–49) is perhaps the most typical of all the laymen who worked for this great religious renewal. He was a follower of the methods of Bérulle rather than of those of François de Sales. Yet his life was fully occupied by the concerns of a family (the father of five children, he wrote a little book on the upbringing of children, and each Saturday held a discussion with his family on that passage of the New Testament which was to be read the next day at Mass); by the demands of professional life—as cavalry officer, as military theorist, as practising physician, as representative of the nobility in the local Estates of Normandy, as Counsellor of State; as a layman active in the Christian apostolate—for ten years he was the life and soul of the vigorous Company of the Blessed Sacrament; and by the devout adoration of a mystic—at the age of twenty-seven, having broken with the vanities of this world, he placed himself under the direction of Fr de Condren, General of the Oratory, and himself was later to become the 'counsellor of the saints'.

De Renty did not escape the censures of the worldlings—in this connection we may recall Molière and his Tartuffe—yet it is the fact that at the end of the seventeenth century his biography (by Fr Saint-Jure) was translated into English by the Anglican Gilbert Burnet, Bishop of Salisbury, and into German by Protestant translators. The new edition of the French original, published in 1704, included a preface by the Reformed pastor Pierre Poiret, who remarks that 'there can be no doubt that, if the labours and the words of Monsieur de Renty were of the highest usefulness to men, this usefulness derived its being and its practical power from his life of ceaseless prayer, and from nothing else.'

The lay apostle had to overcome some resistance on the part of the clergy. A priest was horrified to learn that the layman de Renty was teaching the Catechism to poor folk in the hospital; and at first it was only with some hesitation that the Archbishop of Paris was prepared to admit the incursion of lay people into the affairs of the religious life. Yet it was on de Renty that responsibility for the spiritual direction of a number of houses of religious women in France was to be laid. In the Company of the Blessed Sacrament no attention was paid to distinctions of rank or estate. The elected superior, who held office for three months at a time, could be either a priest or a layman. The Sacrament 'of union and of charity' was at the heart of the life of the Company. Its members, grouped in fifty-two branches and a number of smaller cells, devoted themselves to the care of those condemned to the galleys, to work in the hospitals and prisons, to the provision of free legal aid for those in trouble, to the care of girls who had no protector, to poor wretches, and to the work of missions overseas.

Among the closest friends and fellow-workers of Gaston de Renty in the Company was Henry Michel Buch (1598–1666). Buch was a shoemaker born in Luxemburg. By way of Metz he came to Paris, and at the age of forty-five reached the rank of master-shoemaker. It was in the Company that the artisan became the friend of the baron, and for nine years they were closely associated together. In 1645 Buch founded the 'Shoemakers' Brotherhood', a lay society of which the expressed aim was the development of Christian perfection in and through the exercise of a craft. A little later Buch founded a similar society, the 'Tailors' Brotherhood'. The purpose was the spiritual upbuilding of artisans 'by the practice of the love of God in the exercise of their crafts, of fellowship with their equals, of fidelity towards their neighbours in work and in business, and of watchfulness in dealing with the world in such a way as not to be touched by the corruption which is inseparable from it.'[16]

The reader will expect to find here something about those well-known figures *'les messieurs de Port-Royal'*; but from the point of view of our special interest there is not so very much to be said; in the first place, because the majority of the 'hermits' were in holy orders, or were intending, like Lemaistre de Sacy, to be ordained; and secondly, because Port-Royal was inspired by the idea of flight from the world. Pascal, who regarded the world as a house infected with the plague, affirmed that 'the essential vocation of the Christian is to come out from the world.'

To make use of the illuminating categories worked out by J. Calvet, we may say that in the seventeenth century the 'mystics' and the 'Jansenists' had the least, and the 'Salesians' and the 'Jesuits' had the greatest, interest in the matters which are here our special concern.[17]

Let us take one single example—the Christian attitude to marriage. It was the influence of François de Sales which restored to common estimation the traditional doctrine of the sanctity of marriage. It is the considered opinion of J. Calvet that the saint's most notable work, the *Introduction to the Devout Life*, possesses one incomparable distinction:

> Becoming an intrinsic part of the religious spirit of the race, the book helped to create the pattern of the French matron; that typical mistress of a house, that mother of a family in the ranks of the bourgeoisie or among the common people, who came from the convent school to take up marriage as a kind of religious vocation and constituted herself the guardian of the home.[18]

V · *The Eighteenth Century*

The fragmentary and provisional character of our studies will appear even more clearly than before in the rough and ready fashion in which we have to deal with the eighteenth century. This was a peculiarly unpleasing period in the history of the Church. A survey of church history since the Edict of Milan (AD 313) suggests that the vigour of lay activity in the Church varies inversely with the intimacy of the links connecting Church with State. This is confirmed by the history of the eighteenth century, during which Erastianism was one of the great evils that afflicted the Roman Catholic Church.

In French the word *laïc* is of double significance; it can mean 'the layman in the Church', and it can mean 'the man who violently rejects the Church'. This ambiguity reaches a kind of climax in the eighteenth century. When the intellectuals of the time set themselves against the extravagant privileges accorded to the higher clergy, it is not always possible to distinguish such attacks from attacks on the Christian message itself.

In the seventeenth century, Catholic Europe, with its absolutist organization, was the paragon of civilization as that finds expression in the arts. The new movements in science and philosophy involved a shift in the very foundations of Western culture; the centre of gravity of civilization moved towards the Protestant countries—England, Holland, Prussia, Switzerland. The movement of the times was towards 'political ideals that knew nothing of divine right, towards religion without mystery, towards morals without dogma'. The inner crisis of the Church was grave—the mounting tide of unbelief, the progress of rationalism; contemporaneously with the growing poverty of the lower classes, and the increasing wealth of the ancient and famous monasteries.

It was ebb-tide in religion, and at this time it is hard to distinguish 'layman' ('*laïc*') from 'secularist' ('*laïciste*').[19] The dominant feature of this period is the apostasy of the educated laity, and their determination to promote by every means in their power the complete secularization of society. Yet it is important not to take too simplified a view of the eighteenth century. There were lay writers who dedicated the efforts of their pen to the defence of the traditional positions of the Church. And Paul Hazard has drawn attention to a movement which hitherto has been little studied—that of 'enlightened Christianity', a widespread movement to 'free Christian faith from the incrustations that have gathered upon it, and to present a Christian faith so liberal in its doctrine that no one would be able to accuse it of obscurantism, and so pure in its morality that no one would be able to deny its practical efficacy.'[20] Gustav Schnürer tells us that we have to distinguish two different types among these Christians; on the one hand there are those who hardly go so far as nominal acceptance of the foundation principles of Catholic doctrine; on the other, there are those whose aim it is to fight against the social and cultural backwardness of the Church, while maintaining the right of the Church to declare the basic principles on which civilization rests.[21]

Fr Lenders, S.J., distinguishes yet a third category—a numerous but prudent élite, which had rejected every kind of formalism, and endeavoured to bear Christian witness in life rather than in thought. 'It was as though lay people were endeavouring to compensate, as far as inward spiritual life and outward activities were concerned, for that which was most lacking in the clergy and in the religious orders.'[22]

Active charity, and a concern to raise the moral and intellectual level of the poor, are certainly among the characteristics of the believing laymen of this century. And this brings us to the other side of the medal. If the eighteenth century was the triumphant epoch of 'sense', we must not forget the opposite current, equally violent, of 'sensibility' and sentiment. Here are the first signs of the romantic movement, and of the great lay Christian movements of the nineteenth century.

And now we come to the 'little people' of the century. Against wind and tide they maintained the faith and the spirit of Christian confidence in the future. When they felt that the tension had become too great, they did not hesitate to take to arms. Is it too naïve to think that the revolts in various countries against the revolutionary laws which marked the end of the century are genuinely a part of the history of the laymen of the times?

In the Belgian area of the Low Countries we have to reckon with the Peasants' War (October–December 1798), in France with the rising of La Vendée. It is often difficult to distinguish politics from religion, heroism from banditry; yet of the Vendée sober historians have written that 'the war which had in practice been declared several months earlier was certainly a war of religion.'[23]

At the moment at which Pius VI (1775–99) seemed to be abandoned by the great ones of the earth, it was the simple Catholic people who came to cheer and to salute him, first at Vienna, where he had been very ill received by the Emperor Joseph II, and then in France, at Valence, where he died, deserted and in prison.

VI · The Nineteenth Century and the Beginning of the Twentieth

The history of the lay folk in the Roman Catholic Church of the nineteenth century cannot be summed up in a few pages. This was the century in which 'laicism', the secular spirit, was triumphant. Yet alongside it developed a Christian lay movement, which was extremely vigorous and varied, and so full of vitality that it undoubtedly prepared the way for that more conscious and clearly expressed awakening of the lay people which is evident in the Church today.

The nineteenth century was certainly a great century; yet it was also a century of startling poverty in the field of doctrinal expression. Outside Germany, Roman Catholic theology maintained no more than a pale and shadowy existence. Characteristically, what there was took refuge in an apologetic the rationalizing character of which we of a later century find highly disturbing. On the first page of his book *Celle qui pleure*, Léon Bloy writes, in a strain of prophecy worthy of Kierkegaard: 'What we need are witnesses, not lecturers; martyrs, not demonstrators.' In these words Bloy points forward to Péguy and Bernanos, to a watershed that divides the twentieth century from the nineteenth. The main cause of this deficiency was to become clear after 1914; it is to be sought primarily in the field of *doctrine*. And not only in the field of doctrine; if we except John Henry Newman and a few islets of 'High Church' thinking, the Roman Catholic piety of the nineteenth century seems to us to have been singularly lacking in the living sap of biblical and liturgical reality.

It has to be added that the nineteenth century was the century of a great spiritual disaster—the apostasy of the great mass of the population. In the age of the Encyclopaedists it was the members of the intellectual élite who were the unbelievers. By 1830 this unbelief had penetrated to the level of the bourgeoisie. In the second half of the century the spiritual desolation of the working class in the great cities which sprang up so rapidly in western Europe after the industrial revolution became 'the scandal of our time'—as it still is today.

Finally, the nineteenth century saw the alienation of the physical sciences, in their contemporary development, from Christian faith.

All this casts deep shadows on a century which believed itself to be uniquely the century of light. Yet this was also the century of the awakening of a lay people, which at last began to make its voice heard in the Church, and which consciously became aware of its *Christian* existence in the midst of the world. It is this that makes the nineteenth, in spite of all detrimentals, one of the most attractive of all the Christian centuries.

How did the laymen of this time give expression to their membership of the Church in their life as parents, as professional men, as citizens? In what manner did the Church exercise an influence on society through its lay folk? For the nineteenth century it is easier to answer the second question than the first. The period was markedly 'social' in its thinking, and many of the structures of life as we know it today date from that time.

Space forbids our attempting to record the religious awakening, or the personal conversion, of each of the apostles of lay activity with whom we shall have to deal. But at the outset it is worth while to stress the fact that those Roman Catholics whom we shall find in the van of Christian action in society and in the world were at the same time engaged in efforts for the inward renewal of the Church and in strenuous endeavours to think out for themselves the meaning of the gospel message. It is recorded, for instance, that Princess Gallitzin spent an hour every day in meditation, and that Ozanam, a typical layman of this period, devoted half an hour every morning to the reading of the New Testament in Greek. Laymen produced large works of theology— Joseph Goerres his four volumes on Christian mysticism (1836–42), W. G. Ward *On Nature and Grace* (1860), Louis Veuillot his life of Jesus Christ (1864). These men made history in the field of the outward action of the laymen of the Church; at the same time they were witnesses to the reality of an inner life, enriched from the sources, or steeped in the traditions, of the life of the Church.

We shall find it necessary to consider lay activity under three main headings:

(i) The Life of the City.
(ii) The Social Movement.
(iii) The World of Ideas and of Culture.

The central point of the field of battle remains always the same—the confrontation of the Christian message and the modern world.

One of the best qualified historians of the period, Professor R. Aubert, has summed up the major difference between 'liberal Catholics' and the rigidly orthodox about the middle of the nineteenth century in the following terms:

> One group, taking the term 'modern world' in the sense of a single historical epoch, with its institutions, its ideals, its hopes, felt it to be their duty to go ahead of their time, and to make it plain that the Church was prepared to become incarnate within it, as it had done in earlier periods. . . . The others, taking the term 'modern world' in the sense of that part of the Revolution which had been hostile to the Church, felt it more desirable, in order to be quite sure of not entering into a compromise with error, to blow up the bridges and to strengthen the defences.[24]

It would be hard to give a better summary of the great and often passionate debate which dominated the minds of lay Christians throughout the century. We may link with it the saying of Etienne Gilson, quoted in the great pastoral letter of Cardinal Suhard:[25] 'It is not the business of the Church to prevent the world from passing away; it is its business to sanctify a world which is passing away.'

(i) *The Life of the City*

At a time at which in western Europe many of the higher clergy were failing in the performance of certain important duties to which they were committed by their calling, and in which the intellectual élite was becoming steadily alienated from the Christian faith, we can hear with unusual clearness the *vox populi*, the testimony of the simple believers. Their faithfulness was of the utmost importance in the period of transition between the eighteenth century and the nineteenth.

It is clear that, among the various factors leading to change, by far the most important was the great Revolution of 1789, one consequence of which was the extremely rapid secularization of the life of man, and which in a few years brought about a complete separation between Church and State.

In countries which at the Reformation had adopted a republican form of government, separation of Church and State had made some progress, but in Roman Catholic lands developments had been much slower. It was the French Revolution which precipitated the conflict. The question of the secularization of public and private law was to dominate the nineteenth century; there were many Catholics, who, though far from being in any sense 'secularists', were prepared definitively to justify this change.

Such Catholics were convinced that the Church and the papacy had nothing to fear from this movement of the peoples. According to Lamennais (in *The Affairs of Rome*), the words which the Pope now hears addressed to him by the peoples are these:

You have reigned over kings—now stretch out your hands to the peoples. They will uphold you with their strong arms, and, better still, with their love.

And Chateaubriand, the prophet of the dawn, writes:

A new career awaits the Popes. There are already indications that they will gloriously fulfil it. Rome has gone back to that evangelic poverty, which was its whole treasure in the days of old. By a remarkable parallelism, today too there are Gentiles to be converted.[26]

1. Beyond question it was Germany which played the leading role in this lay renewal of the early nineteenth century.

At the turn of the century, the famous 'Münster Circle' was presided over by Amélie, Princess Gallitzin. This native of Berlin, and wife of a Russian diplomat, had been educated in the school of natural sciences, and in the philosophy of the Dutch scholar Hemsterhuis. In 1779 she went to Münster to visit the pioneer educational institutions, which had been founded by Franz von Fürstenberg, the Vicar-General of the Bishop of Bonn. Not many days passed before the Princess took up permanent residence in Münster, and around her grew up that 'holy family' which was to be the inspiring power of renewal in Catholic Germany. Its influence spread far beyond the limits of the Church, since eminent Protestants, mostly of pietistic tendencies, and many representatives of non-Christian humanism, were received as guests.

It would be an exaggeration to call the spirit of Münster 'non-confessional'; yet it represented a true anticipation of the ecumenical spirit, notably in the close friendship between the Princess and F. H. Jacobi and J. G. Hamann; the latter exercised an abiding influence on her, and came to her house to die. One of the group, Leopold de Stolberg (1750–1819), draws a distinction between 'the charity which makes men indifferent to religions' and 'the charity which embraces members of all religions'. He loathed the first and practised the second. In 1809 he could write:

> Against the person of Luther, in whom I revere not only one of the greatest human spirits that have ever existed but also a profound religious sense which never deserted him, I will never lift a stone.

The group remained in close contact with Goethe, and other leaders in the intellectual and social renaissance of the time. The Bible and the writings of the Fathers played the leading part in this return to inner and spiritual life. But the members of the group were also interested in the great social reforms which were on foot; and those who belonged to the nobility had the opportunity to put their ideas into practice, by bringing to an end the legal status of serfdom on their estates.

A generation later the Catholic bishops in Germany opposed only a timid resistance, if any, to the interference of the state in the affairs of the Church, and showed themselves highly suspicious of the renewed authority of the Popes. The first cause of contention was mixed marriages. The ordinances put out by the Prussian government were generally held to be in direct contradiction to the Canon Law of the

Church; yet the bishops had acquiesced tamely in this state of affairs. But a sharp change in this situation came about when a former disciple of Princess Gallitzin, Clement August Droste-Vischering, became Archbishop of Cologne, and refused to admit the right of a secular government to dictate to the Church.

On 20th November 1837 the Archbishop was arrested, and without trial or condemnation was imprisoned in the fortress of Minden. Pope Gregory XVI protested vigorously; but the chapter of Cologne and the German episcopate remained silent. It was then that the conscience of the Christian people awoke. A layman, Joseph Goerres, set forth a scathing commentary on 'the affair of Cologne' in his *Athanasius*, a booklet which had been hastily composed but had tremendous effects in every direction. In various centres noisy protests were made against the arrest of the Archbishop and public prayers were arranged. 'Under the very eyes of the jailers, the ancient Christian principle of the independence of conscience over against the civil power sprang into new life.'

What was at stake was really the principle of religious liberty; for the affair was no longer a matter of administrative detail; it had become a battle for liberty of conscience.

The 'troubles of Cologne' were brought to an end in 1841 through the conciliatory spirit of the new King of Prussia, Frederick William IV. But they marked the demise of a system of ecclesiastical administration which had lasted for three centuries. In his *Athanasius*, the eloquence of which 'was worth four army corps', Goerres had written: 'The Church has once again found its freedom in the faith of the peoples. . . . Midnight has just struck; a new day has dawned for us.'

But Joseph Goerres (1776–1848) has more than one claim to be included in a study of the Christian layman. After a period of unbelief, he had rediscovered the faith and the Church during the time of his residence at Strasburg (1821–7), and had accepted a professorship of history at the newly founded university of Munich. There, with his wife and children, he was for more than twenty years the centre and inspiration of the 'circle of Munich'—a group which was both international and interconfessional in its outreach. In addition to many outstanding laymen, it included such eminent clerics as J. A. Möhler, Ignaz von Döllinger and F. Windischmann.

In the life of Goerres we recognize one fundamental source of inspiration—the desire to impress on the Catholic revival of the romantic period the idea of a living Church in its universality. Hence his attacks on 'territorialism', an attitude which was all too common among the bishops of the German states; hence his researches into the earlier history of Christendom, and his contacts with the rising generation of Christians in the other countries of Europe.

2. In a very different setting we find rather similar processes of thought at work in France; here, too, these find their expression in the person of a number of eminent lay Christians. The starting-point is the foundation of the periodical *L'Avenir* in 1830.

This movement of 'liberal Catholicism' was closely linked in its earlier period to 'ultramontanism'; but the developments of ultramontanism under the Second Empire led the liberal Catholics into opposition to what they regarded as extreme and almost 'sectarian' tendencies in this movement.

The period was rich in ideas and events. To depict accurately the lines of force is difficult, since each one of the laymen who were its leaders was marked by highly individual characteristics. A brief summary runs the risk of obliterating distinctive qualities, a disregard of which would be fatal to a right understanding of the period. A further danger is that of the backward glance. If we look backwards from the Vatican Council of 1869–70, we are likely to present a distorted picture of the whole development between 1830 and 1870. We must first recall three remarkable writers of a slightly earlier period, not one of whom was a priest—René de Chateaubriand (1768–1848), Joseph de Maistre (1751–1821) and Louis de Bonald (1754–1810).

We may have some reservations as to the theological value of the ideas put forward with such eloquence by de Maistre in his book *On the Pope* (1819). We may recognize that his concept of the theocratic order is based on ideas which are sociological rather than religious in character. In the midst of an upheaval, which is comparable to that of the revolutionary epoch in Russia in 1917, de Maistre and other writers like him failed to make the necessary distinctions between the role of the papacy in the Europe of an earlier day and the pastoral office of the Father of all the faithful, which is independent of time and change. Yet de Maistre is the first in the line of writers who have maintained that the layman, no less than the priest, is an active member of the body of the Church—the layman is to be regarded as the link between the world of 'religion' and the man who has separated himself from the Church.

The generation of 1830 included 'three very great Christians, who fought the good fight in the second third of this century'—Charles de Montalembert (1810–70), Frédéric Ozanam (1813–53) and Fr Lacordaire (1802–61). The first two of the three were laymen. All three had come under the influence of the inspired Abbé Félicité de Lamennais (1782–1854), who had become a liberal in 1826, and the first of whose aims was to reconcile modern society with Catholicism. After his condemnation in 1832 by Pope Gregory XVI, Lamennais separated himself from the Church. But the impulse which he had given did not die away, and the movement continued to grow within the Roman Catholic Church.

De Montalembert, a historian whose chosen field of study was the Middle Ages, was in the fullest sense of the term the Catholic leader of his time. His deepest concern was to break that close alliance between the throne and the altar which hindered the Church in the fulfilment of its apostolic task. Lamennais had earlier complained that the priest had become 'a policeman in the service of the royal power'. De Montalembert, the champion (in 1863) of the idea of 'a free Church in a free State', had on 12th September 1846 dispatched a confidential memorandum to Pius IX, the recently elected Pope, in which he gave powerful expression to the dislike felt by the younger generation for a system which led, albeit indirectly, to the priest being regarded as a public official, as the agent, or even as the auxiliary, of the state.

Ozanam, professor at the Sorbonne, who died in the flower of his age, is perhaps nearer to us than most of his contemporaries by reason of his profoundly religious spirit, and of the contemporary relevance of the views which he championed. As much as a hundred years ago, Ozanam, a republican by conviction, was criticizing 'the Constantinian era' of the Church:

> We are dreaming of a Constantine who all in a moment will bring back the peoples to the fold. . . . The faith prospers only when it encounters governments that are foreign or hostile to it. Let us not ask God to give us evil governments; but equally let us not ask him to give us one which will set us free from our responsibilities by taking upon itself a mission to the souls of our brethren which God has not committed to it.

In 1835 Montalembert was twenty-five, Ozanam twenty-two, and Lacordaire thirty-three. At that time there was living in Paris an outstanding woman who was the centre of great intellectual, social and charitable activity, and whom we shall find concerned in the spiritual undertakings of this whole generation. Madame de Swetchine (Sophie Petrovna Seimonova, 1782–1857) was a Russian Roman Catholic, who kept open house in the Rue Saint-Dominique, and received there 'the most distinguished representatives in Paris of political life, of the law, the clergy, literature and the arts'. The great years of this hospitable home, 1836 to 1848, coincided exactly with the years of the highest influence of the first generation of liberal Catholics.

The influence of Madame Swetchine on the contemporary leaders of Catholic renewal, both priests and laymen, recalls what we have encountered earlier in the seventeenth century. What she gave to Montalembert, to Lacordaire, who wrote that 'her counsels upheld me against the dangers both of loss of courage and of enthusiasm', and to countless others was nothing less than that spiritual direction which is ordinarily given to the layman by the priest. On the day after her death Augustin Cochin bore witness that 'The only thing that I can do is simply to say again how deep has been the impression left upon me by that holy woman, who so fully brought to realization the miracle of holiness in the midst of the world.'

3. It would be impossible to pass in review all the countries of Europe; but a place of special mention must be found for Belgium. Even before the Belgian revolt of 1830, clergy and laity, liberals and conservatives, in Belgium were unanimous in demanding a genuinely constitutional form of government, and the great 'liberties', which the Dutch government of 1815 to 1830 was not prepared to grant. In point of fact, from 1831 onwards Belgium was the only one among the European countries with a deeply Catholic tradition, which had adopted a modern constitution involving the separation of Church and State, and enjoying the support of a public opinion based on the principles of liberal Catholicism before liberal Catholicism had been born. The restoration of the Catholic University of Louvain (1835) was the fruit of yet another liberty—freedom in education.

The entire absence of the Gallican spirit, of 'territorialism' among the Catholic bishops in Belgium; co-operation between the lay folk and the official leadership of the Church; the separation of Church and State—these factors show the extent of the difference between the situation in Belgium and that which prevailed in its neighbours to the south and to the east. Moreover, liberal Catholicism in Belgium was a *pragmatic* attitude (accepting, for instance, freedom of worship as something which appeared to the liberals to be inevitable) rather than a *philosophic conclusion* of universal validity, such as the French school seemed inclined to deduce from a similar situation.

4. The history of the layman in the nineteenth century is intricately involved in the history of ultramontane ideas. It would be a grave

simplification to interpret this history in terms of the opposition between liberal Catholics, mainly laymen, and ultramontanes, mainly
ecclesiastics and supporters of the centralization of the Church in
Rome. The reality does not correspond to this delineation of it. Ideas
developed over the course of the years, and they were much more
varied and delicately shaded than an excessively simplified presentation
of them would suggest.

If we are concerned to trace this history from the point of view of the
laity, our starting-point must be, not the desire for the centralization
of authority in Rome which was characteristic of some of the cardinals
of the Curia, but the pastoral inadequacy of the bishops, whom the
simple clergy of the countryside often found to be too authoritarian,
or too high and mighty, to be truly the shepherds of their dioceses.

So we shall take as our starting-point not Rome itself, but one of the
independent though interlocking factors, the traditional Gallicanism of
many bishops in France, who viewed with disfavour the interventions
of the Pope and the Roman congregations even in purely religious
affairs, and were equally suspicious of the actions of the lay folk,
whether in the religious or in the social sphere. In France after 1830
the episcopate was embarrassed by the unpopularity in which it found
itself involved as a result of the compromises with the régime of the
restored Bourbons on which it had entered, and was paralysed by
the fear of provoking still further the hostility of a new government
(the 'July monarchy') together with the ill-will of an increasingly critical
public opinion. The first obstacle to be encountered by the young
Catholics of the Christian renaissance was the passivity of the bishops,
too deeply committed as these were to the illusion of protection by the
state. It is important to remember that the first person to put forward
ultramontane doctrines was Lamennais himself. It was the judgment of
Ozanam in 1840 that the spiritual renewal of the Church had over a
long period been put in quarantine by the bishops; this judgment
includes the Conferences of Notre Dame, the Benedictines of Solesmes,
the Dominicans of the School of Lacordaire, and the Society of St
Vincent de Paul. When Montalembert set out eagerly to recover for
the Church the liberty of teaching, he in his turn was to meet with
opposition on the part of the great majority of the bishops.

It would be possible to draw up a long list of bishops who manifested
their hostility to the movement of renewal, and to that new loyalty to
the Pope which was one of its countersigns. The movement changed its
character a number of times in the course of the nineteenth century;

L

but all through it was marked by a certain mistrust of the bishops, partly as a result of the renewal of Gallicanism under the authoritarian régime of Napoleon III.

In weighing up the part played by the laity in the history of ultramontanism, it is necessary to bear in mind the actions and attitudes of the Holy See itself.

(*a*) There is the shadow cast on the whole development by 'the Roman question', the question of the retention by the papacy of that political authority over the Papal States, which was being threatened by the progress of Italian unification. This purely political question was to corrupt the genuinely religious motives which underlay the ultramontane movement in its beginnings.

(*b*) It would be a complete mistake to regard the centralization of authority in Rome as due simply to a desire for power, and to a spirit of hostility to progressive tendencies in the Church. Again and again in history we find that the initiatives taken by the Popes have been directed towards the salvation of the faithful; we may adduce as evidence the role of the Roman Curia, which, in the eleventh century, reacting against the decadence of the Churches of Gaul and Germany, undertook from Rome a reform intended to liberate the local episcopate from that control by the lay princes which was signified by the right of investiture. In our own period, the most notable developments in the affairs of the missions overseas (development of the indigenous episcopate, liberation of the Churches from the traditions of colonialism) are due to initiatives taken at Rome, and were for a time frustrated on the middle levels by the conservatism of certain missionary societies, which were able to oppose a passive but effective resistance to the directives of the head.

These instances may serve to throw light on a number of situations of the nineteenth century, now forgotten, in which the interests of the faithful were better served by the intervention of Rome than by the conservative attitude of a large number of bishops.

It has been said, with some justice, that a lay writer like Louis Veuillot, the extremely conservative journalist, was completely out of touch with the modern world; it must not be forgotten that some French bishops who opposed Veuillot were also out of touch with the modern world, though in a different manner. When Veuillot, the 'lay pope', arrived in Rome in December 1869 on the eve of the Vatican Council, he was asked rather contemptuously by a journalist what right he had to allow himself to hold opinions on the Council. He replied,

'In myself I am nothing at all; but when I consider the place which my brethren have given me and the commission which I fulfil, I am *someone* from among the faithful Christian people.'

Speaking of the episcopate, the Abbé Combalet wrote as follows to the Abbé Salinis: 'The spiritual sword has, so to speak, rusted in its hands. Only a Pope can give back to it that energy of power which it no longer possesses' (14th June 1846). The first impulse of the ultramontane movement came from the circumference and not from the centre. We may recall the phrase of de Tocqueville, all the more significant for the criticial tone which underlies it: 'The fact is that the Pope was pushed by the faithful into becoming absolute master of the Church, rather than that they were pushed by him into accepting this absolute domination. The attitude of Rome was an effect rather than a cause' (1856).

(ii) *The Social Movement*

The revolution of 1848 was clearly a turning-point of the utmost importance in the social history of the principal countries of Europe.

1. In Germany the episcopate was freed from its political associations, and in October 1848 was able to meet in full assembly in Würzburg. It is remarkable that the official legal adviser of the assembly was a layman, Moritz Lieber, and that it was his hand which drew up the manifesto which the bishops addressed to the faithful.

The year 1848 was also a year of liberation for public opinion. Democratic associations of Catholics grew up almost everywhere, and before the end of the year, a general assembly brought together nearly 1,400 delegates from every part of Germany. From this time on, the German Catholic Assemblies (*Deutsche Katholikentage*) were well launched and were increasingly successful. Careful steps were taken to maintain a correct relationship with the hierarchy, and to avoid the twin reefs of insubordination and of conventional prudence. But these assemblies had the further advantage that from the beginning they were marked by a deep concern for social problems. As early as 1848 Kress, a delegate from Münster, declared in public session that 'in our gatherings artisans sit side by side with counts and barons, ordinary citizens with officers, workers with officials'. In France, Catholicism came to be more and more closely identified with the conservative bourgeoisie; whereas in Germany the delegates from the industrial regions turned the attention of Christians in the direction of their social responsibilities.

Another notable development was that of the 'associations of comrades' (*Gesellenvereine*), which were founded in 1846 by Adolphe Kolping (1813–65), a former cobbler who had just been ordained priest. Ten years later the association, which concerned itself chiefly with the care and education of young workers, had 12,000 members, and had residences in most of the great cities of Germany. The original feature in this movement was that it had grasped the idea of Christian witness by laymen to laymen.

2. In Austria, the initiative in the Christian social movement came principally from members of the aristocracy, who on the whole were attracted by the ideal of the restoration of Christian society after the medieval pattern. Yet it is important not to underestimate the value of the practical reforms which were brought into effect by the members of this school.

3. In France, the 'liberal Catholics' were succeeded, in the years following 1870, by the 'social Catholics'.

The most important of the pioneers in this movement was without doubt Léon Harmel (1829–1915), industrialist and social reformer, who was far more realistic than others in the attempt to apply the spirit of the gospel to the hard realities of modern industrial life. He is, however, to be counted among the supporters of a new school, which was formed in 1891 after the publication of the Encyclical *Rerum Novarum*, and called itself 'Christian Democracy'. It should be added that this famous Encyclical was largely the work of laymen, whom the Pope had consulted shortly after his election.

4. The social movement was not limited to the few countries which we have singled out for mention; it was rather a general ferment in the whole Roman Catholic world, with representatives in every country who were pioneers and forerunners of the more fully co-ordinated political and social actions that were to follow at a later date.

(iii) *Intellectual and Artistic Life*

If, to repeat the phrase of Etienne Gilson, the business of the Church is not to prevent this world from passing away but to sanctify a world which is passing away, it is easy to see that its task will be more delicate in the world of intellectual life than in that of political and social institutions.

In the world of artistic creation, the claim of the world to liberty is deserving of respect; and the more disinterested the creative search, the greater the respect which is its due. The Christian who enters into this world is bound to identify himself with its claim to liberty, and the message of the gospel which he desires to bring to it must find its own appropriate ways of penetration. It will always be a question not so much of an influence that is to be exercised, as of a witness that is to be borne, with full respect for the liberty of others to take that witness seriously, or to reject it.

1. Higher education and the universities presented endless problems to Roman Catholics, infinitely varied according to the different situations in the different countries of Europe.

Unfortunately we have not the space to trace out in detail the contribution of laymen to the Roman Catholic revival in England. A figure like that of Ambrose March Phillipps de Lisle (1809–78) must at least be mentioned here: he devoted his life to the restoration of monastic life, he organized an international association for prayer (1838) and an 'Association for Promoting the Unity of Christendom' (1857). The institution of the Roman Catholic hierarchy in that country in 1850 brought into being a new generation of lay people, as different as could be imagined from the Roman Catholic families of the old tradition in its vigorous spirit of initiative, in its independence of the clergy, and in a personal attitude (it might be of devoted adherence, it might be of criticism) towards the authority of the Roman See. Many distinguished names could be mentioned; but in the ranks of the Roman Catholic laity in England two stand out beyond all others.

William George Ward (1812–82) is unique in that, although a layman, from 1851 onwards he carried responsibility for theological teaching. An anxious priest protested to Pius IX against the idea that a layman, married and the father of a family, could teach the sacred science of theology. The Pope's reply was: 'It is a novel objection to anyone who is engaged in the work of God that he has received one sacrament of Holy Church which neither you nor I can possibly receive'![27] Ward's hatred of liberal Catholicism turned him into a formidable and somewhat reckless controversialist, the principal field of his activity being the *Dublin Review*. The appointment of H. E. Manning to succeed Cardinal Wiseman as Roman Catholic Archbishop of Westminster was attributed in no small measure to the influence which Ward was able to exercise at Rome.

Sir John Dalberg, Lord Acton of Aldenham (1834–1902), was the most fully accredited representative of liberal Catholicism in England. His own definition of his position was that he was a man 'who has renounced everything in Catholicism that is incompatible with liberty, and everything in politics which is inconsistent with Catholic faith.'[28] Acton had a brilliant mind, cosmopolitan through education, and open in every direction. He made it his aim to draw the English Catholics out of the narrow and restricted world in which they had lived. His dream was the creation in England of a circle comparable to that of Goerres in Munich. For he was convinced that it was only through the excellence of their own scientific and literary work that Catholics could attain to the renewal of the unity of intellectual life.[29] Acton had various means of bringing his influence to bear, notably the two periodicals which he edited one after the other, *The Rambler* and *The Home and Foreign Review*; of the latter it has been written that 'probably no review of the reign of Queen Victoria maintained so high a standard of general excellence'.

During the Vatican Council Acton took all possible steps to prevent the declaration of the infallibility of the Pope; but later, in December 1874, in a letter to his bishop he explicitly declared his acceptance of this dogma. The last and perhaps the best years of his life were spent as Regius Professor of Modern History in the University of Cambridge.

It was in this situation in England that we first encounter the clash of two conflicting ideas among Catholics concerning university education.

John Henry Newman had produced in 1852 his great work *The Idea of a University*, and from 1851 to 1858 had been Rector of the Catholic University of Dublin. Yet he was of the opinion that in England Roman Catholic students should share in the ancient traditions as maintained in the Universities of Oxford and Cambridge. Manning and Ward were opposed to this solution of the problem, which they regarded as 'liberal' and therefore dangerous; they were in favour of the foundation in England of a purely Catholic University. The majority of the thoughtful laity in England were on the side of Newman. A petition signed by a hundred of them was dispatched to Rome in 1864; a second attempt was made in 1866, with no better success than the first.

Disregarding the hesitation of other bishops and the disapproving attitude of the laity, in 1874 Cardinal Manning arranged for the opening of a Catholic University in Kensington. It was not long before it became plain that this enterprise could not be maintained.

2. In the Netherlands the hierarchy was re-established in 1853. For a variety of reasons, the Catholic population continued to exist in a state of cultural paralysis, and the influence of the clergy on the laity was particularly powerful and penetrating. By reaction, the anti-clerical feeling

of many Roman Catholic laymen was (and to some extent still is) more violent than in other countries.

By far the most attractive among these distinguished and independent laymen of the nineteenth century was Jozef Albert Alberdinck Thijm (1820–89). Thijm was a self-educated man, a leader in the work of higher education, a founder of periodicals, and the inspirer of a whole world of intellectual life which was both genuine and original. Above all, he was a Christian with a deep sense of the responsibilities that are proper to the laity, and in his thinking half a century ahead of his own time.

In 1855 Thijm founded the review *Dietse Warande*, which he continued to direct for thirty years; its character and policy are sufficient to indicate the profoundly ecumenical character of his spirit. The review was wide open to the aesthetic and intellectual problems of the time; this openness led to the friendly collaboration in its pages of priests and laymen, Christians and unbelievers, Dutchmen and foreigners.

It is to be noted that when, at a later date, a separate Roman Catholic university was organized, it came into being with its windows open on the world and free from any purely sectarian purpose—thanks to the eirenical spirit of those who had been responsible for the planning.

Thijm and his followers who founded the *Thijmgenootschap*, or 'Society for the Promotion of Scientific Work among Catholics in Holland', were basically in favour of co-operation by Catholics with the existing state universities—an attitude which aroused a good deal of mistrust on the part of the clergy, unaware as these were of the advantages of a university education. A little later the *St Radboud Stichting* was formed with the express purpose of the founding of a separate Catholic university. Was this to lead to tension between two different Catholic attitudes to the world—one open and friendly, the other on the defensive and 'armed to the teeth'? Was Holland to see a repetition of the hostility that had existed between Newman and Manning, between Acton and W. G. Ward?

Happily nothing of the kind took place. Under the guidance of the Archbishop of Utrecht, collaboration between the two groups was an established reality no later than 1906. And the foundation of the Catholic University of Nijmegen was brought about in 1923 in a spirit not of rivalry but of very generous co-operation with the state universities, which continued to be attended by as large a number of Catholic students as in the past.

3. Every other country had problems specially its own. In France the university was a state monopoly, and its work was often carried on in a highly secularist spirit. In such a situation a whole variety of attitudes is possible. Some Catholics felt that the only solution was to create a system of higher education in independence of the state. Philibert Vrau (1829–1907), one of the great lay apostles of the north of France, helped to create the Catholic Institute of Lille (1877). Yet Ozanam wished and chose to teach history at the Sorbonne. And the man who has been described as 'the greatest Catholic layman in France since Ozanam', Léon Ollé-Laprune (1841–98), was professor of philosophy at the École Normale Supérieure for twenty-three years, and resisted all attempts to entice him away, on the ground that he liked 'worlds to conquer more than worlds already conquered'.

It is the attitude of Ollé-Laprune which has proved itself to be best related to the Christian spirit as that has developed in the most recent period. We may think, for example, of E. J. Lotte, the friend of Charles Péguy, who about 1910 gathered around him eighteen professors of university rank, twelve primary-school teachers, and 124 teachers in secondary schools, and undertook the publication of a *Bulletin*. The purpose of this fellowship was to help the laymen to realize their Christian vocation 'by community in feeling and in action, by the upward impulses of the spiritual life, to make their faith more effective in witness, and so to let the influence of their character and their devotion bear fruit in their pupils.'

VII · The End of the Constantinian Era

1. If the twentieth century begins to mark the end of the Constantinian era in the history of the Church, this is to a considerable extent due to the meeting of two independent currents of development, which reach back to the end of the preceding century. On the one hand, there is the development of the Popes themselves, beginning with Leo XIII and Pius X; on the other hand there is the development of lay opinion within the Church in the period which begins with 1890. This means that, from this time onwards, the laity more and more acquire a function which is organic to the life of the whole Church, which is now recognized as such, and which as we can see on the eve of the Second Vatican Council will in course of time make necessary certain modifications in the internal legislation of the Church.

It was this revival which was to usher in the twentieth century, and to give it its special character. In many respects the generation of 1890 is nearer to that of 1920, and even to ourselves, than to that of 1860.

The thing that is most striking in these years is the awakening among laymen of a sense of the responsibility of the Christian for the world, a world which he approaches now in the spirit not of hostility but of friendly encounter. It would be possible to draw up a long list of articles and essays which appeared in these years, and in the title of which the words 'duty' or 'responsibility' occur. Those who speak thus are no longer Catholics of the Constantinian era, engaged in claiming 'rights' which 'the others' must yield to them; these are Catholics who recognize that they themselves have 'duties' and that they cannot afford much longer to fail to fulfil these duties.

The pontificates of Leo XIII and Pius X constitute a new chapter in the history of the Church.

(*a*) In August 1883 Leo XIII gave orders that the immense archives of the Vatican were to be opened to scholars engaged in the labour of contemporary historical research.

(*b*) In May 1891 the Encyclical *Rerum Novarum* was published.

(*c*) In February 1892 the Encyclical commonly called 'Rallying to the Republic' required of Roman Catholics in France that they should definitively separate the cause of the Church from that of the monarchical régime.

The work of Leo XIII was followed up in one direction or another by his successors. The Encyclical of Pius X, *Sacra Tridentina Synodus* (1905), was revolutionary; it gave back to the layman his proper share in the Eucharistic mystery, and prepared the way for a liturgical movement which has done much to shape the form of the Church in the twentieth century. The *Maximum Illud* of Benedict XV gave a new shape to missionary policy overseas, by insisting as early as 1919 on the radical separation of the life of the younger Churches from the interests of the colonizing powers. Pius XII was, more than any other, the Pope of the laity, who gave to the work of the laity an organic form hitherto unknown in the history of the Church; the document *Mystici Corporis* (1943) encourages a fresh doctrinal consideration of the theology of the lay vocation in the life of the Church.

2. In the second half of the nineteenth century, the atmosphere in the Church in Germany underwent considerable changes, and not entirely for the better. Under the influence of neo-Scholasticism, the earlier eirenical spirit was abandoned in favour of a more combative and rigidly confessional attitude. This in its turn produced an unfavourable

reaction, manifest in the abandonment of the faith by many in intellectual and university circles; and this was followed by a certain fatal withdrawal of Catholicism into a ghetto of inferiority.

In the field of culture, both Catholics and orthodox Protestants had suffered a fearful set-back as a result of the secularization of literature and the arts which began in the eighteenth century. From 1837 onwards Roman Catholics had devoted themselves increasingly to militant activity, especially in the social realm, and in the field of letters had lamentably little to show. It can well be understood that towards the end of the century, following up the first attempt at intellectual renewal set in motion by the Goerresgesellschaft in 1877, a number of Catholics with aesthetic and critical gifts desired to free themselves from this impasse of intellectual and artistic mediocrity.

The mouthpiece of this group was Karl Muth (1867–1944), whose essay on 'The Literary Tasks of German Catholics'[30] was the first sign of the awakening. The title that he gave to a book published in 1927, 'The Renewed Encounter between the Church and Culture',[31] gave it the force of a manifesto. The challenge thrown out by Muth led Catholics to realize the possibility of a new evaluation, at the same time favourable and critical, of the national tradition of culture, and especially of Goethe. It is probably difficult for the younger generation in Germany today to picture to themselves the decisive influence of Muth and his periodical *Hochland* on the cultural literature of Catholics in Germany in his day. Yet it is to him that they are indebted, if they have today a faith more fully confident in itself, with readier access to the world outside. Leaders of that generation brought about a new beginning in the history of Catholicism in Germany; they made it plain that the faith has need of other means of expression than the arid combativeness of another school of social action; after the lapse of three-quarters of a century they took up again the spirit of dialogue which had been familiar in the Circle of Münster.

3. A parallel movement can be noted in Holland. In 1899, a free association of young priests and young laymen, called from the place of its annual meeting the 'Klarenbeck Club', came into being, with the aim of fighting against clericalism, 'one of the great curses of our era', and of publicizing the ideas of Pope Leo XIII. One of the most outstanding figures of this time was Gérard Brom (1882–1959), the gifted author of a number of biographies of notable personalities of the nineteenth century. Brom is noteworthy also for his pioneer work in compiling a study of the sources which must be consulted by anyone who

desires to write a history of the laity in the Catholic Church. Fr Yves Congar, in preparing his well-known book on the theology of the laity,[32] made use of this original article of Gérard Brom. It should not be forgotten that Brom also played a leading part in the foundation of a Catholic university for the Netherlands; it was in part due to his influence that this plan could be brought to its fulfilment in a conciliatory and eirenical spirit. In that way the tradition of J. A. Alberdingk Thijm has been followed up to the present day: a detailed history of the lay movement in Holland would have to include a study of the part played by laymen in the production and direction of a number of periodicals which exercised a marked influence on public opinion.

4. When we turn to France, we find that in the second half of the nineteenth century the development of the lay consciousness had been so rapid that, by 1890, it is possible to speak of a definite school of lay thinking within the Church—and this fact alone makes it evident that the Church was entering on a period of renewal. Among the 'young folk' of that time, whom the Pope found more ready than their elders to accept the fact that the Constantinian era had really come to an end, we may mention, in addition to Léon Ollé-Laprune, already a senior in years, the philosopher Georges Fonsegrive, the historian Georges Goyau, such inspirers of the young as Marc Sangnier, and, among the rising generation of authors, Charles Péguy, Paul Claudel and Francis Jammes.

Georges Fonsegrive (1852–1917) has left us written testimony concerning this epoch, based on his own experience of living through it. In 1889 he had been appointed to a professorship in the Collège de France; but signature of the formal document confirming his appointment was withheld, when it came to the notice of the minister in charge that his daughters were being educated in a Christian school. From 1896 to 1907 Fonsegrive was editor of the periodical *La Quinzaine*, which has been described as the meeting-place of the Church and the University. In his book *De Taine à Péguy*, Fonsegrive has described for us the awakening of the Christian laity in France. Montalembert and Ozanam had gathered certain groups of younger spirits about them, but in reality they were generals without soldiers. The law of 1850, which permitted secondary education other than that controlled by the state, made possible the creation of a new atmosphere. Between 1850 and 1890 half the children of the French middle class were being educated in schools inspired by the Christian faith. By 1890 attendance at church had ceased to carry with it a social stigma. We are told that by 1912 a third of the students at the École Normale were Christians who made no secret of their observance of the faith.

A more modern spirit began to take charge of the approach to the world with the message of the gospel. In the closing years of the century the desire to be done for good and all with the Constantinian era, to free the Church from its political commitments, and to separate political and social life from confessional concerns, found open expression. We find ourselves already in touch with that contemporary current of opinion which will find expression in such a periodical as *Esprit*, and other currents associated with the names of J. Maritain, J. Lacroix, H. Guillemin, H. Marrou, and particularly Emmanuel Mounier.

Georges Goyau (1869–1939), whom we have had occasion to mention earlier in the course of this study, is of particular interest to the student of the history of his generation. Committed to the 'Christian socialism' of the period of *Rerum Novarum*, he has proved himself a witness of incomparable value to the thoughts and feelings of his own generation. As a historian he was the interpreter who made available to the reading public in France the lessons that could be learned from *L'Allemagne religieuse* (9 vols) ('Religion in Germany') in the nineteenth century. His work on J. A. Möhler, published at the beginning of this century, shows that this young layman already had an intuitive anticipation of the theology that was destined to develop in the twentieth century, and a sense of the value of the interpretative role that he felt to be his. More than almost any other church historian, Goyau has laid on those aspects which belong to a history of the layman in the Church that emphasis which they deserve.

Is it not an impressive fact that it is in the generation which came to maturity about 1900 that we find the lay historians of the Church and the Catholic movement, and that it is they also who were the first to gather together the materials out of which a history of the laity in the Catholic Church could be written? To take them in chronological order, we encounter the German Gustav Schnürer (1860–1941), professor at the University of Freiburg (Germany) from 1889 onwards; the Frenchman Georges Goyau (1869–1939); and the Dutchman Gérard Brom (1882–1959)—three writers on whom we have drawn heavily for information and instruction in the preparation of this sketch of the part played by the layman in Roman Catholic developments.

VIII · By Way of Conclusion

Looking back rapidly over the three divisions of our study of the nineteenth century—the life of the city, the social movement, the intellectual movement—it is hard to avoid the impression that the social Catholics are more remote from us than the liberal Catholics of the period between 1830 and 1848. Even if it be true that the thinkers of that first period 'failed to realize the complexity of the problem and were inclined to rush ahead too fast', even though these Catholic thinkers were in error in 'failing to make certain necessary distinctions'[33] earlier than they did, even though the social Catholics were the precursors of certain changes in the social domain, it nevertheless remains true that for us in the middle of the twentieth century it is easier to find links of kinship with the former group than with the latter.

The liberal Catholics were nearer to the French Revolution. They felt more keenly the breach with the traditions of 'the Christian order of things', the chasm that separates the Church from modern society, the need to build bridges on new foundations; the link between Church and political party had not been so firmly tied as was the case twenty years later.

By way of contrast, the social Catholics, whose opinions seem to have reached definite form about 1880, maintained a reverence for the Middle Ages, which, though it led to certain conclusions of which use could be made and has been made, nevertheless served as an opaque screen between them and the modern world. They seem at times to have failed to understand that the development of industrialization in the modern world is irreversible, and that the class struggle is not an invention of the Marxists but was implicit in the attitude of the employers in the early days of the modern developments. And, worst of all, a number of them made the grave mistake of linking 'monarchy' and 'corporative state' to their social aspirations. Underlying all this was the nostalgic desire to *restore* a certain type of Christian order. From this arises an attitude which we can only call ambiguous in relation to the 'role of religion in social affairs', and to 'Christianity as the solution for social conflicts'; the result of this was a total unawareness of the situation among the masses who were already completely alienated from the Christian tradition, and even, in certain cases and for the same reasons, a latent anti-Semitism.

But, when all has been said, it is naturally with the intellectual renewal of the concluding years of the nineteenth century that we find without difficulty the largest number of points of contact and sympathy. In Catholic action in the twentieth century, whether officially organized or not, it is impossible not to feel the weight of mass-organizations, and the unfavourable balance of compromise with certain political parties. Since the end of the Second World War there have been increasingly clear signs of the desire for a return to a more personal form of witness—to an active life 'in open order' in the world, and to an inner life of close fellowship within the *Ecclesia*.

IX · *Postscript*

I may be criticized for having distorted the concepts 'lay' and 'laity' through making too sharp an empirical distinction between 'laity' and 'clergy'. I am well aware of the element of precision that has been lacking. I readily accept the principle that any valid definition of the term 'layman' must lead us back to the *laos*: the 'layman' is one who is a member of the *laos*, the people of God, in point of fact one who has been baptized. But in a rapid historical survey such as ours it has not been possible to maintain the delicacy of handling that is required by a theological idea.

Simply as a matter of fact, the lay people, as a constitutive part of the people of God, are often driven to take up a defensive attitude in order to maintain their position against the constant tendency towards clerical domination; such an abnormal attitude certainly involves an impoverishment in the life of the Christian as a member of that fellowship which is the Church. It remains the fact that such an attitude is constantly encountered in history, and that it is one of those historical phenomena of which the student has to take account.

Certainly, to arrive at a completely balanced presentation, it would be necessary to study in equal detail the other aspect—that of brotherly co-operation between clergy and laity within the fellowship of the Church. But in the nineteenth century a balance of that kind had as yet simply not come into existence. It is impossible to pass over in silence such realities as the opposition of Cardinal Wiseman to the *Rambler*; the criticism which W. G. Ward had to endure because of his activities as a lay teacher of theology; the 'quarantine' in which Ozanam and Montalembert were kept; the mistrust which harried J. B. Rossi in Rome, because, although a layman, he took up the study of Christian archaeology—the list could be endlessly extended.

It is, of course, true that another panel of the diptych could be displayed—the influence exercised by laymen, as individuals or as groups, on the clergy and the hierarchy. We may think of the influence of Ozanam on Lacordaire, the favourable response to Fonsegrive when he described the special responsibility of the secular clergy, the authority exercised by L. Ollé-Laprune, who was often invited to lecture to the students in certain major seminaries and to instruct them in the work that later on they were to do as priests. We may recall the influence of certain laymen on the Pope himself. Montalembert, when only twenty-six years old, was given three long audiences by Gregory XVI in the course of a few weeks. Veuillot was received by Pius IX in 1869 on the eve of the Council, at a time when the Pope had already shut his doors and refused to receive anyone, even the cardinals. Yet even such a diptych would not present the picture of a well-articulated and well-balanced community, in which, in accordance with the words of St Paul, each member has his own appointed task.

It will be the task of the twentieth century to move towards this balance by revising the status of the laity within the institutional framework of the Church. Extensive preparation for this adaptation has been made by the work of the nineteenth century, in which the layman, forming part of the prophetic element in the Church, on occasion met with generous-hearted understanding from the side of the institutional element. One part of the Church can never move forward without the other. For both are subject, in common obedience, to one and the same Lord.

NOTES

1. A. Steichele, *Beiträge zur Geschichte des Bistums Augsburgs*, (Augsburg, 1850–52) I, pp. 50–3; quoted by Joh. Janssen, *Geschichte des deutschen Volkes seit dem Ausgang des Mittelalters* (Freiburg i/Br., 1886) V, p. 221.

2. The words 'sects' and 'sectarianism' are used here only from the sociological point of view and without any pejorative colouring; besides, not all lay groups have been unaffected by the development of the sectarian spirit!

3. *Dienst am Glauben* (Freiburg i/Br., 1948).

4. Alfons Auer, *Die vollkommene Frömmigkeit des Christen* (Düsseldorf, 1954), pp. 194–9.

5. L. Febvre and H. J. Martin, *L'apparition du livre* (Paris, 1958), p. 414; Johannes Janssen, *Geschichte des deutschen Volkes* (Freiburg i/Br.) II, p. 22 n. 2.

6. Henri Hauser and Augustin Renaudet, *Les débuts de l'âge moderne—La Renaissance et la Réforme* (Paris, 1929), p. 256.

7. P. Imbart de la Tour, *Les Origines de la Réforme* (Paris, 1909) II, p. vi.

8. Friedrich Heer, *Die dritte Kraft* (Frankfurt a/M., 1959), p. 585.

9. André Duval, O.P., in *La Vie Spirituelle, Supplément*, 15th November 1949, p. 359.

10. André Duval, O.P., *loc. cit.* And see H. Jedin, *Geschichte des Konzils von Trient* II, (Freiburg i/Br., 1949), pp. 384–5 and 433–4.

11. *Histoire littéraire du sentiment religieux en France* I (Paris, 1923), p. 71.

12. Johannes Janssen, *Geschichte des deutschen Volkes* VII, pp. 363–8.

13. *Op. cit.* I, p. 19.

14. J. Calvet, *La Littérature religieuse de François de Sales à Fénelon* (Paris, 1936), pp. 72–3.

15. See H. Bremond, *op. cit.* II, pp. 210 ff.

16. A. Bessières, *Gaston de Renty et Henry Buch* (Paris, 1931), p. 260 (quoting J. A. Vachet).

17. J. Calvet, *op. cit.*, pp. 16–18, 427–8.

18. *Op. cit.*, pp. 55–6.

19. The very neat *laïcs* and *laïciste* can hardly be reproduced in English (Tr.).

20. Paul Hazard, *La Pensée Européenne au XVIIIe Siècle* I (Paris, 1946), p. 116.

21. Gustav Schnürer, *Katholische Kirche und Kultur im 18 Jahrhundert* (Paderborn, 1941), ch. 4, at end.

22. P. Lenders, S.J., 'Leek en Kerk in de 18de eeuw', *Universitas* XVIII.4–5 (Louvain, 1957), pp. 67–8.

23. A. Dansette, *Histoire religieuse de la France contemporaine* I (Paris, 1951), p. 112.

24. Fr Aubert, *Le Pontificat de Pie IX* (Paris, 1952), p. 228. [Our translation, *Edd.*]

25. *Essor ou déclin de l'Eglise?* (ed. du Vitrail), p. 24.

26. *Génie du christianisme*, Part IV, Bk VI, ch. 6. [Our translation, *Edd.*]

27. Maisie Ward, *The Wilfrid Wards and the Transition* (London, 1934), p. 12.

28. Acton to Lady Blennerhassett in 1879 (quoted by R. Aubert, *Pie IX*, p. 244).

29. J. J. Dwyer, *The English Catholics 1850–1950*, pp. 493–4.

30. *Die literarischen Ausgaben der deutschen Katholiken* (1899).

31. *Wiederbegegnung von Kirche und Kultur*.

32. *Jalons pour une théologie du laïcat* (Edition du Cerf, Paris, 1953).

33. R. Aubert, 'L'Enseignement du Magistère ecclésiastique au 19 siècle sur le Libéralisme', *Tolérance et Communauté Humaine* (Tournai-Paris, 1952), p. 102.

14

Hans-Ruedi Weber

THE YOUNGER CHURCHES

Introduction

WHEN in May 1498 Vasco da Gama's fleet landed at Calicut on the Malabar coast in South India, a new era began for Asia. At about the same time the Iberian conquest drew Africa and the Americas also into this new epoch. Both Asia and Africa had already had contacts with the West, and in both continents Churches exist which derive their origins from the earliest Christian centuries. But the Iberian conquest marked a new beginning. It brought radical changes to the non-European world, and lay members of the Christian Church, both those coming from the 'older Churches' and those of the so-called 'younger Churches', played an important role in it.

The Iberian conquest was no mere mercantile and political expansion, but in essence it must be understood as 'the last of the crusades'.[1] When reading the accounts of the cruel colonial warfare in Latin America, of the slave market, and of the acts of 'pacification' of colonial powers in Asia and Africa, we find it hard to believe today that the Christian captains, soldiers and merchants were driven to these regions not only by the lust for gold and adventure but also with a sincere desire to serve God and to be led by him. Yet this was indeed the case. When on the way to India the sailors and pilots of Vasco da Gama's fleet mutinied, the captain threw his charts and nautical instruments into the sea before the eyes of the pilots and said as he pointed his finger in the direction of India: 'That is the route, the pilot is God.'[2] The twenty cannon, however, which stood also on the deck of da Gama's ship, were not thrown overboard. It was these cannon and above them the flag on which a large cross of Christ was painted that became the two symbols of the beginning of Western domination over Asia and the whole non-European world.

The Indian historian and diplomat K. M. Panikkar, at the beginning of his extensive study of what he calls 'the Vasco da Gama Epoch of Asian History' (1498–1945), points to these two significant symbols of the West on da Gama's ship. Panikkar describes then how the Western political power, symbolized by the cannon, made indeed a great impact on Asia but has now been overcome by the Asian revolution. And according to him the same is true of the second power which was symbolized by the cross. The part of his study dealing with the Christian missions—it is significant that a Hindu historian should devote some eighty pages to this subject!—leads up to a chapter on 'The Failure of the Christian Missions', where Panikkar concludes: 'It will hardly be denied that in spite of the immense and sustained effort made by the Churches with the support of the lay public of the European countries and America, the attempt to conquer Asia for Christ has definitely failed.'[3]

Panikkar is historically right when he points to the fact that Christian missions have been very closely interwoven with the Western political, economic and cultural expansion. He is also right when he speaks about a breakdown of traditional Western missionary work in the modern non-Western world. But is his final verdict true to the actual historic development? Is it true that the Christian Church, and therefore the laity, was only an exponent of Western domination and therefore played during the Vasco da Gama period only a temporary role in the history of the non-Western world? Over against this evaluation by an Indian Hindu it is interesting to hear how an Indian Christian evaluates the Asian revolution. Pointing to the origin of the new dynamism in Asian society, M. M. Thomas states that 'the Asian revolution can be interpreted both as a direct and indirect impact of Jesus Christ on Asia.' Organized Western missions were only one, and perhaps only a minor, revolutionary factor. But most of the other movements and aims which brought about the revolution of the non-European world arose in a culture which for centuries had been under the impact of the Christian gospel. Many of the things for which the non-Western world fights today—science and technology, new social values, a view of history which interprets the course of events no longer as fate but as the result of human freedom and tragedy—cannot really be understood as long as one ignores Christ. Therefore, M. M. Thomas observes: 'The more I study social questions in India the more I feel that in every sphere the non-Christian has to face the question "What do you think of Christ?" In this new situation, Asia is going to be on the one hand militantly anti-Christian, and on the other hand, there is going to be much more opportunity for Christian witness. People have to be confronted with this choice, by the preaching, the fellowship, and the service of the Church.'[4]

In this chapter we shall examine how far, since the beginning of the sixteenth century, the lay membership of the Church has played a role in the shaping of the new Asia and Africa, and how far the life, message and service of Christians have made the choice between Christ or Anti-Christ inescapable for persons, groups and nations in those continents. We shall limit ourselves to younger Churches which are the fruit of Protestant missionary work. Studies of this aspect of the history of Churches that have grown out of Catholic missions have already been published.[5]

In the growth of many Churches in Asia and Africa three main periods can be distinguished: the period of the pioneers, which often begins in the pre-colonial era; the period of missionary guidance, which often coincides with the colonial or semi-colonial era; and the period of crisis and renewal, which usually begins with the struggles for independence and nationhood. Different Churches are in different stages of development at different times. But for many Churches the sudden growth of imperialistic expansion of Western nations around 1884 marked the frontier between the first and the second period, and the Second World War, with the ensuing Communist revolution in China and the struggle for nationhood in the whole of Asia and Africa, marked the beginning of the third period.

We shall first examine the question, how far the laity played a role in the break-through of missionary obedience in the West, and then follow the three periods of growth of the younger Churches, examining which type of layman and which understanding of the role of the laity were predominant in each of these periods.

I · The Laity and the Beginnings of Missionary Obedience

While in the Roman Catholic Church the religious orders became the main agents of the missionary task, in the Protestant churches the break-through of missionary obedience is mainly due to the initiative of laymen.

With the exception of John Eliot's missionary work among the indigenous Indians in New England, the earliest Protestant missionary undertakings were initiated by laymen, mainly arising out of the *cuius regio, eius religio* doctrine of that time. It is doubtful whether the tragic episode of 1555/56 should be mentioned here, when upon the instigation of the pseudo-Protestant adventurer Durand de Villegagnon and with the help of Coligny and Calvin a first Reformed missionary attempt was made in Brazil. Better and more lasting results came from another lay initiative: in 1598 some Dutch shipowners requested the city government of Amsterdam to allow theological students to accompany their fleets to the Far East as *ziekentroosters* (ministers to the sick). This initiative led the church synod of Amsterdam in 1599 to create a new ministry in the Church whose task was not only pastoral care among sailors, but 'it was hoped that he (the *ziekentrooster*) would have the opportunity to teach the true Christian religion to the people who are living out there in darkness.'[6] The Dutch colonial mission, which became instrumental for the growth of some Indonesian churches, was thus initiated by laymen. So also was the Danish-Halle mission which had been conceived by King Frederik IV of Denmark, and the first Protestant missionaries to India—Ziegenbalg and Plütschau—were sent out in 1705 'upon the most gracious order of His Majesty the King of Denmark and Norway Frederik IV'.[7]

Among the many laymen who fought for the break-through of missionary obedience Baron Justinian von Weltz (1621–68) has already been mentioned (pp. 163 f.). A little later the Protestant philosopher Gottfried Wilhelm von Leibniz (1646–1716) received more hearing when, impressed by the missionary work of the Jesuits, he proposed to send out a missionary caravan via Russia to China, which would serve not only missionary but also political and scientific ends. His book *Novissima Sinica* (1697) drew the attention of August Hermann Francke to the missionary task. Pastor Francke's significance for the growth of missionary obedience is so well known that this leader of German Pietism is now often called 'the father of Protestant missions'. But one must not forget that Pietism was essentially a lay movement and that the greatest missionary spirit of Pietism was the layman Count Nikolaus Ludwig von Zinzendorf (1700–60). He founded the Moravian mission, one of the most daring missionary ventures in the history of the Church. From the very beginning this mission worked without dependence on or association with the ruling colonial powers. It sent out artisans and settlers along with ordained missionaries, so that the whole membership of the Church became the missionary agent. In Britain the most outstanding example of this lay initiative was the 'Clapham Sect', a group consisting mainly of politicians, business men and some clergy. Their most memorable victories were won in connection with the abolition of slavery. But they fought also with the East India Company for the right of entry of Christian missions to India and many of them were instrumental in founding the Church Missionary Society and the British and Foreign Bible Society.

The further history of Christian missions is full of examples which show to what extent the lay membership of the Church, especially women and students, initiated and sustained Protestant missionary work. The evangelical awakening in Britain and the missionary societies which sprang from it, the creation of many 'women's missionary societies' in the course of the nineteenth century, the famous student conference at Mount Hermon in 1886 with its slogan of 'the evangelization of the world in this generation', and the whole work of the 'Student Volunteer Movements', the foundation of the 'Laymen's Missionary Movement' in 1906, are all examples of this missionary consciousness among the laity. Moreover, many missionary societies began to follow the pattern of the Moravian mission and to send out Christian doctors, nurses, teachers, artisans, administrators and—not to be forgotten— the wives of all these missionaries for full-time missionary service. Such 'lay missionaries' have carried a major burden of the missionary task. However, for the subject of this volume another type of Western laymen is even more important, namely the ordinary Christians in 'secular' jobs.

II · The Period of the Pioneers

'The character of the few foreigners in this country is very detrimental to the cause of Christianity: immorality prevails everywhere, indifference to the Christian religion is the example set before the people; infidelity is openly professed, if not open opposition against the doctrine of Christianity declared. . . .'[8] With these words Bishop Crowther, the African pioneer of the Niger Mission, complained in a personal letter about the behaviour of the merchants who had come from the Christian West. This was not the expression of any anti-Western feeling, for Crowther was an avowed follower of the doctrine that 'the Bible and the plough (*sc.* Western civilization) must regenerate Africa', as was stated as early as 1837 by the British statesman Fowell Buxton.[9] It was a simple statement of facts by a sympathetic African observer.

More often than not Western laymen working in Africa and Asia were a hindrance to the cause of Christ in these continents. It would be wrong, however, to write the history of the younger Churches, and especially of their initial period, merely as the history of organized Western missionary work. Western laymen and above all the first converts have played a vital role. When studying the origin of many younger Churches, one meets indeed not the intentional work and witness of full-time ordained or lay missionaries, but first the spontaneous witness of ordinary men and women who for many different reasons had come to the non-Western world. This will be illustrated by examples taken from the beginning of church history in East Java, Japan and Uganda.

For a long time the Dutch colonial government did not allow missionary work among the Muslim population of Java, because it feared that this might 'involve a risk to beautiful, rich Java, the chief source of revenue from the East Indies'.[10] But when finally in 1848 the first missionary, the Rev. J. E. Jellesma, was allowed to stay in East Java, he found there already two groups of Christians. How had they heard of Christ? At the beginning of the nineteenth century a young German pietist, Johannes Emde, had heard in Holland that in the East Indies there was no winter. He thought this incredible, because it was in contradiction to Gen. 8.22, and he therefore decided to go there and check for himself. After many adventures as a sailor he settled, in 1811, in Surabaja (East Java) as a watchmaker. His work and his Javanese wife brought 'Father Emde' into contact with many Javanese, and he used these contacts for distributing parts of a Javanese translation of the Bible and for talking about Christ. He thus became the instrument to lead the first Javanese group of thirty-five Muslims from the village of Wiung to be baptized by the Dutch minister in Surabaja in 1843. At the same time a former civil servant, Coenraad Laurens Coolen, who had become an independent settler, witnessed to Christ in another part of East Java. While the German pietist Emde had no understanding of the age-old Javanese culture and requested the Javanese converts to conform to European customs, C. L. Coolen had had a noble Javanese for his mother and was from his childhood steeped in the old Hindu-Javanese mysticism. On his estate in Ngoro, Coolen became a Christian religious teacher who was venerated by all the residents. In order to preach the gospel he used the old Javanese *wajang* theatre (a shadow theatre with puppets) and the Muslim way of reciting the Koran. This appealed to the Javanese and soon a quite unique and fully indigenous

Christian community grew up in Ngoro, although Coolen did not, for many reasons, allow anybody to be baptized; he feared, for instance, that through baptism the converts would lose their Javanese character. Meanwhile the Christians of Wiung had come repeatedly to visit the community in Ngoro, and when they were baptized the question of baptism brought the community in Ngoro into a serious crisis. It was providential that at that time the first missionary arrived in East Java. For we can observe in the work of Emde and Coolen not only the great possibilities and blessings of such spontaneous lay witness, but also its limits and dangers. In the tradition of Emde the Church would never have taken roots in the heart of the Javanese people and culture, and in the tradition of Coolen the Church would soon have been lost in syncretism. With prophetic discernment Pastor Jellesma joined neither the group in Wiung nor the group in Ngoro, but went to Modjowarno where the Javanese Paulus Torsari had combined both Coolen's nearness to Javanese culture and Emde's sound biblical doctrine, and where a strong Javanese Christian congregation was growing. The Church in East Java remained true to its origin. It continued as a spontaneously missionary Church where many ordinary members witnessed to Christ without having been especially prepared, set apart or paid for this task. When Modjowarno no longer offered an adequate livelihood to the younger generation, many young Christians began to clear more forests on the south coast of Java. New Christian settlements grew thus in the midst of other Muslim areas, becoming the basis for the work of lay evangelists who had been trained by Jellesma. Alongside the witness of these lay evangelists who already initiated the second period of growth of the Church in East Java, some religious teachers and *wajang* players continued the unorganized spontaneous witness. A typical example was Tunggu Wulung, a Muslim mystic who lived as a recluse on Mount Kelut. Once he found on his sleeping-mat a copy of the Decalogue which Christians of Modjowarno had put there. After having read it he heard a voice ordering him to go to Modjowarno. There he was instructed in the Christian faith in which he recognized the treasure vainly searched for in the Hindu-Javanese religion and the Muslim mystics. After his baptism he became an itinerant Christian teacher who travelled through East, Central and West Java and persuaded many Javanese and Sundanese searchers that the *ratu adil*, the righteous King, who according to old Javanese expectation was to come in order to establish a kingdom of peace, had now appeared in Christ. Until this day the Church in East Java is probably the fastest-growing Church in a Muslim area in the world. One of the major reasons for this is the continuing spontaneous witness by laymen, laywomen and even children.

When in 1868 the decaying Bakufu feudal regime in Japan was overthrown and modernization under the Meiji Restoration began, Japan needed Western specialists. Among those who came first were not only 'disguised' ordained and lay missionaries, as for instance the famous missionary doctor J. C. Hepburn, but also such outstanding American laymen as L. L. Janes and W. S. Clark. Captain Janes became in 1871 the director of a school at Kumamoto, on the island of Kyushu, where a feudal lord who had decided to join the Meiji Restoration wanted to train leaders for future government service. The best students in the area were enlisted and Janes taught them mathematics, geography, history, physics and other subjects. For three years he did not speak about his Christian belief. Only in the fourth year of instruction, when Janes began to speak about the basis and presuppositions of Western culture and civilization, did he mention the Bible and the Christian faith. He began to hold Bible study classes every week in his home. As a result of this, in January 1876, thirty-five students signed a Declaration of Belief in Christianity on Mount Hanaoka; out of this Kumamoto Band came many Christian leaders in Church and society. In the same year Colonel W. S. Clark was on his way to Sapporo in the northern island of Hokkaido, where he had been called to establish an agricultural college. The Japanese government had invited him because he was the president of the agricultural college of Massachusetts. Dr Clark took temporary leave of absence of no more than nine months. Already upon arrival he had informed the Japanese minister of development and colonization that he would make the Bible the basis of his whole instruction and education. In Sapporo Dr Clark selected twenty-four students, mainly from Samurai families, and his rigid Puritan discipline was eagerly accepted by these representatives of the feudal warrior class of Japan who searched for a new way to serve Japan in its new era. But they learned not only botany and zoology. Under the influence of Clark's strong personality and of his teaching about Christ the King, as early as 1877 seven pupils were baptized and formed a small congregation in their dormitory. As in East Java these first converts became immediately witnesses to Christ: the Sapporo group attempted to win all new students; and even before the members of the Kumamoto Band had taken their vow on Mount Hanaoka, they were trying to convert the whole town of Kumamoto. Many hardships came upon these early converts, and in this school of suffering they grew into the maturity of faith. Among them were the well-known church leaders Hiromichi Kozaki, Danjo Ebina, Kanzo Uchimura, and others. But what is less known is the great contribution which these and other early converts made to the building-up of modern Japan. Tokio Yokoi and Tsurin Kanamori, two of the Kumamoto Band, became fervent workers for democracy, and among the Sapporo group were Inazo Nitobe, a famous Christian writer and statesman, and Baron Shosuka Sato who became president for life of Hokkaido Imperial University. 'It was a general pattern that these early Christians, immediately after accepting the Christian faith, sought to express their experience through a new relation to their neighbours. They poured their energies into such fields as education, social work, the temperance movement, civil liberties, and prison reform.'[11] When in 1956 the government was asked to name the four most outstanding leaders in social work during Japanese history, all four nominated were Christians: Juji Ishii, the founder of the large Okayama Orphanage; Kosuke Tomeoka, the leader of the prison reform work; Gumpei Yamamuro, founder of the Japanese Salvation Army and social settlements; and Takeo Iwahashi who founded the Light House in Osaka for those who like himself were blind. But the early Christian leaders were not only led to such charitable work. They also felt responsible for changing social and political structures. Hiromichi Kozaki became not only a great church leader, but was also one of the first to introduce socialist thinking to Japan (as early as 1881), and in his *A New Theory of Politics and Religion* (1886) he severely criticized the feudal structure of society. In 1897, the 'Association for the Formation of Labour Unions' was founded at a meeting in the Tokyo YMCA. Many Christians were among the initiators, among them the secretary of the Association, Sen Katayama, who in 1901 became one of the founders of the Social Democratic Party.

A similar commitment to the social and political struggle on the part of the first converts can be seen in the growth of the Anglican Church in Buganda. It was again a Western layman, the journalist and explorer H. M. Stanley, who first taught the essentials of Christian faith to the Kabaka Mutesa I and his court during two short visits to Buganda in 1875. Stanley even began to translate parts of the Bible into Kiswahili, and he wrote his famous letter to the *Daily Telegraph* (asking for 'a pious practical missionary') which in fact changed the whole missionary policy of the Church Missionary Society in East Africa. As a response to Stanley's letter, the first missionaries arrived at the palace of Mutesa I in 1877. Their household soon came to resemble the household clusters of the chiefs in Buganda society, when groups of pages, mostly sons of chiefs, gathered around them to learn to read and write. Many of them began to respond to the preaching of the gospel, and other Christian clusters or house churches grew in the country. The extent of this response was tested in the course of the next fifteen years in a series of crises and persecutions in which the famous Uganda martyrs gave their lives for the witness to Christ. When, eleven years after the arrival of the first missionaries, all Europeans had been driven out of the country and the young Church stood alone, the early converts not only continued their missionary work, but also took up their political responsibilities. They organized the Church as an underground movement, and prepared the revolutionary action which brought them into warfare, exile and, in 1890, to the political control of Buganda. 'The decisions they made were not those the missionaries would have advised or the Western Churches approved of; but they were their own, and they made them in response to what they believed to be the call of God as it came to them in the things that encompassed them. They knew their Swahili Bibles, and, however limited their interpretation of them, they devoutly believed that the Book should guide their actions.'[12]

It would be easy to add other instances from other parts of the non-Western world where during the period of the pioneers both Western and national laymen and laywomen made vital contributions to the life of their church and society. But is it possible to discern a general pattern in this initial period of church growth in Asia and Africa? One might perhaps say this much: In the period of the pioneers the Western missionaries, both ordained and lay, professional and non-professional, were still foreigners living in a society whose old structures had not yet been broken by the Western impact. Their authority lay only in the authority of their message and personality and had no relation to the power of a colonial government. They were more occupied in missionary itinerations than in missionary institutions. They did not yet train national leaders for a church life whose structures were mainly imported from the West; they rather discerned and collaborated with the given leaders in society as well as in the small groups and 'house churches' of the first converts whose common life had not yet been institutionalized. Among these converts were many strong personalities who dared to break with the old way of life and the old community, for whom baptism became the decisive event in their life, and who often had to go through the hard but strengthening 'school' of persecution.

Many of these first converts were chiefs, heads of villages, 'seekers for truth' or others who had natural gifts of leadership. All these factors explain why during the initial period of growth in most younger Churches the laity played such an important role.

III · *The Period of Missionary Guidance*

In 1884, at a round-table conference in Berlin, nearly the whole of Africa was divided among the major European powers. In the same year an outstanding Japanese politician, Count Itagaki, declared that the hour had come for Japan to accept Christianity because otherwise Japan would never be on equal footing with the Western powers. These two events were symptomatic. Even earlier the Protestant nations of the West had forced the Chinese government to admit them to the Empire and permit their teaching, and in India British colonial rule had already been established since the middle of the nineteenth century. The West was going to complete what 'the last of the crusades' in the sixteenth century had begun. It attempted to take over the non-Western world. This had its effects also on the life of the younger Churches and on their conception of the laity. In his study on *The Growth of the Church in Buganda* John V. Taylor significantly named the time after the period of the pioneers 'The Church in Leading Strings', and 'The Period of Disengagement'. And what happened in Buganda is symbolic for the development of many younger Churches in Africa and Asia.

Soon after the political triumph of Christianity, the key persons in the history of the Church in Buganda became the missionaries and the African evangelists, village catechists and pastors. Inspired by the prayer and work of the missionaries Baskerville and Pilkington, a revival movement began in 1893 in the course of which hundreds of ordinary Christians offered themselves as teachers and evangelists. The outreach of the Church in Buganda during the next twelve years became an amazing demonstration of responsibility. The whole Church was in action guided by its spiritual leaders, the chiefs. The missionaries helped the Church by the translation of the Bible into Luganda (completed in 1896 by Pilkington), by the supply of good commentaries and other substantial Christian literature, and above all by training for Bible study, expository preaching and by the training of catechists. But soon a new generation of missionaries came and, through their protective and possessive love, 'took over'. The handful of pioneer missionaries had had virtually no power to impose their will. But by 1904 there were seventy-nine missionaries of the Church Missionary Society in Uganda, supported by the authority of the colonial government and enjoying an almost unlimited freedom to make, and carry out, their own schemes. 'The old type of African church leadership could not for long be maintained in partnership with this new missionary assertiveness, and it was steadily replaced by a new leadership that was both more clerical and more filial.'[13] This, according to Taylor, had a three-fold result: (1) Paternalism: a revealing sign of this trend was the breakaway of the 'African Orthodox Church' in 1929, which described itself as 'a Church established for all right-thinking Africans, men who wish to be free in their own house, not always being thought of as boys'. (2) Clericalism: when the leadership of the Church was taken over by missionaries and later by African clergy, the Christian chiefs and the other laity—being no longer trusted with spiritual responsibility—tended to relax and become second-class Christians. Soon also the catechists were made to feel the distinction between themselves and the ordained clergy, and a revealing sign of this change was the strike of the catechists of seven districts for double pay in 1905. (3) Centralization and specialization: while the reports of the Uganda mission up to 1904 contain mainly accounts of missionaries' itinerations, of the work of catechists and the outreach of the Church, later reports are almost wholly devoted to educational and medical work. Missionary itinerations were gradually being replaced by missionary institutions and administration. When handing over responsibility into African hands, the missionaries did so by withdrawing into a higher category in the administrative hierarchy. And soon also the best African pastors and evangelists were caught into this 'withdrawal upwards'. The fruit of this process was the building-up of an impressive church structure and the establishment of many Christian institutions, which have made a great contribution to the development of East Africa. But this has happened at the expense of the most important level of church life, the life of the local congregation where most laymen and laywomen get their spiritual food and where they should be helped in their response of obedience to the demands of the gospel. The flock, in its unimportant village church, was left with the poorest quality of shepherds. No wonder that the church membership is now dangerously out of touch with the Word of God (almost all the good theological literature in Luganda for the use of catechists and intelligent laymen is out of print and only Bunyan's *Pilgrim's Progress* has been reprinted). Moreover, more than 80 per cent of the laity is deprived of the sustenance of Holy

Communion because of the unimaginative approach of church leaders to the difficult question of African marriage.

There are of course many variations to this pattern of development in the life of younger Churches during the period of missionary guidance. Even the development of the Anglican Church in Buganda was obviously more complicated than the above short sketch can convey. But in almost all younger Churches at least three features were characteristic of that period: the concentration on the building-up of the membership, structures and ministries of the younger Church; the predominance of missionary institutions; and the prevailing other-worldly piety.

After the 'missionary occupation' of many parts of the non-Western world the first aim was naturally to increase the membership of the younger Churches through systematic evangelistic work. Where the membership did indeed increase rapidly—as for instance in the mass-movement areas of India—the missionary effort was concentrated on organizing the converts into Christian congregations and regional units with appropriate buildings, a disciplined church life and regularly trained and appointed ministers. The classical example of this development was the strategy followed by German missionaries in the growing Batak Church in Sumatra. The rapid growth of that Church was first due to spontaneous expansion. 'The heathen saw the young Christian community and its power, its deliverance from the fear of demons. In the markets they talked with each other about the new religion and by this means heathen became interested in it. Or there were Christians who went to heathen areas to follow their own trade and immediately began to propagate Christianity.'[14] The missionaries began therefore to mobilize and train the most promising of the young Batak Christians and made them 'their native helpers'.[15] The whole missionary work became a model expression of the then prevailing missionary theory of Gustav Warneck, namely the *education* of converts to become an independent Church. The result was the impressive Batak Church, with its well-structured church life and hierarchy of ordained and lay ministries. This 'crown of Protestant missionary work in the Dutch East Indies'[16] did, however, not develop as harmoniously into an independent Church as the missionaries had hoped. The structure was too much imposed from above and from outside. Now, when the outburst of Indonesian nationalism has come, new and more indigenous structures must grow.

Another classic example of growth through missionary guidance was the Nevius plan in the Presbyterian Church in Korea. The China missionary John L. Nevius had published in 1885 a series of articles on the 'Planting and Development of Missionary Churches'.[17] He insisted there on the continuing importance of missionary itineration, took up the Venn-Anderson principles of 'self-propagation, self-government and self-support', laid much stress on strict discipline, regional units, non-interference in lawsuits, on helpfulness in economic life-problems and above all on systematic Bible study for every believer under his group leader and for every leader in the regional Bible classes. This strategy proved to be sound, and perhaps nowhere in the non-Western world has the total membership played a more important role in the life and mission of the Church than in Korea. Yet even this excellent missionary strategy could not save the young Church from serious crises during and after the second world war, when party spirit from within and the temptations of foreign financial aid threatened the further development of the Church.

The second mark of the period of missionary guidance was the predominance of missionary institutions. There is no doubt that during that period the greatest contribution of the Church to the non-Western world was made through these institutions. Where would Africa be today without the pioneering work of Christian schools, hospitals, rural reconstruction schemes and so forth; or India without Alexander Duff's educational policy and the Christian concern for the depressed classes? Non-Christian Asian and African statesmen have often publicly acknowledged this fact. Even Chou En-lai said to the Chinese Christian leaders in 1950 that the Communist Party had come to recognize that by their social and educational services the Protestant Churches had indeed contributed to the well-being of the Chinese people, that the party appreciated this fact and respected the Churches for this pioneering work.[18] These many Christian institutions provided wide possibilities for service, both for Western lay missionaries and even more for Asian and African Christians. Moreover, these institutions brought a great number of Asians and Africans into contact with the Church. Although many of these were never baptized or after baptism lost contact with the Church, they were nevertheless marked by Christian influence. Beside the Church, which in most parts of the non-Western world remained a small minority, there grew what is often called 'the Christian movement'. The phenomenon which Stanley Jones has described in his book on *The Christ of the Indian Road* is by no means limited to India. Out of this 'Christian movement' grew many outstanding Asian and African leaders such as Dr Sun Yat-sen and, to a certain degree, also Mahatma Gandhi. Because of the existence of a Christian movement beside the institutional Church, halfway groups and institutions between the Church and the world, such as the YMCA, the YWCA and the Student Christian Movement, became extremely important. For instance, the great majority of Chinese Christians who had a real impact on Chinese society came out of the Student YMCA's and YWCA's.

The third mark of the period of missionary guidance was the prevalent other-worldly spirituality. Nowhere else has John Bunyan's *Pilgrim's Progress from this World to that which is to come* been translated, read and meditated so fervently as in the younger Churches. The pietist-evangelical background of most missionary preaching and the experience of conversion which for the converts often meant an almost total separation from their natural environment, are the roots of this prevailing spirituality. Even the above-mentioned medical and educational work, which had such a great impact on society, was in many cases conceived not as a Christian service, which in itself is an expression of Christian obedience, but primarily as a means to preach the gospel and to convert. And, as soon as missionaries and national church leaders were faced with the problem of a lax third-generation Christianity, their main answer was the prayer for revival movements. In the history of the younger Churches of that period revival movements play indeed a predominant role. Some of them have become world-famous, such as that which took place on the island of Nias in Indonesia and the revival in East Africa. These revival movements were the place in which the lay membership could recover some of the intiative it had had during the period of the pioneers, but under the impact of missionary guidance the general conception of the role of the laity had meanwhile changed.

The concentration on the building-up of the Church, on Christian institutions and on conversion *out of* this world tended to neglect the aspect of Christian obedience *in* the world, in the 'secular' spheres of life and work. The religious aspect of life—and the religious profession! —overshadowed all the others. When a prominent Brahmin was converted, the tendency was to make him an ordained minister or at least a doctor or teacher in a Christian institution. When he chose engineering, journalism, politics or any other such 'worldly' work, he often found little understanding and support from the Christian community and its leaders. It was indeed extremely difficult to fulfil such professions as a Christian vocation in the midst of a society whose business prac-tices and general ethos had not been under the impact of the gospel for centuries. Many fervent Christians chose therefore 'church-vocations' in Christian institutions. They became the 'key-laymen', helping or opposing the missionaries and the national clergy, while laymen in 'secular' professions tended to be regarded as secondary church mem-bers. This dichotomy developed mainly among the more educated Christians. In rural areas, for instance in the mass-movement areas in India, the Christian community remained far more a unit, and the separation between the religious and other spheres of life was less marked. Yet even there lay-training was in the first place conceived as a training to help in the inner life of the Church, its institutions and evangelism campaigns, rather than as a preparation and nurturing with a view to the Christian's obedience in the world. There were of course notable exceptions—for instance the movements for Christian home and family life and some rural reconstruction schemes; but these did not change the general institution-centred and clerical pattern of the period of missionary guidance.

IV · Crisis and Renewal

'To the Chinese mind, Christianity is synonymous with schools, hospitals, asylums, preaching, church worship, evangelistic campaigns, relief work, etc. We are not using the word "activity" in any dis-paraging sense at all, except that we wish to point out that it is the activities of Christianity rather than its teachings and spiritual experi-ences that have arrested the attention of our people and have won their respect.' This judgment of a Chinese Christian[19] points to a basic weakness of the pattern of missionary guidance. All three of the above-mentioned marks of the second period in the growth of the younger Churches have become points of crisis and renewal. Both the crisis and the renewal in this third phase of their growth are intimately related to the end of the Vasco da Gama period and the growing non-Western self-expression, and to the active participation of the younger Churches in the ecumenical movement.

The patterns of church life, evangelism, paid ministry and worship were essentially foreign to the non-Western world. Already in 1899–1900 the Boxer rebellion flamed up against the 'primary devils', the foreign missionaries, and against the 'secondary devils' equally de-serving death, namely the Chinese Christians. But the protest against the foreignness of church life came also from within the Christian community. It found expression, for instance, in the phenomenal growth of 'Ethiopian churches', African Zionism and the Black-Christ dogma on the whole African continent. Also the creation and steady growth of *Mukyokai*, the Non-Church Movement, in Japan is most significant. The man who inspired that movement, Kanzo Uchimura from the Sapporo group, who became one of the greatest Christian teachers and exegetes of Japan, during his stay in America (1884–8) already voiced his doubts about the profession of a 'seller of religion'. 'If Paul were now living in Japan, he would have said: "It were better for me to die than that I should become a salaried minister." And I am almost tempted to say the same thing.'[20] Azegami, another *Mukyokai* leader, has strongly expressed the view that in the Western church-type Christianity the believer becomes 'the slave of organization', and becomes so involved in the material side of church life and building maintenance that the primacy of spiritual things is lost.[21] *Mukyokai* is today one of the few, perhaps the only Christian group in Japan which is fully indigenous and self-supporting and has developed a strong charismatic leadership. But will it survive, without any sacraments, ordained ministries and regular church structure? Leading Christians in Asia admit that 'the Church in Asia today might well be compared with the youthful David struggling with the well-intended gift of Saul's armour.' 'This is a time, then, in which the Church in Asia is . . . groping after new patterns of life that will equip it better for its tasks.'[22] The crisis of the foreign structures of church life cannot be overcome, however, by sectarian isolation or the rejection of all ministries and structures. What is needed is the renewal of the given structures in view of the total task of the Church in modern Asia and Africa. Church union movements in many parts of the non-Western world, the introduction of a scheme for voluntary presbyters in the Church of South India, the growth of Christian communities (*ashrams*) in India, new forms of industrial evangelism, especially in the Philippines and Japan, the establishment of centres such as the one in India for the study of religion and society, or that in Mindolo, Northern Rhodesia, which serves as a means of reconciliation in a situation marked by explosive racial and social tension—all these are signs of renewal.

The Christian institutions in Asia and Africa contributed much to the foreignness of the younger Churches. The initiative for most of these institutions came from Westerners, and even today many of them rely to a great extent upon Western money and leadership. Their

M

spectacular work tended to overshadow the manifestation of the Spirit in the normal life of Asian and African Christian communities. Only a few of these institutions were really rooted in the spiritual life of the younger Churches, even if legally they were no longer missionary institutions but had become institutions of the Church; and so 'they became object lessons in social service, in modern ways of living and hygiene, but their spiritual mission was on the whole, by the vast majority, unheeded.'[23] For a long time such object lessons were appreciated, but now in the era of growing Asian and African welfare states they are apt to be regarded as competing with national plans for development. At the inaugural assembly of the East Asia Christian Conference in Kuala Lumpur in 1959, an outstanding group of Asian church leaders, theologians and laymen studied this question of 'Christian Service in the Framework of National Welfare and Development Plans'. In their report they said that 'in the situation of rapid social change in Asia accompanied by the awakening of the ancient religions to social values and the development of state programmes for the welfare of the people, the emphasis of the Church should be more on the witness and service of individual Christians in secular institutions of national life than on Christian institutions of service.' 'Christian witness in the world is mainly fulfilled by the lay members of the Church regarding their daily work as a Christian vocation. This means that the Churches' witness in political life is mainly articulated as its members become involved in the responsibilities of citizenship, at the municipal, national and international level.'[24] These statements reveal an important trend in contemporary Asian church life. A few months before the Kuala Lumpur assembly, an East Asian Conference was held in Hong Kong about 'The Christian in Medical Work in East Asia Today'. The majority of the participants came from large mission hospitals. One would have expected that at such a meeting the importance of Christian hospitals would be emphasized. Yet the report stresses 'the consistent emphasis which the Conference expressed as to the strategic witness of the individual Christian in medical work whose field of service lies outside the church-related institutions'.[25] The crisis of Christian institutions is being overcome by a renewal of the conception that all work done to the glory of God and the service of our neighbour is a Christian vocation and genuine Christian witness and service. The necessary polarities in the life of the Church between 'worship and work', organized and 'corporate service and serving presence in the world', organized and 'corporate witness and (spontaneous) gossiping of the gospel', 'the community of the saints and the community with our neighbours'[26] are being rediscovered and the one-sided emphasis on institutions and organized church life during the period of missionary guidance is being corrected.

The crisis and renewal of the structures of church life and the work of Christian institutions went parallel with the crisis and renewal of the type of piety which had developed during the period of missionary guidance. Fitzgerald wrote in his evaluation of the role of Christianity in the Chinese revolution: 'The Protestant failed to ask for the right renunciations, or to gear his demands to the level of the whole society.' 'The sacrifices which the Protestant demanded, wine, theatre and tobacco, seemed irrelevant and merely quaint to the Chinese.'[27] The Communists, however, came with a call to a single-minded, disciplined and selfless devotion to a revolutionary action which was highly relevant to the challenge of the decaying feudal war-lord society. A Christian may wonder whether the piety developed in the East African revival movement was the right response to the Mau-Mau revolution. A West African Christian wrote, after his contacts with revival Christians in Kenya: 'We discovered among the "brethren" of Kenya, under the Mau-Mau tribulation, a sense of living only for the "Other World". One of them told me that he would think it useless to take part in the government of his country with a view to making it more righteous. To him government and the power it wields belong to this world, with which the "sons of light" should have no parley.'[28] This kind of piety is today called in question by many Asian and African Christians, as may be illustrated by the following two statements of the East Asian Christian Conference in Kuala Lumpur and the All African Church Conference in Ibadan. 'The inheritance of a pietistic Christian tradition coupled with escapist tendencies already inherent in the Asian religious traditions have to be counteracted.'[29] 'The Church has a duty to bear witness in humility to its understanding of the will of God for man in organized society. For that reason it dare not assume a passive, indifferent or neutral attitude towards the crucial political and social issues of the time.' It 'has the duty to provide education in Christian citizenship' and 'to give true pastoral care to those of its members who are called to take an active part in the politics of their country'.[30] This is another important trend in the contemporary life of the younger Churches: the crisis of one-sided, other-worldly piety is overcome by the discovery of new dimensions of Christian obedience in the midst of the struggle for a new Asia and Africa.

In the process of the above-mentioned threefold crisis and renewal a new type of layman and a new understanding of the lay ministry has come to the forefront. We see it incorporated in persons such as Sir Francis A. Ibiam, the Governor of Eastern Nigeria who was elected as the first African among the presidents of the World Council of Churches, or in the Christian students of Indonesia who play such a vital role in the life of both their Church and their nation. In contemporary missionary literature one finds the persistent call for 'an increasing flow of Christian lay men and women who go out across the world in business, industry and government, and do so with a deep conviction that God calls to them to witness for Him in all of life'.[31] The emphasis on the vital importance of a mature laity and adequate lay training is a recurrent theme in the reports of recent Asian and African Christian gatherings, and this emphasis is being written into the ecclesiastical structures of younger Churches. As a result of a long and most revealing discussion, in which the concepts of both the ordained ministry and the laity which are traditionally held by the Anglican, Methodist, Congregationalist and Presbyterian churches were mutually corrected, the Constitution of the Church of South India includes a chapter on 'The Ministry of the Laity'. It is there said that the Church of South India 'welcomes and will as far as possible provide for the exercise by lay persons, both men and women, of such gifts of prophecy, evangelization, teaching, healing and administration as God bestows upon them'.[32] When the East Asia Christian Conference was formed, it created a Committee on 'The Witness of the Laity' which has become an important means of interpreting to the Asian Churches the contemporary ecumenical reaffirmation of the ministry of the laity and of making a specific Asian contribution to this reaffirmation.

Will the end of the Vasco da Gama period in the history of the non-Western world bring about the end of the younger Churches? Many believe that the answer to this question depends mainly upon how Asian and African laymen and laywomen respond to the demands of the gospel in their everyday life and work.

NOTES

1. John A. Mackay, *The Other Spanish Christ; A Study in the Spiritual History of Spain and South America* (London, 1932), pp. 23–41.

2. Oliveira Martins, *Historia de la Civilizacion Ibérica*, p. 314. Quoted from John A. Mackay, *op. cit.*, p. 25.

3. K. M. Panikkar, *Asia and Western Dominance* (London, 1953), p. 454.

4. M. M. Thomas, 'The Logic of the Christian Mission', *The Pilgrim* III, No. 1 (1959), pp. 73 f.

5. See especially: 'Das Laienapostolat in den Missionen', *Festschrift für Prof. Dr Johannes Beckmann SMB*, ed. J. Specker SMB and W. Bühlmann OFMCap. (Beckenried, 1961).

6. Quoted by H. D. J. Boissevain, *De Zending in Oost en West* I (s'Gravenhage, 1934), p. 26.

7. Martin Schlunk, *Die Weltmission des Christentums* (Hamburg, 1925), p. 151.

8. Letter of S. A. Crowther to H. Wright, Secretary of the CMS (21st January 1878), quoted in Peter Beyerhaus, *Die Selbständigkeit der jungen Kirchen als missionarisches Problem* (Wuppertal-Barmen, 1959), p. 129.

9. Fowell Buxton, *The Slave Trade and Its Remedy* (London, 1837).

10. C. W. Nortier, 'The Role of the Laity in the Missionary Outreach of the Church in East Java, Indonesia': unpublished paper, p. 4. A summary of this paper has been published in *Laity* 4 (Geneva, 1957), pp. 15–24. Cf. also C. W. Nortier, *Van Zendingsarbeid tot Zelfstandige Kerk in Oost-Java* (Hoenderloo, 1939); Hendrik Kraemer, *From Missionfield to Independent Church* (The Hague, 1958), pp. 73–95.

11. Masao Takenaka, *Reconciliation and Renewal in Japan* (New York, 1957), p. 23. The life of some of these Christian Japanese pioneers is described in M. and N. Prichard, *Ten Against the Storm* (New York, 1957) and Norimichi Ebizawa, *Japanese Witnesses for Christ* (London, 1957).

12. John V. Taylor, *Processes of Growth in an African Church* (London, 1958), p. 10.

13. John V. Taylor, *The Growth of the Church in Buganda* (London, 1958), p. 71.

14. E. Verwiebe in *Tambaram Report* V, p. 430.

15. J. Warneck, *Unsere Batakschen Gehilfen, wie sie arbeiten, und wie an ihnen gearbeitet wird* (Gütersloh, 1908). Cf. also J. Warneck, 'Die Erziehung der Gehilfen in der Batakmission', *Allgemeine Missionszeitschrift* (1902), pp. 305 ff., 353 ff.

16. J. Richter, *Allgemeine Evangelische Missionsgeschichte* V, p. 80. For a careful analysis of the growth of this Church, see Beyerhaus, *op. cit.*, pp. 163–215.

17. Originally published in the *Chinese Recorder*, later brought together in J. L. Nevius, *Methods of Mission Work* (London, 1898). See also C. A. Clark, *The Korean Church and the Nevius Method* (New York, 1930).

18. C. P. Fitzgerald, *Revolution in China* (London, 1952), p. 138.

19. David Z. T. Yui, in *China Today through Chinese Eyes* (London, 1927), pp. 148 ff.

20. Quoted in Raymond P. Jennings, *Jesus, Japan and Kanzo Uchimura; A Brief Study of the Non-Church Movement and its Appropriateness to Japan* (Tokyo, 1958), p. 27.

21. *Ibid.*, p. 75.

22. 'Christ, the Light of the World, and our Unity, Witness and Service—An Asian Perspective', *The South East Asia Journal of Theology* I, No. 2 (1959), p. 55.

23. Fitzgerald, *op. cit.*, p. 142.

24. *Witnesses Together: Report of the Inaugural Assembly of the East Asia Christian Conference at Kuala Lumpur, Malaya, May 1959*, ed. U Kyaw Than, pp. 73, 64.

25. *The Christian in Medical Work in East Asia: Hong Kong, December 28, 1958–January 1, 1959*, published by the EACC, p. 89.

26. These are sub-titles in the report on 'The Form and Nature of the Congregation' of the World's Student Christian Federation Asian Conference in Rangoon (28th December 1958–7th January 1959), published in *Darshan* 4, No. 2 (1959), pp. 17–24.

27. Fitzgerald, *op. cit.*, pp. 128, 127.

28. Edmund Ilogu, *West Meets East* (1955), p. 205, quoted in J. V. Taylor, *Christianity and Politics in Africa* (London, 1957), p. 185.

29. U Kyaw Than, *op. cit.*, p. 63.

30. *The Church in Changing Africa; Report of the All-Africa Church Conference, Ibadan, January 1958*, pp. 57 ff.

31. *Missions under the Cross (Report of the Conference of the I.M.C. at Willingen 1952)*, ed. Norman Goodall (London, 1953), p. 315. For a survey of this discussion on non-professional missionaries and laymen working overseas, see: 'Men and Women Working Abroad', Document No. V of the Department on the Laity, WCC, Geneva, 1957.

32. *The Constitution of the Church of South India* (Madras, 1952), ch. 6, p. 34.

BIBLIOGRAPHY

The histories of Foreign Missions, although often written from a one-sided Western and clerical point of view, contain much relevant material as well as references to detailed studies and primary sources. Cf. especially Kenneth Scott Latourette, *A History of the Expansion of Christianity*, 7 vols (New York, 1937–45); Julius Richter, *Allgemeine Evangelische Missionsgeschichte*, 5 vols (Gütersloh); C. P. Groves, *The Planting of Christianity in Africa*, 4 vols (London, 1948–58).

Among the reports of missionary and church conferences the most important are: *The Tambaram Series* (International Missionary Council Meeting at Tambaram, Madras, 12th–29th December 1938), 7 vols (London, 1939); *The Church in Changing Africa* (Report of the All-Africa Church Conference, Ibadan, Nigeria, January 1958); *Witnesses Together* (Report of the Inaugural Assembly of the East Asia Christian Conference at Kuala Lumpur, 14th–24th May 1959), ed. U Kyaw Than.

Besides the special studies quoted in the text other important publications for the subject of this chapter are: Christian Keysser, *Eine Papuagemeinde* (Kassel, 1929); J. Waskom Pickett, *Christian Mass Movements in India* (Lucknow, 1933); Wilfred Scopes, *Training Voluntary Workers* (Lucknow, 1955); B. G. M. Sundkler, *Bantu Prophets in South Africa* (London, 1948); M. A. C. Warren, *Revival: An Enquiry* (London, 1954); and the publications of the 'Studies in the Life and Growth of the Younger Churches' undertaken by the Department on Missionary Studies of the World Council of Churches.

15

A. E. Fernandez Arlt

THE LAITY IN THE LATIN AMERICAN EVANGELICAL CHURCHES
1806–1961

I · The Layman at the Frontier (1492–1806)

The Roman Catholic Church

CHRISTOPHER COLUMBUS discovered the Americas in 1492. The rulers of Spain who were the sponsors of the expedition wrote: 'We send the knight Christopher Columbus with three well-equipped caravels over the Ocean towards India with a view to certain undertakings for the propagation of the divine Word and the true faith.'[1] This makes it clear that evangelization was included in the commission given by the rulers of Spain to Columbus. Since Columbus and the rulers were alike laymen, we see that from the start laymen undertook responsibility for the evangelization of America. The Christian name of Columbus, Christopher, the bearer of the Christ, symbolically sums up his task.

From another angle also we recognize lay participation in the evangelization of Latin America from the start: the Roman Catholic missionary movement and the establishment of the Roman Catholic Church took place under the law of Patronate. This term *patronate* is defined by Fr Benno Biermann O.P. in the following terms: 'The word Patronate denotes that ancient custom of the Church under which a layman who had built a church, or had provided for ecclesiastical revenues, obtained the right to nominate or to "present" suitably qualified clerics to the ecclesiastical offices in such churches; the nominees could be rejected only if some canonical impediment stood in the way of their appointment.'[2]

In some Latin American countries this law of the Patronate is retained until the present time. We may criticize such a law in the light of a sound Christian doctrine of the relationships between State and Church; but it is clear that it confers on the laity a very important place and responsibility for the extension of the gospel. In this connection we must not forget the remarkable part played by the various orders of lay brothers, which devote themselves especially to such works as hospitals, instruction in Christian doctrine and so forth.[3]

These first steps laid down the lines which were later followed, and helped to impress on Latin American Christianity certain characteristics to which it has remained faithful. Today there is a new awareness among Roman Catholics regarding the responsibility of laymen in the Church and in society. The biblical, theological and liturgical movements are making notable contributions to the development of a lay apostolate adapted to the present age. We shall not follow up further these movements in the Roman Catholic Church, since our first concern here is with the Evangelical Churches of Latin America.

The Evangelical Churches

In the second and third decades of the nineteenth century, the countries of Latin America won independence from Spain and Portugal. It was only after this that the Protestant Churches were able to enter the field and to consolidate their position. But, during the colonial period under the rule of Spain and Portugal, there are three Protestant missionary efforts of which we have to take note.

1. In 1555 a French expedition arrived at Rio de Janeiro under the leadership of Nicolas Durand de Villegagnon, and with the support of Gaspard de Coligny, the famous Admiral and Huguenot leader. The aim of de Villegagnon was to establish a Protestant colony in the New World, on much the same lines as those followed later by the Pilgrim Fathers in North America.

Once the colony was established, Villegagnon wrote to Calvin in Geneva asking for Protestant pastors; in answer to this request, Pierre Richier and Guillaume Chartier were sent out to Brazil—the first Protestant pastors to reach South America. We must stress the fact that it was laymen who asked for pastors and tried to interest the Church of Geneva in this missionary venture.

Unfortunately the colony was not a success, and Villegagnon himself must bear a considerable share of the blame for its failure. Nevertheless a beginning had been made; and this first Protestant venture had also its missionary dimension. Jean de Léry, one of the colonists, in his *Histoire d'un voyage fait en la terre du Brésil*, says that the task of the two pastors was 'to cross the sea to join Villegagnon, in order to proclaim the gospel in America'.[4]

2. For thirty years (1624–54) the Dutch were in North Brazil. About 1634, Justinian von Weltz strove to persuade the Dutch Reformed Church that it was its duty to send out missionaries. At that time the Church had no sense of missionary vocation, and was not able to take this challenge seriously. Once again we note that it is a layman who calls the Church to take up its missionary task.[5]

3. From 1738 onwards there was a third missionary movement in the Guianas, British and Dutch; here the Moravian brethren were active among the Arawak Indians.[6]

II · Laymen and Lay Ventures as Pioneers of the Protestant Churches in Latin America (1806–60)

The influence of Protestantism can be traced in the first days of Latin American history. This influence was certainly indirect; but this Protestant influence is genuinely present in the political and social structures of these countries. That is to say, what confronts us here is a genuine lay ministry. We refer to the influence of the thought of Calvin on the first constitutions of the Latin American countries, in which the democratic and republican orders were established. The basic principles were the will of the people as supreme, and this will as the source of authority.[7]

Beyond question, the principles of the American and French Revolutions exercised a decisive influence on the fundamental ideas of those revolutions which led to the independence of the Latin American countries. When we recall that the ideas of the Puritans, and the Congregationalist understanding of the structure of societies, played a preponderant part in fashioning the principles of the American Revolution, it is not difficult to trace the relationship between these and the basic ideas which underlay the Latin American Revolutions. Similarly, the French Revolution meant a resurgence, in secularized form, of the spiritual forces of the Huguenots, which had been so cruelly repressed in the sixteenth and seventeenth centuries.

Both these Revolutions provided the basic concepts which found expression in the Latin American Revolutions in their struggle for independence from Spain and Portugal. Thus, the *Social Contract* of

Jean Jacques Rousseau was translated by the Argentine hero Mariano Moreno during the first decades of the nineteenth century. The libraries of most of the men who directed the struggle for independence contained, together with the Constitution of the United States, the work of such authors as Adam Smith, Jeremy Bentham, John Locke and others. We must, however, also recognize that in this process of which we are speaking two Spanish Jesuit thinkers, Suarez and Molina, also exercised a considerable influence.

In any case, the indirect influence of Protestantism can be discerned in the sympathy felt by many of the national leaders for the distribution of the Bible, and for Protestant methods of education and Protestant teachers. But, furthermore, our outstanding men believed that only an evangelical form of Christianity, of the kind that was able to sustain the American Revolution, could serve as the solid foundation for the new Republics in the process of the development of their democratic and republican institutions. Thus, the great Argentine educator Domingo Faustino Sarmiento regarded the Bible and the life of Jesus as the sole possible foundation for a democratic form of education that would help the country to emerge from barbarism into civilization.

The famous President of Mexico Benito Juárez, an Indian of pure race, under whose presidency a progressive constitution was promulgated in 1857, declared that the Indians needed a religion which would teach them to read and write, and that for this nothing was better adapted than Protestantism, if it would undertake to Mexicanize itself. On the other hand, Canon Gorriti, a republican leader in Argentina, analysing in his book *Reflexiones*, which was published in 1830, the internal maladies of the Latin American countries which had recently become independent, affirmed that the right solution for these evils could be found in the virtues of Protestantism, as expressed in family life, in the reading of the Bible, and in a serious and responsible morality. The same Gorriti went on to suggest that a book written by the French Protestant M. Necker should be used as a textbook on morals in the schools. This last fact gives clear evidence of the relationship which existed between our leaders and the Protestant thought of their time, and of the extent of their acquaintance with it.

The great adventure of establishing Evangelical Churches in Latin America had its beginnings in the early years of the nineteenth century. Two stages can be distinguished: (*a*) the dissemination of a non-denominational gospel; (*b*) the coming of Protestant immigrants.

We shall attempt to describe the part played by laymen in each of these two stages.

The dissemination of a non-denominational gospel (1806–30)

The preface to the history of evangelical Christianity in Latin America was written by the British and Foreign Bible Society, and a little later by the American Bible Society. Dr Stewart Herman of the Latin American Committee of the Lutheran World Federation has written that 'probably the single most important influence of the whole nineteenth century was the persistent and heroic colportage undertaken by the Bible Societies'.[8] There can be no doubt that this is historically true.

The first attempt at Bible distribution was made by the British Society in 1806, when it sent David Creighton to Uruguay; this was followed in 1817 by the American Society, when through the services of American and British 'travellers' an edition of the New Testament in Portuguese was circulated in Brazil.

But the circulation of the Bible is useless unless people can read. So, closely associated with the work of the Bible Societies was the work of the representatives of the British and Foreign School Society. James Thomson was a Scot, and a lay reader in the Baptist Church. He arrived in Buenos Aires on 6th October 1818, and founded schools on the basis of the Lancastrian method of education, with the Bible as the textbook for reading. Thomson was most warmly welcomed by the political leaders of the time, among them Bernardino Rivadavia, the first constitutional President of Argentina. In 1820 he conducted the first evangelical service of worship ever to be held in Buenos Aires. In 1821 he was in Chile and in 1822 in Peru, where with the support of General José de San Martín, the liberator of the Argentine, Chile and Peru, he was able to found schools and to distribute the Bible. In Peru a Roman Catholic layman of Trujillo, Dr O'Donovan, was inspired by Thomson to undertake the distribution of the Bible in his own country.

Later James Thomson went to Ecuador (1824) and Colombia (1825), and in the following years was in Mexico and the Caribbean Islands. This extensive missionary journeying of Thomson has been described as 'one of the most remarkable missionary travels undertaken since those of Paul with Barnabas and John Mark'.[9] Thus it was the work of this layman, supported by two lay organizations, which, together with the work of other lay representatives of the same societies, sowed the first seeds of evangelical Christianity in the Latin American countries. From these first contacts with the Bible spring two of the main characteristics of Protestant Christianity in these countries—it has always been Bible-centred, and it has been centred in the work of the laity.

a. A Bible-centred Christianity

In support of this first contention, we cannot do better than cite some sentences from a lecture delivered by Dr José Míguez Bonino to the second Latin American Evangelical Conference (July 1961):

> Latin American Protestantism has been built on the Scriptures. It is a Biblical Protestantism. And it is so in two ways; on the one hand we affirm without hesitation that the Scripture is the highest rule of our Faith. No doctrine has the right to be maintained if it is not founded on the message of the Scriptures. On the other hand, Latin American Protestantism has been built by the Scriptures. . . . Literally we were born by the Holy Spirit, from the Word of God.[10]

Rubem Alves and Richard Shaull, in an article on 'The Devotional Life of Brazilian Protestantism', state that 'for several generations the Protestants have been known in Brazil as the "Men of the Bible". This is literally true, for they were formerly called *"os biblias"* by non-Evangelicals.'[11] This is true of all Latin American Protestants.

b. A lay-centred Christianity

An Argentinian Methodist minister, Adam F. Sosa, in an article entitled 'Some Remarks on the Present Theological Position of Latin American Evangelicals'[12] states that the contemporary developments within Roman Catholicism and European Protestantism, with regard to the place of the laity in the life and mission of the Church, are no new thing in Latin American Protestantism. 'Our laymen', he says, 'know that "You shall be my witnesses" (Acts 1.8) is not a commandment limited to the ministers.' He continues, 'When one listens to those who say, for instance, that the Protestant ministers might undertake such experiments as those of the "Priest-Workers" in order to evangelize the workers' milieu, we ask ourselves what has happened to the doctrine of the priesthood of all believers.' He concludes by remarking that the Latin American Evangelical Churches have always maintained that every man in his own environment must be a minister of the gospel.

We shall demonstrate the truth of this affirmation by a few historical examples, in which the Bible-centred and lay-centred character of the

Latin American Churches is made plain. We shall see that again and again it was laymen who called the Church to come to their countries; or that a copy of the Bible in the hands of a layman resulted in the birth of an evangelical congregation without the preaching of foreign missionaries.

Guatemala: It was Justo Rufino Barrios, President of Guatemala, who invited the Evangelical Church to come to his country. The following account of the circumstances is given by Tomas S. Goslin:

> After the Revolution of 1871 the liberal party assumed political power, and immediately the Roman Catholic Church lost many of its privileges. The new President, Justo Rufino Barrios, probably for political rather than spiritual reasons, felt that it would be good that his people should be exposed to influences other than those of the Roman Catholic Church. . . . An outstanding foreign woman, Mrs Francisca de Cleaves, who was a resident of the country, suggested to the new President that it would be advantageous to invite some Evangelical missionaries to come to Guatemala to start educational and religious work. President Barrios asked her to open the necessary negotiations. She entered into correspondence with the Presbyterian Board of Missions; in 1882 the Board decided to send the Rev. John Hill to Guatemala. . . . The first Evangelical Church of Guatemala was organized in 1884, with eight members.[13]

Mexico: We have seen that James Thomson, in his journeys of 1827–30 and 1842, distributed the Bible in Mexico. After his time, other laymen, North American soldiers in the war between Mexico and the United States in 1846–48 and in the Civil War of 1861–65, crossed the Mexican frontier and brought copies of the Bible with them. In 1862 Thomas Westrupp, an Anglican layman, invited to Mexico the first Evangelical missionary, James Hickey, a Baptist.

According to Goslin,[14] the first evangelical service in Mexico was conducted by a man named Blake, a young traveller who happened to be in Mexico City at the moment at which a North American shoe-maker was to be buried. This man had been killed by some fanatics during a Roman Catholic procession, because he had refused to kneel as the procession passed by. Also in 1859, the first service of Holy Communion after the evangelical order was celebrated by a layman, Dr Julius Mallet Prevost, with his wife and a man named José Llaguno. Mallet Prevost had been in touch with a group of Roman Catholic priests who had separated themselves from the Roman Catholic hierarchy, in reaction against the conservative attitude maintained by the Church during the struggle for a liberal constitution in Mexico.

The first evangelical sermon in Mexico City was delivered by Sóstenes Juárez in 1865. Juárez was a layman who, under the influence of the Bible, started to preach and to study with a number of other people. In 1868, the Church which had come into existence around Juárez invited a North American Episcopal clergyman, Henry C. Riley, to come to Mexico. In 1873 Juárez was ordained by a Methodist bishop—the first Protestant minister ever to be ordained in Mexico.[15]

Colombia: George P. Howard tells how the Evangelical Church came to Colombia:

> Many English and Scottish soldiers and officers formed part of the armies that fought for independence in South America. In Bolívar's army there was a British Legion. Many of the officers settled in the South American countries. One of these, Colonel Fraser, settled in Colombia and later became Secretary of War. He married a Colombian lady. He and an influential group of patriots saw that the South American countries would never really be free until Christianity became a vital spiritual force among them. In 1850 they sent to Scotland for a clergyman. But there were no funds then for the sending of missionaries from Scotland. The American Presbyterian Board, however, responded to the call, and in 1856 Horace Pratt went to Colombia.[16]

We may supplement these historical records with one or two examples from more modern times of the part played by the layman and the Bible in the expansion of evangelical Christianity in Latin America.

Bishop Barbieri of the Methodist Church in Argentina, in his book *Land of El Dorado*, tells the following story:

> About thirty years ago, he was preaching in a home in a certain village where the gospel had never been preached by a Protestant minister. The grandmother of the household, after the service was over, came to him with tears in her eyes. Grasping his hands, she exclaimed, 'Thank God that you have come, because now I know that the things that are written in that old book are true.' The writer asked her what book she was referring to. And she answered. 'The Bible.' 'Thirty years ago a man passed by here and left me this book, exhorting me to read it to my family.' A few months afterward, she and some other members of the family were baptized and taken into the Church and a small congregation was formed in that house.[17]

Alberto Rembao, in an article entitled 'Protestant Reality in Spanish America',[18] reports:

Years ago, in a little town in the mountains of Puebla Mexicana, on Sunday at market time the police arrested three people who were 'disturbing the public order'. These men were three country folk who had been witnessing to the gospel. They were put in prison for holding a public meeting without the permission of the police. As they said that they were Baptists, the Protestant minister in Puebla came to ask them about the denomination to which they belonged. Their answer is astonishing: 'We do not belong to any denomination. One of us who can read bought a New Testament. By reading we were converted.'

The coming of Protestant immigrants (*1825–1900*)

Almost from the beginning of the period of independence, many English and Scottish immigrants, settlers and business men, came to Latin America. They were mostly Protestant—Anglican or Presbyterian. They came as laymen on their own affairs, and with no special purpose of preaching the gospel; nevertheless, through their presence the Protestant community became a reality in the Latin American countries. Almost everywhere they asked for religious liberty; this compelled the Latin American governments to revise their constitutional laws. This revision was not easily carried through, since previously these governments had had experience only of one established Church, the Roman Catholic. Not long after their arrival, the immigrants began to ask for pastors of their own traditions. Though many Churches showed little interest in their spiritual needs, in the end their insistence bore fruit and ministers arrived. Latin American history is full of examples of this process; we may think of the Scottish Presbyterians in the Argentine[19] and in Chile,[20] and of the Waldensians in Uruguay.[21]

In Chile David Trumbull was the champion of religious toleration and to a certain extent of religious liberty. His work is an interesting illustration of the way in which the presence of the immigrants compelled Latin American governments to change their laws relating to religious liberty. When Trumbull arrived, his work was naturally limited to people of English speech; but gradually he was drawn into the whole struggle for religious liberty in that country. During his early years in Chile, as in most other Latin American countries,

only the Roman Church was allowed to perform the marriage rite, the cemeteries were completely under its control and were only open to those of its faith, there was no freedom of the press, and all religious observances other than those of the dominant church were prohibited by law. Trumbull set himself to overcome these disabilities. He began a controversy in the press with the Archbishop, circulated Christian literature, and gradually formed a circle of close friends who were influential in political circles. So deeply did he feel the situation that, attached to his own country though he was, he made a vow that if God would give him strength to overthrow the oppressive laws, he would become a citizen of the Republic. Largely due to his influence, in 1880, a liberal government set aside the disabilities under which residents other than Roman Catholics had laboured, and, true to his vow, Trumbull became a Chilean. . . . In 1885 an unusually liberal charter was secured from the government, whereby those who profess the Reformed Church religion according to the doctrines of the Holy Scriptures, may promote primary and secondary instruction according to modern methods and practice, and propagate the worship of their belief obedient to the law of the land. The mission was also authorized to acquire lands and buildings for the expressed object, and retain the same by act of the legislature.[22]

III · The Coming of Historical Churches and Missions
(1860–1961)

Most European Churches did not regard Latin America as a field for Christian missions, since they took it for granted that all the Latin American countries were Roman Catholic. This attitude found expression at the Edinburgh World Missionary Conference of 1910, at which the Latin American Churches were not represented. The North American Churches had never accepted the European thesis, and were driven by their missionary spirit to undertake work in Latin America also. They had discovered a reality, which during the last two decades has been generally accepted in the Christian world, Roman Catholic as well as Protestant—that the Western world, and this includes Latin America, finds itself in a 'post-Constantinian' situation;[23] it is a dechristianized and post-Christian world. This fact is recognized today by all perspicacious Christian leaders.

When the North American Churches at work in Latin America met in conference in Panama in 1916, they discovered this astonishing reality of the situation, with the support and deep insights of many Latin American lay Christian leaders, among them the Uruguayan Monteverde, although they did not formulate their thesis in modern terms. The effect of this wise and accurate understanding of the situation was the strengthening of the older missions, and the coming of new missionary enterprises to Latin America.

Our purpose is not to give a general history of these enterprises, but to concentrate on the element of the lay apostolate among them, or, to use a modern term, their work on the frontiers. This found expression in schools and social work on the one hand, and on the other in the emphasis laid on the doctrine of the priesthood of all believers.

a. Educational and Social Work

In 1944 there were in Latin America 152 Protestant secondary schools, besides many elementary schools. Three universities are of Protestant origin—MacKenzie University in São Paulo, Brazil; Candler University in Cuba; and Interamericana University at San German, Puerto Rico.

The pioneer work of these educational centres has been described by a non-Protestant writer, Fernando de Azeredo. (Although he is writing of Brazil, his remarks have a wider application to the Latin American situation as a whole.)

> The American [*sc.* Protestant] schools introduced into the country in the early days of the Republic, at a time when public instruction was still very retarded, made a notable contribution in São Paulo in the change of methods and the intensifying of teaching. The Protestants founded great colleges like MacKenzie in São Paulo, Gramberry Institute in Juiz de Fora, Gamon Institute in Minas, and the Evangelical High Schools of Bahia and Pernambuco. They gave stimulus to didactic literature which was enriched by works of the first order at that time, such as the grammars of Julio Ribeiro and Eduardo Carlos Pereira, the arithmetic and algebra of Antonio Trajano, the works of Otoniel Mota and the Readers of Erasmo Braga; they made an efficacious contribution to the spread of popular education through their system of Sunday Schools.[24]

The contribution of the Protestant schools can be traced also in the political arena of many Latin American countries, in which former students of the evangelical schools have been pioneers in the development of their countries. A former President of Brazil, Juan Cafe Filho, had been a student at MacKenzie College. One of the Presidents of Bolivia, Hernán Siles Suazo, was an old student of the Instituto Americano in La Paz.

In the field of social work, we may take note of sixty hospitals and clinics, and of mission farms in Brazil, Chile, in the highlands of Bolivia and Peru among the Indians, and other similar efforts.[25] Mauricio López, Secretary for Latin America of the World Student Christian Federation, writes that 'the ministry of the laity in Latin

America is carried out in different spheres of life. Christian agricul-
turalists, engineers and doctors work on the frontiers of the Church to
try and reach the peasant population.'[26]

b. The Priesthood of all Believers

'Every believer an evangelist.' This was the practical side of the
emphasis on the priesthood of all believers which was characteristic
of the evangelical Churches and missions in Latin America. Laymen
took an important place in the preaching and administration of
churches, in Sunday schools and other forms of Christian work.

An Argentinian Methodist minister has published a book,[27] in
which he clearly develops and states the concept of the Christian
commitment of the layman in the inner life of the Church. We shall
see later how this concept is changing positively into a broader and
sounder concept of the Christian layman and his commitment in
relation to the life of the world. The deep and positive aspects of this
emphasis on the laity in the Latin American Churches are a highly
developed sense of Christian stewardship, and serious theological
thought about the relations between Church and State, public education
and similar problems within a non-Christian society.[28]

Faith Missions and indigenous Churches

The numerically strongest Protestant movement in Latin America
must be sought among the Faith Missions, the non-historical groups,
and the indigenous Churches which have come spontaneously into
being. The first representatives of these groups were established in
Latin America in the last decade of the nineteenth century; many
others followed in the early years of this century, and they received
great accessions in strength through the immense increase in missionary
activity in the years following the second world war. Seventy-five
per cent of the missionaries now active in Latin America belong to
these groups.

The secret of the expansion of these groups is that every member is
recognized to have his share in responsibility for the evangelistic task:
'It would seem that the growth of each group is related directly to its
effectiveness in mobilizing its total membership in continuous evangelistic endeavour.'[29] When we consider the indigenous Churches,
especially the Pentecostal movement in Chile and Brazil, we note
further reasons for their success in their structure, forms of worship,
popular character, adaptation to local circumstances and so forth.

Many sociological and religious factors play their part in the growth of the evangelical movement; but the active practice of the priesthood of all believers surpasses all others in importance.

For Latin America as a whole, the following figures display the growth of the evangelical community, including both baptized persons and those more loosely related to it:

1900	12,675
1916	59,360
1949	2,992,314
1957	4,290,349
1961	8,953,000

Whereas the population of Brazil increased threefold over the last sixty years, the Protestant population increased thirty-fivefold.

IV · A New Consciousness in the Latin American Protestant Laity

What we have called a new consciousness may be described as the awakening of a sense of responsible participation in the everyday life of society, and theological reflection on all that is involved in this.

Protestant Christianity in Latin America from its beginning to the third decade of the twentieth century was a 'gathered community', a leaven operating indirectly in the world by means of schools, social work and other forms of service. This was a period of consolidation, during which the body was being built up. Adam F. Sosa says that the Evangelical Churches are 'set apart or separated (from the world). They try to draw out from the community in which they work groups of believers who are genuinely converted and regenerated. Like the apostolic Churches, they regard themselves as "colonies of heaven".'[30]

In consequence we may hear critics affirm that the Latin American Evangelical Churches have been up to the present a kind of ghetto. This may be true. In any case, it is easy to understand why this policy was followed—this was the only way to consolidate a movement the background of which was in striking contrast with that of the Latin American peoples:

The contrast was cultural and religious. Evangelical missions were predominantly from Britain and the United States, lands prevailingly Protestant and with an ethos which was alien to Latin Europe, especially to Spain and Portugal. Moreover they were from the Evangelical wing of Protestantism, even further removed from Roman Catholicism than the

Catholic wing of the Anglican Communion. It stressed conversion of the individual through faith in Christ and a Christ-like life dedicated to God. In general it made little of philosophy and so had slight common ground with the Latin American intellectuals. In England its strength was in the middle class and in the United States the group from which the early Evangelical missions issued were largely of middle-class mentality. In Latin America until the twentieth century the middle class was either non-existent or weak.[31]

Moreover, the Roman Catholic background of Latin America forced the new converts to break with their environment, and in many cases even with their own families:

> The Latin American Evangelical listens to the gospel as a call; when he answers, he cuts the apron-strings of his past, his old customs, his inherited religion, and frequently of his family. Many of them have had the same experience as the Bolivian *mestizo*, who, when he returned home after his baptism, found the door of the house closed against him, and a voice which told him: 'Here we do not want either devils or Protestants.' It was his mother's voice.[32]

Today the situation is changing. The gathered community is realizing that it is necessary to be also a scattered community, that especially through its laymen it must make its presence felt in the cultural, social, economic and political structures of each country.

This change will be at once evident to anyone who takes the trouble to compare the resolutions of the First and Second Latin American Evangelical Conferences (Buenos Aires 1949; Lima 1961).

In the First Conference, we find the traditional emphasis on the work of laymen as helpers to pastors, as instruments for securing individual conversions and the growth of the congregations. The means of evangelism are focused on the same purpose.[33] The Second Conference took seriously the structures of society and the need to change these structures through the presence within them of the Christian laity. This Conference had before it the resolutions of the First Latin American Consultation on Church and Society, which had been held at Huampaní, Peru, some days before the assembling of the Lima Conference.[34]

It can be said that the concept of the role of the layman has been revolutionized. In earlier times, the lay apostolate was understood as a kind of second-class form of the work of a pastor, based often on a misunderstanding of the role and work of the ordained and whole-time ministry and of the priesthood of all believers. Now the lay apostolate is seen as arising from a specific understanding of the lay ministry in the structures of the world, the lay ministry of the scattered congregation, and the real participation of the lay people in the life and mission of the Church.

What is the reason for this change? In the first place, it may be attributed to the inner life of the Latin American Churches themselves, which have now reached their maturity. We must take account also, however, of the influence of the renewal of the Church and of theology which has been going on all over the world. The influence of this movement has reached the Latin American Churches mainly through their contacts with the ecumenical movement in various forms— the Department on Church and Society and the Department on the Laity of the World Council of Churches; the Committee on Co-operation in Latin America, the work of which has been of quite exceptional value; and the International Missionary Council, now the Division on World Mission and Evangelism of the World Council of Churches.

As illustrations of what has here been said, we may outline some aspects of the lay ministry and its present trends:

1. The Latin American Committee on Church and Society

This was formed under a resolution of the First Latin American Consultation on Church and Society (1961). Evangelical Councils in several of the Latin American countries have membership in this Committee. Its task is to strengthen the Christian witness in society, to stimulate the creation of regional commissions on Church and Society, and to collaborate with such commissions in studies, projects, new forms of service and so forth.

A number of consultations on Church and Society have been held in the last five years by Evangelical Councils. We should note four in Brazil, one in the River Plate area, and one on social service in Chile. Much printed material relating to these subjects has been produced; and the Latin American Committee periodically publishes documents and studies on Church and Society in its Bulletin *Iglesia y Sociedad en América Latina*.

2. Associations of Evangelical Professionals and Teachers

Such associations exist in Argentina and Uruguay. Their task is to study the problems of Christian witness in the field of each of the liberal professions.

3. The Student Christian Movement

Almost every Latin American country now has groups of Christian students meeting under the auspices of the World's Student Christian Federation:

> Today, SCMs have been established in all the South American countries except Paraguay and Ecuador, in the Caribbean, in Mexico and in some Central American countries. They are all ecumenical movements, basically Christian but also open to non-Christians. Their object is to make the students familiar with the Christian faith in God . . . to make them live as true disciples of Christ within the life and vocation of the Church.

The SCM has adopted a lay structure in order to preserve its essential nature: that of a movement centred in the university which is its specific field of action. Its lay character derives immediately from its Evangelical nature and this is made even more obvious by its ecumenical character. Such a movement of a missionary nature as the SCM might be expected, in facing the Churches—which are divided over conflicting doctrines of the ministry—to stress the need for a structure in which there would be no room for such questions. Finally the lay character of SCM reflects its concern with calling the faithful to active service in the life of the Church. And during student days, this means the SCM. The SCM in Latin America has been mainly concerned with a direct and indirect effort at evangelization in the university, with leading the Christian students to discover a sense of vocation in university life, developing an ecumenical spirit in them; nourishing them with the spiritual resources of the Word and Sacraments in the life of the Church, and with preparing the students for the building up of a responsible society which would give a day to day witness of what the Scriptures say about Jesus Christ as King of Kings and Lord of Lords.[35]

4. Other lay projects and achievements

Work in the area of the proletariat, political activity, public statements on political, economic and social matters are increasingly developing in the evangelical scene as a contribution to the national life of a number of countries.

Notable work is being done by the Emmanuel Centre in Uruguay. This is an ecumenical centre for spiritual retreats and studies, brought into being under the inspiration and through the financial help of a laywoman, Mrs Galland. This is the first step towards lay training centres, which may be developed in the future, following the European pattern of the lay institute. During the last four years, the International Academy, Alétheia, of the South American Federation of YMCAs has been working on a similar lay and ecumenical basis.

5. The Young Men's Christian Association

In Latin America the YMCA is not considered to be an evangelical movement. Nevertheless the lay apostolate that it has developed must be regarded as among the most remarkable to be found in the Latin American Christian scene.

The YMCA has struck deep roots in the Latin American world, and now has more than ninety centres in the South American countries. These South American YMCAs are an educational institution of service to the community with an ecumenical Christian basis and emphasis. They have been pioneers in the field of physical education, camping, and work among boys and young men; through their influence national committees of physical education and sports fields have been brought into being in almost all the countries of South America. They have also introduced the methods of the 'Finance Campaign', which has today been adopted by almost every service institution, and which has exercised great influence in the creation of a sense of social responsibility.

In a secularized world, the YMCAs have been a bridge between the members of the post-Christian generation and the Christian religion. Bearing witness through their *diakonia* (ministry of service), through conferences, courses for small groups, and through literature, the YMCAs have helped to eliminate a great number of misunderstandings between the people and the Christian faith. At the present time, the YMCAs in South America are carefully studying their position in the Latin American world as a 'Christian, lay and ecumenical movement'.

NOTES

1. Benno Biermann O.P., 'Das spanisch-portugiesische Patronat als Laienhilfe für die Mission', in J. Specker S.M.B. and W. Buehlmann O.F.M.Cap., *Das Laienapostolat in den Missionen* (Schöneck-Beckenreid, 1961), p. 165.

2. *Idem*, p. 161.

3. J. Specker S.M.B., 'Der Spital-Orden der Bethlehemiten in Latein-amerika (1667–1820)', in Specker and Buehlmann, *op. cit.*, pp. 181 ff.

4. Oliver Reverdin, *Quatorze Calvinistes chez les Topinambous* (Editions du Journal de Genève, 1957).

5. On Baron von Weltz, see Arthur T. Pierson, *The New Acts of the Apostles* (London, 1914).

6. K. G. Grubb, *The Lowland Indians of Amazonia* (World Dominion Press, London, 1927), pp. 66 and 71.

7. Alfonso Lopez Michelsen, *La estirpe calvinista de nuestras instituciones* (Bogota), and Guillermo Furlong S.J., *Nacimiento y desarrollo de la filosofía en el Rio de la Plata* (Buenos Aires, 1952).

8. S. Herman, 'The Thirst for the Word of God in Latin America', *Bulletin of the U.B.S.* (No. 33:1958/1), p. 5.

9. Quotation from Dr Webster Browning in Tomas S. Goslin, *Los evangélicos en la América Latina* ('La Aurora', Buenos Aires, 1956), p. 16.

10. *Cristo, la esperanza para América Latina; Segunda Conferencia Evangélica Latino-americana, Lima 1961* (Buenos Aires, 1961), p. 75.

11. In *Student World* (1956/4, Geneva), p. 361.

12. A. F. Sosa, 'Algunas consideraciones sobre la actual posición teológica de los evangélicos latinoamericanos', *Cuadernos teológicos* (No. 34, Buenos Aires, 1960) p. 159.

13. Goslin, *op. cit.*, pp. 84–6.

14. *Op. cit.*, p. 92.

15. *Op. cit.*, pp. 94–5, and B. Camargo and K. G. Grubb, *Religion in the Republic of Mexico* (World Dominion Press, New York, 1935), pp. 62 ff.

16. G. P. Howard, *Religious Liberty in Latin America* (The Westminster Press, Philadelphia, 1944), p. 122. See also Goslin, *op. cit.*, p. 76, and K. G. Grubb, *The Northern Republics of South America* (World Dominion Press, 1931), p. 70.

17. Sante U. Barbieri, *Land of El Dorado* (Friendship Press, New York, 1961), p. 51.

18. A. Rembao, 'La realidad protestanta en la América Hispánica', *Cuadernos teológicos* (No. 21, Buenos Aires, 1957), p. 7.

19. Juan C. Varetto, *El Apóstol de Plata* ('La Aurora', Buenos Aires, 1943), p. 13.

20. Ignacio Vergara, *El Protestantismo en Chile* (Editorial del Pacífico, Santiago de Chile, 1962), pp. 36–40.

21. Ernesto Tron and Emilio H. Ganz, *Historia de las Colonias Valdenses Sudamericanas* (Librería Pastor Miguel Morel, Uruguay, 1958).

22. W. E. Browning, J. Ritchie and K. G. Grubb, *The West Coast Republics of South America* (World Dominion Press, London, 1930), pp. 28–9.

23. Alberto Hurtado Cruchaga S.J., *Es Chile un país católico?* (Editorial Espeudor, Chile, 1941).

24. Fernando de Azevedo, *Brazilian Culture* (The Macmillan Company, New York, 1950); pp. 157 ff. quoted by Alberto Rembao in 'The Reformation comes to Hispanic America', reprinted from *Religion in Life* (Winter 1957–58), p. 10. Note that 'American schools' are here synonymous with 'evangelical schools'.

25. Other examples of church and social work may be found in Raymond A. Dudley, *The Growing Edge of the Church* (Agricultural Missions, Inc., New York), pp. 11, 32, 46, 53, 56 and 63.

26. *The Church and Lay Movements in Latin America* (Documents from the Department on the Laity, WCC, Geneva, Doc. IX, 1960), p. 8.

27. Luis P. Bucafusco, *Laicos activos, Iglesia viva* ('La Aurora', Buenos Aires, 1955).

28. Emilio Castro, 'Bases teológicas del laicismo escolar', *Cuadernos teológicos* (No. 34, Buenos Aires, 1960).

29. Kenneth Strachan, *The Missionary Movement of the Non-historical Groups in Latin America* (CCLA, New York, 1957), p. 9.

30. Sosa, *op. cit.*, p. 160.

31. Kenneth Scott Latourette, *The Early Evangelical Missionary Movement in Latin America* (CCLA, New York, 1958), p. 7.

32. J. Míguez Bonino, *América Latina, un continente descristianizado* (Preparatory Paper, No. 5 for the Second Latin American Evangelical Conference, 1961), p. 6.

33. *El Cristianismo Evangélico en la América Latina; Primera Conferencia Evangélica Latinoamericana* (Buenos Aires, July 1949).

34. *Christians and Rapid Social Change in Latin America* (published by the Latin American Committee on Church and Society, Montevideo, Uruguay, and by the Department on Church and Society of the WCC, Geneva, Switzerland, 1961).

35. *The Church and Lay Movements in Latin America*, p. 10.

16

Hans-Ruedi Weber

THE REDISCOVERY OF THE LAITY
IN THE ECUMENICAL MOVEMENT

This volume reveals how in different periods and streams of church
history different roles and concepts of the laity were predominant. In
this closing chapter we shall examine what distinctive role and concept
of the laity appear in the modern ecumenical movement.

I · A Totally New Phenomenon?

'NEVER in church history, since its initial period, has the role and
responsibility of the laity in Church and world been a matter of so basic,
systematic, comprehensive and intensive discussion in the total *oikoumene* as today.' This discussion 'is a totally new phenomenon', it
'implies a new examination and general reshaping of all ecclesiologies
which we have had for centuries' and it 'is the most important aspect of
the longing for the renewal of the Church which arises in the Churches
all over the world'.[1] These assertions of Hendrik Kraemer may over-
state the case, but the main affirmation is correct. The lay membership
has always played a vital role in the life and mission of the Church, but
has never become so much a subject of theological reflection as it is
today. The ever-growing literature on the subject is a sign of this,[2]
and this chapter will show how intimately this rediscovery of the laity
is related to the development and main concerns of the ecumenical
movement.

There are many varied reasons for this rediscovery. It is partly due
to the biblical and theological renewal which has revealed to us a new
image of the Church: the Church as a people and a body, the Church
which is elected and sent for mission and service in God's world. The

rediscovery also stems partly from our new world situation: the break-down of the *corpus Christianum*; the processes of industrialization and secularization which tend to edge the Church out of daily life into a religious ghetto; the fact that the Church is becoming almost every-where a minority which has great difficulty in communicating with the modern world. Wherever these new insights about the nature and the task of the Church and these challenges of the modern world are taken seriously—and the ecumenical movement attempts to do so—the question of the role of the laity immediately becomes prominent. This is confirmed by a quick glance at the history of the ecumenical move-ment, as it is reflected in its main conferences and institutions.

It was J. H. Oldham who, in the preparatory volume for the Oxford Conference in 1937 on 'Church, Community, and State', pointed to the role of the laity as a crucial matter of ecumenical study and concern. 'In relation to the issues which will come before the Oxford Con-ference,' he wrote, 'nothing could be plainer than that if the Christian faith is in the present and future to bring about changes, as it has done in the past, in the thought, habits and practices of society, it can only do this through being the living, working faith of multitudes of lay men and women conducting the ordinary affairs of life.' Therefore, 'if the Church is to be an effective force in the social and political sphere, our first task is to laicize our thought about it. We stand before a great historic task—the task of restoring the lost unity between worship and work.'[3] This prophecy came true: first of all, in the Oxford Conference itself, where eminent laymen made decisive contributions[4] and where one of the main results was 'the change of the Protestant conception of the responsibility of the laity'.[5] The experiences of the war and the many lay and renewal movements springing from it did much to spread J. H. Oldham's conviction. When in 1948 the First Assembly of the World Council of Churches was convened in Amsterdam, a committee on 'The Significance of the Laity in the Church' was appointed in order 'to meet the widespread need expressed by Churches in many parts of the world for a consideration of the urgent question of the right use and training of the laity in the service of the Church'.[6] There was still a slightly paternalistic tone in the discussions of that Com-mittee (church leaders speaking about how to 'use' their laity), but, especially in the paragraph entitled 'The Laity in the World', the principal points in the present ecumenical reaffirmation of the role of the laity were clearly stated.

Two years before the Amsterdam Assembly, the Ecumenical Institute at the Château de Bossey, near Geneva, had already been created under the leadership of people like Hendrik Kraemer and Suzanne de Diétrich. A report about the origin and purpose of this Institute states: 'The laity, men and women, had discovered a new vision of their responsibility for expressing the true nature and task of the Church, not only within its own fellowship, but in the world in which the Church has been set and their own lives are lived. The Institute, therefore, endeavoured to help the Churches to understand and encourage this new development, and at the same time to give laymen a better grounding for this task and a wider vision of the Church as an ecumenical reality today. This remains one of the primary purposes of the Ecumenical Institute.'[7] Conferences of leaders of European laymen's institutes and groups became instrumental in the creation of a 'Secretariat for Laymen's Work' in 1949, which took up the recommendations of the Amsterdam Laity Commission, and organized the first European Laymen's Conference held in 1951 at Bad Boll, Germany. This was followed in 1952 by a North American laymen's conference at Buffalo with the subject 'The Christian in his Daily Work'. The Ecumenical Institute and the Secretariat for Laymen's Work became increasingly the focal point for much of the pioneer thinking and experimentation regarding the ministry of the laity. Much of this is reflected in the periodical *Laymen's Work*,[8] and is described in the chapters dealing with modern times in this volume. In these post-war years the main focus was on Europe and Great Britain, with North America coming increasingly into the picture. Accordingly, the main leaders of ecumenical thought and action with regard to the laity came from these continents.[9] But it soon became clear that the role of the laity was a burning issue in the Churches of all continents.

When the Second Assembly of the World Council of Churches at Evanston in 1954 had to choose the major issues which should be brought to the attention of Christians all over the world, the rediscovery of the laity became one of the six major subjects. The Evanston Assembly also acknowledged this emphasis on the laity by giving it departmental status within the structure of the World Council of Churches: the provisional 'Secretariat for Laymen's Work' was replaced by a regular 'Department on the Laity', working alongside such classical World Council units as the Departments on 'Faith and Order', 'Church and Society', and 'Evangelism'. The Evanston Section Report on 'The Laity —the Christian in his Vocation' achieved two things: in its second and third chapters it helps Christians living in an industrial society to rediscover their daily work as a Christian vocation; in the first and fourth chapters, which became far more important for the further development of ecumenical thinking and action, an important attempt is made to define the ministry of the laity and to see its implications for the renewal of the life and structures of the Church. This second set of questions became the main concern of the newly created Department on the Laity. In its meetings and publications, especially in the periodical *Laity*, published twice a year, these questions were further explored and thus became a leaven working changes in the thinking and attitudes of many church leaders and members all over the world.[10] The work of the Department became truly world-wide in its response to this quite spontaneous grasping for a new concept of the ministry of the laity and of new kinds of lay training in the Churches of almost all continents and traditions. At the same time it began increasingly to influence most of the other divisions and departments of the World Council of Churches. In all this, the voice of the Asian and African Churches played no small part. Never since the Oxford Conference in 1937 has an ecumenical gathering been so much under the impact of eminent laymen and of the struggle for a new concept of the role of the laity as was the inaugural Assembly of the East Asia Christian Conference in Kuala Lumpur, 1959. The fact that this reaffirmation of the lay apostolate acts as a similar leavening power in the contemporary renewal in the Roman Catholic Church shows that the rediscovery of the laity is indeed intimately related to the whole ecumenical movement.

The Third Assembly of the World Council of Churches at New Delhi in 1961 revealed this in a remarkable way. Looking back at the three Assemblies, H. Berkhof wrote, 'In Amsterdam we spoke about the layman. In Evanston he got his own section. But in New Delhi the layman gave more than ever his own contribution and revealed his own face.'[11] During one of the first evening sessions, three laymen spoke about 'The Laity: the Church in the World'. The impact of their straightforward statements and the leaven of the new thinking about the laity now appears in most of the New Delhi documents. This was no historic accident, for from the beginning there had been an intimate connection between the three main emphases of the ecumenical movement and the rediscovery of the laity.

*II · The Rediscovery of the Laity in the Three Main Currents
of the Ecumenical Movement*

By the selection of the three sections of the New Delhi Assembly—
witness, service, unity—the three main original currents of the ecumenical movement were singled out: God calls his Church to be
renewed in such a way that its whole life be a *witness* to Christ, the light
of the world. This was indeed the main concern of the missionary
movement and the former 'International Missionary Council', the first
ecumenical current which must now penetrate the whole ecumenical
movement. God calls his Church also to *service* with Christ, the light
of the world. This second ecumenical current, until now mainly em-
bedded in the former 'Movement for Life and Work' and the World
Council's units which deal with mutual aid and service in social and
political affairs, has for a long time emphasized this calling to service
which must now penetrate the whole life of the Church universal.
Finally, God calls his Church to manifest its *unity* in Christ, the light
of the world. This was the deepest concern of the third ecumenical
current, the 'Movement for Faith and Order', which must now be a
concern of all who partake in the ecumenical movement. The rediscovery of the laity has taken place in all three original currents and it
helped, therefore, to let these three currents flow together at New
Delhi. Speaking about the interconnection and inner momentum which
led to the integration of the IMC and the WCC, Lesslie Newbigin said,
for instance, at New Delhi, 'Few things have done more to strengthen
the understanding of the missionary task of the Church than the work
of the WCC's Department on the Laity.'[12]

The pioneer of *the missionary emphasis* in the ecumenical movement,
John R. Mott, had already spoken passionately in 1931 about 'Liberating the Lay Forces of Christianity'.[13] But at that time this prophetic
voice got little hearing among Churches and mission boards. Only
twenty years later, the Willingen Conference of the International
Missionary Council (1952) stated, 'We believe that God is calling the
Church to express its mission not only through foreign missionaries
sent by the boards, but also through an increasing flow of Christian
lay men and women who go out across the world in business, industry
and government, and who do so with a deep conviction that God calls
them to witness for him in all of life.'[14] What is far more important,
however, is the emphasis laid on the importance of a mature laity if
the Church as a whole is to become a witnessing community. One of

the main points mentioned in the preparatory survey of the emerging pattern for evangelism discussion at Evanston is that 'laymen are the spearhead of the Church in the world; the true twentieth century evangelist is the instructed and witnessing layman.'[15]

This line of thought was taken up at Evanston and has since been increasingly expressed in modern literature on evangelism and missions, as was shown in H. J. Margull's careful analysis of the ecumenical discussion on evangelism.[16] In the section at New Delhi on witness the role of the laity was so forcefully and one-sidedly expressed that this became the subject of heated discussion where many church leaders expressed their fear that through this emphasis on the spontaneous witness of every Christian in his everyday life, the specific ministry of ordained ministers and organized evangelistic activities might be undervalued. The final report is much weaker, yet avowedly more balanced than the first drafts. It can teach nothing new about the witnessing laity to people like J. H. Oldham, H. Kraemer, or those who followed the laity discussions since Amsterdam. Nevertheless, it now expresses as the opinion of a representative group of church leaders what only a few decades ago had been considered as dangerous and wild statements of a few: 'Within this whole enterprise of corporate witness, every individual Christian will play his own unique part according to the gifts of the Spirit with which he is endowed.' . . . 'It is obvious that, if the Christian witness is to penetrate into all those areas where the work of the world is carried on, it must be carried there by laymen. They alone can bring Christian judgement to bear upon all the issues of life in the spheres of industry and commerce, scientific research and social organization, and all the other activities which make up the workaday world. Their meeting-points in the secular world can become real opportunities for the witness of a living Church in the midst of the busy world's life.' . . . 'The ordained minister can be of great help in the work of preparation for such evangelism. Not only can he assist in such matters as the understanding of the Bible and of doctrine, but he can enter into discussion with laymen and listen to them as they speak of the actual situation in which their witness is to be borne. Together the laymen and the pastors may thus come to a fruitful appreciation of the relevance of the Gospel in the life of the secular world today. The pastor will not attempt to tell the layman how to bear his witness or to do his job, for only the layman can understand its real nature; but there are many ways in which the mutual discussion of the common problem will help to clarify the issues and to stimulate zeal according to knowledge.'[17]

As already mentioned above, it was in the *service emphasis* of the ecumenical movement, on the occasion of the Oxford Conference in 1937 and under the leadership of J. H. Oldham, that for the first time the laity came significantly into the limelight of ecumenical study and action. To a great extent this was so because at Oxford the thinking begun nine years earlier about the emergence of secularism was continued. When preparing the Jerusalem meeting of the IMC in 1928, J. R. Mott and J. H. Oldham became convinced that besides Buddhism, Hinduism, Islam, etc., another 'religion' must be reckoned with which they called 'secularism'. Rufus M. Jones was asked to write the preparatory paper on 'Secular Civilization and the Christian Task',[18] which 'convinced Oldham on his first reading that Christianity's real opponent in the East was not one of the ancient religions but secularism. Consequently he bent every effort to make it a paramount consideration at Jerusalem. His constant attention to the issue after 1928 was in large part instrumental in leading him into the program of Life and Work and the Oxford Conference of 1937.'[19] The struggle with this issue also brought Oldham straight to his new thinking about the double aspect of the Church as 'a society organized for the specific purpose of worship, teaching, preaching and the pastoral ministry' and on the other hand as a 'society of men and women who have been given a new understanding of life and have undergone a change which affects their whole outlook and behaviour, and must colour every action of their lives'. Clergy and laity alike had lost sight of the second aspect and thus clericalized their concept of the Church. Therefore—concluded Oldham at Oxford—we must now 'recognize that the permeation of the social life with Christian motives can be brought about only by the action of those who participate in the conduct of its affairs, that they can discharge this Christian responsibility only as members of the Church, nourished by its tradition, preaching, and sacraments, instructed by its teaching and supported by its fellowship and prayers, and that, in order to do this, they need a kind of help which is not at present being given'.[20]

It was still Oldham who in the preparation of the Amsterdam Assembly carried the rediscovery of the laity a step further. In his paper on 'A Responsible Society'[21] he included the treatment of a subject which had already been raised during the first World Conference on Life and Work in Stockholm in 1925, namely the question of work and vocation.[22] Indeed, all Christian discernment of the real needs of this world, of their roots and remedies, remains sterile until Christians do serve God and their neighbours in their daily work and not only during their free time in a few programmes of the Church for social action and service. This implies that the everyday attitudes, decisions and choices of Christians must reveal God's love. Since the Evanston Assembly these fundamental questions about work and vocation, discernment and decision, solidarity with the world yet refusal to be conformed to it, have been mainly discussed in the Secretariat and later in the Department on the Laity,[23] while the actual needs and issues Christians meet in the world of today were taken up by other units of the World Council of Churches. There exists, therefore, a deep interconnection and interdependence between the work, study and tasks reported in the Evanston section on the laity and the sections on social questions, international affairs and intergroup relations. Often the same persons are involved in both lines of inquiry and action,[24] and this intimate connection has become especially manifest in the WCC study on 'The Common Christian Responsibility towards Areas of Rapid Social Change' which results in an urgent demand for new kinds of lay training in Asia, Africa and Latin America.

The two trends in the service emphasis of the ecumenical movement met again at New Delhi. After speaking to the principal world issues which are a challenge for Christian service, the report ends with a chapter on 'The Service of the Church'. While traditionally in most Churches and missions the main accent is put on corporate Christian service activities and institutions, and only lip-service is paid to service of Christians in their daily work, this chapter begins with the emphasis on 'individual responsibility and involvement'. 'Precisely because government discharges an increasing number of services, we recognize the immense significance of each individual Christian who shares in secular service agencies and in government work by turning what might be impersonal service into truly personal service through a consciousness of the saving presence of Christ.' . . . 'This requires deeper understanding of stewardship in the Church. It should not be narrowly confined but should be seen in the light of total dedication of one's gifts to the glory of God in all spheres of life. More than ever, the Churches must help laymen to realize that their responsibility to serve lies in their daily work and to train them accordingly.'[25]

The Commission on Faith and Order, the main champion of the *unity emphasis* in the ecumenical movement, has been severely criticized because neither in its membership nor in its study does it seem to have been aware of the rediscovery of the laity in contemporary church life—although the movement owes its origin and development to a great extent to an American layman, the indefatigable Robert Gardiner! As will be shown in this paragraph, this criticism is not wholly justified. Yet if one studies Faith and Order documents it is indeed 'striking to find that "Faith and Order", quite rightly demanding a renewed attempt at an ecumenical understanding of the Ministry of the Church, evidently thinks only about Ministry in terms of the Clergy or the body of ordained Ministers'.[26] No wonder, therefore, that in a careful treatise on the ecclesiology of the ecumenical movement— very much based on Faith and Order documents and unity section reports—the laity is hardly mentioned anywhere.[27] As long as the main task of Faith and Order was seen in comparative studies of what different Churches traditionally teach about the Christian message, about the ordained ministry, the sacraments and the Church, this absence of a theological discussion on the laity was to be expected, because little theological reflection had, in fact, been done in most Christian traditions. But at the Lund Conference of 1952 Faith and Order decided to go beyond such comparative studies. The literature on the laity had now to be taken into account if Faith and Order really wanted to be concerned with the wholeness of the Church.[28]

The inner development of Faith and Order with such studies as 'The Nature of the Church', 'Christ and the Church' with its emphasis on baptism, 'Worship' and 'Institutionalism' (to which sociologists, historians and lawyers have contributed so much) will lead Faith and Order to its own discovery of the laity. A sign of this was the 'laity dialogue' during the meeting of the Faith and Order Commission in 1960.[29] The report of the unity section of the New Delhi Assembly points in this direction with its emphasis on the unity of 'all *in each place* who are *baptized*; who *confess* Christ . . . and are brought into one *fully committed fellowship* . . . where ministry *and members* are accepted by all'. The report also recognizes the fact that 'ordinary social life already brings men together into various associations—academic, professional, industrial, political, etc. Within these forms of unity there is need for a Christian unity of those who may learn from each other how to bear their witness in those settings. Ecumenical thought on the calling of the laity needs to be shared in groups of this kind and it has its own bearing on church unity, for denominational divisions are often found to be quite irrelevant on this frontier.'[30] There is still the tendency, however, to skip over a supposedly well-known and worked-out ecumenical agreement on the laity to an extensive and one-sided treatment

N

of what is felt to be the really burning issue: the ordained ministry. 'All agree that the whole Body is a royal priesthood. Yet one of the most serious barriers to unity is our diverse understanding of the nature of the ministry within the corporate priesthood. . . . The achievement of a ministry accepted by all would largely resolve the issues involved in the mutual recognition of members.'[31] Should this last statement not also be turned round? By a comprehensive ecumenical study on what this corporate priesthood of all the baptized implies we would create a sounder and less one-sided setting for a growing mutual recognition of the nature and *task* of the ordained ministry.

There are beginnings of such an ecumenical Faith and Order study on the laity. The report of the second world conference on Faith and Order in Edinburgh 1937 made clear that the (ordained) 'ministry does not exclude but presupposes the "royal priesthood", to which all Christians are called as the redeemed of Jesus Christ'. At one point the report even began to explain what this could imply: 'The Spirit may speak by whomsoever He wills. The call to bear witness to the Gospel and to declare God's will does not come to the ordained ministry alone; the Church greatly needs, and should both expect and welcome, the exercise of gifts of prophecy and teaching by laity, both men and women.'[32] But while in the same year this emphasis became predominant at Oxford, a prominent (Reformed) churchman immediately reacted at Edinburgh by saying, ' "Prophecy" is a very dangerous thing to allow to the laity. . . . I wish to support encouraging the activity of lay people, but not to "prophecy".'[33] The section on 'Christ and His Church' in the report of the Lund Conference is basic for the ecumenical study on the laity,[34] but the Lund Conference did not yet take up seriously the advice given to it by its own theological commission on 'The Church'. Referring to four 'trends in theology which may prove to be of great significance for our thought on the Church or for the hastening of its unity' the first mentioned is 'Laymen's Movements'— and the paragraphs describing this first trend are undoubtedly the best ecumenical statements about the laity before Evanston. These laymen's movements are said to be essentially 'a reaffirmation of the unity of "laity" and "ministry", together constituting the *laos* or People of God, the royal priesthood of all believers, and of the service to God of the Church in the world as lying largely in and through men's daily work.' The report then refers to the emphasis on the apostolate of the laity in the Roman Catholic Church today and welcomes in this an emphasis 'which Luther began to develop in the idea of *Beruf* (calling) and which

Calvin suggested in the service of God *per vocationem*, in the actual work we do in the calling in which we find ourselves. Protestantism, especially in and after the *Aufklärung*, did not sufficiently develop these ideas, though isolated prophets of them were to be found in the nineteenth century, like F. D. Maurice, an Anglican, and R. W. Dale, a Congregationalist, in England, A. S. Talma in Holland or Adolf Stöcker in Germany.' The report then mentions the lay movements and institutes which sprang up in Europe during and after the Second World War, as well as the contribution of J. H. Oldham: 'Concerned, as we are in this Commission of Faith and Order, with the theology of the Church, we welcome this revolutionary re-assessment in life and thought simultaneously, of the Church's nature and its witness in the world. Here are possibilities of understanding afresh the meaning of the "priesthood of all believers", of the relation between "laity" and "ministry" in the one *laos*, and so of the nature of the ministry itself.' The liturgical movement in our times is referred to: 'One of the emphases common to many parts of this movement is the relation between worship and life. As a more primitive pattern of Christian worship is disclosed, the part of the laity in the liturgical action is revealed. The congregation is not merely passive before either the altar or the pulpit, and this share of the people in the action of the liturgy reflects the truth that worship is, in part, an offering to God through Christ of the whole of community life. All that the members of the congregation have been doing all the week, and all the corporate life in which their work has been set, all is offered to God in penitence and praise, and the congregation, by union and communion with Christ, is released into the world again to serve him there in their daily lives. Thus is the sacrament linked with the life of the whole of suffering mankind.' Finally, this Faith and Order Commission said, 'This trend towards a deeper and more serious understanding of the vocation of the laity is full of promise for a better theology of the Church. We welcome it whilst we recognize that it implies a serious challenge to many of our accepted ways. It demands a new depth of co-operation between theologians and laymen, for many of the solutions will never be found by those whose life shelters them from the conflicts and decisions of daily life in modern society. An adequate theology of the Church must in part be the work of those who serve God daily in the struggles of the world.'[35]

III · *The Ecumenical Movement, a Lay Movement?*

One might ask whether the whole ecumenical movement is not such a lay and renewal movement as was referred to in the Faith and Order document quoted above. The answer to this question depends upon what one understands by 'laity' and 'lay movement'. What are then the main assertions of the ecumenical rediscovery of the laity?

1. 'The growing emphasis in many parts of the world upon the function of the laity since the Amsterdam Assembly is not to be understood as an attempt to secure for the laity some larger place or recognition in the Church, nor yet as merely a means to supplement an overburdened and understaffed ordained ministry. It springs from the rediscovery of the true nature of the Church as the People of God.'[36] Two misunderstandings are rejected: lay movements are not anticlerical movements, fighting for a better status of the laity in the Church. A high doctrine of the laity includes rather than excludes a high doctrine of the ordained ministry. Neither are lay movements mere auxiliary troops helping the ordained ministry. The right relationship is rather vice versa: 'The ordained clergy [are] set apart to strengthen and teach, to encourage and unite all the several witnesses in their various callings whose ministry is set in the heart of the secular world's manifold activity.'[37] The wholeness of all members is emphasized. We must 'learn that the laity is really the *laos*, that is, the whole People of God in the world, including, of course, those who have been ordained'.[38] This broad definition, making the term laity virtually a synonym of the term Church, has its difficulties. In fact, even in the literature of the Department on the Laity, the term is used in a more specific way, designating either those who have not received a special ordination and/or theological training, or more often 'those members of the Church, both men and women, who earn their livelihood in a secular job and who, therefore, spend most of their waking hours in a "worldly" occupation.'[39] The important thing, however, is that the nature and task of the laity is no more defined by comparing them with a special group within the Church—the ordained clergy, the theologian, the professional church worker—but by a new appreciation of the Church in the world. At Evanston it was, therefore, said, 'The phrase "the ministry of the laity" expresses the privilege of the whole Church to share in Christ's ministry to the world.'[40] Can this also be said of the ecumenical movement? This movement, seen in its conferences and committees, certainly does not seem to represent the *whole* Church but mainly a group of church

leaders and theologians, mainly men.[41] But the ecumenical movement does not merely or primarily consist of conferences and committees! It probably grows more in ecumenical work camps, in the accomplishment of projects of Inter-Church Aid and Service to Refugees, wherever Christians worship, pray, study, serve and witness together, in ecumenical house-churches and in local congregations which discover themselves as members of Christ's Church in all places and times. It must also be remembered that decisive impulses for the growth of the ecumenical movement came from much older lay movements such as the Young Men's Christian Association, the Young Women's Christian Association, and especially the World's Student Christian Federation. These and more recent lay movements such as the different *Kirchentag* movements, the lay centres, etc., still play a pioneering role.

2. The second main assertion is that the laity shares in Christ's ministry to the world not only when it is assembled for worship and when it collaborates in organized church activities but also, and no less essentially, when it is scattered abroad in every department of life. This was the concern of J. H. Oldham's distinction of two aspects of the Church, taken up by the Faith and Order document on the Church quoted above, and later widely publicized in a statement adopted by the Central Committee of the World Council of Churches in 1956 on 'The Ministry of the Laity in the World'.[42] In reaction to the traditionally prevailing conception of the Church with its focus on organization, activities and building, the emphasis is now sometimes too exclusively laid on the presence of the laity in the structures and institutions of secular society. However, the basic intention is to recover the necessary rhythm of the Church which is being *assembled* and *sent out*. Only through this withdrawal and return does the Church grow in its full apostolicity which includes not only being with Christ in discipleship, but also being sent out by Christ to join his mission. Only in this way can the whole Church's priestly ministry of its presence before God for the sake of the world and of its presence in the world as God's agent be fulfilled. This concern for gathering God's people in the whole *oikoumene* in order to strengthen them and send them out for witness and service unto the ends of the earth and the ends of time certainly lies at the heart of the ecumenical movement.

3. 'God gives his gifts in variety to his people. One of the primary callings of the serving Church is to discover and develop these gifts for the sake of the world.' 'We must understand anew the implications of the fact that we are all baptized, that, as Christ came to minister, so

N*

must all Christians become ministers of his saving purpose according to the particular gift of the Spirit which each has received.'[43] This emphasis on the *charismata* promised to each baptized person and giving each one his own irreplaceable function within Christ's ministry is a third basic assertion of the ecumenical rediscovery of the laity. It is a rediscovery of the charismatic nature of the Church which implies at the same time a new sensitiveness to the spontaneous life of the Church and its members, their spontaneous witness and service. The task of ordained ministers can no more be to enlist the laity for preconceived and set church activities, but to help the charismatic laity to grow fully into its charismatic ministries both in the corporate worship and church work *and* in the daily business at home and when earning a living. W. A. Visser 't Hooft once described the World Council of Churches as 'essentially an attempt to manifest the economy of the *charismata*'.[44] But will the ecumenical movement preserve this spontaneity of a movement where *charismata* are recognized and given space to develop so that the life of the Church is renewed?

4. 'We offer ourselves to serve all men in love' was solemnly affirmed before God by the New Delhi Assembly as a whole at its closing service. This recognition that to be a Christian in and for the world means self-offering (Rom. 12.1) is probably the deepest truth lit up in the ecumenical rediscovery of the laity. To be the *laos* means to abandon all self-glorification and to live by grace. To become a fully *apostolic Church* means to be taken into the apostolic movement from communion with Christ into Christ's mission; and the aim of this mission is not to 'churchify' the world but to witness to Christ so that the world may believe and God's kingdom come. To be a *charismatic Church* means to exist for service, because it belongs to the essence of each *charisma* not to be used for self-edification but to be spent for others. And to fulfil the *priestly ministry* means nothing less than that the priestly people are 'permitted and enabled to share in the continuing high-priestly work of Christ by offering themselves in love and obedience to God and in love and service of men'.[45] True lay movements look beyond the world of the Churches and draw them into the movement of God's love for the world. There are many words in the ecumenical movement which speak about self-sacrifice. But in this matter of self-sacrifice will Churches and Christians really hear the pastoral letter addressed to them in the message of New Delhi: 'The real letter written to the world today does not consist of words. We Christian people, wherever we are, are a letter from Christ to his world'?

The ecumenical movement can be regarded from many other points of view. It loses its true self, however, as soon as it no longer shows these four marks of a genuine lay movement.

NOTES

1. Hendrik Kraemer, 'De wereldomvattende laity-discussie en haar oorzaken', *Wending* (December 1961), pp. 541, 543, 547. For the justification of these statements see: Hendrik Kraemer, *A Theology of the Laity* (London: Lutterworth Press, 1958).

2. *Laici in Ecclesia: An Ecumenical Bibliography on the Role of the Laity in the Life and Mission of the Church* (published by the Department on the Laity, World Council of Churches, Geneva, 1961) refers to more than 1,400 articles, pamphlets and books published on the subject mainly since 1948 in Protestant and Orthodox Churches. A Roman Catholic bibliography (*L'Apostolato dei Laici*, Milan, 1957) has more than 2,200 entries.

3. W. A. Visser 't Hooft and J. H. Oldham, *The Church and its Function in Society* (London: Allen and Unwin, 1937), pp. 117, 118.

4. For a list of these eminent laymen see *The Churches Survey their Task. The Report of the Conference at Oxford, July 1937* (London: Allen and Unwin, 1937), p. 12.

5. Ernst Hornig, *Der Weg der Weltchristenheit* (Stuttgart: Evangelisches Verlagshaus, 1958), p. 53. See also J. H. Oldham's evaluation of this in *The Churches Survey their Task*, pp. 43–6, and *A History of the Ecumenical Movement, 1517–1948*, ed. Ruth Rouse and Stephen C. Neill (London: SPCK, 1954), p. 592.

6. *The First Assembly of the World Council of Churches*, ed. W. A. Visser 't Hooft (London: SCM Press, 1949), p. 153.

7. *The First Six Years: 1948–1954* (Geneva: World Council of Churches, 1954), p. 40; cf. also pp. 58–62.

8. *Laymen's Work*, published twice a year by the Secretary for Laymen's Work, World Council of Churches, Geneva, 1951–55 (Nos. 1–8).

9. Before Amsterdam: J. H. Oldham (Britain); Amsterdam Assembly Committee on the Laity: C. C. Stoughton (USA) and H. Kraemer (Holland) as chairman and secretary resp.; Committee for Laymen's Work: H. Kraemer and H. H. Walz (Germany) as chairman and full-time secretary from 1945–54 resp.; Evanston Assembly Section on the Laity: Kathleen Bliss (Britain) and H. H. Walz as chairman and secretary resp. After Evanston the widening scope of the work was reflected in the appointments: Working Committee of the Department on the Laity until the New Delhi Assembly: R. D. Paul (India) and H. R. Weber (a former missionary in Indonesia) as chairman and full-time executive secretary resp.; New Delhi Assembly Committee: K. von Bismarck (Germany) and V. T. Istavridis (Turkey) as chairman and secretary resp.; full-time executive secretary since New Delhi: R. C. Young (Canada), responsible to a Working Committee with a well-balanced membership representing all continents and all major denominations of the World Council member Churches.

10. Major consultations and publications in the period between the Evanston and New Delhi Assemblies dealt with the training for the ministry of the laity in the world; new structures of church life which are of special importance for the laity (house-churches, regional lay institutes, etc.); the implications of the ministry of the laity for our missionary strategy; our concept of the ordained ministry and our ecclesiologies; the Christian style of

life; discernment and decision; conversion and baptism as the initiation to the ministry of the laity, etc. For a fuller survey, see: *From Evanston to New Delhi* (Geneva: World Council of Churches, 1961), pp. 76–82, 251–3.

11. H. Berkhof, 'Kroniek van New Delhi', *Wending* (February 1962), p. 805.

12. Lesslie Newbigin, 'The Missionary Dimension of the Ecumenical Movement', *The Ecumenical Review* XIV/2, January 1962, p. 209.

13. John R. Mott, *Liberating the Lay Forces of Christianity* (Ayres Lectures), New York and London: Macmillan and SCM Press, 1934.

14. *Missions under the Cross*, ed. Norman Goodall (London: Edinburgh House Press, 1953), p. 315. Cf. also, N. Goodall, *The Ecumenical Movement* (London: Oxford University Press, 1961), pp. 94–8.

15. Ecumenical Survey on *Evangelism—The Mission of the Church to those Outside her Life* (London: SCM Press, 1954), p. 49. See also the survey for the Laity Section, p. 49.

16. Hans Jochen Margull, *Theologie der missionarischen Verkündigung. Evangelisation als ökumenisches Problem* (Stuttgart: Evangelisches Verlagswerk, 1959), *passim*, especially pp. 220–3. (English translation: H. J. Margull, *Hope in Action*, Philadelphia: Mühlenberg Press, 1962.)

17. *New Delhi Speaks* (London: SCM Press, 1962), pp. 24 ff. For an appraisal of the laity discussion in the witness section by the co-chairman of that section and the executive secretary of the Department on Studies in Evangelism, see: G. Brennecke, 'Gesamtübersicht über die Sektion "Zeugnis"', and H. J. Margull, 'Strukturfragen werden wichtig. Anmerkung zur "Laien"-Arbeit und zur missionarischen Verkündigung', both in *Oekumenische Rundschau* (March, 1962), pp. 15 ff. and 17 ff.

18. Published in the Report of the Jerusalem Meeting of the International Missionary Council, 1928, vol. I, pp. 284–338.

19. W. R. Hogg, *Ecumenical Foundations. A History of the International Missionary Council and its Nineteenth-Century Background* (New York: Harper and Brothers, 1952), p. 241.

20. The Report of the Conference at Oxford, 1937, pp. 44 ff.

21. Published in *The Church and the Disorder of Society*, Amsterdam Series on *Man's Disorder and God's Design*, vol. III, pp. 120–54.

22. Three papers on the subject of 'Christian Vocation at the Present Day' were read at the Stockholm Conference by Paavo Virkkunen, D. Mahling and J. A. Marquis. They are published in *The Stockholm Conference 1925*, ed. G. K. A. Bell (London: Oxford University Press, 1926), pp. 259–79.

23. See for instance the Evanston documents about *The Laity—The Christian in his Vocation* and Nos. 5, 10 and 13 of *Laity*, especially the lecture of the Indian lawyer E. V. Mathew at New Delhi, published in *Laity*, No. 13, pp. 9–16.

24. Persons who more recently contributed to both are, for instance, Masao Takenaka, M. M. Thomas, Cameron P. Hall, Klaus von Bismarck.

25. *New Delhi Speaks*, pp. 50 f.

26. H. Kraemer, *A Theology of the Laity*, pp. 10, 81 f., 188.

27. Gustave Thils, *Histoire Doctrinale du Mouvement oecuménique* (Louvain: E. M. Warny, 1955), pp. 125–65. The study of Faith and Order documents gives apparently such a clerical flavour that one of the few non-clerics who contributed to this study, the French lawyer Jacques Ellul, is introduced as 'le *pasteur* J. Ellul' (p. 161)!

28. Besides the already quoted book by H. Kraemer, see especially Yves Congar, O.M.P., *Lay People in the Church—A Study for a Theology of the Laity* (London: Bloomsbury Pub-

lishing Co., 1957), as well as the publications of the Department on the Laity, such as *Laymen's Work*, Nos. 7 and 8, and *Laity*, Nos. 3, 8, 9, 11 and 13.

29. *Minutes of the Faith and Order Commission 1960, St Andrews, Scotland*, Faith and Order Papers, No. 31, pp. 82–8.

30. *New Delhi Speaks*, pp. 55 and 63.

31. *Idem.*, p. 61.

32. *The Second World Conference on Faith and Order, Edinburgh 1937* (London: SCM Press, 1938), pp. 245 and 235.

33. Pastor Marc Boegner in the Edinburgh 1937 Report, p. 160.

34. *The Third World Conference on Faith and Order, Lund 1952* (London: SCM Press, 1953), pp. 17–22. See especially the paragraph on 'The Nature and Mission of the Church', p. 19.

35. *The Church. A Report of a Theological Commission of the Faith and Order Commission of the World Council of Churches in preparation for the Third World Conference on Faith and Order to be held at Lund, Sweden, in 1952*, Faith and Order Papers, No. 7, 1951, pp. 39–41.

36. *The Evanston Report* (London and New York: SCM Press and Harper and Brothers, 1954), p. 161.

37. *New Delhi Speaks*, p. 26.

38. *Idem.*, p. 25. This etymological derivation of the term laity from the biblical content of the Greek word *laos*, i.e. *laikos*, is probably wrong (see Ignatius de la Potterie, 'L'origine et le sens primitif du mot "laïc"', *Nouvelle Revue Théologique* LXXX (1958), pp. 840–53.

39. *The Evanston Report*, p. 161. Cf. also the relevant paragraph in the Report of the Laity Commission at New Delhi, in *Laity*, No. 13, p. 28.

40. *Idem.*, p. 161.

41. Because of the different definitions of the term laity used in different Churches and situations, it is almost impossible to indicate the number of 'laymen' and 'laywomen' in a certain committee or gathering. But the following tentative break-downs may indicate the present situation: the *Commission on Faith and Order* has 120 members, of which there are 111 ordained ministers having studied theology, 5 lay theologians; only 3 are laymen in a 'secular' occupation, and only one is a woman. Of the 19 members of the Working Committee of the *Department on Church and Society*, there are 8 laymen in secular occupations, 7 bishops, pastors or church executives and 4 professors in theology or social ethics, among all of them only 2 women. The Working Committee of the *Department on the Laity* has 7 laymen in secular occupations, 4 pastors or theologians, and 5 ordained or unordained church or lay movement executives, among them all 5 women. For this problem of 'The Participation of Laymen and Laywomen in Ecumenical Discussion', see the paper by W. G. Symons on this subject, in *Documents*, No. III (Geneva: Department on the Laity, World Council of Churches, 1957).

42. *World Council of Churches' Minutes and Reports of the Ninth Meeting of the Central Committee, Galyatetö, Hungary, 1956*, pp. 26 f.

43. *New Delhi Speaks*, p. 50, and *The Evanston Report*, p. 161.

44. W. A. Visser 't Hooft, 'The Economy of the Charismata and the Ecumenical Movement', *Paulus-Hellas-Oikumene, an Ecumenical Symposium* (Athens, 1951), p. 192.

45. T. W. Manson, *Ministry and Priesthood: Christ's and Ours* (London: Epworth Press, 1958), p. 70.

BIBLIOGRAPHY

For the history of the ecumenical movement, see:

Reports of the main conferences of the International Missionary Council, of the Commission on Faith and Order, of the Movement for Life and Work and of the World Council of Churches.

Ruth Rouse and Stephen C. Neill (edd.), *A History of the Ecumenical Movement, 1517–1948* (London, 1954).

W. R. Hogg, *Ecumenical Foundations. A History of the International Missionary Council and its Nineteenth-Century Background* (New York, 1952).

C. P. Shedd, *History of the World's Alliance of Young Men's Christian Associations* (London, 1955).

A. V. Rice, *A History of the World's Young Women's Christian Association* (New York, 1947).

Ruth Rouse, *The World's Student Christian Federation* (London, 1948).

E. Duff, *The Social Thought of the World Council of Churches* (London, 1956).

G. Thils, *Histoire Doctrinale du Mouvement oecuménique* (Louvain, 1955).

H. J. Margull, *Hope in Action* (Philadelphia, 1956).

For the special subject of the Laity in the Ecumenical Movement, see:

The First Six Years: 1948–1954 (Geneva, 1954), pp. 58–62.

From Evanston to New Delhi (Geneva, 1961), pp. 76–82.

Minutes of the Working Committee of the Department on the Laity (Geneva, from 1955 onwards).

H. H. Walz, 'Lay, Theology of the Laity, Laymen's Work', *The Ecumenical Review* VI (1954), pp. 469–75.

K. Bliss, 'The Ecumenical Movement and the Role of the Laity', *The Ecumenical Review* X (1958), pp. 249–54.

H. R. Weber, 'Die Laienfrage in oekumenischer Sicht' and 'Mündige Gemeinde', *Oekumenische Rundschau* VIII (1959), pp. 105–22; IX (1960), pp. 3–20.

Die Religion in Geschichte und Gegenwart[3] IV, 203–6: 'Laienapostolat', 'Laienbewegung, *christliche*', by H. H. Walz.

Weltkirchenlexikon, 818–29: 'Laien', by H. H. Walz.

Laici in Ecclesia: An Ecumenical Bibliography on the Role of the Laity in the Life and Mission of the Church (Geneva, 1961).

INDEX

[The notes are not indexed below]